RESEARCH IN FINANCE

Volume 16 • 1998

RESEARCH IN FINANCE

Editor: ANDREW H. CHEN
Edwin L. Cox School of Business
Southern Methodist University

VOLUME 16 • 1998

United Kingdom – North America – Japan
India – Malaysia – China

Emerald Group Publishing Limited
Howard House, Wagon Lane, Bingley BD16 1WA, UK

British Library Cataloguing in Publication Data
A catalogue record for this book is available from the British Library

ISBN: 978-0-7623-0328-1
ISSN: 0196-3821 (Series)

Awarded in recognition of
Emerald's production
department's adherence to
quality systems and processes
when preparing scholarly
journals for print

INVESTOR IN PEOPLE

CONTENTS

LIST OF CONTRIBUTORS

Mojib V. Ahmed

Department of Finance
Old Dominion University
Norfolk, VA

Jalal D. Akhavein

Department of Economics
New York University
New York, NY

Jeffrey W. Allen

Edwin L. Cox School of Business
Southern Methodist University
Dallas, TX

James S. Ang

Department of Finance
Florida State University
Tallahassee, FL

Jon A. Christopherson

U.S. Equity Research
Frank Russell Company
Tacoma, WA

Raymond A. K. Cox

Department of Finance
Central Michigan University
Mt. Pleasant, MI

Paul Evans

Department of Economics
The Ohio State University
Columbus, OH

Wayne E. Ferson

School of Business
University of Washington
Seattle, WA

Taylor W. Foster III

College of Business Administration
New Mexico State University
Las Cruces, NM

Bill B. Francis   College of Business Administration
                                     University of South Florida
                                     Tampa, FL

Debra A. Glassman   School of Business
                                     University of Washington
                                     Seattle, WA

Iftekhar Hasan   Department of Finance
                                     New Jersey Institute of Technology
                                     Newark, NJ

M. Kabir Hassan   Department of Economics and Finance
                                     University of New Orleans
                                     New Orleans, LA

Richard Yan-Ki Ho   Faculty of Business
                                     City University of Hong Kong
                                     Hong Kong

S.V. Jayanti   Dateware Technologies
                                     Cleveland, OH

Khondkar E. Karim   School of Professional Accountancy
                                     Long Island University
                                     Brookville, NY

Tsong-Yue Lai   Department of Finance
                                     California State University
                                     Fullerton, CA

Van Son Lai   Department of Finance and Insurance
                                     Laval University
                                     Quebec, Canada

John Leusner   Graduate School of Business
                                     University of Chicago
                                     Chicago, IL

Scott L. Lummer   Chief Investment Officer
                                     401k Forum
                                     Naperville, IL

John J. McConnell

Krannert School of Management
Purdue University
West Lafayette, IN

Sia Nassiripour

Department of Accounting
Monmouth University
West Long Branch, NJ

Debra K. Reed

Department of Economics
University of Oklahoma
Norman, OK

Alan K. Reichert

Department of Finance
Cleveland State University
Cleveland, OH

Edmund Scribner

College of Business Administration
New Mexico State University
Las Cruces, NM

Philip H. Siegel

School of Professional Accounting
Long Island University
Brookville, NY

R. Gene Stout

Department of Finance
Central Michigan University
Mt. Pleasant, MI

P.A.V.B. Swamy

Bank Research Division
Comptroller of the Currency
Washington, DC

Sorin Tuluca

College of Business
Fairleigh Dickenson University
Madison, NJ

Kie Ann Wong

Department of Finance and Accounting
National University of Singapore
Singapore

Chi-Keung Woo

Faculty of Business
City University of Hong Kong
Hong Kong

CONDITIONAL MEASURES OF PERFORMANCE AND PERSISTENCE FOR PENSION FUNDS

Jon A. Christopherson, Wayne E. Ferson, and Debra A. Glassman

ABSTRACT

This paper presents evidence on persistence in the relative investment performance of large, institutional equity managers. Similar to existing evidence for mutual funds, we find persistent performance, concentrated in the managers with poor prior-period performance measures. A conditional approach, using time-varying measures of risk and abnormal performance, is better able to better detect this persistence and to predict the future performance of the funds than are traditional methods.

I. INTRODUCTION

The question of whether professional portfolio managers can deliver expected returns in excess of naive benchmarks has long been important, both for academic research and for practical decision making. However, the evidence on the ability of

Research in Finance, Volume 16, pages 1–46.

managers to deliver consistently superior returns, or positive *alphas*, remains controversial. Some studies find that particular open-ended mutual funds, performing relatively well or poorly in the past, tend also to do so in the future. Jensen (1969), Carlson (1970), and a number of more recent studies find evidence of such *persistence* in mutual fund performance.[1]

A large number of studies examine the persistence of mutual fund performance over time, but the evidence for institutional equity managers is sparse. Christopherson and Turner (1991) study pension managers and conclude (p. 10) that "alpha at one time is not predictable from alpha at a previous time." Lakonishok, Shleifer, and Vishny (1992) find some persistence of the relative returns of pension funds for two to three-year investment horizons. They also find that pension fund managers underperform the Standard & Poors Stock Index over the 1983–1989 period. Coggin, Fabozzi, and Rahman (1993) study market timing and stock-picking ability, and provide references to the few additional academic studies of institutional equity manager performance.

It is important to further study the performance of institutional funds for several reasons. First, institutional managers control a larger portion of the aggregate wealth than do mutual funds (Coggin, Fabozzi, & Rahman, 1993). Second, institutional equity managers and mutual fund managers operate in different environments. For example, pension fund managers are reviewed periodically by their clients and pension consultants, who presumably are more sophisticated than the typical individual investor. Mutual fund investors may not monitor a fund manager's behavior as closely, but they can simply withdraw their money or invest in a "hot" fund at any time. The process by which some funds survive and others disappear is thus likely to be different for pension and mutual funds. Mutual funds and pension funds are also taxed differently. Given these differences, it is interesting to compare the persistence in performance for the two types of managers.

Our study is also motivated by an important practical problem. Institutional investors must decide which managers to retain, and attempting to predict the future performance of a manager is a critical part of that decision-making process. If the abnormal investment performance, or alpha, of pension managers is randomly distributed over time—consistent with the findings of Christopherson and Turner (1991)—the past performance of a manager provides no useful information about future performance. While this is consistent with some versions of the efficient market hypothesis, it suggests that investment firms are wasting money trying to measure alphas.

It has been traditional to measure performance by the average portfolio returns, net of a fixed benchmark return, over some historical period. This approach uses *unconditional* expected returns as the performance baseline, assuming that the consumer of the performance evaluation uses no information about the state of the economy to form expectations. Such an assumption is even less tenable for sophisticated institutional investors than for individual investors evaluating mutual funds. Furthermore, unconditional measures of performance are known to be biased when managers react to market indicators or engage in dynamic trading strategies. These well-known biases make it difficult to measure even the average performance; if these biases persist over time they can also distort inferences about the persistence of investment performance.

To address these concerns about unconditional measures, Chen and Knez (1996) and Ferson and Schadt (1996) advocate *conditional performance evaluation*. The idea is to use time-varying conditional expected returns and conditional betas instead of the usual unconditional moments. The expected returns and risks are conditioned on predetermined, publicly available information. A conditional approach can control for biases in the traditional measures when managers trade on public information. Ferson and Schadt find that incorporating public information, such as dividend yields and interest rates, affects inferences about the average performance in a sample of open-ended mutual funds.[2]

In this paper we study persistence in the performance of a sample of 185 U.S. pension fund equity managers over the 1979–1990 period. We extend the approach of Ferson and Schadt (1996) to estimate time-varying *conditional alphas* as well as betas. We find that the returns and excess returns are partially predictable using the predetermined information variables. We also find evidence of time-varying conditional betas, investment style-factor exposures, and time-varying conditional alphas. When we measure the performance of these managers relative to market and style benchmarks, we find—in contrast to Lakonishok, Shleifer, and Vishny (1992)—no evidence that they deliver inferior returns. We attribute much of Lakonishok, Shleifer, and Vishny's negative evidence about pension manager performance to the subperiod they examine.

We compare the predictive ability of a number of measures of alpha for the future relative returns. We find evidence that the investment performance of the managers persists over time. However, unlike Lakonishok, Shleifer, and Vishny (1992), there is little evidence of persistence among the better-performing managers. Instead, we find persistence for poorly performing managers: low-alpha managers in the past tend to be low-return managers in the future. Also, we find that conditional measures of alpha outperform traditional, unconditional measures for predicting the future returns, while past average returns have little explanatory power. Our results suggest that the use of conditional measures may improve upon current practice. We conclude that the best practical use for alphas may not be for picking winners, but for avoiding those managers with persistent inferior performance.

The paper is organized as follows. Section II draws the main distinctions between pension and mutual funds that motivate our analysis of the persistence in pension fund returns. Section III describes the data, section IV describes the empirical methods, and section V presents preliminary results which establish the relevance of the conditional measures. Section VI presents results on the average performance in our sample of pension funds. Section VII addresses the issue of persistence in performance and the economic significance of the persistence. Section VIII offers concluding remarks.

II. PENSION FUNDS VERSUS MUTUAL FUNDS

There are differences between the institutional details surrounding pension fund and mutual fund management, and these differences suggest a number of prior conjectures about the persistence of performance. Pension fund management involves (1) plan sponsors (specifically, the administrators or trustees of pension plans), (2) pension fund consultants, and (3) investment management firms. Typically, a plan sponsor divides funds among a number of managers with various investment styles. Consultants such as the Frank Russell Company advise plan sponsors on manager review and selection, and also on the allocation of funds among different asset classes and investment styles. In order to perform this function the consultant tracks the performance of a large number of money managers.

Superior performance presumes that fund managers have the ability to pick undervalued investments or time market returns. The literature on market timing finds few cases of consistently superior market timers; our sample of pension funds excludes market-timing funds in any case. If some managers are good at picking stocks, then it is reasonable to think that such talents persist over time. Consistently superior managers should gravitate to larger pools of cash, such as in pension funds, where the compensation is higher. This suggests that investment performance may be superior and possibly more highly persistent in pension funds than in mutual funds.

However, with the specialization that is common among pension fund managers, it is likely to be hard to maintain continued superior performance as the size of the pension fund expands. Such considerations may lead to mean-reversion in the relative performance (i.e., a lack of persistent performance) for superior fund mangers.

It is not difficult to imagine that there are inferior fund managers, but there are reasons to think that abnormally poor performance is less likely to persist among pension funds than among mutual funds. The relative sophistication of institutional investors and the large amounts of money involved suggest that lackluster performance should not be tolerated for long in pension funds. Large institutional investors have enough money at stake to provide incentives to monitor their managers; in contrast it is more difficult for individual mutual fund investors to justify these monitoring costs. Some mutual fund investors may be reluctant to sell a fund if they are "locked in" by a previous capital gain. However, pension funds have no such concerns, as pension fund returns are not taxed at the firm level.

There are, however, reasons to expect that low returns can persist among pension fund managers. Pension fund managers deliver services to their clients in addition to investment returns. These include education, research, and reports that the responsible officers at the plan sponsor organization can use in reporting to their superiors. Fund managers develop relationships with their clients that mutual fund investors typically do not enjoy. Agency problems may also allow poor performance to persist. For example, firing a manager may be seen as evidence that the pension plan administrator's previous decision to hire the manager was a poor one.[3] Finally, while no-load mutual funds make switching between funds inexpensive, there are significant transactions costs associated with firing one pension fund manager and hiring another. Consistent with the importance of these costs, pension plan sponsors periodically review their managers, commonly at quarterly to annual frequencies. Flows of money in response to measured performance, typically occur episodically and in large amounts. This is in contrast to mutual fund flows, which occur virtually continuously in response to short-term performance (e.g., Ippolito, 1992; Gruber, 1996; Sirri & Tufano, 1992).

III. THE DATA

A. Pension Fund Returns

We obtained monthly returns for 273 institutional equity managers from the Frank Russell Company's Russell Data Services (RDS) database. The returns are for large accounts of domestic, U.S. equity pension fund managers who have been allocated funds by Frank Russell Company clients. We present most of our results for the January 1979 to December 1990 period. Over this period there are 232 managers with some returns data and 185 managers with more than 12 months of data. We use this latter subsample in our analysis. Managers enter the database at different points in time, but all are present at the end of the sample period. Our sample of 185 managers includes 41 growth managers, 40 value managers, 55 large cap managers, and 49 small cap managers. The style classifications for the managers are determined by RDS, based on the managers' investment philosophies and portfolio characteristics (see Christopherson & Trittin, 1995).

A given money management firm may have a number of portfolios and accounts, but our database includes only one "representative" account per firm. We do not have data on the values of the accounts, but we were told by RDS that most are over $100 million in size. On average, the small cap portfolios tend to be smaller sized accounts. The money management firm chooses which account to designate as its representative account. Representative accounts usually have been in existence for some time, and are subject to fewer investment restrictions than many individual-client accounts. We may therefore expect representative accounts to perform better than a typically restricted client account.

The data measure the total portfolio returns, including any cash holdings. We were told by RDS that cash holdings are typically less than 10%. The returns include the reinvestment of all distributions (e.g., dividends) and are net of trading commissions but not of management fees. Except where indicated, our analysis is performed on the returns net of the monthly return to investing in a one-month Treasury bill. The Treasury bill data are from the Center for Research in Security Prices at the University of Chicago (CRSP).

B. Survivorship Issues

Our database almost certainly has survivorship biases, as it contains only surviving managers. When a manager goes out of business or is dropped by RDS, the entire returns history for that manager is removed from the database (and is unavailable to us). Managers also fall out of the database when their firms stop sending data to the Frank Russell Company, often because Russell has not recommended the manager to its clients. Survivorship creates a number of potential problems affecting both the average levels of performance and the apparent persistence in performance.

One obvious reason for a manager to leave the database is poor performance. To the extent that managers are dropped because of poor performance, the measured performance of the surviving managers is biased upwards. For example, Elton, Gruber, and Blake (1996b) find an average survivorship bias of 0.7–0.9% per year in mutual fund data (see also Brown & Goetzmann, 1995; Malkiel, 1995; Gruber, 1996; Carhart, 1997, and others).

Managers are dropped from pension fund databases for reasons other than poor performance. For example, funds are dropped from our database when the firm has an important change in management personnel, such as when a star performer leaves for another firm. To the extent that managers are dropped from the database because they were star performers, the average measured performance of the surviving managers is biased *downwards*.

Brown, Goetzmann, Ibbotson, and Ross (1992), Hendricks, Patel, and Zeckhauser (1996), and Goetzmann, Brown, Ibbotson, and Ross (1995) consider the effects of survivorship on performance persistence under the simplifying assumptions that: (1) the expected returns of all managers are the same, (2) there are differences in variances, and (3) that managers leave the database when their returns are relatively low. Under these assumptions survivorship is likely to induce a spurious "J-shaped" relation between future and past relative returns. In particular, past poor performers in a sample with survivorship bias are likely to reverse their performance in the future.[4]

The empirical evidence on performance persistence for mutual funds suggests a positive relation between the future and past performance, concentrated in the poorly performing funds. This is not what we would expect if persistence is a spurious result in a simple model of survivorship bias. Brown and Goetzmann (1995), Carhart (1997), and Elton, Gruber, and Blake (1996a) find similar patterns in samples of mutual funds designed to avoid survivorship bias.

Our evidence for pension funds also reveals positive persistence, concentrated in the poorly performing funds. This is interesting, given that we know there are survivorship effects in the database. However, the "death process" for pension funds is likely to differ from that for mutual funds, which leads us to expect a more complex pattern than the J-shaped relation between past and future relative returns.

Since the data that would allow us to model the birth and death processes are not available to us, it is not possible to measure the effects of survivorship on the pension fund evidence. We leave this as a topic for future research.

C. Selection Biases

Our sample is likely to have a selection bias, because managers enter the database after they attract attention from the Frank Russell Company and its clients. When a manager is added to the database, some previous history of the manager's returns may be back-filled. There is evidence consistent with selection bias for the average returns in our sample. The average annual return on an equally weighted portfolio of all managers is 16.11% over 1981–1990. If we exclude the first five years of data for each manager, the average annual return over 1981–1990 drops to 15.45%. In the analysis of performance persistence below we use the returns following the first five years of data for a given manager. This should reduce the effects of selection bias.

D. Money Management Fees

When we evaluate performance by measuring relative investment returns it is important to account for the fees charged by managers. We do not have specific fee data associated with the individual managers, as the managers are not identified to us by name. Halpern and Fowler (1991) find that, for accounts of $100 million, posted management fees average about 50 basis points at the end of our sample period. Internal RDS research shows that average quoted fees vary by investment style. For example, the median (interquartile range) of the quoted fees for $100 million accounts in 1988 varies from 44 (35–58) basis points for the large cap managers to 78 (56–100) basis points for the small cap managers. The figures for growth and value managers are 49 (40–59) and 53 (43–59) basis points, respectively. Fees vary according to account size, and smaller accounts would pay more. There has been a secular decline in management fees over our sample period. According to RDS, the median posted fees of value managers fell from 53 basis points in 1988 to 47 in 1994.

It would be difficult to determine the actual fees paid by plan sponsors, even if posted fee data were available for each manager. "Banner" sponsors are likely to be offered a discount from the posted fees and they prefer not to disclose the details of these discount arrangements (Halpern & Fowler, 1991). In addition, there may be some substitution between fees and other types of costs, such as brokerage commissions. For example, a plan sponsor might pay lower fees and, in exchange, buy research or direct trading to designated brokers, who then rebate a portion of the trading commissions as "soft dollars."

E. Benchmark Portfolios

Performance measurement compares a fund's return to the return of some benchmark. We use the CRSP value-weighted NYSE and AMEX index as an overall market benchmark. This allows us to compare our results with previous studies based on the CAPM, which used similar market portfolios as their benchmarks. Christopherson and Turner (1991) choose manager style indexes as the benchmarks; that is, a manager is classified according to style and a single index which reflects that style is used. Our analysis includes performance measurement relative to style indexes.

The RDS database includes passive benchmarks for four investment styles. These are the Russell growth, value, market-oriented, and small-capitalization indexes. The Russell market-oriented style index is the Russell 1000, a value-weighted index of the stocks of large capitalization firms. The Russell small-capitalization index is the value-weighted Russell 2000 index. These are nonoverlapping subsets of the Russell 3000 index universe. Over the period covered in this study the Growth and Value indexes are formed by further dividing the stocks in the Russell 1000 into two groups of stocks. The stocks are divided at the median market value-weighted ratios of market price to the book value of equity. Stocks with high ratios go into the growth index, and those with low ratios are in the value index.[5]

F. Predetermined Information Variables

The conditional performance models include a vector of lagged information variables. We use the same variables used by Ferson and Schadt (1996). We choose the same variables for comparability with their results for mutual funds and to avoid our own data snooping on this "new" data set. The instruments are (1) the lagged level of the one-month Treasury bill yield (TBILL), (2) the lagged dividend yield of the CRSP value-weighted NYSE and AMEX stock index (DY), (3) a lagged measure of the slope of the term structure (TERM), (4) a lagged quality spread in the corporate bond market (QUAL), and (5) a dummy variable for the month of January.

TBILL is the discount yield of a bill that is the closest to one month to maturity at the end of the previous month. It is drawn from the CRSP RISKFREE files. The bill yield is calculated from the average of bid and ask prices on the last trading day of each month. The dividend yield is the price level at the end of the previous month on the CRSP value-weighted index divided into the previous 12 months of dividend payments for the index. TERM is a constant-maturity 10-year Treasury bond yield less the three-month Treasury Bill yield; both are annualized weekly averages from Citibase. QUAL is Moody's BAA rated corporate bond yield less the AAA rated corporate bond yield, using the weekly average yields for the previous month, as reported by Citibase.

IV. EMPIRICAL METHODS FOR MEASURING PERFORMANCE

A. Unconditional Models

The traditional, or *unconditional alpha*, α_p, is estimated by the following regression:

$$r_{pt} = \alpha_p + \beta_p r_{bt} + v_{pt}. \tag{1}$$

Both the return of the manager, r_{pt}, and the return of the benchmark portfolio, r_{bt}, are measured net of the one-month Treasury bill rate, R_{ft}. That is, $r_{pt} = R_{pt} - R_{ft}$ and $r_{bt} = R_{bt} - R_{ft}$, where R_{pt} is the return of the managed portfolio and R_{bt} is the return of a benchmark. β_p is the unconditional beta and v_{pt} is the regression error. Jensen (1968) proposed the unconditional alpha as a measure of abnormal performance, using a proxy for the "market portfolio" as the benchmark, R_{bt}. Jensen was thinking about the Capital Asset Pricing Model (CAPM, see Sharpe, 1964), but unconditional alphas are commonly estimated using various benchmark portfolios. They can also be estimated using multiple-benchmark models, in which β_p and r_{bt} are vectors.

The average value of the *excess return*, $R_{pt} - R_{bt}$ is sometimes used as a simple alternative performance measure. The past average excess return is a special case of an unconditional alpha, where the beta in equation (1) is assumed to be equal to 1.0.

B. Conditional Models

If expected market returns and managers' betas change over time and are correlated, the regression equation (1) is misspecified. Ferson and Schadt (1996) propose a modification of equation (1) to address such concerns. They assume that market prices fully reflect readily available, public information, which is measured by a vector of predetermined variables, Z_t. Ferson and Schadt also assume a linear functional form for the conditional beta, given Z_t, of a managed portfolio:[6]

$$\beta_{pb}(Z_t) = b_{0pb} + B'_{pb} z_t \tag{2}$$

where $z_t = Z_t - E(Z)$ is a vector of the deviations of Z_t from the unconditional means, and B_{pb} is a vector with dimension equal to the dimension of Z_t. The coefficient b_{0pb} is an "average beta." The elements of B_{pb} measure the response of the conditional beta to the information variables Z_t. A modification of regression (1) follows:

$$r_{pt+1} = \alpha_p + b_{0pb} r_{bt+1} + B'_{pb}[z_t \, r_{bt+1}] + u_{pt+1}. \tag{3}$$

Under the null hypothesis of no abnormal performance, the model implies that the average *conditional alpha*, α_p, is zero (the α_p in equation (3) will differ from equation (1) if B_{pb} is nonzero). In the case of a single benchmark r_{bt+1} and L information variables in the vector Z_t, equation (3) is a regression of the manager's return on a constant and $L+1$ variables. The products of the future benchmark return and the predetermined variables capture the covariance between the conditional beta and the conditional expected market return, given Z_t. Ferson and Schadt (1996) find that this covariance is a major source of bias in the traditional, unconditional alphas of mutual funds. The specification in (3) can easily be extended to the case of a multiple-benchmark model.

Using a single coefficient α_p in equation (3) captures a particular alternative to the null hypothesis of no abnormal performance. The alternative is that the expected abnormal performance is constant over time. But if managers' abnormal returns vary over time and can change signs, this may not provide much power.

C. Time-varying, Conditional Alphas

In a conditional performance evaluation model the conditional alpha should be zero when managers' portfolio weights are no more informative about future returns than the public information variables, Z_t. However, if a manager uses more information than Z_t, causing the portfolio weights to be conditionally correlated with future returns given Z_t, then the conditional alpha is a function of the conditional covariance between the manager's weights and the future returns, given Z_t.[7] This conditional covariance, and therefore the expected abnormal performance, is an unobserved function of Z_t. We therefore modify the regression (3) to include an explicit *time-varying conditional alpha*, allowing the alpha to be a function of Z_t:

$$\alpha_p(Z_t) = \alpha_{0p} + A'_p z_t. \qquad (4)$$

In equation (4) we assume that the conditional alpha is a linear function. The modified regression is therefore:

$$r_{pt+1} = \alpha_{0p} + A'_p z_t + b_{0pb} r_{bt+1} + B'_{pb}[z_t r_{bt+1}] + u_{pt+1}. \qquad (5)$$

Regression (5) allows us to estimate conditional alphas, and to track their variation over time as a function of the conditioning information, Z_t.[8]

We estimate standard errors and t-ratios and construct Wald tests for our models using the heteroskedasticity-consistent estimation techniques of White (1980), Hansen (1982), and Newey and West (1987), because our evidence of time-varying betas implies conditional heteroskedasticity in the data. Lee and Rahman (1990) and Ferson and Schadt (1996) also find evidence of heteroskedasticity effects in mutual fund returns.

V. EMPIRICAL RESULTS

A. Predictability of Pension Fund Excess Returns

Table 1 summarizes time-series regressions which attempt to predict the managers' future monthly returns over the 1979–1990 period. The dependent variables are the managers' returns, in excess of either the one-month Treasury bill, the Russell style index, or the CRSP value-weighted index. The independent variables are the predetermined information variables. The purpose of these regressions is to determine whether managers' returns are related to public information. If so, this provides one motivation for a conditional performance analysis.

When the dependent variables are the returns net of the Treasury bill return, the regressions for equally weighted portfolios of the managers (panel B) and the averages of the individual manager regressions (panel A) produce adjusted R-squares in excess of 12% for each of the four style groups. For small-cap managers, the R-squares are about 17%. These adjusted R-squares are high by conventional standards for monthly predictive regressions (for passive size and industry-grouped portfolios, see Ferson & Harvey, 1991b; Ferson & Korajczyk, 1995). Most of the regressions for the individual managers' returns in excess of the bill are strongly significant at conventional levels. The residual autocorrelations typically are not large; for the equally weighted portfolios they are between .07 and .13, which is within two standard errors of zero.

The excess returns of the value managers produce slightly higher R-squares in Table 1 than those of the growth managers, and the small-cap funds produce higher R-squares than large-cap funds. To check whether these patterns reflect differences in the predictability of the assets held by the funds, panel C reports regressions where the dependent variables are the passive style indexes. The R-squares in panel C follow the same pattern as those in panels A and B: they are higher for value than growth indexes, and they are higher for small-cap than for large-cap indexes.

Table 1 also presents regressions for the managers' returns measured in excess of the CRSP value-weighted index and the Russell index for the manager's style group. The excess returns relative to these benchmarks may be interpreted as measures of ex post abnormal performance, under the assumptions that the benchmark is efficient and that the conditional beta of each manager on the benchmark is identically equal to 1.0. Under this interpretation the return in excess of the benchmark should not differ predictably from zero.

Using the returns in excess of the value-weighted index, the regressions produce adjusted R-squares which average between six and 10 % for the individual managers and vary between 2.6 and 10% for the equally weighted portfolios. The regressions are statistically significant for each of the equally weighted portfolios, excepting the portfolio of the large-cap managers. The equally weighted portfolios mask significant variation across the funds in the degree of predictability. For example, in the case of the large-cap managers, the average right-tail p-value for the

Table 1. Predictability of Returns and Excess Returns of Institutional Equity Manager Portfolios

	Returns Excess of Bill			Returns Excess of Style			Returns excess of CRSP index		
	auto	adjRsq	pval(F)	auto	adjRsq	pval(F)	auto	adjRsq	pval(F)
PANEL A: Averages for the Individual Managers									
Growth	0.132	0.129	0.095	-0.052	0.0387	0.465	0.0031	0.0608	0.369
Value	0.127	0.158	0.064	-0.064	0.0562	0.437	-0.0479	0.0891	0.288
Large	0.127	0.148	0.048	-0.062	0.0729	0.339	-0.0609	0.0656	0.344
Small	0.199	0.175	0.074	-0.047	0.1090	0.227	0.0586	0.0971	0.244
PANEL B: Results for Equally Weighted Portfolios									
Growth	0.077	0.132	0.0004	-0.015	0.0366	0.148	0.0620	0.0656	0.029
Value	0.075	0.136	0.0003	-0.256	0.0238	0.277	0.0288	0.0908	0.006
Large	0.078	0.135	0.003	-0.147	0.0410	0.117	-0.1530	0.0226	0.292
Small	0.123	0.170	0.000	0.056	0.0188	0.001	0.0808	0.0999	0.003
PANEL C: Results for the Indexes									
Growth	0.0679	0.130	0.0004				0.113	0.090	0.006
Value	0.0037	0.131	0.0004				0.094	0.055	0.054
Large	0.0385	0.133	0.0004				0.0147	0.056	0.050
Small	0.138	0.188	0.0000				0.0349	0.123	0.001

Notes: The returns on the managed portfolios in excess of a one-month Treasury bill and in excess of alternative benchmarks are regressed on a vector of predetermined information variables. These variables are the dividend yield of the CRSP index, a yield spread of long versus short term bonds, the yield on a short term Treasury bill, a corporate bond yield spread of low versus high grade bonds, and a dummy variable for Januaries. The adjRsq are the adjusted R-squares of the regressions and the pval(F) are the right-tail probability values of the F tests for the significance of the regression. The auto are the first order sample autocorrelations of the regression residuals. Panel A reports the average results, taken across the regressions for the individual managers. Panel B reports regressions for an equally-weighted portfolio of the funds in each group. The equally-weighted portfolios for each group are formed using every manager whose return is available in a given month. Panel C reports regression results when the dependent variables are the passive style indexes. The data are monthly from 1979:1–1990:12, or the shorter subsample available for an individual manager. Cases with fewer than 13 observations are not included.

significance of the R-square is 0.34, but more than half of the individual fund regressions produce p-values less than 0.05.

The regressions for the returns net of the CRSP index show that the hypothesis that there is no predictable abnormal performance can be rejected, if one assumes that the CRSP index is an efficient benchmark and that all funds have unit betas. The rejection of this joint hypothesis may be due to either time-varying betas or abnormal returns; either reason motivates a conditional performance analysis. Alternatively, the rejection could simply be driven by inefficiency of the CRSP index. The middle columns of Table 1 therefore report regressions for the returns net of the alternative benchmarks provided by the Russell style indexes.

The regressions for the returns in excess of the style indexes deliver typically lower R-squares than the other regressions. At the equally weighted portfolio level the regressions are statistically significant only for the small-cap managers. The style indexes are more closely correlated with the fund returns than a typical market index, which reflects a practical appeal of style indexes as performance benchmarks. (High correlation should reduce the estimation error associated with measures of abnormal performance.) The predictable excess returns of the small-cap managers may indicate that small-cap fund returns are more difficult to capture with a style index than are the other groups.[9] Similar to other regressions in Table 1, the equally weighted portfolios mask cross-sectional variation. The individual-fund regressions net of the style indexes are significant at the 5% level for about half of the managers, and the average adjusted R-square for a small-cap manager is over 10%.

To summarize, the regressions show that the expected excess returns of the managers vary over time with the public information variables. The evidence of predictable returns in excess of a benchmark is not attributed to the use of the CRSP index as the benchmark. This motivates the use of conditional models to study the performance of pension managers.

B. Estimates of Pension Fund Alphas

Section IV described various models for alpha. We estimate unconditional and conditional versions of the CAPM, using the CRSP value-weighted index as the benchmark, as given in equations (1) and (3). The unconditional CAPM assumes that both the betas and the alphas are constant over time but that they may differ across funds. The conditional model (3) allows time-varying betas, but assumes that any abnormal performance is captured by the fixed alpha coefficients. We also estimate models where the Russell style index for a manager replaces the CRSP index as the benchmark. The results are summarized in Table 2, where panels A and B report results using the CAPM benchmark and panels C and D give the results for the style indexes.

The two right-hand columns of Table 2 report right-tail p-values of F-tests and of heteroskedasticity-consistent Wald tests for the hypothesis that the conditional

Table 2. Estimates of Pension Fund Alphas

	Unconditional Models					Conditional Models						
	alpha	t(alpha)	beta	t(beta)	Rsq	alpha	t(alpha)	beta	t(beta)	Rsq	pval(F)	pval(W)
PANEL A: Averages for the Inividual Managers, CAPM Benchmark												
Growth	0.100	0.438	1.11	25.1	0.888	0.087	0.314	1.22	13.7	0.902	0.376	0.184
Fraction of p-values < 0.05											0.56	0.56
Bonferroni P-values											0.011	0.000
Value	−0.034	−0.026	0.91	24.3	0.880	−0.033	−0.038	1.00	13.5	0.899	0.344	0.181
Fraction of p-values < 0.05											0.63	0.63
Bonferroni P-values											0.007	0.000
Large	0.104	0.675	0.95	33.5	0.899	0.099	0.570	0.96	20.9	0.920	0.236	0.066
Fraction of p-values < 0.05											0.84	0.75
Bonferroni P-values											0.000	0.000
Small	−0.105	−0.309	1.15	14.5	0.791	0.031	0.084	1.47	7.88	0.820	0.387	0.186
Fraction of p-values < 0.05											0.55	0.55
Bonferroni P-values											0.103	0.000
PANEL B: Results for Equally Weighted Portfolios of Managers, CAPM Benchmark												
Growth	0.173	1.54	1.09	49.8	0.932	0.162	1.43	1.10	45.3	0.933	0.927	0.878
Value	0.164	2.25	0.87	49.6	0.960	0.130	1.79	0.88	55.0	0.966	0.004	0.032
Large	0.126	2.04	0.91	48.5	0.972	0.113	2.11	0.91	79.0	0.980	0.000	0.000
Small	0.159	0.89	1.12	23.8	0.859	0.251	1.37	1.11	27.5	0.863	0.540	0.311

PANEL C: Averages for the Inividual Managers, Style Index Benchmarks

Growth	0.074	0.521	1.01	30.5	0.918	-0.010	-0.005	0.98	16.2	0.930	0.106	0.101
Fraction of p-values < 0.05											0.68	0.68
Bonferroni P-values											0.000	0.000
Value	0.018	0.109	0.95	24.4	0.884	0.003	-0.010	1.12	14.3	0.901	0.110	0.163
Fraction of p-values < 0.05											0.68	0.55
Bonferroni P-values											0.000	0.000
Large	0.107	0.708	0.930	33.6	0.902	0.064	0.331	0.92	21.3	0.923	0.084	0.084
Fraction of p-values < 0.05											0.80	0.80
Bonferroni P-values											0.000	0.000
Small	0.597	2.11	0.974	23.3	0.887	0.493	1.79	1.14	11.0	0.907	0.075	0.121
Fraction of p-values < 0.05											0.80	0.69
Bonferroni P-values											0.000	0.000

PANEL D: Results for Equally Weighted Portfolios of Managers, Style Index Benchmarks

Growth	0.268	3.34	0.99	63.8	0.968	0.143	1.80	0.99	70.6	0.971	0.014	0.000
Value	0.128	1.92	0.92	49.4	0.964	0.106	1.56	0.92	59.3	0.965	0.206	0.307
Large	0.142	2.30	0.89	47.0	0.973	0.086	1.59	0.89	81.9	0.980	0.000	0.000
Small	0.357	3.50	0.91	45.3	0.954	0.265	2.78	0.91	50.0	0.960	0.004	0.000

Notes: Alpha and beta are the intercept and slope coefficients in market model regressions for the managed portfolio returns net of a one-month Treasury bill. In the unconditional CAPM, the regressor is the excess return of the CRSP Value-weighted market index. In the style index models, the excess return of the Russell Style index is used as the benchmark return. For the conditional models, the portfolios are regressed over time on the excess return of the relevant benchmark index and its product with a vector of predetermined instruments. The instruments are the dividend yield of the CRSP index, a yield spread of long versus short term bonds, the yield on a short term Treasury bill, a corporate bond yield spread of low versus high grade bonds, and a dummy variable for Januaries. Alpha and beta are the intercept and the slope coefficient on the market index. Heteroskedasticity-consistent t-ratios are reported for all coefficients. The Rsq are the R-squares of the regressions. pval(F) is the right-tail probability value of the F test for the marginal significance of the additional lagged variables in the conditional model regression. pval(W) is the right-tail probability value of a heteroskedasticity-consistent Wald test. The Bonferroni P-values are the minimum of the individual p-values in a group multiplied by the number of managers in the group. The data are monthly from 1979:1–1990:12, or the subsample available for a particular manager. The excess returns are percent per month. Panels A and C present averages taken across the regressions for each manager, which may refer to different subperiods. Panels B and D report equally-weighted portfolios for each group, formed using every manager whose return is available in a given month. Cases with fewer than 13 observations are not included.

market betas are constant over time. These are exclusion tests for the additional terms in the conditional models, which are the interaction terms between the benchmark index and the lagged conditioning variables in regression (3). In panel B we see that the incremental explanatory power of the interaction terms is significant for equally weighted portfolios of the value and large-cap funds.

Table 2 includes the average R-squares, taken across the individual funds in a group. The R-squares go up more for a typical individual fund than for the portfolio, when the conditioning variables are brought into the model. This suggests that there is time variation in the individual fund betas that washes out at the aggregate level. The regressions for the individual funds show this to be the case. Using a 5% significance level, the CAPM benchmark and the F (Wald) statistic, the hypothesis of a constant conditional beta is rejected for 23 (23) of 41 growth managers, 25 (26) of 40 value managers, 46 (41) of 55 large-cap managers, and 27 (27) of 49 small-cap managers. Similar results are found using the style index benchmarks.

Table 2 also reports a joint test for the hypothesis that the individual betas are constant, for each fund in each style group. These are based on the Bonferroni inequality.[10] The joint test rejects the hypothesis that all managers have constant conditional betas.

We estimated four-factor models in which the Russell style indexes are used in multibeta generalizations of the models of equations (1) and (3). The factors are the four style indexes, measured net of the Treasury bill return. The results (not reported here) are qualitatively similar to those in Table 2.[11]

The above results imply heterogeneity in the month-to-month market risk dynamics of the individual funds within a style group. Some of the managers reduce their betas at the same time that others increase their betas. Therefore, we would expect that conditional models, which allow for fund-specific risk exposure dynamics, should be able to capture returns across managers better than models which assume that the betas are constant.[12,13] These results motivate further analysis of the performance dynamics.

C. Evidence of Time-varying Conditional Alphas

Table 3 summarizes the results of estimating equation (5) with time-varying conditional alphas. This model approximates the conditional alpha as a linear function of the predetermined information, allowing the function to be different for each manager.[14]

Panel A of Table 3 uses the CRSP value-weighted index as the benchmark portfolio. The two far right-hand columns report right-tail p-values for the F test and for a heteroskedasticity-consistent Wald test of the hypothesis that the conditional alphas are constant over time, against the alternative that they are time-varying. The tests in panel A provide evidence that some managers have time-varying conditional alphas relative to the CAPM. A 5% F test (Wald test) rejects the constant-alpha hypothesis for 27% (24%) of the growth managers, and for 43%

Table 3. Evidence of Time-varying Conditional Alphas

PANEL A: Coefficients of the conditional CAPM alphas:

manager	const	t(const)	dy	t(dy)	term	t(term)	tbill	t(tbill)	Rsq	pval(F) Bonferroni	pval(W) Bonferroni
Growth	0.218	2.00	0.284	1.18	-0.145	-1.69	-0.047	-0.598	0.934	0.656	0.064
										0.000	0.000
Value	0.186	2.47	0.196	1.25	0.057	0.864	0.030	0.594	0.964	0.291	0.002
										0.000	0.000
Large	0.168	2.96	0.184	1.45	0.009	0.192	-0.028	-0.755	0.978	0.719	0.016
										0.000	0.000
Small	0.353	2.02	1.22	3.72	-0.207	-1.850	-0.210	-2.01	0.872	0.134	0.000
										0.024	0.000

(continued)

Table 3. Continued

manager	const	t(const)	dy	t(dy)	term	t(term)	tbill	t(tbill)	Rsq	pval(F) Bonferroni	pval(W) Bonferroni
PANEL B: Coefficients of the conditional style model alphas:											
Growth	0.248	3.16	0.236	1.37	-0.0906	-1.68	-0.0125	-0.220	0.971	0.299	0.003
										0.003	0.000
Value	0.206	3.06	0.310	2.25	0.0185	0.345	-0.007	-0.206	0.967	0.215	0.004
										0.000	0.000
Large	0.179	3.13	0.184	1.44	0.017	0.325	-0.022	-0.578	0.979	0.648	0.006
										0.000	0.000
Small	0.404	4.10	-0.049	-0.207	0.003	0.030	-0.005	-0.071	0.959	0.881	0.001
										0.000	0.000

Notes: Coefficients and heteroskedasticity-consistent t-ratios are shown for the conditional alphas in the following regression model, for equally weighted portfolios of the managers:

$$r_{p,t+1} = \alpha_{0p} + A'_p z_t + b_{0p} r'_{b,t+1} + B'_{pb} [z_t r_{b,t+1}] + u_{p,t+1}$$

where the conditional alpha is a linear function of the information: $\alpha_p(Z_t) = \alpha_{0p} + A'_p z_t$. $r_{p,t+1}$ is the excess return of the fund and $r_{b,t+1}$ is the return of a benchmark index, in excess of a one-month Treasury bill. In panel A, the benchmark is the CRSP value-weighted stock index. In panel B, $r_{b,t+1}$ is the Russell Style index for the manager. The instruments z_t are a constant (denoted by const), the dividend yield of the CRSP index (dy), a yield spread of long versus short term bonds (term), and the yield on a short term Treasury bill (tbill). The Rsq are the R-squares of the regressions. pval(F) is the right-tail probability value of the F test for the hypothesis that the A_p coefficients of the conditional alphas are jointly zero and pval(W) is the right-tail probability value of a heteroskedasticity-consistent Wald test for the hypothesis that the A_p coefficients of the conditional alphas are jointly zero. The second line reports the Bonferroni P-values, which are the minimum p-value in a group multiplied by the number of managers in a group. The data are monthly from 1979:1–1990:12, or the subsample available for a particular manager. The excess returns are percent per month. The equally-weighted portfolios for each group are formed using every manager whose return is available in a given month. Cases with fewer than 13 observations are not included.

18

(48%) of the value managers. The fractions for the large-cap and small-cap managers lie in between these figures. The joint Bonferroni tests reject the constant-alpha hypothesis at the 0.024 level or less. A similar result is found in panel B, where the style index benchmarks are used. The tests therefore provide evidence that the conditional alphas in these models are time-varying.[15]

Table 3 summarizes, using equally weighted portfolios, the estimates of the A_p coefficients and their heteroskedasticity-consistent t-ratios, which measure the sensitivity of the conditional alphas to the public information variables. At the group level the dividend yield and the Treasury bill yield are the more important variables. We also examine the coefficients for the individual managers. Judging by the frequency of t-ratios larger than two, the most important variables are, again, the Treasury bill yield (41 cases), and the dividend yield (37 cases).

Among the small-cap managers, 15 of the 16 significant coefficients for alpha on the dividend yield are positive, and all 13 of the significant coefficients on the Treasury bill are negative. This says that the small-cap managers deliver higher risk-adjusted abnormal performance relative to the CAPM when dividend yields are high and short-term interest rates are low, even after allowing for time-varying risk exposures. Since high dividend yields and low short-term interest rates both predict high stock returns, the conditional alphas tend to be positively correlated with expected stock market returns. While consistent with the conventional wisdom that it is easier for a fund manager to look good in an up market, this result may reflect a misspecification in the conditional CAPM.

Panel B of Table 3 summarizes the results of estimating conditional alphas using the Russell style index for the manager as the benchmark portfolio. Different managers with different style classifications therefore have different benchmarks. The results are similar to what we found using the CAPM, including the tendency for positive coefficients on the dividend yield and negative coefficients on the Treasury bill. A 5% test using the F statistic (Wald statistic), rejects the hypothesis that the alphas are constant for 53 (77) of the 185 managers. The Bonferroni joint p-values are 0.003 or less for each manager group. The significant time variation in the alphas is spread fairly evenly across the groups, which is also similar to the results for the conditional CAPM. Our conclusion is that some pension fund managers have time-varying conditional alphas, and these are not an artifact of using the conditional CAPM as the benchmark model.

VI. UNDERSTANDING THE AVERAGE PERFORMANCE OF PENSION FUNDS

Figure 1 presents the distribution of the alphas from six models—unconditional and conditional versions of the CAPM, the single style index models, and the four-factor models. As described above, the returns in the RDS database do not reflect the cost of management fees, which differ across the style groups. Therefore,

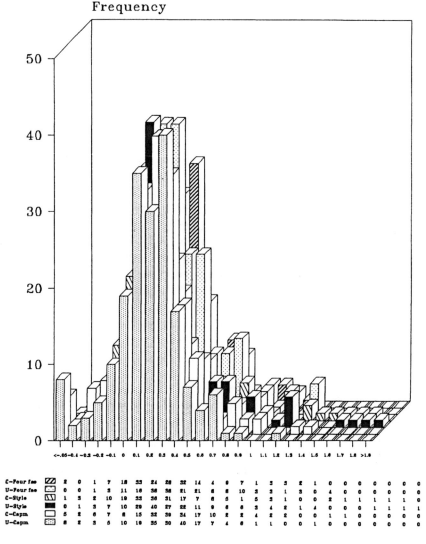

		<-.05	-0.4	-0.3	-0.2	-0.1	0	0.1	0.2	0.3	0.4	0.5	0.6	0.7	0.8	0.9	1	1.1	1.2	1.3	1.4	1.5	1.6	1.7	1.8	>1.8
C-Four fac	▨	2	0	1	7	18	33	24	28	32	14	4	9	7	1	3	3	2	1	0	0	0	0	0	0	0
U-Four fac	▨	0	0	1	3	11	18	38	36	21	21	6	8	10	3	3	1	3	0	4	0	0	0	0	0	0
C-Style	▨	1	3	2	10	19	33	36	31	17	7	6	5	1	5	3	1	0	0	2	1	1	1	1	1	0
U-Style	■	0	1	3	7	10	29	40	27	22	11	9	9	6	3	4	2	1	4	0	0	0	1	1	1	1
C-Capm	☐	5	2	6	7	8	15	32	39	34	17	10	2	2	4	2	2	0	0	1	1	0	0	0	0	0
U-Capm	▦	8	2	3	6	10	19	35	30	40	17	7	4	9	1	1	0	0	1	0	0	0	0	0	0	0

Alpha Values

Notes: The measures of performance are estimated using four alternative models. Each model produces an alpha, which is the average return in excess of the appropriate risk adjusted benchmark. We subtract the median values of posted management fees for 1988 from each alpha; these figures are reported in the text for each investment style. The models are indicated as follows, C-Four fac is a conditional, four factor model in which conditioning information enters in a linear model for the conditional betas. U-Four fac is an unconditional four factor model, with constant betas. C-Style is a conditional model with a single style index as the factor and U-Style is an unconditional version of this model. C-Capm is a conditional capital asset pricing model, using a single market index as the factor and U-CAPM is an unconditional version of this model.

Figure 1. Frequency Distribution of Alphas

we adjust the alphas by subtracting the median 1988 fees reported above for each style group.

While the style index models generally make the managers look better than does the CAPM, the unconditional and conditional versions of the alphas appear similar in Figure 1. This similarity in the distributions is an interesting result, in view of the finding by Ferson and Schadt (1996) that conditional alphas for mutual funds are on average larger than unconditional alphas. Ferson and Warther (1996) show that these differences reflect a positive correlation between expected market returns and the flow of new money into mutual funds over time, combined with a negative relation between new money flows and mutual fund betas.

While we also find time-varying betas for pension funds, it is likely that the flow of pension monies and the cash holdings of these funds do not respond as much in the short run to expected market returns as is the case for mutual funds. This may explain the difference between our results in Figure 1 and the findings of Ferson and Schadt (1996). Future research comparing the dynamic relations between performance and the flow of funds to pensions funds, in comparison with mutual funds, is clearly called for.

Our findings of positive relative performance for the pension managers seem to be at odds with the conclusions of Lakonishok, Shleifer, and Vishny (1992), who find that the managers they study consistently underperformed the S&P 500 by an average of over 1% per year over 1983–1989. Since our universe of managers, sample period, benchmarks, and methodology all differ from those of Lakonishok, Shleifer, and Vishny, we address the reasons for the differing conclusions in this section. In Table 4 we present results using Lakonishok, Shleifer, and Vishny's methodology: a simple comparison of average annual returns (without subtracting fees) for equally weighted portfolios of the managers to the average annual return on the S&P 500. We also report, for comparison purposes, some of the figures from their tables.[16]

Table 4 confirms the positive average performance in our sample of managers, relative to the S&P 500. Over our sample period of 1979–1990 the average return on the equally weighted portfolio of all managers is 18.95%, as compared to an average annual S&P return of 16.45%. By contrast, Lakonishok, Shleifer, and Vishny find an average return of 17.73% for their managers over 1983–1989, compared to an S&P average return of 18.96%. Over the 1983–1989 period they find that 54.1% of the managers in their sample earned lower returns than the S&P, whereas we find only 50% over the same period. Furthermore, over the 1979–1990 sample period only 40.6% of the managers in our universe earned returns below that of the S&P. Clearly, the different results of the two studies reflect both differences in the sample period and differences in the samples of pension managers.[17]

To determine to what extent the differing results are a function of the sample period and of the universe of managers studied, we decompose the difference between the average returns in the two studies. Let $r_{study, \, sample \, period}$ denote the

Table 4. Annual Returns of Equally Weighted Portfolios of Funds and Percentage of Funds with Returns less than the S&P 500

Year	CFG number of managers[a]	S&P 500 return (percent)	CFG equal-weighted return (percent)	CFG % less than S&P 500[b]	LSV equal-weighted return (percent)[c]	LSV % less than S&P 500
79	26	18.62	32.04	11.5		
80	31	32.63	34.23	54.8		
81	41	−4.96	5.50	2.4		
82	47	21.65	27.89	19.1		
83	71	22.57	25.53	36.6	17.8	59
84	84	6.18	3.93	54.8	3.8	63
85	100	31.88	32.74	44.0	33.3	38
86	120	18.69	17.76	52.5	18.1	50
87	140	5.21	3.60	60.0	4.0	61
88	155	16.50	19.49	38.7	17.9	47
89	174	31.67	28.71	63.2	29.2	61
90	189	−3.13	−4.03	49.7		
Mean	79–90	16.45	18.95	40.6		
Mean	83–89	18.96	18.82	50.0	17.73	54.1

Notes: [a] The number of managers out of 273 with return data for all months in a given year. All CFG return data are from the Russell Data Services data base, in percent per year.

[b] The fraction of the managers whose return over the period was less than the return of the Standard and Poors 500 stock index.

[c] LSV figures are based on Lakonishok, Shliefer and Vishny, 1992, Table 2 (the performance data base).

average returns, measured in excess of the S&P 500 return, in a study (Lakonishok, Shleifer, and Vishny LSV, or the present, CFG) over a particular sample period (1983–1989 or 1979–1990). The decomposition is:

$$r_{LSV,83-89} - r_{CFG,79-90} = (r_{CFG,83-89} - r_{CFG,79-90}) + (r_{LSV,83-89} - r_{CFG,83-89})$$
$$-3.73 \quad = \quad (-2.64) \quad + \quad (-1.09)$$

The first term in the decomposition captures the average *sample period effect*, and the second term captures the *manager universe effect*. While the managers in our sample have excess returns 3.73% higher than those in the Lakonishok, Shleifer, and Vishny sample, over 70% of this difference, or 2.64%, is attributed by our decomposition to the sample period effect. For the years in our sample but not in the Lakonishok, Shleifer, and Vishny sample (1979–1982 and 1990), our managers earned an average annual return of 24.92%.

The remaining difference between the excess returns in our sample and the Lakonishok, Shleifer, and Vishny sample is 1.09%. As this is measured over a common subperiod, we attribute it to differences in the population of managers in the two studies. We can rule out one potential explanation for this manager universe effect. Since the returns in Table 4 and in the Lakonishok, Shleifer, and Vishny study do not subtract out management fees, higher fees in our sample could potentially explain the difference. However, it is unlikely that the managers in our sample charged higher fees than those in the Lakonishok, Shleifer, and Vishny sample, because fees are lower for larger accounts. As described above, the average account size for the managers in our sample is in the range of $100 million. The Lakonishok, Shleifer, and Vishny database has more accounts in the $25–$50 million range.[18]

Although smaller account sizes do not necessarily imply that the accounts hold the shares of smaller firms, it is possible that our sample of large accounts is more concentrated in large firm stocks than are the accounts examined by Lakonishok, Shleifer, and Vishny. If this is the case, then the poor performance recorded by Lakonishok, Shleifer, and Vishny may be partly explained by the fact that small firms did not perform well, relative to the S&P 500, over part of their sample period. We provide an additional decomposition of the differences in average returns to investigate this possibility. Using our sample of small-cap managers instead of our overall sample, we compare the results to the Lakonishok, Shleifer, and Vishny universe (they do not report results for small-cap managers separately). The results of the decomposition are as follows:

$$r_{LSV,83-89} - r_{small,79-90} = (r_{small,83-89} - r_{small,79-80}) + (r_{LSV,83-89} - r_{small,83-89})$$
$$-4.81 \quad = \quad (-4.66) \quad + \quad (-0.15)$$

Using our small-cap universe, most of the differences in average returns between the two studies are attributed to the sample period effect. The small-cap managers in our sample earn 4.81% more per year, in excess of the S&P 500, than the managers in Lakonishok, Shleifer, and Vishny's sample. For the years in our sample but not in the Lakonishok, Shleifer, and Vishny sample (1979–1982), our small-cap managers earned an average annual return of 30.5%.

In summary, the results using average returns show that the evidence on the average performance of pension managers is sensitive to the sample period. The 1983–1989 period studied by Lakonishok, Shleifer, and Vishny was a period in which small stocks performed poorly relative to the S&P 500, which they choose as the benchmark. Using a longer sample period than Lakonishok, Shleifer, and Vishny, we find no evidence that the pension managers as a group perform poorly. Indeed, we find essentially the opposite result. We suggest, therefore, that Lakonishok, Shleifer, and Vishny's conclusions about the poor performance of the industry are premature.[19]

VII. THE PERSISTENCE OF INVESTMENT PERFORMANCE

A. Methods for Measuring Persistence

We next address the question of whether good (or bad) performance persists over time. Our approach to measuring persistence is based on cross-sectional regressions of future excess returns on a measure of past performance, or alpha:

$$r_p(t,t+\tau) = \gamma_{0,t,\tau} + \gamma_{1,t,\tau}\alpha_{pt} + u_p(t,t+\tau), \quad p = 1, \ldots n \qquad (6)$$

where $r_p(t,t+\tau)$ is the compounded return from month t to month $t+\tau$ for manager p, measured net of the return to rolling over one-month Treasury bills. The symbol τ denotes the return horizon, for $\tau = 1, 3, 6, 12, 18, 24,$ and 36 months. The regressor, α_{pt}, is a measure of past abnormal performance, estimated using time-series data up to month t. The term $u_p(t,t+\tau)$ is the regression error. The cross-sectional regression is estimated for a number of months, resulting in a time series of the slope coefficients, $\gamma_{1,t,\tau}, t = 1, \ldots T-\tau$. The hypothesis that the alpha cannot be used to predict the future return (i.e., no persistence) implies that the expected value of the coefficient $\gamma_{1,t,\tau}$ is zero.

The regression (6) is a predictive cross-sectional regression, since the alpha is based on past data only. Similar regressions are used in asset pricing studies (e.g., Fama & MacBeth, 1973; Ferson & Harvey, 1991a), where a risk measure like beta is the independent variable. Regression (6) is estimated by GLS, using a computationally feasible weighted least squares (WLS) approach. The weight for each observation is the inverse of the standard deviation of the residuals from the time-series model that was used to estimate the alpha. This has two advantages. Note that the deflated alpha is essentially an appraisal ratio. Because deflating by the standard error reduces cross-sectional differences related to variance, Brown and colleagues (1992) suggest using the appraisal ratio as a partial adjustment for survivorship bias. Roll and Ross (1994) and Kandel and Stambaugh (1995) also show that generalized least squares (GLS) is preferable to ordinary least squares (OLS) in cross-sectional stock return regressions.

Because the slopes of the cross-sectional regressions are invariant to any additive factors, the results are robust to any additive bias in returns that is common across the funds at a given date (for example, a misspecified risk-free rate). By using the future return as the dependent variable in (6), the regressions focus directly on the question of the most practical interest: to what extent can the past alpha be used to predict future relative returns? The alternative approach of using the alpha for a future subperiod as the dependent variable, as in some previous studies, is problematic for the following reason. Most of the likely sources of bias in alphas (e.g., missing priced factors, size effects, book-to-market or earnings yield effects, etc.) are correlated over time. If future alphas were used as the dependent variable, such biases in alpha are likely to be correlated over time, which can generate spurious evidence of persistent performance.

While the cross-sectional regression approach has some attractive features, it also implies some complications. The regression errors are cross-sectionally correlated, making the usual regression statistics, such as R-squares and OLS standard errors, unreliable. Therefore, we use the methodology of Fama and MacBeth (1973) to test the hypothesis that the expected value of $\gamma_{1,t,\tau}$ is zero against the alternative hypothesis that the mean value of the coefficient is not zero. A t-statistic is formed, where the sample mean of the time series of the $\gamma_{1,t,\tau}$ estimates is the numerator and the standard error for the mean is the denominator.

When the future return horizon is longer than one month ($\tau > 1$), the time series of the $\gamma_{1,t,\tau}$ estimates will be autocorrelated due to the overlapping data. We adjust the standard errors in the t-statistics to account for this autocorrelation, using the approach of Newey and West (1987) with $\tau-1$ moving average terms.

B. Evidence that Performance Persists

Table 5 summarizes the results of the cross-sectional regressions, using various measures of the past performance to predict the future returns. Each row of the table uses a different measure of alpha. The simplest measures are the past average returns and the returns in excess of the manager's style index, based on the most recent 60 (or 36) months. We also measure the past average return net of the return for an equally weighted portfolio of the other managers in the same Russell style group (denoted in the tables as "net of group mean"). The "60-month unconditional CAPM" alphas use equation (1), the previous 60 months of data and the market index as the benchmark, to estimate an alpha. The "60-month unconditional style alphas" are similar, but use the passive style indexes as the benchmarks. The "time-varying conditional CAPM" alphas use equation (5) and the previous 60 months of data to estimate the parameters. The most recently available values of the information variables Z_t are then used to determine the conditional alpha. The "time-varying conditional style" alphas are similar, but they use the style indexes as the benchmark.

A final set of alphas are the "timing-adjusted" conditional and unconditional alphas. The unconditional models are based on the classic market timing regressions of Treynor and Mazuy (1966):

$$r_{pt+1} = a_p + b_p\, r_{bt+1} + \gamma_{tmu}[r_{b,t+1}]^2 + v_{pt+1},$$

where the coefficient γ_{tmu} measures market timing ability. Admati, Bhattacharya, Ross, and Pfleiderer (1986) describe a model in which this coefficient is positive if the manager increases beta when he or she receives a positive signal about the benchmark. Alternatively, the coefficient may capture nonlinearities which arise due to derivative securities or dynamic trading strategies (Jagannathan & Korajczyk, 1986; Glosten & Jagannathan, 1994). The intercept coefficient, a_p, is the *timing-adjusted unconditional alpha*.

Table 5. Measures of the Persistence of Institutional Equity Manager Performance

Measure of Prior Performance	T-ratios for Future Returns, by Horizon							Bonferroni pval		Wald
	1 mo.	3 mo.	6 mo.	12 mo.	18 mo.	24 mo.	36 mo.	Minimum t-ratio	Maximum t-ratio	Joint pvalue
PANEL A: Unconditional Models										
36-month past average return	-0.353	-0.148	0.419	0.616	0.211	0.211	0.009	1.00	1.00	0.998
36-month average excess return	0.076	0.141	0.669	0.962	1.31	1.52	2.10	1.00	0.128	0.741
60-month past average return	-0.717	-0.633	-0.700	-1.05	-2.05	-1.24	-1.13	0.145	1.00	0.999
60-month net of group mean	1.40	1.59	1.72	2.78	3.57	3.38	3.54	0.566	0.001	*
60-month unconditional CAPM	-0.005	0.025	0.095	0.328	0.072	0.195	0.579	1.00	1.00	1.00
60-month unconditional style	-0.285	0.067	0.531	1.27	2.23	3.21	2.77	1.00	0.005	0.0289
Timing-adjusted unconditional CAPM	-0.629	-0.971	-0.996	-0.717	-0.958	-1.36	-1.06	0.608	1.00	*
Timing-adjusted unconditional style	-0.094	0.081	0.244	0.741	1.49	2.55	2.48	1.00	0.39	0.147
PANEL B: Conditional Models										
60-month conditional CAPM	-0.449	-0.665	-0.848	-0.581	-0.586	-0.564	-0.113	1.00	1.00	*
60-month conditional style	-0.487	-0.149	0.142	0.760	1.81	3.50	3.16	1.00	0.0018	0.00
Timing-adjusted conditional CAPM	-0.0678	-0.262	-0.397	-0.263	-0.306	-0.230	0.195	1.00	1.00	1.00
Timing-adjusted conditional style	0.456	0.559	0.664	1.26	2.27	3.89	3.66	1.00	0.0004	0.00051
Time-varying conditional CAPM	2.20	2.11	1.39	2.69	0.958	0.729	2.67	1.00	0.026	*
Time-varying conditional style	2.14	1.66	1.31	1.77	2.22	2.19	1.88	0.664	0.095	*

Notes: *indicates that the covariance matrix was not positive definite.

T-ratios for time-series averages of the slope coefficients in monthly cross-sectional regressions of the future excess returns of the funds on predetermined measures of the funds' alphas. The t-statistic for the average coefficient is calculated similar to Fama and MacBeth (1973), using the time-series standard error of the mean. The standard error of the mean is adjusted for autocorrelation induced by overlapping data for horizons τ longer than one month, using $\tau-1$ Newey-West lags. The "Bonferroni pvals" are the individual right-tail pvalue from a normal distribution, for the minimum (or maximum) t-ratio across the investment horizons, and multiplied by the number of horizons, which is seven. (Values larger than 1.0 are shown as 1.0). The joint Wald Test is a heteroskedasticity-consistent test of the hypothesis that the regression coefficients for all seven horizons are zero. The different models for alpha, one for each row of the table, are described in the text. The data are monthly from 1979:1–1990:12. The cross-sectional regression for each month and horizon, τ, uses all managers with 60 past (36 in the case of 36-month past return alphas) and τ future returns available.

Ferson and Schadt (1996) propose a conditional version of the Treynor-Mazuy regression:

$$r_{pt+1} = a_p + b_p \, r_{bt+1} + C'_p(z_t \, r_{bt+1}) + \gamma_{tmc}[r_{b,t+1}]^2 + v_{pt+1},$$

where the coefficient vector C_p captures the response of the manger's beta to the public information, Z_t, and the term $C'_p(z_t \, r_{bt+1})$ controls for the public information effect. The coefficient γ_{tmc} measures the sensitivity of the manager's beta to the private market timing signal, conditional on the public information Z_t. The intercept, a_p, is the *timing-adjusted conditional alpha*. In this model the conditional alpha is assumed to be a fixed parameter over time. We estimate the model using a 60-month moving window, which allows ad hoc time variation. We also estimate conditional and unconditional versions of market timing regressions in which the Russell style indexes are used in place of the CRSP index as the benchmark portfolio. These models imagine that managers attempt to time their movements between cash and a portfolio of stocks which is well approximated by their Russell style index.

We estimated the conditional and unconditional versions of the market timing regressions over the 1979–1990 sample period (tables available by request). We find more positive alphas and negative timing coefficients than can be attributed to chance, in both versions of the market timing model. This is similar to the findings of Coggin, Fabozzi, and Rahman (1993). The negative timing coefficients could indicate a perverse market timing ability. However, negative timing coefficients are more likely to indicate the importance of derivative securities or dynamic strategies, which induce nonlinearities in the relation between managers' returns and the benchmark.

In panel A of Table 5 the unconditional measures of alpha are used in the persistence regression. In panel B the conditional measures of alpha are used. The middle columns of the table show the Fama-MacBeth t-ratios, which are adjusted for autocorrelation if the future return horizon τ is longer than one month. As a number of comparisons are made, and the results are likely to be correlated across the horizons, joint tests across the horizons are appropriate. The right hand columns of Table 5 report the results of joint tests. The first is the Bonferroni p-value, based on the collection of the individual p-values for the seven horizons, using the t-distribution (see note 10). The far right-hand columns report right-tail p-values for Wald tests of the hypothesis that the vector of the slope coefficients for all of the horizons is zero. The Wald test statistic is a quadratic form in the vector of the sample means of the cross-sectional regression slopes, where the matrix is the inverse of the covariance matrix for the mean values of the slopes. The covariance matrix is formed using the standard errors of the means, as described above, and the correlation across the horizons is estimated from the time series of the cross-sectional regression slopes. The Wald test is asymptotically distributed as a Chi-square variable, with degrees of freedom equal to the number of horizons examined.

The results of Table 5 are interesting in a number of respects. Using the unconditional models of alpha, there is little evidence of predictive ability. Only when the unconditional alphas are calculated relative to the style indexes or the group average returns do they produce significant coefficients in the cross-sectional regressions. The unconditional alphas relative to the CAPM have little information about the future returns. The past average returns seem to contain no useful information.

Using conditional models, the alphas appear more informative about the future returns. Both the style models and the time-varying conditional version of the CAPM alphas show some predictive ability. There is a pattern in the *t*-ratios over the horizons of the future returns: the coefficients are not significant for the shorter horizons, and they are typically larger at the longer horizons.

Table 5 is based on the full set of managers who have enough data to estimate alpha over the previous 60 (36) months. Studies of open-end mutual funds find that persistence is concentrated in the poorly performing funds (Goetzmann & Ibbotson, 1994; Shukla & Trzcinka, 1994: Carhart, 1997). However, these studies use unconditional methods. Table 6 therefore repeats the persistence analysis using only the funds whose prior alphas are negative each month. The upper panel of the table shows that the lagged average returns have little predictive ability, unless they are measured net of the group means. The regressions are significant (jointly across the horizons) for four of the eight unconditional models. The significant coefficients are almost always positive, and they are clustered at the longer horizons. This says that, among the negative-alpha funds, those with relatively low prior alphas in a given month tend to have relatively low returns for many months into the future.

The second panel of Table 6 reports the results of persistence regressions using conditional alphas. The results are impressive, in that the regression coefficients are jointly significant across the horizons for five of the six conditional models. The conditional models also have more explanatory power at shorter horizons than the unconditional models. All of the significant coefficients are positive, indicating positive persistence in the relative performance of the negative-alpha managers. In other words, among those managers who have performed poorly by the conditional measures, the worst are likely to deliver significantly lower returns in the future.

Hendricks, Patel, and Zeckhauser (1993) consider the effects of survivorship bias under the simplifying assumptions that the expected returns of all managers are the same, but there are differences in variances. They argue that survivorship bias induces a U-shaped pattern in the relation between future and past performance. Past poor performers are likely to reverse rankings in the future, because a poor performer that remains in the database is one that is more likely to have performed better in the future. In Table 6 the cross-sectional correlation between past and future performance is positive and significant. This suggests that our estimates of the predictive ability may be conservative, if survivorship bias could be accounted for.

The *t*-ratios in Tables 5 and 6 suggest that persistence becomes stronger as the future return horizon increases out to three years. This pattern could reflect more

Table 6. Measures of the Persistence of Institutional Equity Manager Performance: Using Only Negative Prior Period Alphas

| Measure of Prior Performance | T-ratios for Future Returns, by Horizon | | | | | | | Bonferroni pval | | Wald |
	1 mo.	3 mo.	6 mo.	12 mo.	18 mo.	24 mo.	36 mo.	Minimum t-ratio	Maximum t-ratio	Joint pvalue
PANEL A: Unconditional Models										
36-month past average return	-1.05	-0.81	-1.20	-1.30	-1.11	-1.89	-1.70	0.21	1.00	*
36-month average excess return	-1.04	-0.50	-0.39	-0.20	-0.48	-0.62	-0.52	1.00	1.00	*
60-month average excess return	-3.02	-0.29	0.466	0.845	1.17	1.90	2.31	1.00	0.074	0.980
60-month net of group mean	1.32	1.89	2.19	3.26	3.41	3.73	5.04	0.657	0.000	0.076
60-month unconditional CAPM	1.58	1.01	0.50	1.31	2.39	3.09	2.74	1.00	0.008	0.039
60-month unconditional style	0.55	0.768	0.571	0.62	1.14	1.54	2.75	1.00	0.022	0.108
Timing-adjusted unconditional CAPM	0.07	0.11	0.66	1.68	1.99	2.12	4.04	1.00	0.000	0.007
Timing-adjusted unconditional style	-0.60	0.06	0.98	1.84	1.71	1.44	1.08	1.00	0.233	*

(continued)

29

Table 6. Continued

Measure of Prior Performance	T-ratios for Future Returns, by Horizon							Bonferroni pval		Wald
	1 mo.	3 mo.	6 mo.	12 mo.	18 mo.	24 mo.	36 mo.	Minimum Minimum t-ratio	Maximum t-ratio	Joint pvalue
PANEL B: Conditional Models										
60-month conditional CAPM	0.38	0.54	1.21	2.03	2.14	2.36	4.73	1.00	0.00	*
60-month conditional style	0.745	0.886	0.907	1.53	1.93	2.22	4.10	1.00	0.00175	0.0311
Timing-adjusted conditional CAPM	1.72	1.07	1.33	2.85	3.36	2.96	2.14	1.00	0.003	*
Timing-adjusted conditional style	1.12	1.54	2.47	2.43	3.20	2.86	2.80	0.929	0.002	*
Time-varying conditional CAPM	1.57	2.02	1.21	1.77	1.36	1.55	2.52	0.79	0.04	*
Time-varying conditional style	1.62	1.55	0.711	1.06	1.31	1.43	1.82	1.00	0.244	*

Notes: * indicates that the covariance matrix was not positive definite.

T-ratios for time-series averages of the slope coefficients in monthly cross-sectional regressions of the future excess returns of the funds on predetermined measures of the funds' alphas. Only the managers with negative prior period alphas are used. The t-statistic for the average coefficient is calculated similar to Fama and MacBeth (1973), using the time-series standard error of the mean. When the horizon of the future return, τ, exceeds one month, the standard error of the mean is adjusted for the autocorrelation induced by the overlapping future returns data using τ–1 Newey-West lags. The "Bonferroni pvals" are the individual right-tail pvalue from a normal distribution, using the minimum (or maximum) t-ratio across the investment horizons, multiplied by the number of horizons, which is seven. (Values larger than 1.0 are shown as 1.0). The joint Wald Test is a heteroskedasticity-consistent and autocorrelation-adjusted test of the hypothesis that the regression coefficients for all seven horizons are zero. The different models for alpha, one for each row of the table, are described in the text. The data are monthly from 1979:1–1990:12. The cross-sectional regression for each month and horizon, τ, uses all managers with 60 past (36 past, in the case of 36-month past return alphas) and τ future returns available.

precision of the estimates for the longer horizons, or finite sample biases in the estimators. The Newey-West estimator places declining weights on the autocovariances at longer lags. While the estimator is consistent, it could place too little weight on the longer lags in finite samples. We therefore replicated a number of the cases from Table 6 using Hansen's (1982) covariance matrix, which gives equal weights to all of the lags. We find that this alternative estimator typically produces slightly smaller *t*-ratios for the shorter horizons, similar numbers in the one- to two-year range, and larger *t*-ratios at the longest horizons. These patterns are consistent with the negative autocorrelations that are typically found in longer-horizon portfolio return data, and the weak or positive autocorrelation in shorter-horizon returns (e.g., Fama & French, 1988).

We also examine the point estimates of the cross-sectional regression coefficients, in order to see how much of the pattern across the horizons is attributed to larger coefficients, as opposed to smaller standard errors at the longer horizons. The magnitudes of the coefficients have an interesting economic interpretation (Fama, 1976), under the simplifying assumption that the managers' returns can be sold short. The cross-sectional coefficient in a given month is the return of a portfolio with short and long positions, such that the net investment is zero. The position is constructed to have an historical alpha equal to 1 (% per month). The average coefficient is the time-series average return to such a strategy. Figure 2 shows the average values of the cross-sectional coefficients, taken across the models which produce significant positive coefficients, and expressed as a return per month (the coefficient is divided by the number of months in the return horizon). Figure 2 uses all available managers with negative prior alphas, from Table 6. The average coefficients range from over 0.2% per month to more than 0.6% per month.[20] The figures show that the larger *t*-ratios for the longer horizons are not simply a result of more precise estimates. The magnitudes of the coefficients are also larger. The figures show the smallest coefficient at the six-month horizon. The magnitudes of the coefficients are uniformly larger in the sample of negative-alpha managers, which suggests that the economic significance of the persistence is larger for this group of managers. (When we look at the coefficients for each model of alpha separately, a similar pattern is found in most of the models.)[21]

It is conceivable that the weak relation of alphas to future returns in the full sample of managers (Table 5) and the strong positive relation in the subsample of negative-alpha managers (Table 6) masks a significant pattern among the high-alpha managers. Table 7 explores this possibility, replicating the analysis using the subset of managers with alphas in the top third each month. The table reveals no strong evidence of persistence in the performance of the high-alpha managers. Most of the coefficients are negative at the shorter horizons, which suggests some mean reversion in the performance of the top managers, but the negative coefficients are not significant. Only 10 of the 91 *t*-ratios in the table are larger than two, and all but one of these are positive coefficients at the longer horizons. Table 7 therefore

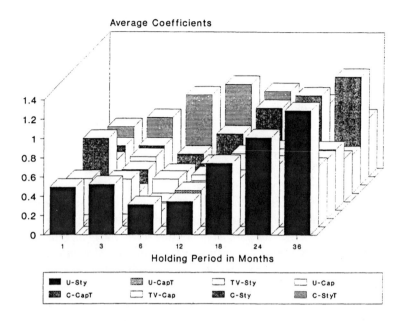

Notes: Measures of performance are estimated using four alternative models and past data, then future returns are regressed cross-sectionally on the performance measures. The holding period of the future returns is shown on the x-axis. The graph shows time-series averages of the cross-sectional regression coefficients normalized to percent excess return per month, for cases with significant negative performance. The models are indicated as follows: C-Sty is a conditional model with a single style index as the factor, assuming a constant conditional alpha, TV-Sty is a version of this model that assumed a time-varying alpha and U-Sty is an unconditional version of the style model. C-Cap is a conditional capital asset pricing model, using a single market index as the factor and assuming a constant conditional alpha, TV-Cap assumes a time-varying alpha and U-Cap is an unconditional version of this model. C-CapT and C-styT are timing adjusted versions of the conditional CAPM and Style models, assuming constant conditional alphas.

Figure 2.   Persistence Regression Coefficients

confirms the impression that the evidence of persistence in the performance of these managers is concentrated in the poorly performing group.

C.   The Economic Significance of Persistence

The interpretation of the cross-sectional regression coefficients as portfolio strategies is hypothetical because, unlike mutual funds, it is not possible to sell short pension funds. Furthermore, the regressions do not account for differences in the risk of the future returns. If the alphas are related to risk because of some systematic bias, then the evidence of persistence may reflect persistence in the expected compensation for this risk. Adjusting the cross-sectional regressions for risk is

Table 7. Measures of the Persistence of Institutional Equity Manager Performance: Using Only the Top Third Prior Period Alphas

| Measure of Prior Performance | T-ratios for Future Returns, by Horizon | | | | | | | Bonferroni pval | | Wald |
	1 mo.	3 mo.	6 mo.	12 mo.	18 mo.	24 mo.	36 mo.	Minimum t-ratio	Maximum t-ratio	Joint pvalue
PANEL A: Unconditional Models										
36-month past average return	1.26	1.09	1.83	2.23	2.38	1.70	0.99	1.00	0.06	0.963
36-month average excess return	−0.25	−0.10	0.34	1.09	1.11	0.98	0.82	1.00	0.93	0.996
60-month average excess return	−0.67	0.35	−0.04	−0.54	1.36	4.08	2.86	1.00	0.00	0.000
60-month unconditional CAPM	−1.93	−2.24	−1.82	−0.72	−0.40	−0.09	0.14	0.09	1.00	1.000
60-month unconditional style	−1.11	−0.98	−1.30	−1.20	−0.43	0.37	2.58	0.68	0.04	0.118
Timing-adjusted unconditional CAPM	−0.93	−0.56	−0.86	−0.77	−0.06	−0.43	−1.43	0.54	1.00	*
Timing-adjusted unconditional style	−0.55	−1.29	−1.14	−0.68	0.27	1.37	0.89	0.70	0.60	0.045

(continued)

Table 7. Continued

Measure of Prior Performance	T-ratios for Future Returns, by Horizon							Bonferroni pval		Wald
	1 mo.	3 mo.	6 mo.	12 mo.	18 mo.	24 mo.	36 mo.	Minimum t-ratio	Maximum t-ratio	Joint pvalue
PANEL B: Conditional Models										
60-month conditional CAPM	−1.27	−1.15	−0.98	−0.29	1.58	3.19	5.67	0.71	0.00	*
60-month conditional style	−0.57	−1.35	−1.43	−1.13	0.05	2.09	3.14	0.54	0.01	0.003
Timing-adjusted conditional CAPM	−0.67	−0.86	−1.19	−0.89	−0.29	−0.61	−1.63	0.36	1.00	0.687
Timing-adjusted conditional style	−0.77	−1.04	−1.02	−0.22	0.19	1.45	0.36	1.009	0.52	0.345
Time-varying conditional CAPM	−0.16	1.21	0.62	0.15	0.38	0.20	0.64	1.00	0.80	0.766
Time-varying conditional style	−0.05	1.21	0.44	0.64	1.19	3.26	1.83	1.00	0.01	0.987

Notes: *indicates that the covariance matrix was not positive definite.

T-ratios for time-series averages of the slope coefficients in monthly cross-sectional regressions of the future excess returns of the funds on predetermined measures of the funds' alphas. Only the managers with prior period alphas in the top third are used. The *t*-statistic for the average coefficient is calculated similar to Fama and MacBeth (1973), using the time-series standard error of the mean. When the horizon of the future return, τ, exceeds one month, the standard error of the mean is adjusted for the autocorrelation induced by the overlapping future returns data using τ − 1 Newey-West lags. The Bonferroni p-values are the individual right-tail pvalue from a normal distribution, using the minimum (or maximum) t-ratio across the investment horizons, multiplied by the number of horizons, which is seven. (Values larger than 1.0 are shown as 1.0). The joint Wald Test is a heteroskedasticity-consistent and autocorrelation-adjusted test of the hypothesis that the regression coefficients for all seven horizons are zero. The different models for alpha, one for each row of the table, are described in the text. The data are monthly from 1979:1–1990:12. The cross-sectional regression for each month and horizon, τ, uses all managers with 60 past (36 past, in the case of 36-month past return alphas) and τ future returns available.

problematic, as discussed above, because errors in the risk adjustment are likely to be correlated over time, which could actually produce—instead of control for— spurious persistence.

To address these issues we construct simple trading strategies, designed to facilitate risk adjustments and to provide a further economic interpretation for the persistence effects. Each trading strategy uses an estimate of alpha based on the past 60 months of data for each eligible manager. The alpha estimates are ranked, grouped according to quintiles and an equally weighted portfolio is formed from each quintile group. This portfolio is held for one month, and the procedure is repeated. The monthly returns and the cumulative investment values are tracked. If there is persistence in performance, then the high-alpha portfolios will generate higher future returns than low-alpha portfolios.

To adjust for risk, the performance of each quintile portfolio is evaluated using both unconditional and conditional models. The conditional models allow for time-varying risk exposures of the quintile strategies. The first date of the trading strategy returns is January 1984, and there are 84 monthly returns for each trading strategy.

Table 8 shows results when the quintiles are formed using three alternative measures of past performance. These are based on a time-varying conditional CAPM, an unconditional CAPM, and on past average returns with no risk adjust- ment. For each trading strategy Table 8 reports the alphas of the strategy's future returns, measured relative to four risk models (unconditional and conditional CAPM and three-factor models),[22] unconditional and conditional betas, and other performance statistics. The first two rows present comparable figures for the CRSP value-weighted index and an equally weighted portfolio of all managers.

When past average returns are used to form quintiles, the extreme high and low quintiles produce the riskiest future returns measured by standard deviation, uncon- ditional beta, or conditional beta. This is consistent with persistence in the volatility of funds, as assumed in the model of survivorship used by Hendricks, Patel, and Zeckhauser (1996) and Goetzmann, Ibbotson, and Ross (1995). However, the expected J-shaped relation between future and past returns or between future returns and volatility is not evident. If anything, the means present an "inverted-U" shaped pattern, with the extreme past return quintiles delivering the lowest future returns.

Figure 3 depicts the cumulative value of an initial investment of one dollar in each of the quintiles formed on the basis of the past average returns. It shows some weak evidence of mean reversion in the high average return quintile, depicted as decile 1 (+ signs). That is, the high return funds earn lower future returns. However, the difference between the ending value of the high- and low-return quintiles is only $0.18, which is not economically or statistically significant.

Using the unconditional CAPM alphas to drive the strategies, the lowest-alpha quintiles have the largest standard deviations of their future returns and the largest betas. These patterns are consistent with a systematic bias in the unconditional CAPM. An inverse relation between alphas and betas is also observed in the early

Table 8. Simple Trading Strategies using Past Alphas

Strategy	Mean	STD	Uncond. Beta	Average Condit. Beta	Unconditional Alphas		Conditional Alphas		Cum Value	Fraction Positive	Min-Max Returns
					3FAC	CAPM	3FAC	CAPM			
CRSP VW-index	0.599	4.89	1.00	1.00	0.56	0.00	0.81	0.00	2.45	56.9%	−22.2+12.4
Hold all managers	0.553	5.05	1.02	1.03	0.51	−0.06	0.73	−0.07	2.34	59.5%	−22.8+11.8
Time-varying conditional CAPM:											
Q1 - high alphas	0.744	5.17	1.03	1.00	0.68	0.126	0.93	0.221	2.73	60.7%	−25.4+11.7
Q2	0.638	4.83	0.97	0.99	0.59	0.057	0.81	−0.016	2.54	57.1%	−20.1+11.3
Q3	0.578	4.78	0.96	0.98	0.53	0.001	0.77	−0.012	2.42	57.1%	−20.8+10.7
Q4	0.467	5.34	1.07	1.07	0.42	−0.175	0.65	−0.182*	2.15	56.0%	−25.3+12.9
Q5 - low alphas	0.333	5.33	1.05	1.09	0.28	−0.297*	0.46	−0.397*	1.93	54.8%	−22.5+12.6
Unconditional CAPM:											
Q1 - high alphas	0.443	4.81	0.96	0.99	0.40	−0.132	0.58	−0.190	2.16	56.0%	−20.8+11.1
Q2	0.650	4.74	0.96	0.98	0.59	0.076	0.79	0.063	2.58	58.3%	−20.9+10.5
Q3	0.627	4.85	0.97	1.00	0.58	0.044	0.81	−0.010	2.52	58.3%	−20.1+11.2
Q4	0.599	5.23	1.05	1.05	0.55	−0.030	0.82	−0.028	2.41	56.0%	−24.2+12.9
Q5 - low alphas	0.461	5.87	1.15	1.12	0.40	−0.228	0.65	−0.165	2.08	58.3%	−28.6+13.7

Past average returns:

Q1 - high past returns	0.454	5.37	1.07	1.07	0.39	-0.189	0.61	-0.154	2.12	57.1%	-25.3+12.0
Q2	0.594	4.86	1.01	0.97	0.55	0.010	0.75	-0.025	2.45	58.3%	-20.5+11.4
Q3	0.596	4.89	0.99	0.98	0.54	0.006	0.76	0.001	2.45	60.7%	-22.4+11.3
Q4	0.589	4.93	0.98	0.99	0.55	-0.004	0.80	-0.002	2.43	56.0%	-22.7+12.6
Q5 - low past returns	0.548	5.38	1.08	1.06	0.50	-0.087	0.73	-0.156	2.30	58.3%	-23.2+12.5

Notes: Each trading strategy uses an estimate of performance, or alpha, based on the past 60 months of data for each eligible manager. The alpha estimates are ranked, grouped according to quintiles and an equally-weighted portfolio is formed from each quintile group. This portfolio is held for one month, and the procedure is repeated. The different models for alpha are described in the text. The data are monthly from 1979:1–1990:12, and the first date of the trading strategy returns is 1984:1. There are 84 monthly returns for each trading strategy measured net of a one-month Treasury bill return. The excess returns are percent per month. The first two rows show comparable results for the CRSP value-weighted index and an equally-weighted portfolio of all managers. Uncond. beta is the unconditional beta against the CRSP value-weighted index, and Condit. beta is the time series average of the time-varying conditional beta. All of the beta have t-ratios in excess of 25.0. The unconditional alpha for the CAPM is the intercept in a regression of the excess return of the strategy on the CRSP value-weighted excess return over the 84 month period. The unconditional 3FAC alpha is the intercept in a regression on the Standard and Poors 500 excess return, the Russell value index less the growth style index, and the small stock less the large stock index. The conditional alpha is the intercept when the regression also includes the product of the factor(s) and a vector of predetermined variables. These variables are the dividend yield of the CRSP index, a yield spread of long versus short term bonds, the yield on a short term Treasury bill, a corporate bond yield spread of low versus high grade bonds, and a dummy variable for Januaries. In the three-factor models, the corporate bond yield spread and the January dummy are excluded. The alpha coefficients have a * when their heteroskedasticity-consistent t-ratios are larger than 1.94.

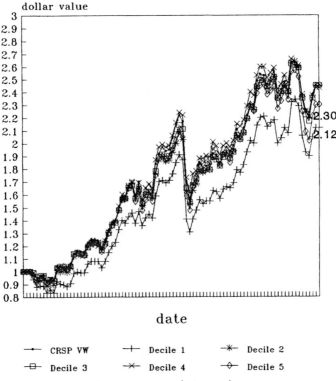

Figure 3. Cumulative Values
60-Month Average Return Quintiles

classic studies of the CAPM (e.g., Black, Jensen, & Scholes, 1972; Fama & MacBeth, 1973). The relation of the future returns to the past unconditional alphas again resembles an inverted U. The difference between the average future returns of the high-alpha and the low-alpha quintile is only 0.2% per year, and the alphas of the future returns are not statistically different from zero. Figure 4 depicts the cumulative values of investing one dollar in each of the quintile strategies. The figure suggests some weak persistence in the worst performing decile, but the difference between the bottom and top deciles is only $0.08 at the end of the period. Thus, unconditional CAPM alphas appear to provide little reliable information about future abnormal performance.

Focusing on the time-varying conditional CAPM, the results of the trading strategies are strikingly different. The average future returns are now monotonically decreasing across the alpha quintiles, and the difference between average returns of the high-alpha and low-alpha quintile is 4.9% per year. The cumulative value of a one-dollar investment made in 1984 and held until the end of 1990, ranges from

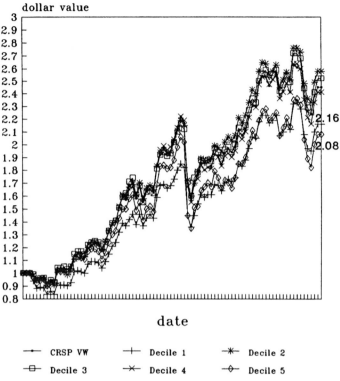

Figure 4. Cumulative Values
Unconditional CAPM Alpha Quintiles

$2.73 for the high-alpha to $1.93 for the low-alpha quintile, as depicted in Figure 5. The fraction of the 84 excess returns that are positive is monotonic across the conditional-alpha quintiles, ranging from 60.7% for the high-alpha to 54.8% for the low-alpha quintile.

Table 8 also provides risk-adjusted returns for the trading strategies. Simple measures of risk are not monotonic across the conditional-alpha quintiles. The standard deviations of the future excess returns, their unconditional betas, and the time-series averages of the conditional CAPM betas are all lower in the middle quintiles and higher at the extreme quintiles. All of the risk measures are the largest for the low-alpha quintile.

Estimates of CAPM alphas (unconditional and conditional versions) for the conditional quintile-strategy returns are positive for the highest-return quintile and ordered nearly monotonically across the quintiles. The return differences generated by the conditional alpha strategies do not appear to be explained by these measures of risk. Significantly negative alphas are found for some of the low conditional-per-

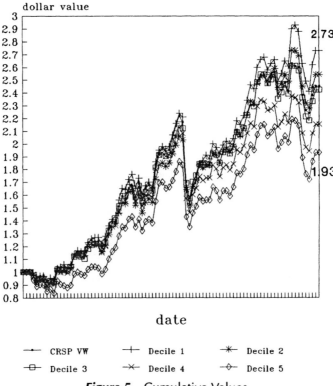

Figure 5. Cumulative Values
Conditional CAPM Alpha Quintiles

formance quintiles. This is consistent with our previous observation that persistence is concentrated in the poorly performing managers. In summary, these are not the patterns that would be expected if there were a simple survivorship bias or a bias related to risk measurement. We conclude that the persistence in pension fund performance is most likely to be an economically meaningful phenomenon.

VIII. CONCLUDING REMARKS

This paper reports on the first analysis of the performance of institutional equity managers using conditional performance evaluation techniques. We use time-varying conditional alphas as well as betas in our models. Our analysis documents a striking persistence in the relative performance of the managers, which appears to be of economic significance. The additional information used by a conditional measure allows us to better detect persistence in the performance of pension funds. Similar to the previous evidence for mutual funds, we find that poor performance tends to be followed by low future returns, so that persistence is concentrated in the poorly performing managers. Finally, we find that previous evidence that equity pension funds perform worse, on average, than the Standard & Poors 500 is not robust to a longer sample period. Over the 1979–1990 period the managers in our sample outperform the S&P.

Finding that a conditional measure can detect persistence in pension fund performance is consistent with the view that more sophisticated techniques are used to successfully evaluate pension fund managers than a typical investor uses to evaluate mutual funds. However, the finding that poor conditional performance is followed by poor future returns is puzzling. While it may not be surprising to find that some managers can generate consistently poor returns, the survival of such managers suggests that plan sponsors do not take action to remove their money from a fund with predictably poor performance. This raises a number of interesting questions for future research. Why do the poorly performing managers survive? Is this an inefficiency in the market for pension manager services, as Lakonishok, Shleifer, and Vishny (1992) suggest? Are the costs of firing low-return managers high enough to justify this persistence? Do the poorly performing managers deliver valuable services to their sponsors which offset their poor investment returns? What strategies for trading and trade execution characterize these persistently poor performers? Conditional models seem to provide a more powerful signal than has previously been available to measure risk-adjusted investment performance. Future research is needed, using conditional methods, to address these issues.

ACKNOWLEDGMENTS

This paper is based in part on our paper, "Conditioning Manager Alphas on Economic Information: Another Look at the Persistence of Performance," 1998 *Review of Financial Studies* (11, 111–142). We are grateful to Robert Bliss, Mark Carhart, Diane Del Guercio, Chris Hensel, Paula Tkac, Sheridan Titman, David Myers, and Ravi Jagannathan for helpful comments. Part of this research was conducted while Ferson was a visiting scholar at Arizona State University. Ferson also acknowledges financial support from the Pigott-Paccar professorship at the University of Washington. We are grateful to the Frank Russell Company for providing data.

NOTES

1. See, for example the studies by Ippolito (1992), Grinblatt and Titman (1994), Goetzmann and Ibbotson (1994), Shukla and Trzcinka (1994), Hendricks, Patel and Zeckhauser (1993, 1996), Brown and Goetzmann (1995), Malkiel (1995), Gruber (1996), Elton, Gruber and Blake (1996a), and Carhart (1997).

2. An alternative approach, directed at capturing nonlinearities in managed portfolio returns, is to include option payoffs as additional "factors" when calculating alphas (see Glosten & Jagannathan, 1994).

3.   While it has been argued that individual investors may stick with a "loser" fund due to a cognitive dissonance (e.g., Goetzmann & Peles, 1993), an individual investor is unlikely to lose his job over the issue.

4.   Goetzmann, Ibbotson, and Ross (1995) show that a J-shape can fail to occur with nontrivial probability, in a sample satisfying the assumptions of Hendricks, Patel, and Zeckhauser (1997), when there is correlation across the funds.

5.   Newer versions of these indexes provided by RDS use a nonlinear weighting scheme and allow stocks near the median to be in both the value and growth indexes.

6.   Many previous studies in the asset pricing literature have used linear functional forms to model time-varying betas and second moments. Examples include Ferson (1985), Shanken (1990), Ferson and Harvey (1993), Cochrane (1996), and Jagannathan and Wang (1996). The approach is especially attractive for fund performance for two reasons. First, linear betas can be motivated by theoretical models of manager behavior such as Admati, Ross, and Pfliederer (1986). Second, the linear regression models which result from this assumption are easy to interpret, as illustrated by Ferson and Schadt (1996).

7.   To see this, assume that the underlying assets follow

$$r_{t+1} = \beta(Z_t)r_{bt+1} + u_{t+1},$$

where $E(u_{t+1}|Z_t) = E(u_{t+1}\, r_{bt+1}|Z_t) = 0$, r_{t+1} is a vector of the underlying asset returns and $\beta(Z_t)$ is the vector of their conditional betas. The underlying assets' alphas are equal to zero. Let the manager's portfolio weight vector be x, so that the portfolio excess return is $x'r_{t+1}$. Taking the conditional expectation of the portfolio return given Z_t, and allowing that x may be a random variable given Z_t, it is easy to see that the manager's alpha in the conditional model is a function of $Cov(x;\, u_{t+1}|Z_t)$ and $Cov(x;\, r_{bt+1}|Z_t)$. The first term may be considered as conditional "security selection" and the second term as conditional "market timing." Both terms should be functions of Z_t.

8.   The approach of modeling alphas by a linear function goes back in the asset pricing literature at least to Rosenberg and Marathe (1979), but our paper is the first to use economy-wide conditioning variables for conditional alphas to measure portfolio manager performance. Ferson and Harvey (1994) use a similar approach in a study of international equity market returns.

9.   Consistent with this view, we learned shortly after beginning this study that RDS was experimenting with using the Russell 2500 instead of the Russell 2000 as a small-cap index.

10.   Consider the event that any of N statistics for a test of size p rejects the hypothesis. Given dependent events, the joint probability is less than or equal to the sum of the individual probabilities. The Bonferroni p-value places an upper bound on the p-value of a joint test across the equations. It is computed as the smallest of the N p-values for the individual tests, multiplied by N, which is the number of funds in a group. The Bonferroni p-values are one-tailed tests of the hypothesis that all of the slope coefficients are zero against the alternative that at least one is positive (maximum value) or negative (minimum value).

11.   For parsimony and to reduce collinearity of the regressors, we reduce the number of instruments in these models to a constant and the two most important variables, based on the previous analysis, which are the Treasury bill yield and the stock market dividend yield. In the conditional four-factor models, the regression equation has twelve regressors: a constant, the four style indexes, and the products of the two information variables with the four style indexes.

12.   Recent studies show that conditional versions of the CAPM do a better job at capturing cross-sectional differences in passive portfolio expected returns than unconditional versions of the CAPM (e.g., Jagannathan & Wang, 1996; Carhart et al., 1996).

13.   Note that the alphas of the equally-weighted portfolios are larger than the averages of the individual managers' alphas. The equally weighted portfolios combine the data for every manager that exists in the data base for a given month. Therefore, a manager with a longer data history gets more weight in these results, and each date in the sample period gets equal weight. The averages for the individual manager regressions give unit weight to each manager, provided there are more than 12 observations of the manager's returns. Since there are more managers at the end of the sample period,

dates at the end of the sample period get more weight. Finding that the alphas of the equally-weighted portfolios are larger is consistent with the view that managers with longer data series are the better performing managers. It may also reflect better performance for the managers in general in the latter part of the sample.

14. To keep the number of coefficients manageable, we use a subset of the original instruments in these models, deleting the January dummy variable and the quality-related bond yield spread. These two variables were typically the least important in the predictive regressions.

15. Since the time variation can occur in the alphas and the betas, we conduct tests of the hypothesis that the betas are constant, allowing for time-varying alphas. Using an F (Wald) test, the average p-value is 0.09 (0.12) and there are 122 (114) funds with individual p-values below 0.05. Bonferroni joint tests produce p-values of 0.000 based on either the F or the Wald statistics. We conclude that time-varying alphas alone are not sufficient to capture the role of the lagged variables.

16. Lakonishok, Shleifer, and Vishny also look at value-weighted portfolio returns. We could not do this, as we have no data on individual account size.

17. Coggin, Fabozzi, and Rahman (1993) examine pension manager performance using Frank Russell data for 1983-1990, but they only report separate results for timing and selectivity measures, using unconditional models. Their results are therefore not directly comparable to ours or to Lakonishok, Shleifer, and Vishny's.

18. One other factor that might account for a portion of the manager universe effect is that the RDS database includes only representative accounts—one per management firm—while the SEI database used by LSV includes multiple accounts per firm. As noted above, representative accounts are relatively unrestricted, and therefore may be expected to have higher returns on average. Another difference between the two databases is that Lakonishok, Shleifer, and Vishny exclude cash holdings when calculating manager returns, while our managers' portfolios include any cash holdings. Since average cash returns are lower than equity returns, this means that the returns in our database would be even higher if equity-only data were used.

19. The Lakonishok, Shleifer, and Vishny study includes a second database (the "search" database), which tracks returns by money management firm, rather than by individual manager. Using this second database, Lakonishok, Shleifer, and Vishny report average returns that are uniformly higher than those for the first database over 1983–1989, and even higher than ours. Arguing that the search database is more likely biased, they emphasize the results using the first database in which the returns are lower.

20. It is interesting to note that these are large relative to the magnitudes of survivorship bias, as estimated for mutual funds by Grinblatt and Titman (1988)—0.1% to 0.4% per year—by Brown and Goetzmann (1995)—about 0.8% per year, and by Malkiel (1994)—about 1.4% per year. Of course, we do not know how these estimates for mutual funds compare to the survivorship bias in our sample of institutional managers.

21. We conduct an additional experiment in which we compare the ability of conditional and unconditional models to forecast the managers' future returns through time, out of sample. We estimate the models using past data, and we use the estimates of the coefficients to construct conditional predictions of the future returns, given the ex post future value of the market or style index return. Each month we roll the procedure forward to produce one-step-ahead conditional forecasts, and we compare the bias and mean square prediction errors of the models over time. We find a tradeoff between estimation error, which increases with the larger numbers of parameters in a conditional model, and model specification error, which is likely to be worse in a simpler model. Our experiments suggest that the tradeoff between the two types of errors results in roughly similar overall mean square prediction errors for the conditional and unconditional models. The bias in the conditional models is typically much smaller, which is consistent with a smaller specification error. However, the error variance is larger, presumably because of the larger number of parameters.

22. The conditional three factor alphas are the intercepts in regressions of the quintile portfolio returns on three factors and their products with three lagged instruments. (We do not use the yield spread QUAL or the January dummy as instruments in the three-factor models.) The three factors roughly

follow Fama and French (1993). They are: (1) the Standard & Poors 500 excess return, (2) the difference between the small-cap and the large-cap style index returns, and (3) the difference between the value and the growth style index returns.

REFERENCES

Admati, Anat R., Bhattacharya, S., Ross, S., & Pfleiderer, P. (1986). On timing and selectivity. *Journal of Finance, 41*, 715–30.

Black, F., Jensen, M. C., & Scholes, M. (1972). The capital asset pricing model: some empirical tests. In M. C. Jensen, (Ed.), *Studies in the Theory of Capital Markets* (pp. 79–121). New York: Praeger.

Brown, S. J., & Goetzmann, W. N. (1995). Performance persistence. *Journal of Finance, 50*, 679–98.

Brown, S. J., Goetzmann, W. N., Ibbotson, R., & Ross, S. (1992). Survivorship bias in performance studies. *Review of Financial Studies, 5*, 553–580.

Carhart, M. (1997). On persistence in mutual fund performance. *Journal of Finance, 52*, 57–82.

Carhart, M., Krail, R., Stevens, R., & Welch, K. (1996). *Testing the conditional CAPM*. Working paper, University of Southern California.

Carlson, R. S. (1970). Aggregate performance of mutual funds, 1948–1967. *Journal of Financial and Quantitative Analysis, 5*, 1–32.

Chen, Z., & Knez, P. J. (1996). Portfolio performance measurement: theory and applications. *Review of Financial Studies, 9*, 511–556.

Christopherson, J. A., Ferson, W., & Glassman, D. (1988). Conditioning manager alphas on economic information: Another look at the persistence of performance. *Review of Financial Studies, 11*, 111–142.

Christopherson, J. A., & Trittin, D. J. (1995). Equity style classification system. In T. D. Coggin & F. J. Fabozzi (Eds.), *The Handbook of Equity Style Management*. New Hope, PA: Frank J. Fabozzi Associates.

Christopherson, J. A., & Turner, A. L. (1991, Fall). Volatility and predictability of manager alpha: Learning the lessons of history. *Journal of Portfolio Management*, 5–12.

Cochrane, J. (1996). A cross-sectional test of a production-based asset pricing model. *Journal of Political Economy, 104*, 572–621.

Coggin, T. D., Fabozzi, F. J., & Rahman, S. (1993). The investment performance of U.S. equity pension fund managers. *Journal of Finance, 48*, 1039–1056.

Elton, E. J., Gruber, M. J., & Blake, C. R. (1996a). The persistence of risk-adjusted mutual fund performance. *Journal of Business, 69*, 133–158.

Elton, E. J., Gruber, M. J., & Blake, C. R. (1996b). Survivorship bias and mutual fund performance. *Review of Financial Studies, 9*, 1097–1120.

Fama, E. F. (1976). *Foundations of Finance*. New York: Basic Books.

Fama, E. F., & French, K. R. (1988). Permanent and temporary components of stock prices. *Journal of Political Economy, 96*, 246–273.

Fama, E. F., & French, K. R. (1993). Common risk factors in the returns on stocks and bonds. *Journal of Financial Economics, 33*, 3–56.

Fama, E. F., & MacBeth, J. D. (1973). Risk, return and equilibrium: Empirical tests. *Journal of Political Economy, 72*, 607–636.

Ferson, W. E. (1985). *Changes in expected risk premiums and security risk measures*. Proceedings of the European Finance Association, August.

Ferson, W., & Harvey, C. R. (1991a). The variation of economic risk premiums. *Journal of Political Economy, 99*, 385–415.

Ferson, W., & Harvey, C. R. (1991b, May/June). Sources of predictability in portfolio returns. *Financial Analysts Journal, 3*, 49–56.

Ferson, W., & Harvey, C. R. (1993). The risk and predictability of international equity market returns. *Review of Financial Studies, 6,* 527–566.

Ferson, W., & Harvey, C. R. (1994). An exploratory investigation of the fundamental determinants of international equity returns. In J. A. Frankel (Ed.), *Internationalization of equity markets* (pp. 59–148). University of Chicago Press.

Ferson, W., & Korajczyk, R. A. (1995). Do arbitrage pricing models explain the predictability of stock returns? *Journal of Business, 68,* 309–350.

Ferson, W., & Schadt, R. (1996). Measuring fund strategy and performance in changing economic conditions. *Journal of Finance, 51,* 425–462.

Ferson, W., & Warther, V. A. (1996). Evaluating fund performance in a dynamic market. *Financial Analysts Journal, 52* (6), 20–28.

Glosten, L., & Jagannathan, R. (1994). A contingent claims approach to performance evaluation. *Journal of Empirical Finance, 1,* 133–164.

Goetzmann, W. N., Brown, S. J., Ibbotson, R. G., & Ross, S. A. (1995). *Rejoinder: The J-shape of performance persistence given survivorship bias.* Working paper, Yale School of Management.

Goetzmann, W. N., & Ibbotson, R. G. (1994,Winter). Do winners repeat? *Journal of Portfolio Management,* 9–18.

Goetzmann, W. N.,& Peles, N. (1993). Cognitive dissonance and mutual fund investors. Working paper, Columbia Business School.

Grinblatt, M., & Titman, S. (1988). The evaluation of mutual fund performance: An analysis of monthly returns. Working paper, University of California at Los Angeles.

Grinblatt, M., & Titman, S. (1994). The persistence of mutual fund performance. *Journal of Finance, 47,* 1977–1984.

Gruber, M. J. (1996). Another puzzle: The growth in actively managed mutual funds. *Journal of Finance, 60,* 783–810.

Halpern, P., & Fowler, I. I. (1991, Winter). Investment management fees and determinants of pricing and structure in the industry. *Journal of Portfolio Management,* 74–79.

Hansen, L. P. (1982). Large sample properties of generalized method of moments estimators. *Econometrica, 50,* 1029–1054.

Hendricks, D., Patel, J., & Zeckhauser, R. (1993). Hot hands in mutual funds: short-run persistence of relative performance, 1974–88. *Journal of Finance 48,* 93–130.

Hendricks, D., Patel, J., & Zeckhauser, R. (1997). The J-shape of performance persistence given survivorship bias. *Review of Economics and Statistics, 79,* 161–166.

Ippolito, R. A. (1992). Consumer reaction to measures of poor quality: evidence from the mutual fund industry. *Journal of Law and Economics, 35,* 45–70.

Jagannathan, R., & Wang, Z. (1996). The conditional CAPM and the cross-section of expected returns. *Journal of Finance, 51,* 3–54.

Jensen, M. C. (1968). The performance of mutual funds in the period 1945–1964. *Journal of Finance, 23,* 389–416.

Jensen, M. C. (1969). Risk, the pricing of assets and the evaluation of investment portfolios. *Journal of Business, 42,* 167–247.

Kandel, S., & Stambaugh, R. F. (1995). Portfolio inefficiency and the cross-section of expected returns. *Journal of Finance, 50,* 157–184.

Lakonishok, J., Shleifer, A., & Vishny, R. (1992). The structure and performance of the money management industry. *Brookings papers: Microeconomics,* 339–391.

Lee, C., & Rahman, S. (1990). Market timing, selectivity and mutual fund performance. *Journal of Business, 63,* 261–278.

Malkiel, B. (1995). Returns from investing in equity mutual funds 1971–1991. *Journal of Finance, 50,* 549–572.

Newey, W., & West, K. D. (1987). A simple, positive semi-definite, heteroskedasticity and autocorrelation-consistent covariance matrix. *Econometrica, 55,* 703–708.

Roll, R., & Ross, S. A. (1994). On the cross-sectional relation between expected returns and betas. *Journal of Finance, 49,* 101–121.

Rosenberg, B., & Marathe, V. (1979). Tests of capital asset pricing hypotheses. *Research in Finance, 1,* 115–224.

Shukla, R., & Trzcinka, C. (1994). Persistent performance in the mutual fund market: tests with funds and investment advisors. *Review of Quantitative Finance and Accounting, 4,* 115–136.

Shanken, J. (1990). Intertemporal asset pricing: an empirical investigation. *Journal of Econometrics, 45,* 99–120.

Sharpe, W. F. (1964). Capital asset prices: A theory of market equilibrium under conditions of risk. *Journal of Finance, 19,* 425–42.

Sirri, E., & Tufano, P. (1992). *Buying and selling mutual funds: flows, performance, fees and service.* Working paper, Harvard University.

Treynor, J., & Mazuy, K. (1966). Can mutual funds outguess the market? *Harvard Business Review, 44,* 131–136.

White, H. (1980). A heteroskedasticity-consistent covariance matrix estimator and a direct test for heteroskedasticity. *Econometrica, 48,* 817–838.

CREATING AND DESTROYING VALUE:
SPIN-OFFS OF PRIOR ACQUISITIONS

Jeffrey W. Allen, Scott L. Lummer,
John J. McConnell, and Debra K. Reed

ABSTRACT

This paper examines excess stock returns at announcements of spin-offs that originated as acquisitions by parent firms. We evaluate whether pre- and post-spin-off
acquisitions destroy value and whether the positive stock returns at spin-off announcements represent the re-creation of value destroyed in an earlier acquisition. At
both pre- and post-spin-off acquisitions the combined bidder and target excess stock
returns are negative and significant. We also find that excess stock returns to spin-off
announcements are negatively correlated with pre-spin-off acquisition announcement
returns.

I. INTRODUCTION

Several research studies in the finance literature report significant increases in stock
prices to announcements of corporate spin-offs. Hite and Owers (1983), Miles and
Rosenfeld (1983), Schipper and Smith (1983), and Daley, Mehrotra, and Sivakumar

Research in Finance, Volume 16, pages 47–70.
ISBN: 0-7623-0328-X

(1997) find significant positive excess stock returns between 2 and 3% during a two-day period surrounding spin-off announcements. These authors investigate a number of hypotheses to explain how spin-offs could increase shareholder value including wealth transfers from senior claimholders, the relaxation of regulatory or tax constraints, enhanced contracting efficiencies between the parent, subsidiary, and other third-party entities, and streamlining of an unwieldy managerial structure (improved focus) in parent firms.

This study also investigates an alternative explanation of how spin-offs might create value. We examine whether stock price increases in corporate spin-offs come about because the parent firm is correcting an acquisition mistake. If the spun-off entity was an acquisition of the parent that destroyed shareholder value, the gains at spin-off may represent the undoing of that unwise takeover. The roots of this explanation can be found in Porter (1987), Ravenscraft and Scherer (1987), Scherer (1988), Kaplan and Weisbach (1992), and Allen, Lummer, McConnell, and Reed (1995).

In particular, Porter studies 33 major U.S. corporations over the period 1950 through 1986 and finds that more than half of their acquisitions were subsequently divested. In a detailed analysis of acquisitions that occurred between 1971 and 1982, Kaplan and Weisbach (1992) classify acquisitions that are later divested as being either successful or unsuccessful. Among other things, they compare the announcement period stock returns of the acquirer and the combined returns of the acquirer and the acquired firms for those acquisitions in the unsuccessful group with those in the successful group. They find that average announcement period returns to the acquirer are significantly lower for the unsuccessful than for the successful set of acquisitions. They interpret these results to indicate that when an unwise acquisition is undertaken, investors revise their expectations downward for the performance of the combined entity and the stock price of the acquirer declines appropriately.

In a related study Mitchell and Lehn (1990) examine the announcement period returns of the acquisitions of a large sample of firms, some of which later became acquisition targets themselves and some of which did not. They report that acquisition announcement period returns are more negative for acquisitions that are subsequently divested relative to acquisitions that are not divested regardless of whether the acquirer later became an acquisition target. In short, both targets and nontargets tend to divest unsuccessful takeovers. Mitchell and Lehn do not relate acquisition announcement period returns to subsequent divestiture announcement period returns nor do they distinguish their sample according to whether the divestitures were by means of a sell-off or a spin-off.

To motivate the investigation in this paper, suppose that the motive for some corporate spin-offs is to unwind an unsuccessful prior acquisition. Under this supposition the average positive stock price reaction that has been observed around the announcements of corporate spin-offs generally may merely represent the re-creation of wealth that was destroyed (or expected to be destroyed) as a result of the earlier (unwise) acquisition. We investigate the "correction-of-a-mistake" hypothesis as an alternative explanation of the positive excess returns that accompany corporate spin-off announcements generally. Support for this hypothesis does not mean, of course, that all spin-offs are undertaken to correct an unwise acquisition. It only means that the average positive stock price response across a large sample of spin-offs contains a component that represents the re-creation of wealth dissipated in the subset of unwise acquisitions and, as a consequence, provides an upward bias to the average stock price response around spin-off announcements.

We conduct the investigation with a sample of 94 spin-offs in which the spun-off entity had been previously acquired by the parent firm. The predictions of the hypothesis are threefold. First, the acquirer's stock price reaction around the announcement of a takeover that becomes spin-off is negative. A stronger version of this prediction is that not only are the stock returns to the acquiring firm negative, but that the loss in value to the shareholders of the acquiring firm is greater than the gain to the shareholders of the target. In this case the post-announcement value of the combined firm would be less than the sum of the preannouncement values of the separate entities. Second, the average stock price reaction around spin-offs of prior acquisitions is more positive than the average stock price reaction around spin-offs generally. That is, if the value gain documented for spin-offs generally can be attributed to the re-creation of value from the undoing of unwise acquisitions, then the spin-off announcement period returns for the spin-offs in this sample should be greater than those for spin-offs of non-acquired subsidiaries. Third, the stock price reaction around the announcement of spin-offs of prior acquisitions is positive, but negatively correlated with the stock price reaction around the original acquisition. That is, the "bigger" the acquisition "mistake," the greater the rebound in price when the spin-off is announced.

Both the first and third of these predictions are supported by the data. Over $(-1, 0)$ and $(-4, +4)$ intervals relative to the initial acquisition announcement, and over the interval from 10 days prior to the date of the initial announcement through the date on which the acquisition agreement is announced, the average excess returns to the acquiring firm are negative and significantly different from zero. The magnitudes of the average excess returns over the three intervals are -0.7, -1.1, and -3.1%, respectively, with associated p-values of 0.05, 0.10, and 0.00. Furthermore, even the stronger variation of the first prediction is supported by the data: for a subsample of 40 cases in which stock price data are available for both the acquirer and the target firm, the combined average excess return is negative and significantly different from zero. The magnitudes of the combined bidder and target excess returns for the $(-1, 0)$, $(-4, +4)$, and -10 through acquisition agreement date intervals are -0.7, -1.9, and -2.1%, respectively, with p-values of 0.10, 0.04, and 0.06.

Regarding the second prediction, both the $(-1, 0)$ and the $(-4, +4)$ announcement period average excess returns surrounding the spin-off announcement are positive $(+2.2$ and $+2.5\%$, respectively) and highly significant (p-value = 0.00 for both), but the average excess returns for this sample of spin-offs is not much different from that of spin-offs generally or from that of a matched sample of spin-offs which did not originate as takeovers. The average excess returns over the (−1, 0) and (−4, +4) announcement periods for the matched sample of spin-offs are +1.8 and +2.9%, respectively.

Finally, regarding the third prediction, when a cross-sectional regression is estimated in which the dependent variable is the (−4, +4) spin-off excess return and the independent variables include the acquirer's announcement period return, measured over the (−1,0) or (−4, +4) announcement intervals or over the interval from 10 days before the initial announcement through the acquisition agreement date (and several control variables), the coefficient of the acquirer's announcement period excess return is always negative and significantly different from zero. Similarly, when the dependent variable is the spin-off announcement period return and the independent variable is the combined excess return of the bidder and target firms at the acquisition (and certain control variables), the coefficient of the combined bidder and target excess return is always negative and significantly different from zero. In short, the bigger the acquisition mistake (i.e., the more negative the acquisition returns), the greater the wealth creation at the announcement of the spin-off.

We interpret the results to indicate that, at least in part, the positive stock price reaction around the announcement of corporate spin-offs represents the recapturing of wealth that is lost (or expected to be lost) as the result of an unwise acquisition, rather than a wealth gain associated with the spin-offs, per se. It is possible that analyses of stock price increases associated with announcements of corporate spin-offs would prove more powerful if they were to control for the increase in share price due to the re-creation of value lost in those spin-offs that began as acquisitions. The results do not indicate that all gains in corporate spin-offs are the result of undoing unwise acquisitions. Indeed, our failure to support the second prediction of the "correction-of-a-mistake" hypothesis points in the opposite direction. But, the results do indicate that studies which attempt to explain spin-off announcement period returns should control for this effect.

A recent contribution in the literature concludes that spin-offs which increase the focus of the parent firm realize substantial increases in stock prices while spin-offs that do not increase focus do not have a significant effect on the stock price of the parent (Daley, Mehrotra, & Sivakumar, 1997). A contribution of this paper is to determine whether cross-industry (focus increasing) spin-offs have a significant impact on excess returns to spin-off announcements in our sample of spin-offs and in the presence of several control variables. The other hypotheses noted earlier do not appear to fully explain the shareholder wealth gains associated with spin-offs.

We find that cross-industry (focus increasing) spin-offs experience greater positive excess stock returns during a two-day (−1,0) announcement window (2.7 vs. 1.1%). The difference, however, is not significant. We find that the results change when stock returns are calculated during a nine-day (−4, +4) announcement window. During this period, excess returns are 2.4% for focus-increasing spin-offs and 2.7% for spin-offs that do not increase the focus of the parent in our sample. An indicator variable representing industry relatedness between the parent and subsidiary is not significant in cross-sectional regressions.

We also examine spun-off subsidiaries during a five-year period following spin-off to determine whether these firms are subsequently acquired by other firms. We find that 20% of the spin-offs in our original sample are involved in post-spin-off acquisitions. Further, excess stock returns are negative for post-spin-off acquiring firms. Combined returns between the acquirer and target in post-spin-off acquisitions are also negative indicating that these transactions also destroy value in the aggregate.

There are some managerial implications that follow from the results. First, the negative correlation between acquisition returns and spin-off returns suggests that managers who ignore negative stock market returns at the time of an acquisition can redeem themselves, at least partially, by divesting the same acquisition. Second, the results indicate that one potential source of gains in "bust-up" takeovers is the recapturing of stock market losses that were sustained earlier in value-reducing acquisitions undertaken by the firm that later becomes the target of the bust-up takeover. Finally, post-spin-off acquisitions destroy value for both acquiring firms and overall including the gains to target shareholders.

The next section provides further background discussion of spin-offs and acquisitions to motivate the empirical analysis that follows. Section III describes the sample and Section IV reports the empirical results. The final section summarizes and concludes the paper.

II. BACKGROUND

In a corporate takeover—whether by means of a merger or an acquisition—two free-standing companies are joined to comprise one entity. In those cases in which the acquired firm is later spun-off, the combined enterprise once again becomes two free-standing companies.

In the typical corporate spin-off a corporation (customarily called the "parent") forms a new, separate corporation and ownership to a subset of the assets of the parent is transferred to the newly created corporate entity. The shares in the new corporation are then distributed on a pro rata basis to the shareholders of the parent firm. When the spin-off involves the divestiture of a previous acquisition, it is often the case that the acquired firm had been operating as a wholly owned subsidiary of the parent firm. In these cases the parent need not create a new corporate entity. Rather, the shares in the wholly owned subsidiary are distributed directly to shareholders of the parent firm—again on a pro rata basis.

Evidence from the stock market indicates that the shareholders of acquiring firms do not gain and, perhaps, lose a little at the time of the acquisition. Evidence to this effect is presented in Dennis and McConnell (1986), Bradley, Desai, and Kim (1988), Asquith, Bruner, and Mullins (1983), and Jarrell and Poulsen (1989), among others. However, with a comprehensive sample of mergers and acquisitions that took place over the period 1965 through 1988, Loderer and Martin (1990) report an apparent time dependency in the stock market reaction to corporate takeovers. Roughly speaking, during the 1960s acquirers earned positive abnormal returns; during the 1970s acquirer returns are not significantly different from zero; and during the 1980s takeover announcements were accompanied by significantly negative announcement returns to acquiring firms.

Explanations that have been postulated to explain the lack of a positive valuation effect for acquirers include the inability of the acquirer's management to foresee the undesirable effects of the acquisition or managerial motives to undertake the acquisition despite the undesirable consequences for shareholders. These motives include hubris (Roll, 1986), growth-based compensation (Jensen, 1986), entrenchment (Shleifer & Vishny, 1989), and other forms of self-serving behavior (Morck, Shleifer, & Vishny, 1990). These explanations offer a corollary that is tempting to apply when interpreting the documented positive returns that accompany spin-off announcements—a correction-of-a-mistake hypothesis. According to this hypothesis the negative effect of an acquisition is unwound by a spin-off, thereby, "causing" a positive effect on stock price, when the spin-off of a previously acquired company is announced. In a large sample, of course, only a fraction of the spin-offs derive from prior acquisitions. Still, if the wealth gains associated with this subset is substantial enough, it could increase the announcement period return in an entire sample of spin-offs even if the spin-off of subsidiaries that did not previously result from a prior acquisition generate a zero wealth effect. Specifically, it is possible that "generic" spin-offs do not create value, per se, rather it is the subset of spin-offs made up of prior acquisitions that is largely responsible for the average positive stock price reaction across a large sample of spin-offs. If so, then the average announcement period abnormal return for this subset of spin-offs would be larger than the average return across a random sample of spin-offs.

Additionally, if it is assumed that the re-creation of value at the spin-off is roughly proportional to the value lost at the announcement of the original takeover, the spin-off announcement period returns should be negatively correlated with the acquisition announcement period returns. That is, if bigger acquisition mistakes result in a larger negative wealth effects at the announcement of the acquisition, then correction of these mistakes should give rise to larger positive wealth effects at the announcement of the spin-off.

Of course, acquirers can divest themselves of acquisition mistakes by means other than spin-offs. The most popular, but not the only alternative is by sale of the subsidiary to another firm. For our purposes, though, that is not as clean an experiment because the positive abnormal returns that accrue to the seller in a "sell-off" may represent "overpayment" by the second acquirer.[1]

III. SAMPLE SELECTION

To conduct our investigation, an initial list of 1,142 stock distributions that took place over the period 1962 through 1991 was identified from a search of the S&P Quarterly Dividend Record.[2] To be considered a spin-off, we require that the distribution be a pro rata distribution of the stock of a wholly owned subsidiary. This criterion, thus, excluded 451 distributions of stock in publicly traded companies and 131 distributions that involved a voluntary self-liquidation. We also eliminated 92 distributions in which the spin-off could not be confirmed in CCH's Capital Changes Reporter and 38 nonvoluntary spin-offs. These criteria reduced the sample to 430 confirmed voluntary spin-offs. To be included in the sample for further analysis, we require that the spin-off be announced in the *WSJ* and that the parent firm's shares be traded on the NYSE, the AMEX, or the OTC/NASDAQ System at the time of the spin-off. These criteria reduced the sample to 342. Of these, eight were deleted because the spin-off announcement was accompanied by an earnings announcement (3), a change in dividend policy (2), or the spin-off was used as a takeover defense (3).[3] We further determined that 13 of these spin-offs were undertaken expressly for the purpose of facilitating the acquisition of the subsidiary by another company. Because our focus is on spin-offs that give rise to two free-standing entities, these 13 observations (both the spin-off and the acquisition) are removed from the analysis. If the spin-off is undertaken to facilitate acquisition of the subsidiary by another company, the positive announcement period stock price returns may merely represent "overpayment" by the new acquirer of the spun-off subsidiary. Or, to put it another way, the second acquisition may be a mistake. We exclude these from the sample to avoid contaminating the results with such a possibility.[4]

For the 321 spin-offs that remain in the sample, three avenues of inquiry were pursued to determine whether the spun-off entity originated with an earlier acquisition. First, the *WSJ* article describing the spin-off was read to discover whether it contained any reference to an original acquisition. The second avenue of inquiry was Moody's Manuals. The entry for each company in the manuals includes a "corporate history" section that presents an abbreviated history of the company's origins, its acquisitions, and certain other significant events in the life of the corporation. The history also gives the year in which the acquisition was consummated. Because the history is updated at regular intervals and because certain events that occurred a number of years earlier are occasionally dropped from the most recent history, the history of each parent was read at three-year intervals retrogressively from the year of the spin-off through 1955 to identify whether a spun-off entity originated with an earlier acquisition.

The third, and most fruitful source of acquisition information, is the "company history" section of the spun-off subsidiary's 10K filings following the spin-off. Of the 321 spin-offs with stock returns data and with an "uncontaminated" announcement in the *WSJ*, 94, or nearly 30% of the sample, were identified from the various sources as having originated with an acquisition.

To determine whether an announcement of the acquisition appeared in the *WSJ*, both the acquiring and the acquired firm's entry in the *WSJ* Index was searched for the year of and (if necessary) the two years prior to the takeover consummation date identified in Moody's Manuals or the spun-off company's 10K. Because the index begins in 1958, for the years 1955–1957, the *WSJ* itself was searched to identify acquisition announcement dates.

As is well known, the initial announcement date of some acquisitions is ambiguous because some acquisitions are first announced as "talks have begun" followed by subsequent progress reports on the status of negotiations until an "agreement in principle" is announced. In other cases, the first announcement is the announcement of an "agreement in principle." In some cases the ambiguity regarding the initial "information" date is heightened because there appears to be "leakage" of information regarding the takeover prior to any public announcement. There is, thus, the question as to when the market first learns of the acquisition and the related question as to when the full valuation effect of the takeover is impounded in the stock price. Because of this ambiguity, care must be taken in identification of acquisition announcement dates. For acquirers, we identify the initial announcement date as the first date that the bidder and target are mentioned in the same *WSJ* article. For targets, the initial announcement date is the first date that the target is mentioned as a takeover candidate prior to the takeover by the successful bidder firm. We follow this procedure because there are some instances in which the target is identified as an acquisition candidate prior to any identification of the bidder.

Finally, to enter the acquisition sample, we require that either the acquirer or the target firm have shares listed on the NYSE, the AMEX, or the OTC/NASDAQ System at the time of the acquisition and that there be no "contaminating" information about the firm in the *WSJ* over the three-day interval surrounding the initial acquisition announcement.[5]

Of the 94 spin-offs that could be identified as having originated with an acquisition, 78 have uncontaminated acquisition announcement dates in the *WSJ* and stock price data are available for 73 of the acquirers and for 40 of the acquired firms at the time of the initial acquisition announcement. For all 40 cases in which stock price data are available for the target, stock price data are also available for the acquirer. Thus, the acquisition sample includes 40 observations in which it is possible to calculate the combined announcement effect for the bidder and target firms. In 52 of the 73 cases for which we have returns for the acquiring firm, the initial announcement is an announcement of an agreement in principle. These 52 include 19 of the 40 cases in which stock price data are available for both the bidder and the target firms. In 21 cases the first article mentions that negotiations are underway, but an agreement on terms is not reached until a later date. We identify this later date as the "acquisition agreement" date.[6] In those cases in which the initial announcement is the announcement of an agreement in principle, we use the initial announcement date as the acquisition agreement date.

In 36 of the 40 cases for which we have returns for the target, both the bidder and target firm are identified in the same initial announcement. As noted above, in 19 of these the initial announcement is an announcement that an agreement in principle has been reached by the two parties. In 17 other cases the initial announcement indicates that talks have begun, but terms of the agreement are not announced until a later date. Finally, for four cases only the target is identified in the initial article discussing the takeover and the bidder is not identified until a later date. In these four cases the initial announcement date differs for the bidder and the target firms. For all the acquisitions in the sample the time elapsed between the initial announcement date and the acquisition agreement date ranges from one day to 162 days with a mean of 60 days and a median of 43 days.

As might be expected, the mean and median market values of bidder firms ($804 million and $381 million, respectively) are substantially larger than those of target firms ($118 million and $60 million, respectively). One other interesting statistic is the time interval between acquisition and spin-off. The mean (median) time elapsed between acquisition and spin-off is 88 months, the maximum is 356 months, and the minimum is nine months.

IV. STATISTICAL ANALYSIS

To conduct the analysis of stock price reaction to the announcements of takeovers and spin-offs, the CRSP daily stock returns file is used in conjunction with the market model procedure, as described, for example, in Brown and Warner (1985) or Linn and McConnell (1983). When sufficient data are available, market model parameters are estimated over the period from 160 days before through 61 days before the announcement. In two cases stock data are not available for this entire time period. In those cases all available data prior to 61 days before the event are used. In five cases daily stock data are not available on the CRSP file. These are events that occurred prior to the beginning date of the NYSE/AMEX daily file (i.e., prior to 1962) for firms listed on the NYSE or the AMEX or prior to the beginning date of the OTC/NASDAQ daily file for firms listed on the OTC/NASDAQ System (i.e., prior to 1972). For these observations daily stock price data were collected from the *WSJ*. For both spin-offs and acquisitions, announcement period excess returns are computed over a (−1, 0) interval and over a (−4, +4) interval centered on the initial *WSJ* publication date. For acquisition announcements, excess returns are also calculated over the interval that begins 10 days before the initial announcement date and ends on the acquisition agreement date. This longer time interval is used to capture the "full" valuation effect of the takeover. By beginning 10 days prior to the initial announcement, the interval should capture any preannouncement leakage of information. By ending on the acquisition agreement date, this interval should account for the resolution of any residual uncertainty that may occur between the time the negotiations commence and the time at which they are completed.

A. Stock Valuation Effects for Acquiring Firms

As reported in Table 1, for the sample of acquiring firms for which stock price data are available, the average announcement period returns over the (−1, 0) and (−4, +4) intervals surrounding the initial acquisition announcement and over the interval from 10 days before the initial announcement through the acquisition agreement date are −0.7, −1.1, and −3.1%, respectively, with p-values of 0.05, 0.10, and 0.00. Thus, the announcement period returns of takeovers that become spin-offs are negative and significantly different from zero regardless of the acquisition announcement interval considered. These results are consistent with the hypothesis

Table 1. Announcement Period Excess Returns to Acquirers for Acquisitions during the Period 1955–1991 that Became Spin-offs during the Period 1962–1991 (p-values in parentheses)

	Sample Size	(−1, 0)	Fraction Positive	(−4, +4)	Fraction Positive	Day −10 through Agreement[a]	Fraction Positive
Full sample	73	−0.7% (0.05)	0.45	−1.1% (0.10)	0.44	−3.1% (0.00)	0.32
1955–1969	27	1.0% (0.24)	0.56	0.2% (0.56)	0.44	−0.7% (0.40)	0.30
1970–1979	29	−1.1% (0.16)	0.55	−0.2% (0.44)	0.55	−2.6% (0.11)	0.45
1980–1990	17	−2.1% (0.00)	0.12	−4.1% (0.00)	0.24	−6.9% (0.00)	0.12
Target firm's operations related to those of the acquiring firm[b]	24	0.1% (0.77)	0.50	−0.6% (0.31)	0.46	−2.5% (0.14)	0.33
Target firm's operations unrelated to those of the acquiring firm	49	−1.1% (0.02)	0.43	−1.3% (0.12)	0.43	−3.3% (0.00)	0.31
Acquisitions with stock data for both acquiring and target firms	40	−1.6% (0.00)	0.35	−2.7% (0.01)	0.35	−4.8% (0.00)	0.30

Notes: [a]Average holding-period excess return from 10 days before the first announcement in the *WSJ* through the date the merger or acquisition was approved by both firms.

[b]The parent and target firms are considered to be related if any of the SIC codes of the four primary lines of business in each firm overlap at the two digit level. SIC information was obtained from Dun and Bradstreets' Million Dollar Directory for the year prior to the acquisition.

that the documented shareholder gains surrounding corporate spin-offs merely represent the re-creation of value destroyed at the time of the acquisition.

There are, however, other ways to consider the stock price reaction for acquisitions that later become spin-offs. One is according to the time interval in which the takeover occurred. When the takeover sample is divided into three time periods— 1955–1969, 1970–1979, and 1980–1989—the announcement period returns, also displayed in Table 1, can be compared to those documented by Loderer and Martin (1990) over roughly similar time periods. For example, using a $(-1, 0)$ interval for the period 1955–1969, the average announcement period return is $+1.0\%$ (p-value $= 0.24$); for the period 1970–1979, the announcement period return is -1.1% (p-value $= 0.16$); and for the period 1980–1989, it is -2.1% (p-value $= 0.00$). For the interval beginning 10 days prior to the initial announcement and ending with the acquisition agreement date, the returns are more negative, but display a similar time-series pattern: For the period 1955–1969 the average announcement period return is -0.7% (p-value $= 0.40$); for the period 1970–1979, it is -2.6% (p-value $= 0.11$); and for the period 1980–1989, it is -6.9% (p-value $= 0.00$). Over roughly similar time periods, Loderer and Martin (1990) report higher announcement period returns for each "decade" for a large sample of various types of takeovers. For their three time intervals, the announcement period excess returns are $+1.7\%$ (t-statistic $= 8.52$), $+0.6\%$ (t-statistic $= 5.49$), and -0.1% (t-statistic $= -0.34$).[7] Thus, the market reaction to the takeovers in our sample is more negative than for the population of takeovers generally.

Another way in which to consider acquisitions is whether the bidder and target come from the same industry. Porter (1987) argues that diversifying takeovers are more likely to result in failure than are those in which the bidder and target come from the same industry. Kaplan and Weisbach (1992) find scant support for this contention. They classify a sample of acquisitions into diversifying acquisitions and related acquisitions. A related acquisition is one in which the acquirer and target share a two-digit SIC code in any of their four primary lines of business. All others are classified as diversifying acquisitions. They report that the announcement period returns to the acquirer and target are not significantly different between the two samples. When we use the same classification scheme for our sample, we have 24 related and 49 diversifying acquisitions. As shown in Table 1, announcement period returns are mildly different between the two samples with the mean announcement period return being modestly lower for diversifying acquisitions than for related acquisitions, but the p-values for the differences between the mean returns of the two samples over the three time intervals considered are only 0.45, 0.81, and 0.78.

B. Stock Valuation Effects for Target Firms

A third way in which to consider takeovers is by analyzing returns to the shareholders of the target firm. Announcement period returns for target firms are reported in Table 2. These results are similar to those reported for target firms in prior studies (see, for example, Bradley, Desai, & Kim, 1988; Dennis & McConnell, 1986). Specifically, announcement period returns are significantly positive for every announcement period considered, for the full sample of target firms, for acquisitions during the 1960s, the 1970s, and the 1980s, and regardless of whether the acquisition is classified as related or diversifying. Additionally, the target's announcement period excess returns are much larger when measured over the interval from 10 days before the initial announcement through the acquisition agreement date than when measured over the announcement periods suggesting that this interval more accurately gauges the full valuation effect of the takeover.

C. Stock Valuation Effects for Combined Acquirer and Target Firms

To this point, the analysis considers returns separately for bidder and target firms. As we noted at the outset, a stronger test of the "correction of a mistake" hypothesis

Table 2. Announcement Period Excess Returns to Targets in Acquisitions during the Period 1955–1991 that Became Spin-offs during the Period 1962–1991 (*p*-values in parentheses)

	Sample Size	(–1, 0)	Fraction Positive	(–4, +4)	Fraction Positive	Day –10 through Acquisition Agreement[a]	Fraction Positive
Full Sample	40	6.4% (0.00)	0.70	9.0% (0.00)	0.72	16.2% (0.00)	0.85
1955–1969	9	5.1% (0.02)	0.67	7.8% (0.02)	0.78	15.4% (0.00)	0.89
1970–1979	16	4.8% (0.07)	0.63	8.3% (0.04)	0.63	15.1% (0.00)	0.81
1980–1990	15	8.9% (0.00)	0.80	10.6% (0.00)	0.80	18.8% (0.00)	0.87
Target firm's operations related to those of the acquiring firm[b]	12	5.2% (0.00)	0.50	8.9% (0.00)	0.75	13.6% (0.00)	0.83
Target firm's operations unrelated to those of the acquiring firm[b]	28	6.9% (0.00)	0.79	9.1% (0.00)	0.71	17.4% (0.00)	0.86

Notes: [a] Average holding-period excess return from 10 days before the first announcement in the *WSJ* through the date the merger or acquisition was approved by both firms.

[b] The parent and target firms are considered to be related if any of the SIC codes of the four primary lines of business in each firm overlap at the two digit level. SIC information was obtained from Dun and Bradstreets' Million Dollar Directory for the year prior to the acquisition.

is whether the combined value of the bidder and the target decline at the time of the acquisition. To consider this question, we compute a value-weighted excess return for the combined acquirer and target firms where the weights are the market values of the bidder and target firms measured five days prior to the takeover announcement. Equivalently, we have computed the market-adjusted change in the aggregate market values of the bidder and target firm during the acquisition announcement period and divided that by the sum of their market values five days prior to the takeover announcement. This value is computed for the 40 cases in which stock price data are available for both the bidder and the target firm. The results are reported in Table 3.

Regardless of the announcement period considered, the average excess return is negative and statistically significantly different from zero. The average values of this statistic for the $(-1, 0)$ and the $(-4, +4)$ periods, and for the interval from 10 days before the initial announcement through the acquisition agreement date are -0.7% (p-value $= 0.10$), -1.9% (p-value $= 0.04$), and -2.1% (p-value $= 0.06$). On

Table 3. Combined Value-Weighted Announcement Period Excess Returns to the Bidder and Target Firms for Acquisitions that Became Spin-offs during the Period 1962–1991 (*p*-values in parentheses)

	Sample Size	(−1, 0)	Fraction Positive	(−4, +4)	Fraction Positive	Day −10 through Acquisition Agreement[a]	Fraction Positive
Full Sample	40	−0.7% (0.10)	0.48	−1.9% (0.04)	0.48	−2.1% (0.06)	0.45
1955–1969	9	1.7% (0.19)	0.67	1.1% (0.26)	0.67	4.3% (0.05)	0.67
1970–1979	16	−1.7% (0.15)	0.38	−3.4% (0.05)	0.38	−4.7% (0.02)	0.38
1980–1990	15	−0.9% (0.31)	0.47	−2.1% (0.10)	0.47	−3.2% (0.09)	0.40
Target firm's operations related to those of the acquiring firm[b]	12	0.0% (0.98)	0.50	−1.0% (0.25)	0.50	−2.9% (0.13)	0.42
Target firm's operations unrelated to those of the acquiring firm[b]	28	−0.9% (0.12)	0.46	−2.3% (0.06)	0.46	−1.8% (0.17)	0.46

Notes: [a]Average holding-period excess return from 10 days before the first announcement in the WSJ through the date the merger or acquisition was approved by both firms.

[b]The parent and target firms are considered to be related if any of the SIC codes of the four primary lines of business in each firm overlap at the two digit level. SIC information was obtained from Dun and Bradstreets' Million Dollar Directory for the year prior to the acquisition.

average, it appears that acquisitions that result in spin-offs actually destroy value in the combined firms—keeping in mind, of course, that this analysis is conducted with only the 40 observations for which data are available for both the bidder and the target firm.

We also separate this sample into those that occurred during the period 1955–1969, 1970–1979, and 1980–1989 and according to whether the acquisitions are related or diversifying. As shown in Table 3, the combined average excess returns to acquirers and targets are negative and generally significantly different from zero during the 1970s and the 1980s and they are positive and significantly different from zero during the 1955–1960 period using the extended window around the acquisition announcement. Finally, as also shown in Table 3, combined average excess returns tend to be negative, although not always significantly different from zero, regardless of whether the acquisition is related or diversifying.

D. Stock Valuation Effects of Spin-offs

The results to this point are generally consistent with the first prediction of the "correction of a mistake" hypothesis—on average, acquisitions that end up as spin-offs generate stock valuation losses at the time of the original acquisition. We now turn to the second prediction—that announcement returns are more positive for spin-offs that originated as a takeover than for spin-offs generally. To test this prediction, announcement period excess returns are calculated for our sample of spin-offs for the $(-1, 0)$ and the $(-4, +4)$ announcement intervals surrounding the spin-off announcement. The results are presented in Table 4.

As shown, the average announcement period returns are +2.2 and +2.5% for the $(-1, 0)$ and the $(-4, +4)$ intervals, respectively, with associated p-values of 0.00 and 0.00. Thus, the spin-off announcement period returns for takeovers that become spin-offs are comparable to those reported by Hite and Owers (1983), Miles and Rosenfeld (1983), Schipper and Smith (1983), and Daley, Mehrotra, and Sivakumar (1997) for a more inclusive set of spin-offs that may include some spin-offs that began as acquisitions and some that are the result of a divestiture of an internally developed subsidiary.

For a more direct look at the question of concern here, we assemble a sample of spin-offs that did not originate as acquisitions and that occurred over the same time period and are of roughly the same relative size as those in the sample of spin-offs that did begin as takeovers. Specifically, we reviewed all spin-offs not identified as beginning with an acquisition for evidence that the subsidiary was internally developed. In those cases in which there is ambiguity, the spin-off was dropped from further consideration. Of the remaining set, a sample of 120 spin-offs was constructed such that the relative sizes of the spin-offs in this sample and the decades in which the spin-offs occurred match those of the spin-offs in the original sample of spin-offs that began as acquisitions. The $(-1, 0)$ and the $(-4, +4)$ announcement period returns for the "non-acquisition" sample of spin-offs are +1.8 and +2.9%,

Table 4. Announcement Period Excess Returns Surrounding Spin-offs during the Period 1962–1991 of Acquisitions that Occurred during the Period 1955–1991 (*p*-values in parentheses)

	Sample Size	(–1, 0)	Fraction Positive	(–4, +4)	Fraction Positive
Full sample	94	2.2% (0.00)	0.73	2.5% (0.00)	0.71
1962–1969	7	2.3% (0.02)	0.86	5.0% (0.00)	0.71
1970–1979	16	1.0% (0.23)	0.50	1.5% (0.35)	0.56
1980–1991	71	2.4% (0.00)	0.77	2.5% (0.00)	0.75
Target firms' operation related to acquiring firm[a]	31	1.1% (0.00)	0.71	2.7% (0.00)	0.71
Target firms' operations unrelated to acquiring firms	63	2.7% (0.00)	0.75	2.4% (0.04)	0.71
Acquisitions with stock data for both acquiring and target firms	40	1.8% (0.00)	0.72	2.9% (0.02)	0.75
Two-day acquisition announcement period:					
Positive excess returns to the parent at acquisition announcement	33	1.7% (0.00)	0.58	3.3% (0.00)	0.58
Negative excess returns to the parent at acquisition announcement	40	2.6% (0.00)	0.63	3.4% (0.00)	0.63
Value-increasing acquisitions[b]	19	1.0% (0.91)	0.63	3.1% (0.01)	0.68
Value-decreasing acquisitions[c]	21	2.4% (0.00)	0.81	3.3% (0.00)	0.81
Day –10 through acquisition agreement date:					
Positive excess returns to the parent at acquisition announcement	25	1.6% (0.02)	0.56	3.2% (0.01)	0.60
Negative excess returns to the parent at acquisition announcement	48	2.4% (0.00)	0.63	3.6% (0.00)	0.60
Value-increasing acquisitions[b]	18	0.3% (0.83)	0.56	1.7% (0.38)	0.61
Value-decreasing acquisitions[c]	22	3.0% (0.00)	0.86	4.4% (0.00)	0.86

Notes: [a]The parent and target firms are considered to be related if any of the SIC codes of the four primary lines of business in each firm overlap at the two-digit level. SIC information was obtained from Dun and Bradstreets' Million Dollar Directory for the year prior to the acquisition.

[b]For this sample, the combined weighted average excess return of the bidder and target firms was positive during the acquisition announcement period.

[c]For this sample, the combined weighted average excess return of the bidder and target firms was negative during the acquisition announcement period.

respectively, and neither is significantly different from the corresponding statistic for the sample of spin-offs that began with an acquisition. The p-values for the differences between the average announcement period returns for the two samples over the two-day and nine-day announcement periods are 0.84 and 0.71, respectively.

Given the apparent time dependency in announcement period returns to acquirers and the lack of any difference in returns for related and diversifying acquisitions, it is interesting to conduct a parallel analysis for spin-offs. These results are presented in Table 4. There does not appear to be any pronounced periodicity in the announcement period returns or, at least, not one that parallels that for acquisitions. For spin-offs, the average announcement period returns are lower during the 1970s than either the 1960s or the 1980s, but all are positive and significantly different from zero. Similarly, the classification of spin-offs as related or unrelated to the parent does not reveal any strong pattern in returns. For the $(-1, 0)$ announcement period, the average excess return to unrelated (focus increasing) spin-offs is greater than the $(-1, 0)$ return for related spin-offs (+2.7 vs. +1.1%), but this pattern is not sustained over the $(-4, +4)$ interval in which the excess return to related spin-offs is slightly greater than the excess return to unrelated spin-offs (+2.7 vs. +2.4%). These results contradict those presented in Daley, Mehrotra, and Sivakumar (1997) who conclude that unrelated spin-offs have significantly higher excess stock returns at spin-off announcements that do related-industry spin-offs. Our study, however, examines only spin-offs that originate as acquisitions of the parent, not a full sample of spin-offs from any origin. The Daley, Mehrotra, and Sivakumar study, however, is based on a smaller sample of spin-offs than the sample of spin-offs used in this analysis.

A primary concern of this study is whether the observed wealth gains at spin-off announcements represent the re-creation of value destroyed (or expected to be destroyed) at the time of the acquisition. To this point, based on average announcement period returns, the data provide only modest support for that contention. We consider that issue further by separating the sample of spin-offs into those for which the acquirer's announcement period return at acquisition was positive and those for which it was negative and then examine the announcement period returns at spin-off. In so doing, we are conditioning spin-off announcement period returns on the market's reaction at the time of the acquisition. If the correction-of-a-mistake hypothesis is correct, spin-off announcement period returns should be significantly more positive for those spin-offs in which the acquisition return is negative than those for which the acquisition announcement period return is positive.

As shown in Table 4, spin-off announcement period returns are positive and significantly from zero regardless of whether the acquisition announcement period return is positive or negative and regardless of the interval over which acquisition or spin-off returns are measured. Additionally, and consistent with the correction-of-a-mistake hypothesis, the average spin-off announcement period return is larger for acquirers that experienced a negative market response at the acquisition announcement than for acquirers that experienced a positive announcement period return at acquisition. For example, for the set of acquirers for which the $(-1, 0)$ acquisition announcement period return is positive, the average $(-1, 0)$ spin-off announcement period return is $+1.7\%$ (p-value = 0.00) and the average $(-4, +4)$ spin-off announcement period return is $+3.3\%$ (p-value = 0.00). For the sample of acquirers for which the $(-1, 0)$ acquisition announcement period return is negative, the average $(-1, 0)$ spin-off announcement period return is $+2.6\%$ (p-value = 0.00) and the average $(-4, +4)$ return is $+3.4\%$ (p-value = 0.00). However, the p-values for the differences between the spin-off announcement period returns for two samples are only 0.58 and 0.98. When acquirer returns are measured over the interval from 10 days before the initial announcement date through the acquisition agreement date and the sample is separated into those with positive and negative acquisition announcement period returns, the $(-1, 0)$ spin-off announcement period return for the former set is $+1.6\%$ and the $(-1, 0)$ spin-off announcement period return for the latter set is $+2.4\%$. The p-value for the difference between the two is 0.54. Similarly, when the spin-off announcement returns are measured over the $(-4, +4)$ interval, the average excess return is higher for the sample that for which the acquirer experienced a negative excess return at the acquisition than for the sample that experienced a positive excess return at the acquisition, but the difference between the two has a p-value of only 0.89. Thus, while the average spin-off announcement period return is higher when the bidder experiences a negative excess return at acquisition then when the bidder experiences a positive excess return at the time of acquisition, the differences are not statistically significant.

The same experiment is conducted for the 40 takeovers in which stock returns are available for both the bidder and target firms at the acquisition date. That is, the 40 takeovers in this sample are separated according to whether the combined excess return of the bidder and target was positive or negative during the various acquisition announcement periods. As shown in Table 4, the spin-off announcement period returns are higher for the "value-decreasing" acquisitions than for the "value-increasing" acquisitions when acquisition announcement period returns are measured over the $(-1, 0)$ interval around the acquisition announcement, but the differences between the spin-off announcement period returns are often not significantly different from each other at the 0.10 level. The differences between the sample are larger at the spin-off announcement date when the acquisition returns are measured over the interval from 10 days before the initial announcement through the acquisition agreement date, but they are still not significantly different from each other at the 0.10 level. For the set with negative acquisition announcement period excess returns for this interval, the two-day average spin-off announcement period excess return is $+3.0\%$; For the set with positive excess returns over this interval, the $(-1, 0)$ average spin-off announcement period excess return is only $+0.3\%$.[8] The p-value for the difference is 0.18. Similar results are obtained when the spin-off announcement period returns are measured over the $(-4, +4)$ interval surrounding the spin-off announcement. In this case, the p-value for the difference between the two samples is 0.26.[9]

E. Multivariate Tests

Although the differences are not statistically significant, the univariate tests suggest that value-decreasing takeovers are associated with larger spin-off returns than are value-increasing takeovers. However, there may be other phenomena at work in the data as well (for example, a periodicity effect) which may influence the apparent relation between acquisition announcement returns and spin-off announcement returns. To control for other factors that may influence returns, we estimate cross-sectional multivariate regressions using the maximum likelihood regression procedure of Eckbo, Maksimovic, and Williams (1990). In the regressions (reported in Table 5), the dependent variable is the (−4, +4) spin-off excess return. In the first regression in each set the independent variables include dummy variables to indicate whether the spin-off occurred during the 1970s or the 1980s, the dollar market value of the spun-off subsidiary as a fraction of the dollar market value of the pre-spin-off parent firm (i.e., to control for differences in the relative sizes of the parent and the subsidiary), and a dummy variable to indicate whether the acquirer and the target are in the same industry according to their two-digit SIC code (i.e., were the original acquisitions diversifying or related). One other factor that may influence the relation between the spin-off and acquisition announcement period excess returns is the relative length of time between the original acquisition and the spin-off. For example, the effect may be stronger for acquisitions and spin-offs that occur relatively closer in time to each other. To control for this effect, two dummy variables are included in the regressions. The first indicates whether the number of months that elapsed between the acquisition and the spin-off is 0 to 44. The second indicates whether the number of months lies between 45 and 88. Recall that the median number of months between the acquisition and the spin-off is 88.

The independent variables in the second regression include all those in the first regression plus the acquirer's (−1, 0) acquisition announcement period excess return. The independent variables in the third regression in each table include all those in the second except that the acquirer's (−4, +4) excess return replaces the acquirer's (−1, 0) excess return. In the fourth regression the independent variables are the same as those in the second, except that the acquirer's excess return calculated over the interval from 10 days before the initial announcement through the acquisition agreement date replaces the acquirer's (−1, 0) excess return. The sample size for these four regressions is 73. The results are reported in columns (1) through (4) of Table 5.

According to the tables, relative size is a significant explanatory variable in each regression (all p-values 0.01). The time period of the spin-off and the dummy variable for whether the parent and the subsidiary are related are not statistically

Table 5. Cross-Sectional Regression Analysis of Nine-Day Announcement Period Excess Returns at the Spin-off Announcement of Previously-Acquired Subsidiaries, 1962–1991

Independent Variable	[1]	[2]	[3]	[4]	[5][a]	[6][a]	[7][a]
Intercept	.0182	.0122	.0183	.0198	−.0035	.0027	.0051
	(0.50)	(0.65)	(0.50)	(0.48)	(0.94)	(0.95)	(0.92)
Spin-off in 1970s	.0058	.0120	.0075	.0070	0.574	.0486	.0440
	(0.85)	(0.69)	(0.80)	(0.82)	(0.25)	(0.30)	(0.39)
Spin-off in 1980s	−.0112	−.0073	−.0075	−.0103	.0074	.0014	.0013
	(0.65)	(0.77)	(0.76)	(0.68)	(0.87)	(0.97)	(0.97)
Size of spin-off[b]	.1467	.1417	.1378	.1335	.0915	.0980	.0900
	(0.00)	(0.00)	(0.00)	(0.00)	(0.12)	(0.07)	(0.13)
Related acquisition[c]	−.0083	.0059	.0004	.0025	.0255	.0259	.0213
	(0.57)	(0.69)	(0.98)	(0.89)	(0.10)	(0.07)	(0.18)
Interval from acquisition to spin-off: 0–44 Months	.0074	.0056	.0054	.0001	.0023	−.0040	.0040
	(0.65)	(0.74)	(0.75)	(0.99)	(0.88)	(0.80)	(0.81)
Interval from acquisition to spin-off: 45–88 mos.	−.0021	−.0014	−.0076	−.0074	.0095	.0022	.0058
	(0.90)	(0.93)	(0.65)	(0.66)	(0.57)	(0.89)	(0.52)
Acquirer's (−1,0) excess return		−.4903					
		(0.02)					
Acquirer's (−4,+4) excess return			−.2074				
			(0.04)				
Acquirer's day −10 through agreement date excess return				−.1843			
				(0.06)			
Acquirer and target combined (−1,0) excess return					−.2272		
					(0.07)		
Acquirer and target combined (−1,0) excess return						−.2553	
						(0.01)	
Acquirer and target combined day −10 through agreement excess return							−.1940
							(0.05)
Sample size	73	73	73	73	40	40	40
R^2	.121	.185	.197	.191	.211	.322	.218

Notes: The independent variable is the nine-day spin-off announcement period excess return. Regressions are estimated using the procedure of Eckbo, Maksimovic, and Williams (1990) (*p*-values are in parentheses).

[a]Includes the 40 observations where stock price data are available for the acquiring and target firms at the acquisition date.

[b]Calculated as the market value of the spun off firm measured on the first day of trading following the spin-off divided by the market value of the parent firm on the day prior to the spin-off ex date.

[c]The parent and target firms are considered to be related if any of the SIC codes of the four primary lines of business in each firm overlap at the two digit level. SIC information was obtained from Dun and Bradstreets' Million Dollar Directory for die year prior to die acquisition.

significant in any of the regressions. There is little evidence that the relative time elapsed between the takeover and the spin-off is important.[10] Most importantly for the question addressed in this paper, the coefficient of the acquisition announcement period return is negative in each of the relevant regressions indicating that higher spin-off returns are associated with lower returns to the acquiring firm at the acquisition. The significance level of this relation across the regressions are 0.02, 0.04, and 0.06.

The regressions in columns (5) through (7) of the tables parallel those in columns (2) through (4), except that the acquirer's acquisition excess return is replaced as an independent variable by the combined excess return to the bidder and the target firm. As might have been anticipated from the univariate tests of Table 4, the relation between spin-off announcement period excess returns and takeover announcement period excess returns is slightly stronger when the independent variable is the combined change in value of the bidder and target firms. In Table 5 the p-values are 0.07, 0.01, and 0.05. The overall picture that emerges from the analysis is that there is a negative relationship between spin-off announcement period returns and acquisition announcement period returns and that the relationship is more significant for the analysis that uses the longer announcement period.[11]

F.   Post Spin-off Events

A useful extension of our analysis is to examine the extent to which spun-off subsidiaries that originated as acquisitions were acquired by outside firms (including the former parent), became insolvent and delisted, or were liquidated following spin-off. We examine a five-year period beginning on the spin-off ex-dates using the CRSP delisting codes and articles appearing on Dow Jones Newswire. Of the 94 spin-offs that were identified as prior acquisitions of the (initial) parent, 67 (71%) remain independent, publicly traded firms during the five-year period. Eight spin-offs (9%) delisted during the post-spin-off period including one firm (Handyman Corp.) that liquidated its assets. The remaining 19 spin-offs (20%) were merged or otherwise acquired by another firm following their spin-off from the original parent. No parent firms reacquired a subsidiary that was previously spun off.

To examine post-spin-off mergers and acquisitions in more detail, we calculate the announcement period excess returns to acquirers and targets in post-spin-off transactions over both a (−1, 0) and (−4, +4) interval surrounding acquisition announcement dates. The results are reported in Table 6. Excess stock returns to targets of post-spin-off acquisitions are substantial and similar to the excess returns earned by shareholders of target firms in pre-spin-off acquisitions (where those data are available). For the 18 acquirers with available stock data, excess returns are negative in both the two- and nine-day intervals and statistically significant using the latter window. As in Table 3, we compute the combined value-weighted excess return to both bidders and targets in these transactions and find results that are

Table 6. Announcement Period Excess Returns to Acquisitions Completed during
the Five-year Period Following Spin-offs
(*p*-values in parenthesis)

	Sample Size	(–1, 0)	Fraction Positive	(–4, +4)	Fraction Positive
Spun off targets	19	8.3%	0.89	11.4%	0.89
		(0.00)		(0.00)	
Acquirers	18	–2.9%	0.22	–4.3%	0.17
		(0.13)		(0.06)	
Value-weighted combined at post spin-off acquisitions	18	–2.0%	0.28	–3.5%	0.22
		(0.18)		(0.08)	
Value-weighted combined at pre spin-off acquisitions	7	–0.7%	0.43	–1.7%	0.29
		(0.81)		(0.60)	
Previous acquirers	11	–1.1%	0.45	–1.8%	0.36
		(0.63)		(0.46)	
Spin-offs	19	5.1%	0.89	3.4%	0.79
		(0.05)		(0.13)	

similar to pre-spin-off acquisitions—namely that post-spin-off acquisitions destroy value in the aggregate. In the (–1, 0) period, the average combined excess return is –2.0% (*p*-value of 0.18), while the average in the (–4, +4) interval is –3.5% (*p*-value of 0.08).

In Table 6 we also report that pre-spin-off acquisitions of the firms that were acquired following spin-offs also destroyed value (in cases where those data are available). The combined excess return, however, is not significant. The original acquiring firms also experienced negative returns at the original acquisitions. Finally, excess returns to the 19 spin-offs that became targets of subsequent acquisitions were 5.1% over the (–1, 0) period (*p*-value of 0.05) and 3.4% over the (–4, +4) period (*p*-value of 0.13). These excess spin-off returns are slightly higher than the remainder of the sample, but the differences are not statistically significant.

This evidence suggests that the history of firms that have been targets of two acquisitions separated by a spin-off from the original parent appears to repeat itself. Value-destroying acquisitions of these firms are followed by value-increasing spin-offs and subsequently by value-destroying acquisitions. Apparently, managers of firms that acquire spun-off firms that were previously acquisition mistakes of another firm must believe that they are engaging in a value-increasing transaction. The capital markets, however, appear to disagree.

V. CONCLUSIONS

Several prior studies document average positive excess returns of +2 to +3% around announcements of corporate spin-offs. While a number of hypotheses have been explored to explain this effect, none is able to fully explain the shareholder gains associated with corporate spin-offs. This paper considers the conjecture that the gains associated with spin-offs generally come about because some spin-offs represent the undoing of an earlier unwise acquisition. According to this "correction-of-a-mistake" hypothesis, the average stock price increases surrounding spin-offs merely represent the re-creation of wealth lost at the time of the original acquisition. The primary predictions of this hypothesis are as follows. First, at the time of acquisitions the announcement period excess returns to the bidding firm are negative for acquisitions that later result in spin-offs. A stronger version of this prediction is that the combined announcement period excess return to the bidder and the target at the time of the acquisition are negative for acquisitions that later become spin-offs. Second, the average spin-off announcement period excess return for a sample of acquisitions that subsequently became spin-offs is larger than for spin-offs generally and for a sample of spin-offs that did not begin as acquisitions. Third, the spin-off announcement period excess return for spin-offs that began with an acquisition is negatively correlated with the original acquisition announcement period excess returns. That is, the greater the original mistake, the greater the rebound when the spin-off is announced.

We test the various predictions of the correction-of-a-mistake hypothesis with a sample of 94 spin-offs that occurred over the period 1962 through 1991. In general, the results are consistent with the first and third predictions of the hypothesis, but not the second.

We also find that post-spin-off acquisitions destroy value for the shareholders of acquiring firms. The combined change in value in these transactions during a (-4, +4) interval relative to announcement is negative and significant at the 0.10 level. Finally, we do not find evidence that supports the conclusions of Daley, Mehrotra, and Sivakumar (1997) that only focus-increasing spin-offs experience positive excess stock returns at spin-off announcements. In our sample, whether or not the spin-off increases focus is not a significant determinant of excess stock returns.

There are both managerial implications and implications for researchers that follow from the results. For managers the results suggest that managers who undertake poor acquisitions can redeem themselves, at least partially, by subsequently divesting the unwise acquisition. For researchers the results suggest that future investigations of the source of gains associated with spin-offs may be more successful if the investigators control for whether the spun-off subsidiary was the target of a prior acquisition.

ACKNOWLEDGMENT

A significant portion of the results reported here also appear in an article published previously by the *Journal of Financial and Quantitative Analysis* (Allen, Lummer, McConnell, & Reed, 1995).

NOTES

1.   Analyses of the wealth effects of corporate sell-offs have been conducted by Alexander, Benson, and Kampmeyer (1984), Hite, Owers, and Rogers (1987), Jain (1985), Klein (1986), and Rosenfeld (1984) among others.

2.   These sources identify many share distributions as spin-offs that do not qualify as spin-offs for our purposes. To qualify as a spin-off for possible inclusion in our sample, we require that the spin-off be a tax-free pro rata distribution of a wholly owned subsidiary. This criterion excludes partial distributions and the return of capital contributions.

3.   We determined that the spin-off was used as a takeover defense if the *WSJ* article announcing the spin-off indicated that the spin-off was intended to thwart a hostile takeover (2) or if a hostile bidder discontinued a bid shortly after the spin-off announcement (1).

4.   We concluded that a spin-off was undertaken to facilitate acquisition of the subsidiary if the *WSJ* article indicated that the purpose of the spin-off was to facilitate acquisition of the subsidiary by another firm or if the subsidiary was acquired by another company within 60 days of the spin-off.

5.   Two observations were deleted because of concurrent announcements of dividend increases by the acquiring firm.

6.   In all 33 acquisitions in which the target was not publicly traded, the initial article in the *WSJ* states that the target "has been acquired" or "has agreed to be acquired." In the 19 of the 40 cases in which the target is publicly traded and the initial announcement is an announcement of an agreement in principle, the *WSJ* article cites either "board approval by both firms," "an agreement in principle between both firms," the signing of a "definitive agreement," or "agreement on the terms of a proposed merger."

7.   Loderer and Martin employ a six-day announcement period to compute excess returns.

8.   For the set with negative acquisition announcement period returns, the average acquisition announcement period excess return is −8.99%. For the set with positive acquisition announcement period excess returns, the average acquisition announcement period return is +5.24%.

9.   Although not reported in the table, when the sample is split according to the acquirer's nine-day (or combined firm nine-day) announcement period return, the results are very similar to those in Table 4.

10.   We also counted the number of months that elapsed between the takeover and the spin-off and included that as a measure of time between the two events. That variable also does not show up as significant in the regressions.

11.   Each of the regressions was checked for outlier observations. In each case where the residuals gave evidence of an outlier, those observations were dropped from the analysis and the regression was reestimated. In no case did the sign of any coefficient change and, in no case did a coefficient that was significant at the 0.05 level become insignificant at that level. The regressions were also estimated using the (−1,0) excess return as the dependent variable with similar results to those reported in Table 5.

REFERENCES

Alexander, G. J., Benson, P. G., & Kampmeyer, J.M. (1984, June). Investigating the valuation effects of announcements of voluntary corporate sell-offs. *Journal of Finance, 39*, 503–517.

Allen, J. W., Lummer, S. L., McConnell, J. J., & Reed, D. K. (1995, December). Can takeover losses explain spin-off gains? *Journal of Financial and Quantitative Analysis, 30*, 465–485.

Asquith, P., Bruner, R. F., & Mullins, D. W. (1983, April). The gains to bidding firms from mergers. *Journal of Financial Economics, 11*, 121–139.

Bradley, M., Desai, A., & Kim, E. H. (1988, May). Synergistic gains from corporate acquisitions and their division between the stockholders of target and acquiring firms. *Journal of Financial Economics, 21*, 3–40.

Brown, S. J., & Warner, J. B. (1985, March). Using daily stock returns: The case of event studies. *Journal of Financial Economics, 14*, 3–31.

Daley, L., Mehrotra, V., & Sivakumar, R. (August 1997). Corporate Focus and Value Creation: Evidence from Spin-offs *Journal of Financial Economics, 45*, 257–281.

Dennis, D. K., & McConnell, J. J. (1986, June). Corporate mergers and security returns. *Journal of Financial Economics, 16*, 143–187.

Eckbo, B. E., Maksimovic, V., & Williams, J. (1990). Consistent estimation of cross-sectional models in event studies. *Review of Financial Studies, 3* (3), 343–365.

Hite, G. L., & Owers, J. E. (1983, December). Security price reactions around corporate spin-off announcements. *Journal of Financial Economics, 12*, 409–436.

Hite, G. L., Owers, J. E., & Rogers, R. C. (1987, June). The market for interfirm asset sales: partial sell-offs and total liquidations. *Journal of Financial Economics, 18*, 229–252.

Jain, P. C. (1985, March). The effect of voluntary sell-off announcements on shareholder wealth. *Journal of Finance, 40*.

Jarrell, G., & Poulsen, A. (1989, Fall). Stock trading before the announcement of tender offers: insider trading or market anticipation? *Journal of Law, Economics and Organization, 5*, 225–248.

Jensen, M. C. (1986, May). Agency costs of free cash flow, corporate finance and takeovers. *American Economic Review, 76*, 323–29.

Kaplan, S. N., & Weisbach, M. S. (1992, March). The success of acquisitions: evidence from divestitures. *Journal of Finance, 47*, 107–138.

Klein, A. (1986, July). The timing and substance of divestiture announcements: individual, simultaneous and cumulative effects. *Journal of Finance, 41*, 685–696.

Linn, S. C., & McConnell, J. J. (1983, April). An empirical investigation of the impact of antitakeover amendments on common stock prices. *Journal of Financial Economics, 22*, 361–399.

Loderer, C., & Martin, K. (1990). *Corporate acquisition announcements: time series patterns.* Unpublished working paper, University of Iowa.

Miles, J. A., & Rosenfeld, J. D. (1983, December). The effect of voluntary spin-off announcements on shareholder wealth. *Journal of Finance, 38*, 1597–1606.

Mitchell, M. L., & Lehn, K. (1990, April). Do bad bidders become good targets? *Journal of Political Economy, 98*, 372–398.

Morck, R., Shleifer, A., & Vishny, R. W. (1990, March). Do managerial objectives drive bad acquisitions? *Journal of Finance, 45*, 31–48.

Porter, M. (1987, May–June). From Competitive advantage to corporate strategy. *Harvard Business Review, 65*, 43–59.

Ravenscraft, D. J., & Scherer, F. M. (1987). *Mergers, selloffs and economic efficiency.* Washington, DC: The Brookings Institute.

Roll, R. (1986, April). The hubris hypothesis of corporate takeovers. *Journal of Business, 59*, 197–216.

Rosenfeld, J. D. (1984, December). Additional evidence on the relation between divestiture announcements and shareholder wealth. *Journal of Finance, 39*, 1437–1448.

Scherer, F. M. (1988, Winter). Corporate takeovers: The efficiency arguments. *Journal of Economic Perspectives, 2*, 69–82.

Schipper, K., & Smith, A. (1983, December). Effects of recontracting on shareholder wealth: the case of voluntary spin-offs. *Journal of Financial Economics, 12*, 437–467.

Shleifer, A., & Vishny, R. W. (1989, November). Management entrenchment: The case of manager-specific investments. *Journal of Financial Economics, 25*, 123–139.

SOLVING AN EMPIRICAL PUZZLE IN THE CAPITAL ASSET PRICING MODEL

John Leusner, Jalal D. Akhavein, and
P. A. V. B. Swamy

ABSTRACT

A long standing puzzle in the Capital Asset Pricing Model (CAPM) has been the inability of empirical work to validate it. Roll (1977) was the first to point out this problem, and recently, Fama and French (1992, 1993, 1996) bolstered Roll's original critique with additional empirical results. Does this mean the CAPM is dead? This paper presents a new empirical approach to estimating the CAPM. This approach takes into account the differences between observable and expected returns for risky assets and for the market portfolio of all traded assets, as well as inherent nonlinearities and the effects of excluded variables. Using this approach we provide evidence that the CAPM is alive and well.

I. INTRODUCTION

The Capital Asset Pricing Model (CAPM) of Sharpe (1964), Lintner (1965), and Black (1972) in its various formulations provides predictions for equilibrium-

Research in Finance, Volume 16, pages 71–94.
ISBN: 0-7623-0328-X

expected returns on risky assets. More specifically, one of its formulations states that the expected excess return over the risk-free interest rate of an asset (or a portfolio of assets) equals a coefficient, denoted by β, times the (mean-variance-efficient) market portfolio's expected excess return over the risk-free interest rate. This relatively straightforward relationship between various rates of return is difficult to implement empirically because expected returns and the efficient market portfolio are unobservable. Despite this formidable difficulty, a substantial number of tests have nonetheless been performed, using a variety of ex post values and proxies for the unobservable ex ante variables. Recognizing the seriousness of this situation quite early, Roll (1977) emphasized correctly that tests following such an approach provide no evidence about the validity of the CAPM. The obvious reason is that ex post values and proxies are only approximations and therefore not the variables one should actually be using to test the CAPM. The primary purpose of this paper is to provide a new approach to testing the CAPM that overcomes this deficiency.

Recently, Fama and French (1992, 1993, 1996) conducted extensive tests of the CAPM and found that the relation between average stock return and β is weak, and that average firm size and the ratio of book-to-market equity do a good job capturing the cross-sectional variation in average stock returns. These findings suggest, among other things, that a formal accounting of the effects of "excluded variables" may resurrect the CAPM. This will be the central issue in this paper.

According to Fama and French (1993), some questions that need to be addressed are: (i) how are the size and book-to-market factors in returns driven by the stochastic behavior of earnings?; (ii) how does profitability, or any other fundamental, produce common variation in returns associated with size and book-to-market equity that is not picked up by the market return?; (iii) can specific fundamentals be identified as state variables that lead to common variation in returns that is independent of the market and carries a different premium than general market risk? This paper attempts to answer these questions.

In an interesting article, Black (1995) gives three theoretical explanations of the measured flat line relating expected return and β: (i) mismeasuring the market portfolio, (ii) restricted borrowing, and (iii) reluctance to borrow. Even if such reasoning is correct, we have found that the relation between the observed counterparts of expected return and β is nonlinear. Finally, we shall provide some possible answers to questions posed by Black (1995) concerning the future prospects of the CAPM: (i) will the line be flat in the future? (ii) will it be steep as the CAPM says it should be? and (iii) will it be flatter, but not completely flat?

First, the CAPM is modified to take into account the differences between expected and observable returns and between the market portfolio and its proxy. In this modified model β is not required to be a constant, but instead is permitted to vary. Second, the effects of excluded variables and departures from a linear functional form are taken into account. Third, all the modifications are then expressed in terms of observable variables. Finally, the coefficients on the observable regressors are modeled as stochastic functions of the variables that Fama and French (1992) include in their test of the CAPM and find to have reliable power in explaining a cross-section of average stock returns. Once this has been done, the resulting model is estimated using data for 10 stock portfolios formed on the basis of both firm size and the ratio of book-to-market equity. (This procedure of forming portfolios was originated by Fama & French, 1993.)

The specific model to be estimated is developed in Section II. The issue regarding what constitutes a reasonable inference based upon this model is addressed in Section III. A brief description of the data used to estimate the model is presented in Section IV. Section V discusses the empirical results and their applications. Section VI contains the conclusions.

II. IMPROVING THE SPECIFICATION OF THE CAPM

A. Problems With the Original Formulation of the CAPM

The original CAPM may be expressed as

$$Er_{it} - r_{ft} = \beta_{it}(Er_{Mt} - r_{ft}), \tag{1}$$

where Er_{it} is the (subjective) expected return on an asset (or a portfolio of assets) an investor chooses to hold, Er_{Mt} is the (subjective) expected return on the mean-variance efficient market portfolio, r_{ft} is the risk-free rate, i indexes assets or portfolios of assets, t indexes time, and β_{it} is equal to the ratio of the covariance between r_{it} and r_{Mt}, denoted by $cov(r_{it}, r_{Mt})$, and the variance of r_{Mt}, denoted by σ_M^2. The time variability of this variance and covariance implies that β_{it} is time varying. It is important to note that as in the case of Er_{it} and Er_{Mt}, both $cov(r_{it}, r_{Mt})$, and σ_M^2 are the moments of a subjective distribution. Alternative definitions of β_{it} are provided in Ingersoll (1987, pp. 92, 124, 134) and Constantinides (1989).

Sufficient conditions under which the minimum-variance portfolios exist and each investor holds such a portfolio are given in Ingersoll (1987, p. 92). These conditions may not hold if investors' expectations or beliefs are heterogeneous in the sense that their subjective distributions of future returns on risky assets are different. Equation (1) implies that in a market equilibrium, the value-weight market portfolio is mean-variance efficient which, in turn, implies that β_{it} is the only risk needed to explain expected returns and there is positive expected premium for β_{it} risk (see Fama & French, 1996, pp. 1947–1948).

A difficulty with empirically testing whether the implications of the CAPM are true or whether β_{it} is significantly different from zero in equation (1), from a statistical standpoint, is that it represents a statement about expected returns, which are not observable. To transform the relationship into observable variables for testing purposes, we introduce the following two equations relating observable returns to expected returns:

$$r_{it} = Er_{it} + v_{it}, \qquad (2)$$

$$r_{Mt} = Er_{Mt} + v_{Mt} \qquad (3)$$

where r_{it} and r_{Mt} are the observable returns, and v_{it} and v_{Mt} are random disturbances. These latter variables will be distributed with zero means only if the data-generating processes and subjective processes of returns possess the same means. Substituting equations (2) and (3) into equation (1) yields

$$r_{it} - r_{ft} = \beta_{it}^*(r_{Mt} - r_{ft}) + v_{it}, \qquad (4)$$

where $\beta_{it}^* = \beta_{it}[1 - v_{Mt}/(r_{MT} - r_{ft})]$.

Although equation (4) is not expressed in the form of an errors-in-variables model, it reduces to such a model if the means of v_{it} and v_{Mt} are zero and β_{it} is a constant. Models possessing these properties have been extensively studied in statistics and econometrics literature (see Lehmann, 1983, pp. 450–451). As it turns out, estimation of equation (4) when it is not restricted as an errors-in-variables model is relatively straightforward, as will be shown in Section III. Furthermore, the now classic "Roll's (1977) critique" of tests of the CAPM noted earlier does not apply to the estimation of equation (4) because v_{Mt} accounts for any differences between the (unobservable) mean-variance-efficient market portfolio and the particular portfolio that is chosen as a proxy. Further, v_{Mt} is permitted to have a nonzero and time-varying mean to cover situations where these differences are systematic and time varying. The presence of v_{Mt} in equation (4) makes the effects of mismeasurements noted by Black (1995) explicit, although equation (3) indicates that r_{Mt} is a good proxy for Er_{Mt} only if the mean of v_{Mt} is zero. With this definition, it is impossible for anyone to try to decide whether the proxies for the market portfolio used in empirical tests are good or bad because the v_{Mt} are unobservable.

Even if the mismeasurement issue is resolved, equation (4) may nonetheless still be criticized insofar as important regressors are excluded. For example, no asset is perfectly liquid because all trades required to convert assets into cash involve some transaction cost. As a result, investors may choose to hold more liquid assets with lower transaction costs than otherwise. If so, an illiquidity premium should be taken into account. This can be done by allowing for trading costs to enter the right-hand side of equation (4) (see Amihud & Mendelson, 1986). Other potentially important variables, excluded from equation (4), are discussed below.

Another issue in the CAPM is whether investors face only one risk arising from uncertainty about the future values of assets. In all likelihood, investors face many sources of risk, as shown by Merton's (1973) inter-temporal asset pricing model. In such instances, investors would supplement the market portfolio with additional positions in hedge portfolios to offset these risks. This results in separate β_{it}s and risk premiums for every significant source of risk that investors try to hedge. Equation (4), therefore, should be extended to account for the effects of extra-market hedging transactions on equilibrium rates of return. Such an expanded version of equation (4) would recognize the multidimensional nature of risk and thereby show that some important regressors are necessarily excluded from equation (4).

B. A New Formulation of the CAPM

Including previously excluded regressors in equation (4) is not trivial because the functional form of the relationship between them and the dependent variable is unknown. This difficulty is resolved in principle by modifying equation (4) as follows:

$$r_{it} - r_{ft} = \beta_{it}^*(r_{Mt} - r_{ft}) + v_{it} + \sum_{j=1}^{m} \zeta_{ijt} x_{jt}, \tag{5}$$

where the x_{jt} represent excluded variables, the ζ_{ijt} denote their coefficients, and m denotes the number of excluded variables. Since m cannot be known with certainty, one may assume without restricting it to be equal to a specific number that the regressors of equation (5) form a sufficient set in the sense that they exactly determine the values of $r_{it} - r_{ft}$ in all periods.

As a general rule, by allowing all the coefficients in a linear equation to be different for each and every observation, the equation is permitted to pass through every data point and hence it coincides, for certain variations in the coefficients, with the actual process generating the data on its dependent variable. Because of this rule, equation (5) provides the only reliable way to capture unknown functional forms without relying upon strong prior information. One may assume that the coefficients of equation (5) are constants only when this equation is known with certainty to be linear. In contrast, with varying coefficients, equation (5) is truly nonlinear.

Obviously, equation (5) cannot be empirically estimated if the data on the x_{jt} are not available. What is not so obvious is that when the x_{jt} are not observable, one cannot prove they are uncorrelated with $(r_{Mt} - r_{ft})$ (see Pratt & Schlaifer, 1984). An approach for resolving this problem is to avoid making such uncorrelated assumptions and assume instead that

$$x_{jt} = \psi_{0jt} + \psi_{1jt}(r_{Mt} - r_{ft}), \quad j = 1, , 2, \ldots, m, \tag{6}$$

where ψ_{0jt} is the portion of x_{jt} remaining after the effect of the variable $(r_{Mt} - r_{ft})$ has been removed. Accordingly, even if the variable $(r_{Mt} - r_{ft})$ is correlated with the x_{jt}, it can nonetheless be uncorrelated with the remainders, ψ_{0jt}. Also, for certain variations in ψ_{0jt} and ψ_{1jt}, equation (6) exactly coincides with the true relationship between the x_{jt} and $(r_{Mt} - r_{ft})$, if such a relationship exists. Once again, however, one cannot assume the ψ_{0jt} and ψ_{1jt} are constants unless equation (6) is known with certainty to be linear. Equation (6) should be recognized as an auxiliary equation, a linear form of which has been used to analyze the effects of excluded variables in the econometrics literature (see Greene, 1993, pp. 245–247). Since this equation does not impose any constraints on the coefficients of equation (5), it does not prevent the latter equation from coinciding with the true relationship between the variables. Substituting equation (6) into equation (5) yields

$$r_{it} - r_{ft} = \gamma_{0it} + \gamma_{1it}(r_{Mt} - r_{ft}), \tag{7}$$

where $\gamma_{0it} = (v_{it} + \Sigma_{j=1}^{m} \zeta_{ijt}\psi_{0jt})$ and $\gamma_{1it} = (\beta_{it}^{*} + \Sigma_{j=1}^{m} \zeta_{ijt}\psi_{1jt})$.

The coefficient, γ_{1it}, has a relatively straightforward economic interpretation. It consists of three parts, the "true" beta, β_{it}, of the CAPM, a mismeasurement effect, $-\beta_{it}v_{Mt}/r_{Mt} - r_{ft}$, and an omitted-variable bias, $\Sigma_{j=1}^{m} \zeta_{ijt}\psi_{1jt}$. More so than the "true" beta, the omitted-variables bias changes over time because the set of excluded variables undoubtedly changes quite frequently, lending further real-world, economic plausibility to time variability of γ_{1it}. Similarly, the connection of γ_{0it} with the intercepts of equations (5) and (6) clarifies its real-world origin.

The preceding discussion proposes the introduction of varying coefficients and auxiliary equations into the estimation procedure as an important approach to dealing with unknown functional forms and the effects of omitted variables. Equation (7) provides a useful formulation that does not suffer from various specification errors when testing the CAPM, and it avoids such serious errors by not relying on any definitions of γ_{0it} and γ_{1it} other than those provided by equation (7).[1]

III. ECONOMETRIC UNDERPINNINGS OF THE NEW CAPM

Estimation of equation (7) requires specific stochastic assumptions about γ_{0it} and γ_{1it}. The permissible set of assumptions is, however, restricted. For example, one cannot assume that γ_{1it} is a constant because doing so would contradict the assumption that v_{Mt} is a random variable, even ignoring any variations in β_{it} and any omitted-variable bias. In addition, the fact that γ_{1it} depends on $(r_{Mt} - r_{ft})$ via β_{it}^{*}, and γ_{0it} and γ_{1it} are functions of the common set of time-varying coefficients ζ_{ijt} prohibits one from assuming that the variables γ_{0it}, γ_{1it}, and $(r_{Mt} - r_{ft})$ are uncorrelated with one another. (Remember that the nonlinearities involved in equation (5) cannot be captured without the time-varying ζ_{ijt}.) In other words, one cannot assume that $E[(r_{it} - r_{ft})|(r_{Mt} - r_{ft})] = \alpha + \beta(R_{Mt} - r_{ft})$, where α and β are constants, without contradicting the definitions of γ_{0it} and γ_{1it}. By the same logic, in each regression run by Fama and French (1993) and Kothari, Shanken, and Sloan (1995) the right-hand side with the disturbance suppressed does not give the conditional expectation of the left-hand variable given the values of the right-hand side variables. This argument lies at the heart of Roll's (1977) criticism of earlier tests of the CAPM. In principle, generalizing the set of assumptions about γ_{0it} and γ_{1it} in equation (7) can help in this respect. The reason is that general assumptions are more likely to encompass true assumptions as special cases than more restrictive assumptions. We shall proceed therefore by weakening the assumptions about γ_{0it} and γ_{1it}.

Suppose that r_{it} of equation (7) refers to the rate of return on the ith portfolio of assets held by an investor. Then $r_{it} = \sum_{j=1}^{n} w_{ijt} r_{ijt}$, where r_{ijt} is the rate of return on the jth asset held as a part of the ith portfolio, one of the r_{ijt} is equal to r_{ft}, and w_{ijt} is the proportion of the investor's total budget allocated to the jth asset in the period t. It follows that the variance of r_{it} is

$$\sigma_i^2 = \sum_{\substack{j=1 \\ j \neq k}}^{n} \sum_{k=1}^{n} w_{ijt} w_{ikt} cov(r_{ijt}, r_{ikt}) + \sum_{j=1}^{n} w_{ijt}^2 var(r_{ijt}), \tag{8}$$

where $var(r_{ijt})$ denotes the variance of r_{ijt} and $cov(r_{ijt}, r_{ikt})$ denotes the covariance between r_{ijt} and r_{ikt}.

The variance of r_{it} can also be obtained directly from equation (7). It is

$$\sigma_i^2 = var(\gamma_{1it}(r_{Mt} - r_{ft})) + var(\gamma_{0it}) + 2cov(\gamma_{0it}, \gamma_{1it}(r_{Mt} - r_{ft})). \tag{9}$$

Equation (9) eases the computational burden compared to equation (8) because the latter equation involves a large number of variances and covariances that may be time varying and cannot be estimated unless one knows how they vary over time even if the data on all n securities in equation (8) are available. However, it does not have the advantage of parsimony (in terms of a preference for a model with fewer parameters and in all other respects almost as good as other competing models) and may be false if these two equations are inconsistent. Ideally, one should only make those assumptions about γ_{0it} and γ_{1it} that preserve the consistency between equations (8) and (9).

Such assumptions might be the following:

Assumption 1.   The coefficients of equation (7) satisfy the stochastic equation

$$\gamma_{it} = \Pi z_{it} + \varepsilon_{it}, \tag{10}$$

where γ_{it} denotes the two-element column vector $(\gamma_{0it}, \gamma_{1it})'$; Π denotes the 2 $\times 7$ matrix $[\pi_{kj}]$, $k = 0, 1, j = 0, 1, \ldots, 6$; z_{it} denotes the seven-element column vector $(1, z_{i1,t-1}, z_{i2,t-1}, z_{3,t-1}, z_{4,t-1}, z_{5,t-1}, z_{6t})'$,

$z_{i7,t-1}$ = the log of average size over all firms in the ith portfolio (a firm's size is equal to its market equity, ME = a stock's price times shares outstanding, for June of year $t-1$),

$z_{i2,t-1}$ = the average of book-to-market ratio over all firms in the ith portfolio (a firm's book-to-market ratio is equal to its book equity, BE = book value of its common equity as measured by Fama and French (1993, p. 11), for the fiscal year ending in calendar year $t-1$, divided by its market equity, ME, in December of $t-1$),

$z_{3,t-1}$ = the dividend price ratio (dividend/price) for the S&P 500,

$z_{4,t-1}$ = the default premium (Moody's Baa bond rate minus Moody's Aaa bond rate),

$z_{5,t-1}$ = the yield on the 10-year Treasury bill minus the one-year Treasury bill rate,

z_{6t} = a dummy variable that is one in January and zero in other months,[2]

and ε_{it} denotes the two-element column vector $(\varepsilon_{0it}, \varepsilon_{1it})'$ that satisfies the stochastic difference equation

$$\varepsilon_{it} = \Phi\varepsilon_{i,t-1} + a_{it}, \tag{11}$$

where Φ denotes the 2×2 diagonal matrix (ϕ_{00}, ϕ_{11}) with $-1 < \phi_{00}, \phi_{11} < 1$ and $a_{it} = (a_{0it}, a_{1it})'$ is distributed with mean zero and variance-covariance matrix $\sigma_a^2\Delta_a = \sigma_a^2[\delta_{kja}]$, $k = 0, 1, j = 0, 1$.

Assumption 2.   The $(r_{Mt} - r_{ft})$ are independent of the ε_{it} given a value of z_{it}.

Assumptions 1 and 2 are unlike any assumptions made in the previous studies of the CAPM. Assumption 1 is weaker than the assumption that the $(r_{Mt} - r_{ft})$ are independent of the γ_{0it} and γ_{1it} (see Dawid, 1979, p. 5) and both Assumptions 1 and 2 are weaker than the assumptions made by Jagannathan and Wang (1996), Harvey, and others in testing the CAPM.

Note that Assumption 1 permits the v_{it} and v_{Mt} of equations (2) and (3) to have nonzero and time-varying means. Fama and French (1992, 1993) found that the current values of z_{it} have reliable power to explain the cross-section of average returns, even though their chosen variables do not appear directly in the CAPM. They also found that stock risks are multidimensional and the elements of z_{it} proxy for different dimensions of risk. As discussed earlier, the coefficients of equation (7) capture the multidimensional nature of risk. For all these reasons, equation (10), relating the coefficients of equation (7) to z_{it} is an appropriate specification. We have used Fama and French's (1996) discussion of the CAPM average-return anomalies for guidance as to an adequate list of zs that should be included in equation (10).

The elements of z_{it} are called "concomitants" in Pratt and Schlaifer (1988) and form a sufficient set of regressors for equation (10) if they completely explain all the variation in γ_{1it}. Algebraically, this condition can be expressed as

$$|\phi_{11}| = 0 \text{ or } 1, \delta_{01a} = \delta_{10a} = \delta_{11a} = 0,$$

$$\pi_{kj} \neq 0 \text{ for } k = 0, 1 \text{ and } j \neq 0. \tag{12}$$

The implication of these conditions on Φ and Δ_a is that the distribution of ε_{1it} is degenerate. If it is degenerate and if the expectation of ε_{0it}, given the values of z_{it} and $(r_{MT} - r_{ft})$, is zero, as implied by Assumptions 1 and 2, then the third term on the right-hand side of equation (9) is zero given a value of z_{it}, and model (7) reduces to a regression model with first-order autoregressive errors. In this case the usual consistency proofs apply to Swamy, Mehta, and Singamsetti's (1996) parameter estimators of model (7).[3]

Let us interpret the variances and covariances in equations (8) and (9) as the conditional second-order moments given a value of z_{it}. Suppose that given a value of z_{it}, the third term on the right-hand side of equation (9) is equal to zero. In this case the right-hand side of equation (9) can be equal to that of equation (8). If, in addition, the right-hand side of equation (8) can be expressed as a sum of two terms with one term tending to a nonzero value and the other tending to zero as $n \to \infty$, then the former term represents the systematic (or nondiversifiable) risk and the latter term represents nonsystematic (or diversifiable) risk components of the portfolio variance (see Swamy, Lutton, & Tavlas, 1997). If the first term on the right-hand side of equation (9) is equal to the term of equation (8) with a nonzero limit, then it too represents systematic risks. These definitions are more comprehensive than the corresponding definitions found in the finance literature because, as has been shown above, equation (7) captures all sources of risk whereas equation (1) captures only one such source. Note that if both the terms on the right-hand side of equation (8) go to zero as $n \to \infty$, then equation (7) with nonzero γ_{1it} does not hold (see Swamy, Lutton, & Tavlas, 1997).

Under Assumptions 1 and 2,

$$E\left[\left(\beta_{it} - \beta_{it}\frac{v_{Mt}}{(r_{Mt} - r_{ft})} + \sum_{j=1}^{m} \zeta_{ijt}\psi_{1jt}\right) \middle| z_{it}\right]$$

$$= \left[\pi_{10} + \sum_{j=1}^{2} \pi_{1j}z_{ij,t-1} + \sum_{j=3}^{5} \pi_{1j}z_{j,t-1} + \pi_{16}z_{6t} + E(\varepsilon_{1it} \mid z_{it})\right]. \tag{13}$$

If the sum of the second and third terms on the left-hand side of this equation is equal to the sum of all the terms on its right-hand side other than π_{10} and $E(\beta_{it}|z_{it})$ is a constant, then $E(\beta_{it}|z_{it}) = \pi_{10}$. Thus, Assumptions 1 and 2 can aid in the estimation of the conditional mean of β_{it} in the original CAPM, given z_{it}. Even when $E(\beta_{it}|z_{it}) = \pi_{10}$, the average $\pi_{10} + (1/T)\Sigma_{t=1}^{T} (\Sigma_{j=1}^{2} \pi_{1j}z_{ij,t-1} + \Sigma_{j=3}^{5} \pi_{1j}z_{j,t-1} + \pi_{16}z_{6t})$ is preferable to π_{10} as a measure of the risks inherent in the ith asset (or portfolio of assets) if $E((1/T)\Sigma_{t=1}^{T} - \beta_{it} v_{Mt}/(r_{Mt} - r_{ft}) \mid z_{it})$ is equal to $(1/T)\Sigma_{t=1}^{T} E(\varepsilon_{1it} \mid z_{it})$, since equation (5), unlike equation (1), covers all sources of risk. For large T, $E((1/T)\Sigma_{t=1}^{T} \gamma_{1it} \mid z_{it})$ will be equal to $\pi_{10} + (1/T)\Sigma_{t=1}^{T} (\Sigma_{j=1}^{2} \pi_{1j} z_{ij,t-1} + \Sigma_{j=3}^{5} \pi_{1j} z_{j,t-1} + \pi_{16} z_{6t})$ if both $E((1/T)\Sigma_{t=1}^{T} - \beta_{it} v_{Mt}/(r_{MT} - r_{ft}) \mid z_{it})$ and $(1/T)\Sigma_{t=1}^{T} E(\varepsilon_{1it} \mid z_{it})$ tend to zero as $T \rightarrow \infty$. Under these conditions the conditional estimates of $(1/T)\Sigma_{t=1}^{T} \gamma_{1it}$ given z_{it} provide good estimates of the risks inherent in the ith asset (or portfolio of assets).

Estimation of equation (7) under Assumptions 1 and 2 is performed with and without the restrictions that[4]

$$\pi_{kj} = 0 \text{ for } k = 0, 1 \text{ and } j \neq 0. \tag{14}$$

These restrictions, when imposed, eliminate the time-varying zs from equation (10).

Note that assumption (11) does not permit the restriction on ϕ_{11} given in (12) to be exactly satisfied. Such a restriction can only be nearly satisfied if the estimate of $|\phi_{11}|$ is equal to the boundary value 0.99 utilized in our computer program. If this restriction is more closely satisfied when the restrictions on Π given in (14) are not imposed than when they are imposed, then one can conclude that the regressors included in equation (10) are appropriate in the sense that they adequately explain the variation in the coefficients of equation (7).

Equations (7) and (10) jointly describe the time-series model being estimated to explain the excess returns $r_{it} - r_{ft}$ in Section V. Thus, substituting equation (10) into equation (7):

$$r_{it} - r_{ft} = [1(r_{Mt} - r_{ft})] \begin{pmatrix} \pi_{00} & \pi_{01} & \cdots & \pi_{06} \\ \pi_{10} & \pi_{11} & \cdots & \pi_{16} \end{pmatrix} \begin{pmatrix} 1 \\ z_{il,t-1} \\ \vdots \\ z_{6t} \end{pmatrix} + [1 \ (r_{Mt} - r_{ft})] \begin{pmatrix} \varepsilon_{0it} \\ \varepsilon_{1it} \end{pmatrix}. \tag{15}$$

This equation is not linear and contains an error term that is both heteroscedastic and serially correlated. The explanatory variables in this equation are the excess market return $r_{Mt} - r_{ft}$, the six concomitants, z, (introduced in Assumption 1 that includes firm size and the ratio of book-to-market equity), and the interactions between the excess market return and each of the concomitants. Used alone without these interactions, the concomitants may not have adequate power to explain stock returns because of the multidimensional nature of stock risks. Previous tests of the CAPM neglect to consider these interactions. They also use two-pass regressions (see Bodie, Kane, & Marcus (1993, chap. 11) for a survey of these tests). In principle, applying a single-pass regression to (15) is superior to two-pass regressions, even when the second-pass regression overcomes the measurement error problem created by the β estimates. Under Assumptions 1 and 2, the conditional mean of the dependent variable of equation (7), given the values of z_{it} and $(r_{Mt} - r_{it})$, is equal to the first term on the right-hand side of equation (15). For empirical estimation of equation (15), any one of three data sets (time-series data, cross-section data, and time-series-cross-section data) may be used, although Assumptions 1 and 2 are well suited only to time-series data (see Swamy & Tavlas, 1995).[5]

Now suppose that Assumptions 1 and 2 and the restrictions given by (12) hold. It follows that: (i) equation (15) explains how firm size and the ratio of book-to-market equity influence the excess returns, $r_{it} - r_{ft}$, which, in turn, influence the stochastic behavior of earnings, (ii) the sum $\pi_{01}z_{i1,t-1} + \pi_{02}z_{i2,t-1}$ measures variation in excess returns, $r_{it} - r_{ft}$, associated with firm size and *BE/ME* that is not captured by the market return, and (iii) the ε_{it} can be identified as state variables that lead to common variation in the excess returns, $r_{it} - r_{ft}$, that is independent of the market and thus carries a different premium than general market risk. Note that (i)–(iii) are directly responsive to issues (i)–(iii) raised by Fama and French (1993) and restated in the Introduction.

It is useful here to consider some variants of the model proposed above. Clearly, the conjunction of the model given by equation (7) and Assumptions 1 and 2 is false if it cannot explain and predict the underlying phenomenon better than the following inconsistent or restrictive alternatives introduced earlier,

$$\pi_{kj} = 0 \text{ for } k = 0, 1 \text{ and } j \neq 0, \ \phi_{11} = 0,$$

$$\delta_{01a} = \delta_{10a} = \delta_{11a} = 0, \delta_{00a} = 1, \tag{16}$$

or,

$$\pi_{kj} = 0 \text{ for } k = 0, 1 \text{ and } j \neq 0, \ \Phi = 0,$$

$$\delta_{01a} = \delta_{10a} = \delta_{11a} = 0, \delta_{00a} = 1. \tag{17}$$

Restriction (16) implies that equation (7) is a fixed-coefficient model with first-order autoregressive (AR(1)) errors, while restriction (17) implies that equation (7) is a fixed-coefficient model with white-noise errors.

It is useful to digress for a moment to the subject of model validation based on forecast comparisons. A rationale for this type of comparison is provided by the cross-validation approach—which consists of splitting the data sample into two subsamples. The choice of a model, including any necessary estimation, is then based on one subsample and its performance is assessed by measuring its prediction against the other subsample. The premise of this approach is that the validity of statistical estimates should be judged by data different from those used to derive the estimates (see Mosteller & Tukey, 1977, pp. 36–40). Friedman and Schwartz (1991, p. 47) also indicate that a persuasive test of a model must be based on data not used in its estimation. Furthermore, formal hypothesis tests of a model on the data that are used to choose its numerical coefficients are almost certain to overestimate performance: the use of statistical tests leads to false models with probability one if both the null and alternative hypotheses considered for these tests are false, as shown by Swamy and Tavlas (1995, p. 171 and footnote 7). That this is a problem in the present case follows from the lack of any guarantee that either a null or an alternative hypothesis will be true if the inconsistent restrictions (14) or (16) or (17) are necessary parts of the maintained hypothesis. Conversely, a hypothesis is true if it is broad enough to cover the true model as a special case. This is the motivation for extending the CAPM: to make it broad enough so that there is a better chance of encompassing the true model as a special case. Accordingly, in Section V, model (7) and Assumptions 1 and 2 with or without restrictions (14) or (16) or (17) are evaluated based upon forecast comparisons.

Model (7), Assumptions 1 and 2, and the three sets of restrictions can be combined as conjunctions, listed here in decreasing order of generality regarding the restrictiveness of assumptions.

Conjunction I: model (7), Assumptions 1 and 2.

Conjunction II: model (7), Assumptions 1 and 2, and set (14).

Conjunction III: model (7), Assumptions 1 and 2, and set (16).

Conjunction IV: model (7), Assumptions 1 and 2, and set (17).

The reason for considering conjunctions II–IV—even though they are inconsistent—is to examine how they perform in explanation and prediction relative to conjunction I. Doing this is especially useful for understanding earlier empirical work leading to the CAPM puzzle.

The accuracy of the model, or its validity, is determined as follows. Let $R_{it} = r_{it} - r_{ft}$. After estimating the models defined by conjunctions I–IV, forecasts of the out-of-sample values of R_{it} are generated from each of the estimated models. Let these forecasts be denoted by $\hat{R}_{it}$. Then two formulas are used to measure the accuracy of $\hat{R}_{it}$,

$$(i) \text{ root mean–square error} = RMSE = \sqrt{\frac{1}{F} \sum_{s=1}^{F} (\hat{R}_{i,T+s} - R_{i,T+s})^2} \tag{18}$$

and

$$(ii) \text{ mean absolute error} = MAE = \frac{1}{F} \sum_{s=1}^{F} |\hat{R}_{i,T+s} - R_{i,T+s}|, \tag{19}$$

where F is the number of periods being forecasted and T is the terminal date of the estimation period.

IV. DATA

The r_{it} are the monthly value-weighted stock returns on each of 10 portfolios that are formed following Fama and French's (1993, p. 11) procedure: "Each year t from 1963 to . . . [1993] NYSE quintile breakpoints for size (ME, . . .), measured at the end of June, are used to allocate NYSE, Amex, and NASDAQ stocks to five size quintiles. Similarly, NYSE quintile breakpoints for BE/ME are used to allocate NYSE, Amex, and NASDAQ stocks to five book-to-market equity quintiles." The 10 portfolios are formed as the intersections of the five-firm size and the lowest and highest BE/ME quintiles, denoted $nsibje$, $i = 1, 2, \ldots, 5$ and $j = 1, 5$. For example, the $ns1b1e$ portfolio contains the stocks in the smallest ME quintile that are also in the lowest BE/ME quintile, and the $ns5b5e$ portfolio contains the biggest ME stocks that also have the highest values of BE/ME.

The proxies for r_{ft} and r_{Mt} are the same as those employed by Fama and French (1993). That is, r_{ft} = the one-month Treasury bill rate, observed at the beginning of the month, and r_{Mt} = the value-weighted monthly percent return on the stocks in their 25 size-BE/ME portfolios, plus the negative BE stocks excluded from the portfolios.

The sources of the data employed here on the $z_{i1,t-1}$ and $z_{i2,t-1}$ are explained in Fama and French (1992). The variables $z_{3,t-1}$, $z_{4,t-1}$, and $z_{5,t-1}$ were obtained from the FAME database maintained by the Board of Governors of the Federal Reserve System. The index t denotes the months that occurred in the period from July 1963 through December 1993. The subscript i of variables in equations (7), (10), and (11) should not be confused with the i of $nsibje$.

V. EMPIRICAL RESULTS AND APPLICATIONS

Tables 1a–c show the estimates for conjunction I. The maxima, minima, and ranges of the estimates ($\hat{\gamma}_{0it}$) of γ_{0it} in Table 1a show considerable variation over time for all 10 portfolios. By contrast, for the same portfolios, the volatilities of the estimates ($\hat{\gamma}_{1it}$) of γ_{1it} are quite low. When estimated without the nonnegativity constraint, the estimates of γ_{1it} were negative only for five of 341 months and for one ($ns1b5e$) of 10 portfolios. For each size quintile of stocks, the arithmetic mean of $\hat{\gamma}_{0it}$ increases and the arithmetic mean of $\hat{\gamma}_{1it}$ decreases from the lowest to highest BE/ME quintiles. This pattern justifies the use of equation (10).

Black (1995) provides three theoretical reasons why the line relating expected return and β is flatter than suggested by the CAPM, as stated in the Introduction. The question arises then, do the values in Tables 1a–1c support such a flat line? The answer is "no," as is shown below. Under the conditions stated below equation (13), the arithmetic means of $\hat{\gamma}_{1it}$ in Table 1a give measures of portfolio risks. These arithmetic means are positive for all 10 portfolios and are significantly different from zero for seven of these portfolios, implying that for these seven portfolios the relation between expected return and β is not flat. The arithmetic means of $\hat{\gamma}_{0it}$ are

Table 1a. Summary Statistics for the Estimates of the γ_{0it} and γ_{1it} When Conjunction I Holds

Estimation Period: August 1963 to December 1991, 341 months

(t ratios in Parentheses, * denotes statistically significant t ratio at the 0.05 level, and $\text{Mean}(\hat{\gamma}_{jit}) = \frac{1}{341}\sum_{t=1}^{341}\hat{\gamma}_{jit}$ $j = 0, 1$)

Portfolio	$\text{Min}(\hat{\gamma}_{0it})$	$\text{Max}(\hat{\gamma}_{0it})$	$\text{Range}(\hat{\gamma}_{0it})$	$\text{Min}(\hat{\gamma}_{1it})$	$\text{Max}(\hat{\gamma}_{1it})$	$\text{Range}(\hat{\gamma}_{1it})$	$\text{Mean}(\hat{\gamma}_{0it})$	$\text{Mean}(\hat{\gamma}_{1it})$	Log Likelihood
ns1b1e	-14.45	13.76	28.21	0.71	2.32	1.61	0.05 (0.15)	1.39 (8.00)*	-976.73
ns1b5e	-6.28	19.61	25.89	-0.89	3.62	4.51	0.76 (1.91)	0.98 (15.27)*	-930.89
ns2b1e	-12.61	10.78	23.38	0.97	2.00	1.03	-0.06 (-0.23)	1.43 (21.58)*	-890.23
ns2b5e	-8.34	13.02	21.35	0.47	1.86	1.39	0.66 (2.83)*	1.15 (1.03)	-854.05
ns3b1e	-6.71	10.01	16.72	1.01	1.98	0.97	-0.06 (-0.28)	1.33 (36.48)*	-805.04
ns3b5e	-6.20	11.72	17.92	0.40	1.91	1.51	0.65 (3.26)*	1.10 (0.96)	-835.90
ns4b1e	-6.41	8.57	14.98	1.09	1.42	0.33	0.00 (0.02)	1.23 (13.45)*	-721.41
ns4b5e	-6.35	9.14	15.49	0.44	1.79	1.35	0.52 (2.50)*	1.18 (1.24)	-813.86
ns5b1e	-4.03	4.33	8.37	0.67	1.36	0.69	-0.12 (-1.04)	1.04 (48.32)*	-654.99
ns5b5e	-8.47	9.70	18.18	0.07	1.42	1.35	0.20 (1.08)	0.90 (6.54)*	-830.90

Table 1b. Estimates of the Coefficients of Equation (10) When Conjunction I Holds

Estimation Period: August 1963 to December 1991, 341 months

(t ratios in Parentheses; * denotes statistically significant t ratio at the 0.05 level)

Portfolio	π_{00}	π_{01}	π_{02}	π_{03}	π_{04}	π_{05}	π_{06}	π_{10}	π_{11}	π_{12}	π_{13}	π_{14}	π_{15}	π_{16}
ns1b1e	5.33	-1.89	-0.97	0.33	-0.65	0.26	4.56	3.53	-0.39	-0.49	-0.22	0.16	-0.09	-0.09
	(1.26)	(-1.80)	(-0.23)	(0.76)	(-0.90)	(0.90)	(5.50)*	(2.24)*	(-1.10)	(-0.38)	(-1.39)	(0.59)	(-0.95)	(-0.51)
ns1b5e	2.94	-1.41	-1.20	0.76	0.01	0.46	5.50	3.23	-0.55	-0.37	-0.03	0.04	-0.00	-0.13
	(0.87)	(-1.68)	(-0.89)	(1.55)	(0.12)	(1.49)	(8.01)*	(4.63)*	(-3.20)*	(-1.37)	(-0.29)	(0.23)	(-0.02)	(-0.68)
ns2b1e	3.97	-1.41	-0.15	0.19	-0.48	0.20	0.68	2.33	-0.18	-0.17	0.02	-0.03	0.00	-0.15
	(1.39)	(-2.04)*	(-0.28)	(0.57)	(-0.74)	(0.84)	(1.04)	(3.11)*	(-1.06)	(-1.31)	(0.20)	(-0.18)	(0.02)	(-1.18)
ns2b5e	2.10	-0.69	-0.74	0.61	-0.02	0.24	3.85	1.16	0.16	-0.43	-0.25	0.60	-0.01	-0.03
	(1.27)	(-2.24)*	(-0.97)	(2.06)*	(-0.04)	(1.26)	(6.76)*	(0.40)	(0.34)	(-1.10)	(-1.47)	(2.50)*	(-0.15)	(-0.24)
ns3b1e	0.06	-0.31	-0.07	0.43	-0.24	0.12	0.14	2.57	-0.19	-0.12	-0.01	0.02	-0.02	0.01
	(0.04)	(-1.00)	(-0.20)	(1.67)	(-0.52)	(0.74)	(0.26)	(6.37)*	(-2.76)*	(-1.67)	(-0.22)	(0.16)	(-0.56)	(0.10)
ns3b5e	0.13	-0.20	-0.28	0.52	-0.26	0.07	2.91	0.68	0.20	-0.13	-0.28	0.44	-0.06	-0.00
	(0.10)	(-0.99)	(-0.49)	(2.26)*	(-0.65)	(0.51)	(5.41)*	(0.22)	(0.46)	(-0.36)	(-1.73)	(2.01)*	(-0.81)	(-0.03)
ns4b1e	-0.55	0.07	-0.30	0.24	-0.19	-0.06	-0.61	1.57	-0.03	0.03	-0.07	0.05	-0.02	-0.01
	(-0.46)	(0.40)	(-1.03)	(1.22)	(-0.48)	(-0.43)	(-1.50)	(3.39)*	(-0.47)	(0.55)	(-1.58)	(0.57)	(-0.70)	(-0.15)
ns4b5e	0.52	-0.05	0.90	-0.22	-0.13	-0.02	2.77	1.04	0.05	-0.15	-0.10	0.43	-0.03	-0.02
	(0.29)	(-0.20)	(1.34)	(-0.83)	(-0.28)	(-0.11)	(5.45)*	(0.28)	(0.10)	(-0.43)	(-0.68)	(2.03)*	(-0.37)	(-0.18)
ns5b1e	0.67	0.13	-0.43	-0.30	0.37	-0.01	-1.12	0.88	-0.01	0.02	0.06	-0.07	0.06	-0.03
	(0.66)	(0.94)	(-1.99)	(-2.16)*	(1.39)	(-0.07)	(-3.38)*	(3.26)*	(-0.29)	(0.44)	(1.77)	(-1.09)	(2.43)*	(-0.50)
ns5b5e	2.24	-0.23	0.43	-0.48	0.69	-0.13	1.97	3.50	-0.27	-0.49	-0.02	0.31	0.02	0.03
	(1.31)	(-1.15)	(1.22)	(-2.49)*	(1.94)	(-0.97)	(3.59)*	(3.22)*	(-2.16)*	(-3.30)*	(-0.21)	(2.01)*	(0.45)	(0.27)

Table 1c. Estimates of the Parameters of Equation (11) and Forecasting Performance of Equation (7) When Conjunction I Holds, Estimation Period: August 1963 to December 1991, 341 months, and Forecasting Period: January 1992 to December 1993, 24 months

Portfolio	$\hat{\phi}_{00}$	$\hat{\phi}_{11}$	$\hat{\sigma}^2_a\delta_{00a}$	$\hat{\sigma}^2_a\delta_{10a}$	$\hat{\sigma}^2_a\delta_{11a}$	RMSE	MAE
$ns1b1e$	0.15	0.88	15.04	0.57	0.07	4.36	0.87
$ns1b5e$	0.51	−0.35	6.02	1.02	0.61	4.25	0.82
$ns2b1e$	0.13	0.76	9.86	0.20	0.02	3.63	5.17
$ns2b5e$	0.11	0.99	6.69	0.17	0.03	3.05	0.77
$ns3b1e$	0.07	−0.32	5.80	0.07	0.04	3.05	0.77
$ns3b5e$	0.05	0.99	6.16	0.32	0.03	2.49	12.44
$ns4b1e$	0.12	0.99	4.00	0.03	0.00	2.23	0.83
$ns4b5e$	0.11	0.99	5.31	0.09	0.02	2.15	1.21
$ns5b1e$	−0.01	−0.99	2.08	0.01	0.01	2.15	2.76
$ns5b5e$	−0.10	0.94	6.97	0.24	0.01	4.59	1.74

not significantly different from zero for these seven portfolios and are significantly different from zero for the three highest *BE/ME* portfolios ($ns2b5e$, $ns3b5e$, and $ns4b5e$) for which the arithmetic means of $\hat{\gamma}_{1it}$ are insignificant. The significant means of $\hat{\gamma}_{0it}$ and the insignificant means of $\hat{\gamma}_{1it}$ for the three portfolios cannot be interpreted as evidence of a flat expected return-β line because they arise as a direct consequence of the significant estimates of some of the coefficients on zs and on the interactions between $(r_{Mt} - r_{ft})$ and each of the zs that are discussed, in detail, below.

Table 1b shows that the estimates of the intercept (π_{00}) of equation (15) are insignificant for all 10 portfolios. What does this finding say about conjunction I? The answer follows from Merton's (1973) work, revealing that a well-specified, asset-pricing model produces intercepts that are indistinguishable from zero. Fama and French (1993, p. 5) also state that "judging asset-pricing models on the basis of the intercepts in excess-return regressions imposes a stringent standard." The insignificance of the $\hat{\pi}_{00}$ in Table 1b shows that, at least in the cases considered here, conjunction I shares a property with a well-specified, asset-pricing model and meets Fama and French's stringent standard.

Table 1b also shows that the estimates of the coefficient (π_{01}) on log(size) are significant only for two portfolios ($ns2b1e$ and $ns2b5e$), the estimates of the coefficient (π_{03}) on the dividend-price ratio of the S&P 500 are significant for four portfolios ($ns2b5e$, $ns3b5e$, $ns5b1e$, and $ns5b5e$), and the estimates of the coefficient (π_{06}) on the January dummy variable are significant for seven portfolios ($ns1b1e$, $ns1b5e$, $ns2b5e$, $ns3b5e$, $ns4b5e$, $ns5b1e$, and $ns5b5e$). This result shows, among other things, that except for three portfolios ($ns2b1e$, $ns3b1e$, and *ns4b1e*), the strong January seasonals in the returns on seven stock portfolios are not absorbed by strong seasonals in the explanatory variables of equation (15) other than the January dummy variable (z_{6t}). The estimates of the coefficients on $z_{i2,t-1}$, $z_{4,t-1}$, and $z_{5,t-1}$ are insignificant for all 10 portfolios.

Furthermore, the estimates of the coefficient (π_{10}) on ($r_{Mt} - r_{ft}$) are significant for seven portfolios (*ns1b1e, ns1b5e, ns2b1e, ns3b1e, ns4b1e, ns5b1e,* and *ns5b5e*) (see Table 1b). For the remaining three portfolios (*ns2b5e, ns3b5e,* and *ns4b5e*), the estimated coefficients on the interaction between ($r_{Mt} - r_{ft}$) and the default premium ($z_{4,t-1}$) are significant (see Table 1b). The interactions, the estimates of whose coefficients are significant, are ($r_{Mt} - r_{ft}$)*log(size) for three portfolios (*ns1b5e, ns3b1e,* and *ns5b5e*), ($r_{Mt} - r_{ft}$)*(BE/ME) for one portfolio (*ns5b5e*), ($r_{Mt} - r_{ft}$)*(default premium) for four portfolios (*ns2b5e, ns3b5e, ns4b5e,* and *ns5b5e*), and ($r_{Mt} - r_{ft}$) *$z_{5,t-1}$ for one portfolio (*ns5b1e*). The estimates of the interaction coefficients π_{13} and π_{16} are insignificant for all 10 portfolios.

Under the conditions stated below equation (13), the estimates of π_{10} can be viewed as the estimates of $E(\beta_{it}|z_{it})$ and the difference between the arithmetic mean of $\hat{\gamma}_{1it}$ in Table 1a and $\hat{\pi}_{10}$ in Table 1b gives an estimate of the arithmetic mean of the sum of mismeasurement effects and omitted-variable biases. These differences do not appear to be insignificant for most of the 10 portfolios.

All the estimates in Tables 1a and 1b unambiguously support only one conclusion: during our estimation and forecasting periods the relation between the observable counterparts of Er_{it} and β is not a flat line but is a significant part of a nonlinear relationship. There is no a priori reason to believe that this nonlinear relationship will not continue to hold in future. These findings provide possible answers to Black's (1995) questions stated in the Introduction. From the estimates given in Table 1b we cannot conclude that the size and *BE/ME* variables add even more significantly to the explanation of stock returns provided by ($r_{Mt} - r_{ft}$) and its interaction with the default premium. The cross-section of average returns on U.S. common stocks probably shows little relation to the $\pi_{10} + \mu_{1i}$ defined in note 3 and shows significant relation to the z_{it}, as implied by Fama and French's (1992) results, if the interactions between ($r_{Mt} - r_{ft}$) and each of the z_{it}, and the heteroscedasticity and serial correlation of the error term in equation (15) are neglected.

Table 1c indicates the extent to which conjunction I satisfies set (12) of restrictions. In seven of 10 cases shown in this table, the whole set is nearly satisfied. In addition, in all 10 cases the estimated variance of a_{1it} and the estimated covariance between a_{1it} and a_{0it} are very small in magnitude relative to the estimated variance of a_{0it}. It should be noted that exclusion of a concomitant variable from equation (10) because its estimated coefficient is insignificant is improper if the variable is needed to explain the variation in γ_{1it}. It is better to include a concomitant that substantially explains the variation in γ_{1it} than to exclude it even if its inclusion means reducing the *t* ratios of the estimates of the coefficients of equation (10).

Tables 2ab and 2c display the results for conjunction II. These results provide information on the effects of set (14) of restrictions on the estimates in Tables 1a–1c.

Table 2ab. Summary Statistics for the Estimates of the γ_{0it} and γ_{1it} When Conjunction II Holds Estimation Period: August 1963 to December 1991, 341 months

(t ratios in Parentheses, * denotes statistically significant t ratio at the 0.05 level)

Portfolio	$Min(\hat{\gamma}_{0it})$	$Max(\hat{\gamma}_{0it})$	$Range(\hat{\gamma}_{0it})$	$Min(\hat{\gamma}_{1it})$	$Max(\hat{\gamma}_{1it})$	$Range(\hat{\gamma}_{1it})$	$\hat{\pi}_{00}$	$\hat{\pi}_{10}$	Log Likelihood
ns1b1e	−15.15	14.03	29.18	0.73	2.38	1.65	−0.10 (−0.34)	1.35 (4.28)*	−1004.99
ns1b5e	−7.97	19.01	26.98	0.09	2.07	1.98	0.59 (2.36)*	0.97 (20.43)*	−955.58
ns2b1e	−12.08	11.90	23.98	1.11	1.77	0.66	−0.11 (−0.56)	1.41 (32.29)*	−889.15
ns2b5e	−8.24	13.11	21.34	0.22	2.06	1.84	0.53 (2.91)*	1.14 (0.96)	−890.06
ns3b1e	−6.37	10.94	17.30	0.94	1.97	1.03	−0.09 (−0.60)	1.39 (19.50)*	−832.23
ns3b5e	−6.15	11.73	17.88	0.18	1.97	1.79	0.54 (3.54)*	1.09 (1.14)	−847.29
ns4b1e	−5.97	8.46	14.44	1.01	1.41	0.40	−0.00 (−0.02)	1.21 (49.07)*	−736.48
ns4b5e	−6.24	8.85	15.09	0.28	1.77	1.50	0.48 (3.22)*	1.21 (1.48)	−830.63
ns5b1e	−4.17	4.77	8.93	0.70	1.40	0.71	−0.08 (−0.89)	1.04 (48.90)*	−670.84
ns5b5e	−7.34	9.77	17.11	0.50	1.32	0.82	0.19 (1.32)	0.88 (25.52)*	−845.95

Table 2c. Estimates of the Parameters of Equation (11) and Forecasting Performance of Equation (7) When Conjunction 11 Holds, Estimation Period: August 1963 to December 1991, 341 months, and Forecasting Period: January 1992 to December 1993, 24 months

Portfolio	$\hat{\phi}_{00}$	$\hat{\phi}_{11}$	$\hat{\sigma}_a^2\hat{\delta}_{00a}$	$\hat{\sigma}_a^2\hat{\delta}_{10a}$	$\hat{\sigma}_a^2\hat{\delta}_{11a}$	RMSE	MAE
ns1b1e	0.18	0.96	100.29	74.67	126.77	5.07	1.44
ns1b5e	0.26	−0.99	10.84	0.63	0.11	4.89	0.79
ns2b1e	0.13	0.28	9.98	0.11	0.04	3.70	3.02
ns2b5e	0.18	0.99	7.45	0.39	0.07	3.53	0.66
ns3b1e	0.07	0.86	6.92	0.36	0.03	2.88	0.88
ns3b5e	0.11	0.99	6.10	0.31	0.05	2.71	5.59
ns4b1e	0.15	−0.99	4.38	0.02	0.00	2.24	1.19
ns4b5e	0.10	0.99	5.57	0.16	0.04	2.54	1.23
ns5b1e	0.08	−0.99	2.16	0.05	0.01	2.03	2.26
ns5b5e	−0.04	−0.99	7.19	0.16	0.01	4.61	3.26

The values in every column of Table 2ab can be compared with those in the corresponding column of Table 1a. Plots (not included here) show that while the time profiles of $\hat{\gamma}_{0it}$ in Tables 2ab and 1a are the same in all 10 cases, those of $\hat{\gamma}_{1it}$ in these tables are the same only in four of 10 cases. The t ratios of $\hat{\pi}_{00}$ and $\hat{\pi}_{10}$ in Table 2ab are generally higher in magnitude than those of the arithmetic means of $\hat{\gamma}_{0it}$ and $\hat{\gamma}_{1it}$ in Table 1a. It is possible that the extra precision obtained by imposing set (14) of restrictions is spurious because several of the estimates of π in Table 1b are significant. In four of 10 cases the estimates of π_{00} in Table 2ab are significant. This shows that conjunction II does not always satisfy the property of a well-specified, asset-pricing model noted by Merton (1973). In three of 10 cases shown in Table 2ab, the estimates of π_{00} and π_{10} are significant and insignificant, respectively, supporting the conclusion that a relation between expected return and β is flat. However, such a conclusion is not credible because it is based on conjunction II, which is inconsistent.

Tables 1c and 2c might be compared to determine whether the regressors of equation (10) are appropriate and sufficient. It can be seen from these tables that for eight of the 10 portfolios, set (12) of restrictions is better satisfied when set (14) of restrictions is not imposed than when it is imposed. This result supports the conclusion that the regressors of equation (10) are the appropriate explanatory variables for γ_{1it} but some additional concomitants are needed to completely explain all the variation in γ_{1it} for all portfolios. Further work is needed to find such additional concomitants.

Tables 3 and 4 show parameter estimates for conjunctions III and IV, respectively. The t ratios of $\hat{\pi}_{00}$ and $\hat{\pi}_{10}$ in these tables are generally higher than those of

$\hat{\pi}_{00}$ and $\hat{\pi}_{10}$ in Table 2ab in absolute value. The spuriousness of the extra precision obtained by imposing inconsistent sets (16) and (17) of restrictions is more pronounced than that of the extra precision obtained by imposing inconsistent set (14) of restrictions. Since the explanatory variables of equation (15) are not orthogonal to one another, and its error covariance matrix is not equal to a scalar times an identity matrix under all conjunctions I–IV, the estimates $\hat{\pi}_{00}$ in Tables 2ab, 3, and 4 are not comparable to the estimates $\hat{\pi}_{00}$ in Table 1b. The estimates of ϕ_{00} in Tables 1c, 2c, and 3 offer little support for the presence of serial correlation among the ε_{0it}. The estimates $(\hat{\sigma}_a^2\hat{\delta}_{00a})$ of the variance of a_{0it} in Table 1c are generally smaller than the estimates $\hat{\sigma}_a^2\hat{\delta}_{00a}$ in Table 2c and the estimates $\hat{\sigma}_a^2$ in Tables 3 and 4, indicating that in most cases the variance of a_{0it} is reduced as the zs are added to equation (10). This reduction in variance helps to weaken the correlations between γ_{0it} and $(r_{Mt} - r_{ft})$.

The values of log likelihood in Tables 1a, 2ab, 3, and 4 might be compared to determine whether one of the conjunctions I–IV has greater support of the time-series data used for estimation than other conjunctions. With one exception, these values in Table 1a are higher than those in Tables 2ab, 3, and 4. The exception corresponds to the portfolio *ns2b1e* in Table 2ab. Even in this case the value of the log likelihood in Table 1a is only slightly smaller than that in Table 2ab. This shows that the support of the data to conjunction I is either greater or only slightly less than the support to conjunctions II–IV.

Since the *t* ratios in Tables 1a and 1b are based on a consistent set of general assumptions that are not used by earlier tests of the CAPM in the literature, they do not fall into Black's (1995, p. 2) category of "the simplest kind of data mining." Still, it is appropriate to seek RMSE and MAE measures for each portfolio of a conjunction's success in predicting the out-of-sample values of the dependent variable of equation (7). Tables 1c, 2c, 3, and 4 report for each portfolio the values of such measures in the RMSE and MAE columns. The RMSEs for conjunction I are smaller for seven portfolios and slightly higher for three portfolios than those for conjunctions II–IV. For a conjunction which has at least 10 more unknown parameters and hence uses up at least 10 more degrees of freedom than any of conjunctions II–IV, this is not a bad performance. Perhaps conjunction I would have produced lower RMSEs than conjunctions II–IV for all 10 portfolios if all the parameters of equations (11) and (15) were known. Based on the RMSEs, conjunctions II–IV cannot be preferred to conjunction I. Even though the MAEs for conjunction I are smaller than those for conjunctions II–IV in five of 10 cases, they are much bigger than those for conjunctions II–IV in two of the remaining five cases. Two reasons for this result are: (i) the predictor used to generate forecasts of the dependent variable of equation (7) is optimal relative to a quadratic loss function but is not optimal relative to an absolute error loss function, and (ii) sometimes inconsistent models appear to predict better than consistent models if inappropriate formulas are used to measure the accuracy of forecasts. In the long run, only consistent models are able to tell the truth.

Table 3. Estimates of the Parameters of Equations (7)–(11) and Forecasting Performance of Equation (7) When Conjunction III Holds, Estimation Period: August 1963 to December 1991, 341 months, and Forecasting Period: January 1992 to December 1993, 24 months
(t ratios in Parentheses; * denotes statistically significant t ratio at the 0.05 level)

Portfolio	$\hat{\pi}_{00}$	$\hat{\pi}_{10}$	$\hat{\phi}_{00}$	$\hat{\sigma}_a^2$	Log Likelihood	RMSE	MAE
ns1 b1 e	−0.25	1.36	0.15	19.73	−992.30	5.13	1.55
	(−0.89)	(25.86)*					
ns1 b5 e	0.54	1.03	0.15	14.69	−942.00	4.84	0.72
	(2.22)*	(22.69)*					
ns2 b1 e	−0.14	1.39	0.16	10.99	−892.53	3.73	3.04
	(−0.65)	(35.44)*					
ns2 b5 e	0.53	1.11	0.11	10.30	−881.44	3.53	0.68
	(2.72)*	(29.09)*					
ns3 b1 e	−0.14	1.32	0.09	6.95	−814.34	2.91	0.86
	(−0.92)	(42.18)*					
ns3 b5 e	0.53	1.06	0.08	8.21	−842.83	2.68	5.68
	(3.12)*	(30.93)*					
ns4 b1 e	−0.02	1.22	0.15	4.04	−722.15	2.24	1.17
	(−0.16)	(51.20)*					
ns4 b5 e	0.53	1.11	0.06	8.04	−839.33	2.55	1.30
	(3.21)*	(32.93)*					
ns5 b1 e	−0.04	1.02	0.05	2.83	−660.97	2.00	1.98
	(−0.37)	(51.07)*					
ns5 b5 e	0.21	0.89	−0.03	7.77	−833.41	4.57	3.09
	(1.41)	(26.81)*					

Any empirical result that holds for all four conjunctions can be considered robust. The arithmetic means of the estimates of γ_{1it} under conjunction I and the estimates of π_{10} under conjunctions II–IV are the estimates of the conditional and unconditional expectations, $E(\gamma_{1it}|z_{it})$ and $E(\gamma_{1it})$, respectively. It can be seen from Tables 1a, 2ab, 3, and 4 that these estimates are close to one another and hence are robust.

Fama and French (1993, p. 53) list four applications—(a) selecting portfolios, (b) evaluating portfolio performance, (c) measuring abnormal returns in event studies, and (d) estimating the cost of capital—that require estimates of risk-adjusted stock returns. The estimates in Table 1b can be substituted into the first term on the right-hand side of equation (15) to obtain the estimates of risk-adjusted stock returns because γ_{1it} is a comprehensive descriptor of stock risk. The preceding discussion shows that these estimates do a better job in all four applications than those of previous studies. The methodology used to obtain the estimates in Tables

Table 4. Estimates of the Parameters of Equations (7)–(11) and Forecasting Performance of Equation (7) When Conjunction IV Holds, Estimation Period: August 1963 to December 1991, 341 months, and Forecasting Period: January 1992 to December 1993, 24 months

(*t* ratios in Parentheses; * denotes statistically significant *t* ratio at the 0.05 level)

Portfolio	$\hat{\pi}_{00}$	$\hat{\pi}_{10}$	$\hat{\sigma}_a^2$	Log Likelihood	RMSE	MAE
ns1b1e	−0.26	1.40	20.18	−996.12	4.97	1.58
	(−1.08)	(26.22)*				
ns1b5e	0.53	1.07	14.97	−945.30	4.63	0.73
	(2.51)*	(23.24)*				
ns2b1e	−0.15	1.42	11.26	−896.62	3.67	3.11
	(−0.81)	(35.53)*				
ns2b5e	0.53	1.13	10.42	−883.41	3.48	0.68
	(3.00)*	(29.33)*				
ns3b1e	−0.15	1.34	7.00	−815.61	2.90	0.86
	(−1.04)	(42.53)*				
ns3b5e	0.53	1.06	8.27	−843.99	2.66	5.61
	(3.37)*	(31.02)*				
ns4b1e	−0.03	1.23	4.13	−725.74	2.23	1.17
	(−0.24)	(51.06)*				
ns4b5e	0.53	1.11	8.08	−840.01	2.53	1.30
	(3.42)*	(32.92)*				
ns5b1e	−0.04	1.02	2.83	−661.38	1.99	1.97
	(−0.40)	(51.13)*				
ns5b5e	0.21	0.89	7.78	−833.55	4.57	3.09
	(1.36)	(26.80)*				

1a–1c can also be used to obtain accurate predictions about as-yet unobserved values of the dependent variable of equation (15). The discussion in this section and in Sections II and III shows that the measures of market or "systematic" risks of portfolios given by the arithmetic means of $\hat{\gamma}_{1it}$ in Table 1a are theoretically and empirically superior to estimates of β presented so far in the literature.

VI. CONCLUSIONS

This paper has extended the CAPM to account for the effects of differences between unobservable and observable stock and market portfolio returns, of excluded variables, and of departures from a linear relationship between the observable returns on individual stock and market portfolios. The extended CAPM is tested using a stochastic-coefficient methodology. For purposes of comparison, both consistent and inconsistent sets of assumptions are made in these tests. Tests based on a consistent set of assumptions show that the relation between the observable returns on stock and market portfolios is nonlinear.

ACKNOWLEDGMENTS

The views expressed in this paper are those of the authors, not necessarily those of the Comptroller of the Currency, or the Department of the Treasury. The authors thank James Barth, Peter von zur Muehlen, Thomas Lutton, Larry Mote, and Andrew Chen whose comments considerably improved the paper. John Leusner died on March 5, 1996. We mourn his tragic death and will miss our good friend.

NOTES

1. The main difference between this approach and the previous approaches to estimating the CAPM lies in equations (3)–(6) which do not appear in the latter approaches (see Jagannathan & Wang, 1996 and the previous studies by Harvey, Shanken, and others referred to therein). The linear least squares residuals introduced in these previous studies cannot represent measurement errors and the effects of omitted variables (see Pratt & Schlaifer, 1984, p. 11–12).

2. The variable z_{6t} proxies for the January effect which is explained in Bodie, Kane, and Marcus (1993, pp. 380–381).

3. The conjunction of Assumptions 1 and 2 and restrictions (12) is weaker than the assumptions given in Greene (1993, pp. 375–379) for the consistency of instrumental variable estimators (see Pratt & Schlaifer, 1988, pp. 47–48).

4. Equation (7) is estimated under Assumptions 1 and 2, using a computer program developed by I-Lok Chang and Stephen Taubman. This program uses an algorithm developed by Chang, Hallahan, and Swamy (1992) and is based on a methodology introduced by Swamy and Tinsley (1980). For further discussion of this methodology, see Swamy, Mehta, and Singamsetti (1996).

5. If time-series-cross-section data are used to estimate equation (7), then equation (10) may be changed to $\gamma_{it} = \Pi z_{it} + \mu_i + \varepsilon_{it}$, where $\mu_i = (\mu_{0i}, \mu_{1i})'$ is a constant through time; it is an attribute of the *i*th asset (or portfolio of assets) which is unaccounted for by the included variables but varies across *i*. When equation (7) is estimated separately for different *i*, the vector μ_i gets absorbed into $(\pi_{00}, \pi_{10})'$. So π_{00} and π_{10} in equation (15) are implicitly allowed to vary across *i*.

REFERENCES

Amihud, Y., & Mendelson, H. (1986). Asset pricing and the bid-ask spread. *Journal of Financial Economics, 17*, 223–249.

Black, F. (1972, July). Capital market equilibrium with restricted borrowing. *Journal of Business, 45*, 444–455.

Black, F. (1995). Estimating expected return. *Journal of Financial Education, 21*, 1–4.

Bodie, Z., Kane, A., & Marcus, A. J. (1993). *Investments* (2nd ed.). Boston, MA: Irwin.

Chang, I., Hallahan, C., & Swamy, P. A. V. B. (1992). Efficient computation of stochastic coefficient models. In H. M. Amman, D. A. Belsley & L. F. Pau (Eds.), *Computational Economics and Econometrics* (pp. 43–53). Boston: Kluwer Academic Publishers.

Constantinides, G. M. (1989). Theory of valuation: Overview and recent developments. In S. Bhattacharya & G. M. Constantinides (Eds.), *Frontiers of Modern Financial Theory* (Vol. 1, pp. 1–23). Savage, Maryland: Rowman & Littlefield.

Dawid, A. P. (1979). Conditional independence in statistical theory. *Journal of the Royal Statistical Society* Series B, 41, 1–31.

Fama, E. F., & French, K. R. (1992, June). The cross-section of expected stock returns. *The Journal of Finance, 47*, 427–465.

Fama, E. F., & French, K. R. (1993). Common risk factors in the returns on stocks and bonds. *Journal of Financial Economics, 33*, 3–56.

Fama, E. F., & French, K. R. (1996, December). The CAPM is Wanted, Dead or Alive. *The Journal of Finance, 51*, 1947–1958.

Friedman, M., & Schwartz, A. J. (1991, March). Alternative approaches to analyzing economic data. *The American Economic Review, 81*, 39–49.

Greene, W. H. (1993). *Econometrics analysis.* New York: Macmillan Publishing Company.

Ingersoll, Jr., J. E. (1987). *Theory of financial decision making.* Savage, Maryland: Rowman & Littlefield.

Jagannathan, R., & Wang, Z. (1996, March). The conditional CAPM and the cross-section of expected returns. *The Journal of Finance, 51*, 3–53.

Kothari, S. P., Shanken, J., & Sloan, R. G. (1995, March). Another look at the cross-section of expected stock returns. *The Journal of Finance, 50*, 185–224.

Lehmann, E. L. (1983). *Theory of point estimation.* New York: John Wiley & Sons.

Lintner, J. (1965, February). The valuation of risk assets and the selection of risky investments in stock portfolios and capital budgets. *Review of Economics and Statistics, 47*, 13–37.

Merton, R. C. (1973). An intertemporal capital asset pricing model, *Econometrica, 41*, 867–887.

Mosteller, F., & Tukey, J. W. (1977). *Data analysis and regression.* Reading, MA: Addison-Wesley.

Pratt, J. W., & Schlaifer, R. (1984, March). On the nature and discovery of structure. *Journal of the American Statistical Association, 79*, 9–21, 29–33.

Pratt, J. W., & Schlaifer, R. (1988, September/October). On the interpretation and observation of laws. *Journal of Econometrics, Annals, 39*, 23–52.

Roll, R. (1977). A critique of the asset pricing theory's tests: Part I: On past and potential testability of the theory. *Journal of Financial Economics, 4*, 129–176.

Sharpe, W. F. (1964, September). Capital asset prices: a theory of market equilibrium under conditions of risk. *Journal of Finance, 19*, 425–442.

Swamy, P. A. V. B., & Tinsley, P. A. (1980, February). Linear prediction and estimation methods for regression models with stationary stochastic coefficients. *Journal of Econometrics, 12*, 103–142.

Swamy, P. A. V. B., & Tavlas, G. S. (1995, June). Random coefficient models: Theory and applications. *Journal of Economic Surveys, 9*, 165–196.

Swamy, P. A. V. B., Mehta, J. S., & Singamsetti, R. N. (1996, February). Circumstances in which different criteria of estimation can be applied to estimate policy effects. *Journal of Statistical Planning and Inference, 50*, 121–153.

Swamy, P. A. V. B., Lutton, T. J., & Tavlas, G. S. (1997). How should diversifiable and nondiversifiable portfolio risks be defined? *Journal of Economics and Finance.*

FINITE HORIZONS AND THE CONSUMPTION CAPITAL ASSET PRICING MODEL

Paul Evans and Iftekhar Hasan

ABSTRACT

The paper modifies the consumption capital asset pricing model (CCAPM) to allow for the possibility that households have finite horizons. According to the modified CCAPM, shortening the horizon of households raises the expected rate of return on every asset by the same amount ceteris paribus. As a result, risk is priced independently of how long the horizon is. Allowing households to have finite horizons therefore does not enhance the ability of CCAPM to explain either the large size of the equity premium or the coexistence of low rates of return on riskless assets with high growth rates of aggregate consumption.

I. INTRODUCTION

The simplicity and elegance of the consumption capital asset pricing model (CCAPM) have made it a basic building block in theoretical macroeconomic

Research in Finance, Volume 16, pages 95–106.
Copyright © 1998 by JAI Press Inc.
All rights of reproduction in any form reserved.
ISBN: 0-7623-0328-X

models.[1] Financial economists have also been attracted to CCAPM because it simply and elegantly solves two important problems with the capital asset pricing model (CAPM). First, CAPM must assume that the return on some broad-based portfolio of common stocks can proxy for the return on the market portfolio of risky assets. In reality, investors hold portfolios that include not only other claims on physical capital but also human capital. By contrast, the growth rate of consumption is a perfect proxy for the rate of return on the market portfolio in CCAPM. Second, CAPM is derived in a static framework. By contrast, CCAPM fully accounts for the intertemporal nature of portfolio choices; see Merton (1973), Breeden (1979), Jagannathan (1985), Breeden, Gibbons, and Litzenberger (1989), Heaton and Lucas (1992), and Cooper (1993).

Unfortunately, CCAPM is not very successful in explaining assets returns. The overidentifying restrictions implied by CCAPM are rejected at very small significance levels by Hansen and Singleton (1983); Mankiw, Rotemberg, and Summers (1985); Grossman, Melino, and Shiller (1987) and others. Mehra and Prescott (1985) and Hansen and Jagannathan (1991) show that CCAPM requires an enormous relative risk aversion in order to explain the large U.S. equity premium. Weil (1989) has shown that it cannot explain the coexistence of a low average rate of return on riskless assets and a high average growth rate of aggregate consumption in the United States.[2]

The CCAPM is derived on the assumption that a constant population of infinitely lived households maximize time-additive von Neumann-Morgenstern objective functions while facing perfect capital and insurance markets.[3] It could therefore fail to explain asset pricing merely because one or more of these very strong assumptions is too strong. For this reason, financial economists have attempted to fix CCAPM by relaxing some of its maintained assumptions. Eichenbaum and colleagues (1988), Constantinides (1990), and Heaton (1990) have relaxed the assumption that utilities are temporally independent. Epstein and Zin (1989, 1991) have relaxed the assumption that households have von Neumann-Morgenstern objective functions. Although these authors find that their models dominate the standard CCAPM, the overidentifying restrictions implied by their models are also often rejected.[4] In addition, their models do not resolve all of the anomalies described in the previous paragraph.

In this paper we investigate whether the ability of CCAPM to explain the pricing of assets is enhanced by relaxing the assumption that the economy is inhabited by a constant population of infinitely lived households. Using a stochastic version of Blanchard's (1985) model, we modify CCAPM in order to allow for the possibility that households have finite horizons. We obtain two basic results. First, risk is priced identically whether horizons are finite or infinite. As a result, our modification of CCAPM cannot resolve the equity premium puzzle. Second, our modified CCAPM implies that the expected rates of return are higher, the shorter is the horizon of households ceteris paribus. In particular, the riskless rate of return is higher if households have finite horizons than if they have infinite horizons. Consequently, our modification of the CCAPM cannot resolve the puzzle of the coexistence of a low average rate of return on riskless assets with a high average growth rate of aggregate consumption.

II. THE MODEL

In this section we modify CCAPM to allow for the possibility that households have finite horizons. We perform this task in a stochastic version of Blanchard's model. Our discussion of many of the assumptions below is cursory because we believe that familiarity with this model is widespread. For a more complete discussion of these assumptions, see Blanchard and Fischer (1989).

We assume that each household has a constant probability p of dying per unit of time. As a result, the probability that any given household will live from time s until at least time t is always $e^{-p(t-s)}$, and every household has an expected lifetime $\int_S^\infty (t-s)e^{-p(t-s)}$ that is independent of age and time and equal to $1/p$. Hence households have finite horizons unless $p=0$. Furthermore, because we assume the population to be constant, the birth rate is constant and equal to p per unit of time.[5] Consequently, with population normalized to one, the population density of households born at time s and alive at time t is always $pe^{-p(t-s)}$ since $\int_{-\infty}^t pe^{-p(t-s)}\, ds = 1$.

Each household born at time s is assumed to maximize an objective function of the form

$$\int_S^\infty e^{-(\theta+p)(t-s)} E_s u(c_{st})dt \tag{1}$$

with

$$u(c_{st}) = \begin{cases} c_{st}^{1-\alpha}/(1-\alpha), & \alpha \neq 1 \\ \ln ct_{st}, & \alpha = 1 \end{cases} \tag{2}$$

where c_{st} is the consumption that the household will choose in period t if it is still alive then; E_s is the expectation operator conditional on the information available at time s; and α and θ are the household's relative risk aversion and subjective discount rate.[6] Households base their expectations on the same information and to have identical objective functions. The factor $e^{-p(t-s)}$ appears in the objective function because each household has that probability of surviving until period t. Note also that the household cares only about its own consumption and hence has no bequest motive.[7]

Two types of assets exist in the economy: human capital and physical capital. Upon being born, each new household is endowed with human capital, which generates the stochastic wage income $\{y_t\}$ during the household's lifetime and zero thereafter. By assumption, all households alive at a given time receive the same wage income.[8] Physical capital, which must be obtained by each new household after its birth, is immortal, perfectly divisible, and equivalent to the consumption good. We assume that the rate of return on physical capital can be represented as

$$r_k dt + \sigma_k dz_{kt},$$

where r_k and σ_k are the mean and standard deviation of the instantaneous rate of return on physical capital and z_{kt} is a Wiener process.[9]

Consider the pricing of a mutual fund of all human capital that exists at time t.[10] Let h_t be the market value of this mutual fund. The return to the fund between times t and $t + dt$ is

$$y_t dt + dh_t - ph_t dt$$

since the fund receives wage income $y_t dt$, experiences a capital gain dh_t, and loses $h_t(pdt)$ because pdt households die. We assume that the stochastic process $\{y_t\}$ has the property that this return can be represented by $h_t(r_h dt + dz_{ht})$, where r_h and σ_h are the constant mean and standard deviation of the instantaneous rate of return on human capital and z_{ht} is a Wiener process. We then have

$$dh_t = [(r_h + p)h_t - y_t]dt + h_t \sigma_h dz_{ht}. \tag{3}$$

Because insurance markets are perfect, each household can costlessly eliminate all diversifiable risks. For this reason, each newly arriving household can immediately exchange its undiversified endowment of human capital for a diversified portfolio of human and physical capital. Furthermore, in perfect insurance markets annuities yield p more than the underlying assets that are being annuitized. As a result, households with no bequest motives prefer annuities to assets that may pay a return after they have died. We therefore assume that each household born at time s and surviving until time t has holdings h_{st} and k_{st} of human and physical capital that evolve according to

$$dh_{st} = [(r_h + p)h_{st} - y_t]dt + h_{st}\sigma_h dz_{ht} \tag{4}$$

and

$$dk_{st} = [y_t + (r_k + p)k_{st} - c_{st}]dt + k_{st}\sigma_k dz_{kt} \tag{5}$$

Adding these two equations ((4) and (5)) together then yields the budget constraint

$$dw_{st} = \{[(1 - x_{st})r_h + x_{st}r_k + p]w_{st} - c_{st}\}dt + w_{st}[(1 - x_{st})\sigma_h dz_{ht} + x_{st}\sigma_k dz_{kt}]. \tag{6}$$

where w_{st} is the household's total wealth at time t and x_{st} is the fraction of its wealth allocated to physical capital. The initial condition for equation (6) is

$$w_{ss} = h_s \tag{7}$$

since the household begins life with only human capital.

Bellman's equation for the problem of maximizing (1) subject to (2), (6), and (7) is[11]

$$(\theta + p)v(w_{st}) = \max_{\{c_{st}, x_{st}\}} \{c_{st}^{1-\alpha}/(1 - \alpha) + v'(w_{st})[\{(1 - x_{st})r_h + x_{st}r_h + p\}w_{st} - c_{st}]$$

$$+ \frac{1}{2}[(1 - x_{st})^2 \sigma_h^2 + 2(1 - x_{st})x_{st}\sigma_{hk} + x_{st}^2\sigma_k^2]w_{st}^2 v''(w_{st})\}, \tag{8}$$

where $v(w_{st})$ is the value function for this problem and σ_{hk} is the covariance between the returns on human and physical capital. Differentiating the maximand in (8) with respect to c_{st} and x_{st} and equating the resulting expressions to zero yields the following first-order conditions:

$$c_{st}^{-\alpha} = v'(w_{st}) \tag{9}$$

and

$$(r_h - r_k)w_{st}v'(w_{st}) + 2w_{st}^2 v''(w_{st})[(x_{st} - 1)\sigma_h^2 + (1 - 2x_{st})\sigma_{hk} + x_s\sigma_k^2] = 0. \tag{10}$$

We verify below that the value function

$$v(w_{st}) = \begin{cases} bw_{st}^{1-\alpha}/(1 - \alpha), & \alpha \neq 1 \\ b \ln w_{st}, & \alpha = 1 \end{cases} \tag{11}$$

satisfies the Bellman equation (8) and the first-order conditions (9) and (10) for a value of the parameter b derived below. To do so, we first substitute equation (11) into equation (10) and solve for x_{st}.[12]

$$x_{st} = x \equiv \frac{(r_k - r_h)/\alpha + (\sigma_h^2 - \sigma_{hk})}{\sigma_h^2 - 2\sigma_{hk} + \sigma_k^2}. \tag{12}$$

Therefore, each household always holds annuities that are claims on the market portfolio of human and physical capital, which consists of fixed fractions $1 - x$ and x of human and physical capital. Next, we substitute equations (9), (11), and (12) into equation (8) and solve for b:

$$b = [(\theta + p)/\alpha - (1 - \alpha)(r_m + p)/\alpha + (1 - \alpha)\sigma_m^2/2]^{-\alpha}, \tag{13}$$

where $r_m \equiv (1 - x)r_h + xr_k$ and $\sigma_m^2 \equiv (1 - x)^2 \sigma_h^2 + 2(1 - x)x\sigma_{hk} + x^2 \sigma_k^2$. The parameters r_m and σ_m are the mean instantaneous return and standard deviation of rate of return on the market portfolio of human and physical capital. Note that b is indeed a fixed parameter. Finally, we substitute equations (11) and (13) into equation (9) and solve for

$$c_{st} = [(\theta + p)/\alpha - (1 - \alpha)(r_m + p)/\alpha + (1 - \alpha)\sigma_m^2/2]w_{st}. \tag{14}$$

Therefore, consumption is proportional to total wealth with a factor of proportionality that is identical across households.

Although in equilibrium households hold only annuities that are claims on the market portfolio, they are free to hold other portfolios. Consider, for example, a portfolio consisting of a fraction $1 - \lambda$ of an annuity backed by claims on the market portfolio and a fraction λ of an annuity backed by claims on any asset j. In that case the budget constraint (6) takes the form

$$dw_{st} = [[(1 - \lambda)r_m + \lambda r_j + p]w_{st} - c_{st}\}dt + w_{st}[(1 - \lambda)\sigma_m dz_{mt} + \lambda\sigma_j dz_{jt}], \quad (15)$$

where r_j is the mean instantaneous rate of return on the asset, and σ_j is the standard deviation of its return, and z_{jt} is a Wiener process. Employing analysis similar to that used to derive equation (12), we obtain

$$\lambda = \frac{(r_j - r_m)/\alpha + (\sigma_m^2 - \sigma_{jm})}{\sigma_j^2 - 2\sigma_{jm} + \sigma_m^2}, \quad (16)$$

where σ_{jm} is the covariance between the returns on the other asset and the market portfolio. Because every household chooses $\lambda = 0$ in equilibrium, equation (16) implies that

$$r_j = r_m + \alpha(\sigma_{jm} - \sigma_m^2). \quad (17)$$

Because the parameters and r_m, σ_{jm}, σ_m^2 are difficult to measure, we relate them to parameters that are directly measurable in principle. Aggregating equation (14), we obtain

$$c_t = [(\theta + p)/\alpha - (1 - \alpha)(r_m + p)/\alpha + (1 - \alpha)\sigma_m^2/2]w_t, \quad (18)$$

where $c_t = \int_{-\infty}^t pe^{-p(t-s)} c_{st}\, ds$ and $w_t = \int_{-\infty}^t pe^{-p(t-s)} w_{st} ds$. Aggregate wealth w_t equals the market value all human and physical capital. As a result,

$$w_t = h_t + k_t, \quad (19)$$

where h_t and k_t are the aggregate stocks of human and physical capital. The assumptions made above imply that the aggregate stock of human capital evolves according to equation (3) and the aggregate stock of physical capital evolves according to

$$dk_t = (y_t + r_k k_t - c_t)dt + \sigma_k dz_{kt}. \quad (20)$$

Unlike equation (5), equation (20) does not have a term $pk_t dt$ because this term is merely a redistribution from dying households to surviving households. Equations (18)–(20) and (3) imply that

$$dc_t/c_t = dw_t/w_t = (dh_t + dk_t)/w_t$$

$$= \{[(r_h + p)h_t + r_k k_t - c_t]/w_t\}dt + [\sigma_h h_t dz_{ht} + \sigma_k k_t dz_{kt}]/w_t$$

$$= \{[(1-x)(r_h + p) + xr_k] - c_t/w_t\}dt + [(1-x)\sigma_h dz_{ht} + x\sigma_k dz_{kt}]$$

$$= \{r_m + (1-x)p - (\theta + p)/\alpha - (1-\alpha)(r_m + p)/\alpha$$

$$+ (1-\alpha)\sigma_m^2/2]\}dt + \sigma_m dz_{mt}$$

or

$$dc_t/c_t = [(r_m - \theta)/\alpha - (1-\alpha)\sigma_m^2/2 - px]dt + \sigma_m dz_{mt} \tag{21}$$

Using Ito's Lemma to solve the stochastic differential equation (21) produces[13]

$$\Delta \ln c_t = [(r_m - \theta)/\alpha + (\alpha/2 - 1)\sigma_m^2 - px] + \sigma_m(z_{mt} - z_{m,t-1}), \tag{22}$$

Equation (22) implies that

$$r_m = \theta + \alpha(\mu_c + px) + (\alpha - \alpha^2/2)\sigma_m^2, \tag{23}$$

$$\sigma_m^2 = \sigma_c^2, \tag{24}$$

and

$$\sigma_{jm} = \sigma_{jc}, \tag{25}$$

where μ_c is mean growth rate of aggregate consumption, and σ_c^2 is the variance of consumption growth, and σ_{jc} is the covariance between the rate of return on asset j and the growth rate of consumption. Substituting equations (23)–(25) into equation (17) then gives us

$$r_j = \theta + \alpha(\mu_c + px) - \frac{1}{2}\alpha^2 \sigma_c^2 + \alpha\sigma_{jc}. \tag{26}$$

The term px appears in equation (26) because $\mu_c + px$ is the common mean growth rate of consumption for all surviving households and hence for all asset holders. To see why, not that between times t and $t + dt$, pdt households with wealths and consumptions averaging w_t and c_t die and are replaced by newly born households with wealths consisting solely of human capital valued at $(1 - x)w_t$. Because consumption is proportional to wealth, the newly born households consume $(1 - x)c_t$. Therefore, the mean growth rate of consumption for the $1 - pdt$ surviving households is

$$[\mu_c - (pdt)\{(1/c_t)[(1-x)c_t - c_t]/dt\}]/(1 - pdt)$$

which approaches $\mu + px$ as dt approaches zero.

Let r_f be the rate of return on riskless assets; (that is, assets for which $\sigma_{jc} = 0$). With this definition, equation (26) can be rewritten in the form

$$r_j = r_f + \alpha\sigma_{jc} \tag{27}$$

with

$$r_f = \theta + \alpha(\mu_c + px) - \frac{1}{2}\alpha^2\sigma_c^2. \tag{28}$$

According to equation (27), the risk premium for any asset j is the product of α, the relative risk aversion, and σ_{jc}, which measures the riskiness of asset j. Since p does not enter the equation (27), the risk premium does not depend on how long the horizon of households is. As a result, allowing for the possibility that households have finite horizons does not enhance the ability of CCAPM to price risk and does not eliminate any of the anomalies that the literature has found for how it prices risk.

Equation (26) implies that the shorter the horizon is, the higher is the mean instantaneous rate of return on every asset, holding constant the mean and variance of the growth rate of aggregate consumption, the covariance of the asset's rate of return with growth rate of aggregate consumption, and the fraction of wealth held as claims on physical capital. In particular, (28) implies that the rate of return on riskless assets is an increasing function of p. The reason is that the larger p is, the higher is $\mu_c + px$, the common mean growth rate of consumption for asset holders. The CCAPM, however, predicts a rate of return on riskless assets that is too high, not too low. Therefore, positing that households in the CCAPM have finite horizons worsens its overprediction of the rate of return on riskless assets.

III. EMPIRICAL RELEVANCE

In this section we obtain some idea of the empirical importance of the effect of p on the rate of return on riskless assets for plausible values of the other parameters. We equated μ_c to .0179, the annual average growth rate of real per capita expenditures on nondurable and services between 1948 and 1993, and σ_c^2 to .000214, three-halves of the variance of the series.[14] We assigned x the value .308, Kendrick's (1976) estimate of the fraction of wealth held as claims on physical capital. We used a conventional value, .02, for the subjective discount rate θ. We considered the values 1, 3, 5, 10, and 25 for α and .00, .01, .02, .03, and .04 for p. These parameter values imply the values of r_f reported in Table 1. Even for a coefficient of relative risk aversion as low as 1, r_f increases about .3 percentage points for each percentage point that p increases, an appreciable amount. For larger values of α, the effect is proportionally larger. For values large enough to rationalize the equity premium easily (around 25), each percentage point increase in p raises the rate of return on riskless assets by about 8 percentage points.

Table 1. Rates of Return on Riskless Assets

	$\alpha = 1$	$\alpha = 3$	$\alpha = 5$	$\alpha = 10$	$\alpha = 25$
$p = .00$	.0378	.0726	.1067	.1880	.3998
$p = .01$	.0408	.0819	.1221	.2188	.4768
$p = .02$	.0439	.0911	.1375	.2496	.5538
$p = .03$	.0470	.1004	.1529	.2804	.6308
$p = .04$	.0501	.1096	.1683	.3112	.7078

Note: The figures in the table are based on the assumption that
$r_f = \theta + \alpha + (\mu_c + px) - \alpha^2 \sigma_c^2/2$
with $\mu c = .0179$, $\sigma_c^2 = .000228$, $x = .308$, and $\theta = .02$.

Using Blanchard's model, Evans (1991) has shown that government debt policy produces negligible effects on aggregate demand unless p exceeds four percent per annum. Values of p that high require very large rates of return on riskless assets even for values of α as low as 3. Alternatively, if θ is permitted to be negative as Kocherlakota (1990) advocates, values of p exceeding 4% per annum and a rate of return on riskless assets of one percent per annum would require subjective discount rates less than −4.01, −9.96, −15.83, and −30.08% per annum for coefficients of relative risk aversion of 3, 5, 10, and 25, respectively.[15]

IV. SUMMARY AND CONCLUSION

In this paper we have introduced finite horizons into the CCAPM using the basic framework of Blanchard. Our modified CCAPM prices risk in exactly the same way whether horizons are finite or infinite. It does, however, have implications for the level of asset returns in general and for the rate of return on riskless assets in particular. As the horizon for households falls, mean rates of return on all assets rise ceteris paribus. Because the CCAPM already appears to predict mean rates of return that are too high, our modified CCAPM becomes less capable of explaining asset prices as the horizon of households becomes shorter. As a result, introducing finite horizons into the CCAPM does not enhance its ability to price assets. So, we conclude that the assumption of infinite horizons should be retained in the CCAPM.

ACKNOWLEDGMENT

The authors thank the editor (Andrew Chen), Sashi Murti, Latha Ramchand, Stephen D. Smith, and an anonymous reviewer for their helpful comments.

NOTES

1. Although a massive literature could be cited here, citing Blanchard and Fischer (1989), the standard graduate textbook in macroeconomics, suffices.

2. For analyses on German and Canadian market see Sauer (1992) and Carmichael and Sampson (1993), respectively.

3. Grossman and Shiller (1982) have shown that one need not assume households have identical momentary utility functions and identical probability beliefs.

4. Lewis (1991) suggests that rejections in the intertemporal consumption-based asset-pricing relationship at short horizons arises from an adequate auxiliary assumption not necessarily from the relationship itself. Detemple and Zapatero (1991) on the other hand have shown that in economies with habit formation, the consumption capital asset pricing model need not hold when the coefficients of the endowment process are stochastic processes.

5. Allowing for population growth at a constant nonzero rate g as in Weil (1987) is straightforward. Let q be the birth rate, which equals $p + n$ by construction. The analysis below is valid with $n \neq 0$ if $r_k - n$ replaces r_k in equation (20) and q and $\theta + n$ replace p and θ in equations (21)–(23) and (26). Ricardian equivalence then holds if all new individuals in the economy become members of existing households; that is $q = 0$. If instead households act as if their memberships are growing, then Blanchard's alternative to Ricardian equivalence holds. For expositional convenience, the theoretical analysis assumes that $n = 0$.

6. We also impose the restrictions $\alpha > 0$ and $\theta > (1 - \alpha) r_m - \alpha p + (\sigma^2 - \alpha)\sigma^2 m/2$ so that the utility function (2) is strictly concave and the objective function (1) exists, where r_m and σ_m are parameters below.

7. It may be appropriate to interpret p metaphorically as a measure of how disconnected current households feel from future households rather than literally as the birth rate of the population. Under this interpretation, current households have operative altruistic bequest motives and infinite horizons if $p = 0$ and have no operative altruistic bequest motives and finite horizons if $p > 0$.

8. It is straightforward to allow for an exponentially declining age-earnings profile. Doing so replaces r_h in all equations below by $r_h + \delta$, where r_h is the instantaneous rate of return on human capital and δ is the proportional rate at which the age-earnings profile slopes downward. Because r_h does not enter the empirical models developed below, we can abstract from δ without loss.

9. For expositional convenience, we assume that there is only one capital good and no government. Introducing many heterogeneous capital goods, each with its own return process, would add nothing important to the analysis. Moreover, government can be introduced merely by reinterpreting k and y as the stock of physical capital plus the government debt and wage income minus taxes.

10. No such mutual fund exists in the real world because of adverse selection and moral hazard in the markets for human capital. These problems arise because human capital is heterogeneous, each household's work effort and productivity cannot be monitored costlessly, and households have private incentives to shirk. We abstract from these features of actual markets for human capital in order to focus on the implications of finite horizons for the pricing of financial assets.

11. See section 21 of Kamien and Schwartz (1981).

12. We assume that dz_{ht} and dz_{kt} are not perfectly correlated and hence that the expression in the denominator below is positive. If they are perfectly correlated, we must impose the restrictions $r_h = r_k$ and $\sigma_h = \sigma_k$ in order for the portfolio problem to have a solution in which both assets are held.

13. Again see Section 21 of Kamien and Schwartz (1981).

14. Let time be measured in years, and let year t be defined to be the interval $(t - 1, t]$. We calculate our growth rates as $\Delta \ln \bar{c}_t$ rather than $\Delta \ln c_t$, where $\bar{c}_t$ is $\int_0^1 c_{t-\tau} d\tau$. To a first approximation,

$$\Delta \ln \bar{c}_t = \int_0^1 \left[\mu_c + \sigma_c \left(z_{m,t-\tau} - z_{(m,t-\tau-1)} \right) \right] d\tau = \mu_c + \sigma_c \left[\int_0^1 dz_{m,t-\tau-1+\xi} d\xi \right] d\tau$$

$$= \mu_c + \sigma_c \left[\int_0^1 v \, dz_{m,t-v} \, dv + \int_0^1 v \, dz_{m,t-2+v} \, dv \right]$$

As a result, the mean of $\Delta \ln \bar{c}_t$ is μ_c and its variance is

$$2\sigma_c^2 \int_0^1 v^2 \, dv = (2/3)\sigma_c^2$$

15. For a related empirical discussion using 19-country data see Evans and Hasan (1997).

REFERENCES

Blanchard, O. J. (1985, December). Debt, deficits, and finite horizons. *Journal of Political Economy, 93,* 223–247.

Blanchard, O. J., & Fischer, S. (1989). *Lectures in macroeconomics.* Cambridge, MA: MIT Press.

Breeden, D. (1979, September). An intertemporal asset pricing model with stochastic consumption and investment opportunities. *Journal of Financial Economics, 7,* 265–296.

Breeden, D., Gibbons, M. R., & Litzenberger, R. H. (1989, June). Empirical tests of the consumption-oriented CAPM. *Journal of Finance, 44,* 231–262.

Carmichael, B., & Samson, L. (1993). Excess returns determinations: Empirical evidence from Canada. *Journal of Economics and Business, 45,* 35–48.

Constantinides, G. M. (1990, June). Habit formation: A resolution of the equity premium puzzle. *Journal of Political Economy, 98,* 519–543.

Cooper, R. (1993). Risk premium in the futures markets. *Journal of Futures Markets 13,* 357–371.

Detemple, J. D., & Zapatero. (1991). Asset prices in an exchange economy with habit formation. *Econometrica, 59,* 1633–1657.

Eichenbaum, M. S., Hansen, L. P., & Singleton, K. J. (1988, February). A time series analysis of representative agent models of consumption and leisure choice under uncertainty. *Quarterly Journal of Economics, 103,* 51–78.

Epstein, L. G., & Zin, S. E. (1989, July). Substitution, risk aversion, and the temporal behavior of consumption and asset returns: A theoretical framework. *Econometrica, 57,* 937–969.

Epstein, L. G., & Zin, S. E. (1991, April). Substitution, risk aversion, and the temporal behavior of consumption and asset returns: An empirical analysis. *Journal of Political Economy, 99,* 263–286.

Evans, P. (1991, October). Is Ricardian equivalence a good approximation? *Economic Inquiry, 29,* 626–644.

Evans, P., & Hasan, I. (1998). *CCAPM: International evidence.* The consumption-based capital asset pricing model: International evidence. *Journal of Multinational Financial Management, 8,* 1–22.

Grossman, S., & Shiller, R. (1982, July). Consumption correlatedness and risk measurement in economies with non-traded assets and heterogeneous information. *Journal of Financial Economics 10,* 195–210.

Grossman, S., Melino, A., & Shiller, R. (1987, July). Estimating the continuous time consumption-based asset pricing model. *Journal of Business and Economic Statistics, 5,* 315–327.

Hansen, L. P., & Singleton, K. (1983, April). Stochastic consumption, risk aversion, and the temporal behavior of stock market returns. *Journal of Political Economy, 91,* 249–265.

Hansen, L. P., & Jagannathan, R. (1991, April). Implications of security market data for models of dynamic economies. *Journal of Political Economy, 99,* 225–262.

Heaton, J. (1990). *An empirical investigation of asset pricing with temporally dependent preference specifications.* Manuscript, MIT.

Heaton, J., & Lucas, D. (1992). The effects of incomplete insurance markets and trading costs in a consumption-based asset pricing model. *Journal of Economic Dynamics and Control, 16,* 601–620.

Jagannathan, R. (1985). An investigation of commodity future prices using the consumption-based intertemporal capital asset pricing model. *Journal of Finance, 40,* 175–191.

Kamien, M. I., & Schwartz, N. L. (1981). *Dynamic optimization.* New York: North Holland.

Kendrick, J. W. (1976). *The formation and stocks of total capital.* New York: National Bureau of Economic Research.

Kocherlakota, N. R. (1990, January). On the "discount" factor in growth economies. *Journal of Monetary Economics, 25,* 43–48.

Lewis, K. K. (1991). Should the holding period matter for the intertemporal consumption–based CAPM? *Journal of Monetary Economics, 28,* 365–389.

Mankiw, N. G., Rotemberg, J. J., & Summers, L. H. (1985, February). Intertemporal substitution in macroeconomics. *Quarterly Journal of Economics, 100,* 225–251.

Mehra, R., & Prescott, E. C. (1985, March). The equity premium: A puzzle. *Journal of Monetary Economics, 15,* 145–162.

Merton, R. (1973, September). An intertemporal capital asset pricing model. *Econometrica, 41,* 861–887.

Sauer, A. (1992). An empirical comparison of alternative models of capital asset pricing in Germany. *Journal of Banking and Finance, 16,* 183–196.

Weil, P. (1987, September). Permanent budget deficits and inflation. *Journal of Monetary Economics, 20,* 393–410.

Weil, P. (1989, November). The equity premium puzzle and the risk-free rate puzzle. *Journal of Monetary Economics, 24,* 401–422.

MUTUAL FUNDS AND ASSET PRICING
MODELS IN A FINITE ECONOMY

James S. Ang and Tsong-Yue Lai

ABSTRACT

This paper shows that if an asset's return can be decomposed into k factor risks and an idiosyncratic risk in a linear factor generating process and if the idiosyncratic risks are not dependent, then (i) there are k factor risk mutual funds and an idiosyncratic risk mutual fund; these $k + 1$ mutual funds are not idiosyncratic risk free, and (ii) there are k factor risk premiums and an idiosyncratic risk premium in an equilibrium asset pricing model in a finite economy. An explicit error bound from the exact APT is negligible if factors can be extracted exactly. However, the error bound could be substantial if there are missing factors or idiosyncratic risks in the generating process. The resulting model allows some factors to be missed in the linear factor-generating process, as they are captured by the idiosyncratic risk factor, which is priced in our model.

I. INTRODUCTION

Although asset risk is decomposable into k factor risks and an idiosyncratic risk in a k factor linear generating process, there are only k factor risk premiums in the

Research in Finance, Volume 16, pages 107–125.
ISBN: 0-7623-0328-X

Arbitrage Pricing Theory (APT) derived by Ross (1976b, 1977) and extended by Huberman (1982), Stambaugh (1983), Chamberlain and Rothschild (1985), Ingersoll (1984), Connor (1984), and others in a limit economy with an infinite number of assets. The idiosyncratic risk premium is absent in the APT because the idiosyncratic risk is diversifiable in a limit economy. However, the testability of the APT in a limit economy with an infinite number of assets has been questioned by Shanken (1982, 1985).[1]

On the other hand, the APT in a finite economy has been investigated by Chen and Ingersoll (1983), Grinblatt and Titman (1983, 1987), and Wei (1988). Chen and Ingersoll show that an idiosyncratic risk-free optimal portfolio held by an investor is a sufficient condition for the exact APT.[2] A risky portfolio with the idiosyncratic risk-free property can occur only if the covariance matrix of idiosyncratic risks is singular in a linear factor model. That is, a linear combination of random variables (the idiosyncratic risks) has to become nonrandom, that is, its standard deviation approaches zero (risk free). Grinblatt and Titman (1983) derive the exact APT under the existence of an idiosyncratic risk-free basis portfolios assumption. A necessary and sufficient condition derived by Grinblatt and Titman (1987) for the exact APT is the existence of reference portfolios, in which all asset returns are generated without the idiosyncratic risk term.[3]

However, idiosyncratic risk-free basis portfolios (or optimal portfolios) do not exist in a finite economy where idiosyncratic risks have positive definite covariance matrix, because any linear combination of random variables is still a random variable except when they are dependent. Furthermore, the procedure for constructing these basis (or reference) portfolios is absent in their work. Wei (1988) adds the market rate of return as a common factor in the linear factor model to derive the exact APT. The crucial assumption is that market portfolio is idiosyncratic risk free, which implies that the idiosyncratic risks are dependent and their covariance matrix is singular. On the other hand, in a finite economy with a positive definite covariance matrix, if the idiosyncratic risk cannot be diversified away, then it should be priced by an equilibrium asset pricing model within the risk aversion framework. Yet, the idiosyncratic risk premium has not been formally incorporated in previous equilibrium asset pricing models.

This paper develops an equilibrium asset pricing model with an idiosyncratic risk premium. We decompose asset risk into k factor risks and an idiosyncratic risk to construct $k + 1$ risk mutual funds. These are derived from solving the necessary condition for an optimal portfolio that maximizes the expected excess rate of return subject to k constraints on factor risks and a constraint on the idiosyncratic risk. These $k + 1$ risk mutual funds in a finite economy are not idiosyncratic risk free and can be used to construct the mean-variance efficient portfolio held by investors, who need not make any distinction among k factor risks and the idiosyncratic risk in their assessment of a portfolio's riskiness.

The expected excess return in the model is determined not only by k factor risk premiums but also by an idiosyncratic risk premium. The equivalent relationship between an optimal portfolio and assets in an equilibrium asset pricing model, implies that tests of an equilibrium asset pricing model can also be conducted by testing the optimality of this portfolio.[4] This is similar in spirit when, testing for the APT by investigating the existence of arbitrage portfolios. Current tests of the APT use factor analysis to extract the common factors and then regress expected return against factor loadings to determine whether risk premiums are significantly different from zero. Testing whether coefficients of factor loadings are significantly different from zero may not be sufficient and may not have enough power to reject Ross's (1976b, 1977) APT. The results of empirical APT tests thus far are at best, mixed, and certainly not definitive.[5]

The necessary and sufficient condition for the exact APT is that the expected excess return's vector is linearly dependent of the factor loadings matrix. Any of the following conditions could produce the exact APT. These are: (i) a zero idiosyncratic risk premium due to the presence of idiosyncratic risk neutral investors, (ii) the existence of an idiosyncratic risk-free optimal portfolio held by some investor, and (iii) the investor's optimal portfolio can be constructed from the k factor risk mutual funds (defined later). The error bound deviation from the exact APT derived by Dybvig (1983) and Grinblatt and Titman (1983) depends on the value of the relative risk aversion measure, which could vary from -26.3 to 25.6 (see Hall, 1981). To circumvent the use of both the measure of relative risk aversion and the multivariate normality assumption, such as those employed in Grinblatt and Titman (1983), this paper uses only the market parameters (e.g., expected excess market rate of return) to calculate an error-bound deviation from the exact APT. The error bound is negligible if all factors can be extracted with high degree of precision. However, it could be substantial if there are missing factors in the linear factor generating process of asset returns.

This paper is organized as follows. A portfolio optimization problem is solved in Section II to derive an asset pricing model within the framework of the linear factor generating process in a finite economy. Given that the covariance matrix of idiosyncratic risks is non-singular, optimal portfolios that can be used as substitutes for the aggregate portfolio are constructed in Section III. In this section the mutual funds are also developed and constructed. A necessary and sufficient condition for an equilibrium asset pricing model is determined in Section IV. Section V examines an error bound deviation from the exact APT and Section VI concludes.

II. THE MODEL

Assume there are n risky assets in a finite economy. Following Ross's linear k factors generating process, the risks in asset returns can be decomposed into k factor risks and an idiosyncratic risk as:

$$\tilde{R} = R + BF + \tilde{\varepsilon}, \tag{1}$$

where the $k \times 1$ vector F represents the systematic factors influencing asset returns, B is the $n \times k$ matrix of factor loadings, $\tilde{R}$ is the $n \times 1$ vector of n stochastic asset returns; the expectation of $\tilde{R}$ is denoted by R, and $\tilde{\varepsilon}$ is the $n \times 1$ vector of the idiosyncratic noise term. It is also assumed that B has rank $k < n$ and there exists a risk-free asset in the economy.

The set of assumptions concerning the expectations of $\tilde{\varepsilon}$ and F are:

$$E(\tilde{\varepsilon}) = 0, \tag{1-a}$$

$$E(F) = 0, \tag{1-b}$$

$$E(FF^T) = I_k, \tag{1-c}$$

$$E(\tilde{\varepsilon}\tilde{\varepsilon}^T) = V, \tag{1-d}$$

$$E(F\tilde{\varepsilon}^T) = 0, \tag{1-e}$$

where I_k is a $k \times k$ identity matrix, V is a $n \times n$ covariance matrix of the idiosyncratic term $\tilde{\varepsilon}$, 0 is a vector or matrix, and a superscript T denotes the transpose operation.

A result commonly found in both theoretical and empirical studies is that V is positive definite in a finite economy. V is not required to be a diagonal matrix in this paper. For example, if there are missing factors in the formulation of (1), then the effects of these missing factors on asset returns will be absorbed by the term $\hat{\varepsilon}$ and could result in nonzero off-diagonal entries of the positive definite V. A positive definite V implies V is invertible and hence an idiosyncratic risk-free risky portfolio cannot exist.

Let X be a $n \times 1$ vector with ith element x_i denoting the percentage invested in ith risky asset. Thus, the percentage invested in the risk-free asset is, $1 - (x_1 + x_2 + \ldots + x_n)$. According to (1), the expected return on the portfolio X is the sum of $X^T R$ and the return from the risk-free asset. In other words, the expected return on the portfolio X is determined as, $X^T(R - r) + r$, where r is the return on the risk-free asset. $R - r$ is a $n \times 1$ vector of expected excess return with ith component $R_i - r$, and R_i is the expected return on ith risky asset.

Since there are k different factors and an idiosyncratic risk in the asset return (1), the portfolio risk of $X^T\tilde{R}$ can be separated into k different factor risks, $X^T BB^T X$, and an idiosyncratic risk, $X^T V X$. More specifically, the ith factor risk in the portfolio X is determined from $(X^T B_i)^2$, for $i = 1, \ldots, k$, where B_i is the ith column vector of B, based upon the uncorrelated assumption of F in (1-c). The process of minimizing factor risks is equivalent to minimizing individual $X^T B_i$. The economic meaning of $X^T B_i$ follows from Chamberlain (1983) and Ingersoll (1984) who show that the factor loadings matrix B is the covariance matrix of asset return R with k factors F. The factor loadings B measure the sensitivity of asset returns to the factors' changes.

Like the beta in the market model in CAPM, if $E(FF^T) = I_k$, B may be interpreted as the factor beta matrix in APT and $X^T B$ is the factor beta vector of the portfolio X. The ith element of $X^T B$, $X^T B_i$, is ith factor beta of portfolio X.

Although there are $k + 1$ different risks in the portfolio return, if the total risk and the expected return are the only concerns to the investors, then the optimal portfolio must be the mean-variance efficient portfolio, which will be explored later. However, if investors can differentiate and impose different restrictions on these risks, then the investors' investment decision can be formulated to find an optimal portfolio which maximizes its expected excess rate of return subject to the $k + 1$ constraints on its factors and idiosyncratic risks.

$$\text{Max} \qquad X^T(R - r) \qquad\qquad (2)$$

$$\text{subject to} \qquad X^T B = b, \qquad\qquad (3)$$

$$X^T V X \le \xi, \qquad\qquad (4)$$

where b is the $1 \times k$ predetermined factor constraints, and nonnegative scalar ξ is the predetermined idiosyncratic risk constraint. Both b and ξ are determined by the investor, for example, the maximum risk, as a limit, an investor can tolerate from a risk management viewpoint. No restriction on the sign of X indicates that short sales are allowed. Equation (2) is the expected excess rate of return on portfolio X, equation (3) is the constraint on the portfolio's factor beta in the linear factor structure, and equation (4) is the constraint on the portfolio's idiosyncratic risk.

It is noteworthy that $X^T B = b$ is the set of systematic linear equations with n variables. There exist nonzero portfolios to satisfy $X^T B = b$ for any given b. In the case of $b = 0$, there may exist many portfolios with zero factor risk, but a full rank V implies that there is no idiosyncratic risk-free portfolio when $X \ne 0$.

Applying the Lagrangian method, the necessary and sufficient condition for X to be an optimal solution to the above problem is[6]

$$R - r = B \lambda + \delta V X, \qquad\qquad (5)$$

where λ is the $k \times 1$ vector of shadow prices (or Lagrangian multipliers) of factor betas in (3), and $\delta/2$ is a positive shadow price of the idiosyncratic risk in (4).[7]

Different restrictions on factor beta constraints are allowed in the portfolio selection because different investors may have different sensitivities to common factors. However, regardless of how different investors differ on their constraints on factor betas and idiosyncratic risk, their first order condition must have the same form as in (5). It is worth noting that the constraints b and ξ must be finite for risk averters. The finite constraint b (ξ) is important because it represents the factor betas (idiosyncratic risk) which the investor is willing to bear in his portfolio selection. A finite vector b (ξ) implies a finite factor (idiosyncratic) risk of portfolio. For a risk neutral investor, the portfolio decision can be reformulated so as to maximize the expected excess rate of return subject to both infinite factor betas and idiosyncratic risk constraints. In this case the constraints are not binding. Consequently, the λ and δ in (5) must be zero and the expected returns on risky assets must be the same as the risk-free rate in the risk neutral world.

III. MUTUAL FUNDS IN A LINEAR FACTOR MODEL

This section examines the mutual funds and their applications in a finite economy with a linear k factor model. An important implication of (5) is stated in the following mutual funds separation theorem.

> **Proposition 1 ($k + 1$ mutual funds separation theorem).** Under the condition of positive definite covariance matrix for idiosyncratic risks, an investor may obtain his optimal portfolio that satisfied (2)–(4) (for any finite b and ξ) by choosing either from the original assets or from at most $k + 2$ mutual funds. The $k + 2$ mutual funds consist of: (i) the risk-free asset, (ii) the optimal idiosyncratic risk mutual funds, $V^{-1}(R - r)$, and (iii) the k factor risk mutual funds, $V^{-1}B$.[8]

Proof: The optimal portfolio X must satisfy (5), and can be rewritten as:

$$\delta X = V^{-1}(R - r) - V^{-1}B\,\lambda.$$

Q.E.D.

The $k + 1$ risk mutual funds in Proposition 1 can be used to construct all optimal portfolios that satisfied (2)–(4) in the finite economy with k common factors. A merit of these risky $k + 1$ mutual funds is that they can be explicitly constructed from $V^{-1}(R - r)$ and $V^{-1}B$, incorporating idiosyncratic risk. The previous k-linear factor models studied by Ross (1978), Connor (1984), and Chamberlain (1983) assume k idiosyncratic risk-free mutual funds exist while the procedure of their construction was left unspecified.

The mutual fund $V^{-1}(R - r)$ can be obtained by solving the necessary condition for minimizing the portfolio's idiosyncratic risk subject to an expected excess return constraint on the portfolio. The solution provides optimal diversification of idiosyncratic risk. Similarly, maximizing the absolute correlation of the portfolio returns with factors F yields portfolios $(BB^T + V)^{-1}B$, which are constructed from $V^{-1}B$.[9] That is, the mutual funds $(BB^T + V)^{-1}B$ provide optimal hedge, in terms of minimum total risk, against changes in factors F. Since the mutual funds $(BB^T + V)^{-1}B$ are not perfectly correlated to factors F, they are unlikely to hedge completely the changes of each factor in F. Nevertheless, the returns on k mutual funds $V^{-1}B(B^TV^{-1}B)^{-1}$ constructed from $V^{-1}B$ are positively and perfectly correlated to the factors F that minimizes idiosyncratic risk. In other words, the k risk mutual funds $V^{-1}B$ can be used in the finite economy to hedge the factors' changes completely with a minimum level of idiosyncratic risk even though the exact APT may not hold. In this sense, $V^{-1}B$ may be interpreted as the k factors risk mutual funds.

Three portfolios among the set of $k + 1$ risk mutual funds deserve further exposition because of their intuitive appeal. And, as will be shown later, they can be used as the substitute for the aggregate supply portfolio in an equilibrium asset pricing model. The features of these portfolios may allow the researcher to test additional restrictions implied by equilibrium asset pricing models.

The first is the optimal zero factor risk portfolio[10] that is, a portfolio X satisfying $B^T X = 0$ in (3), where, 0 is a $1 \times n$ zero vector. Since the only risk in the zero factor beta portfolio will be idiosyncratic, and since the zero factor risk portfolio (except $X = 0$) can always be rescaled to have variance of one, the optimal zero factor risk portfolio is the solution which maximizes expected excess return among all zero factor risk portfolios with variance equal to (or less than, if $X = 0$) one after rescaling.[11]

$$\text{Max} \qquad X^T(R - r), \qquad (6)$$

$$\text{subject to} \qquad X^T B = 0, \qquad (7)$$

$$X^T V X \le 1. \qquad (8)$$

Mathematically, zero factor risk portfolios are possible because the rank of factor loadings for matrix B is $k < n$. Since $X = 0$ is a feasible solution, the feasible solution set is thus nonempty. The necessary condition for an optimal zero factor risk portfolio is that it must satisfy (5). The optimal zero factor risk portfolio X_{GLS} and the factor risk premiums λ_{GLS} must be uniquely determined, respectively, by

$$X_{GLS} = V^{-1}[I - B(B^T V^{-1} B)^{-1} B^T V^{-1}](R - r)\kappa^{-1/2}$$

$$= \{V^{-1}(R - r) - V^{-1}B[(B^T V^{-1} B)^{-1} B^T V^{-1}(R - r)]\}\kappa^{-1/2} \qquad (9)$$

and[12]

$$\lambda_{GLS} = (B^T V^{-1} B)^{-1} B^T V^{-1}(R - r), \qquad (10)$$

where, $\kappa = (R - r)^T[I - V^{-1}B(B^T V^{-1} B)^{-1} B^T V^{-1}](R - r) > 0$ and that it satisfies $X_{GLS}^T V X_{GLS} = 1$, I is a $n \times n$ identity matrix. Equation (9) shows that the optimal zero factor risk portfolio X_{GLS} is constructed from the $k + 1$ mutual funds: $V^{-1}(R - r)$ and $V^{-1}B$. Multiplying X_{GLS}^T to both sides of the first-order condition (5), the expected excess return on portfolio X_{GLS} is determined as, $X_{GLS}^T(R - r) = \delta_{GLS} X_{GLS}^T V X_{GLS} = \delta_{GLS} = (R - r)^T[I - V^{-1}B(B^T V^{-1} B)^{-1} B^T V^{-1}] (R - r)\kappa^{-1/2} = \kappa^{1/2} > 0$, where $\delta_{GLS}/2$ is the Lagrangian multiplier of the idiosyncratic risk constraint (8). The expected excess return on optimal portfolio X_{GLS} must be positive, that is, not dominated by the portfolio $X = 0$, whose excess return is zero. In addition, the combination of (5), (9) and (10) implies,

$$X = V^{-1}B(\lambda_{GLS} - \lambda)/\delta + (\delta_{GLS}/\delta)\,X_{GLS} \qquad (11)$$

Equation (11) shows that in addition to the k factor risk mutual funds $V^{-1}B$, the optimal zero factor risk portfolio X_{GLS} in (9) can be used to substitute for $V^{-1}(R - r)$ as one of the mutual funds to generate investors' optimal portfolio, that satisfies (2)–(4). A feature of X_{GLS} is that the return on optimal portfolios satisfying (5) must be positively correlated to the optimal zero factor risk portfolio's return.[13] In fact, the portfolio X_{GLS} (except for a constant scalar) in the linear factor model is also the minimum variance zero factor beta portfolio.

The second portfolio of interest to empiricists is the portfolio X_{OLS} which is obtained by minimizing the mean square error term $(R - r - B\lambda)^T(R - r - B\lambda)$ in (5). The optimal portfolio (except for a positive scalar δ_{OLS}), and the factor risk premiums λ that minimize mean square error in (5) are, respectively,[14]

$$\delta_{OLS}X_{OLS} = V^{-1}[I - B(B^TB)^{-1}B^T](R - r)$$

$$= V^{-1}(R - r) - V^{-1}B[(B^TB)^{-1}B^T(R - r)], \qquad (12)$$

and

$$\lambda_{OLS} = (B^TB)^{-1}B^T(R - r). \qquad (13)$$

Equation (12) shows that portfolio X_{OLS} is in the space generated by $k + 1$ mutual funds in Proposition 1. The portfolio X_{OLS} is important because the procedure of testing APT by regressing the excess return $R - r$ against the factor loadings B with the ordinary least square method is equivalent to testing whether X_{OLS} satisfies (12). Since λ_{OLS} is derived from minimizing the mean square error term $(R - r - B\lambda)^T(R - r - B\lambda)$ within a finite economy and a positive definite V, $\delta_{OLS}VX_{OLS}$ in (18) is the lowest error bound deviation from exact APT, if X_{OLS} and δ_{OLS} can be estimated (or observed).

Finally, despite the presence of $k + 1$ risks in both asset and portfolio returns, if investors do not differentiate among these $k + 1$ risks in their portfolio selection, then the mean-variance efficient portfolio X_{MV} should be chosen by investors. The mean-variance efficient portfolio (up to a positive scalar δ_{MV}) and the factor risk premiums are,

$$\delta_{MV}X_{MV} = [BB^T + V]^{-1}(R - r)$$

$$= V^{-1}[I + BB^TV^{-1}]^{-1}(R - r)$$

$$= V^{-1}[I - BB^TV^{-1}(I + BB^TV^{-1})^{-1}](R - r)$$

$$= V^{-1}(R - r) - V^{-1}B[B^T V^{-1}(I + BB^T V^{-1})^{-1}(R - r)]$$

$$= V^{-1}(R - r) - V^{-1}B[B^T(BB^T + V)^{-1}(R - r)], \qquad (14)$$

and

$$\lambda_{MV} = B^T(BB^T + V)^{-1}(R - r), \qquad (15)$$

respectively. Equation (14) shows that the mean-variance efficient portfolio X_{MV} could also be constructed from the portfolios $V^{-1}(R - r)$ and $V^{-1}B$. The expected excess return on the portfolio X_{MV} is positive because $\delta_{MV} X_{MV}^T(R - r) = (R - r)^T(BB^T + V)^{-1}(R - r) > 0$. The importance of X_{MV} can be seen from the studies of the relations between exact APT and mean-variance efficient portfolio by Chamberlain (1983) for the infinite economy and by Grinblatt and Titman (1987) for a finite set of assets. It should be noted that portfolios X_{GLS}, X_{OLS} and X_{MV} in (9), (12), and (14), satisfy (5), are optimal from some investors' perspective, and can substitute for the aggregate supply portfolio in an equilibrium asset pricing model in the following section.[15]

IV. AN EQUILIBRIUM ASSET PRICING MODEL

Since all optimal portfolios satisfying (5) can be constructed from the k factor risk mutual funds $V^{-1}B$ and the optimal idiosyncratic risk mutual funds $V^{-1}(R - r)$, an equilibrium asset pricing model can be obtained by aggregating over all investors' optimal portfolio. More precisely, dividing (5) by δ, aggregating over all investors' optimal portfolio, and then equating the aggregate demand to the aggregate supply, yield the following equilibrium asset pricing model:[16]

$$R - r = B \lambda_m + \delta_m V X_m^*, \qquad (16)$$

where X_m^* is the aggregate supply in the economy, δ_m is the reciprocal of the summation of positive $1/\delta$, and λ_m is the $k \times 1$ vector of the ratio of summation of λ/δ to the summation of $1/\delta$ over all investors.

The λ_m and δ_m terms in (16) may be interpreted as the factor risk premiums and idiosyncratic risk premium, respectively. The existence of risk premiums for λ_m and δ_m in (16) shows that the aggregate portfolio X_m^* is also an optimal portfolio because X_m^* satisfies the necessary and sufficient condition (5). In addition, since X_m^* is the aggregation of all investors' portfolios satisfying (5), X_m^* may not have to be the same as the portfolio X_{MV} in (14). The mean-variance efficient portfolio is a special case of X_m^* in (16) because if all investors possess the mean-variance (or quadratic) utility function, then the mean-variance efficient portfolio X_{MV} will be held by all investors and the aggregation X_m^* would be identical to X_{MV}.

The expected excess return is (i) proportional to the factor betas and (ii) positively related to the sensitivity of asset returns to the nondiversifiable aggregate portfolio's idiosyncratic risk. The higher the correlation of asset return to the aggregate portfolio's idiosyncratic risk, ceteris paribus, the greater should the expected return on the asset be to compensate for the additional risk contributed by the asset to the idiosyncratic risk of the aggregate supply portfolio, $X_m^{*T}\varepsilon$. Thus, the undiversified idiosyncratic risk is priced in our model.

The aggregate supply portfolio X_m^* in (16) can be generated from the $k + 1$ risk mutual funds $V^{-1}B$ and $V^{-1}(R - r)$. It may be replaced by any optimal portfolio satisfying (5), particularly, X_{GLS}, X_{OLS}, X_{MV}. Therefore, to contrast to Wei's (1988) model the portfolio X_m^* in (16) plays no special role here. Replacing the portfolio X_m^* in (16) with X_{GLS}, X_{OLS}, and X_{MV} in (9), (12), and (14) yields the following set of equivalent equilibrium asset pricing models:[17]

$$R - r = B\,\lambda_{GLS} + \delta_{GLS}\,VX_{GLS}, \tag{17}$$

$$R - r = B\,\lambda_{OLS} + \delta_{OLS}\,VX_{OLS}, \tag{18}$$

$$R - r = [BB^T + V]\delta_{MV}\,X_{MV}, \tag{19}$$

$$= B\lambda_{MV} + \delta_{MV}\,VX_{MV}, \tag{20}$$

Note that the coefficients δ_{GLS}, δ_{OLS}, and δ_{MV} in (17), (18), and (20) need not be identical. They can be obtained by pre-multiplying the optimal zero factor risk portfolio X_{GLS} in (9) to both sides of (17), (18), and (20).[18]

The expected excess return in (19) is positively related to the covariance of asset returns with the mean-variance portfolio return. From equations (19) and (20), the equilibrium asset pricing models (16)–(18) and CAPM are identical if the market portfolio is the mean-variance efficient portfolio X_{MV} in (19). This implies testing the mean-variance efficient (or optimal zero factor risk) portfolio is equivalent to testing the equilibrium asset pricing models (16)–(18). It is also equivalent to testing the CAPM if the market portfolio used in the CAPM is the portfolio X_{MV}. The results can be summarized into the following set of proposition and corollary:

Proposition 2. In a finite economy and a linear k factor model with a positive definite idiosyncratic risk matrix V, if investors' investment decision can be formulated by (2)–(4), then there exists an optimal portfolio X_m^* such that an equilibrium asset pricing model satisfies (16). The optimal portfolio X_m^* can be replaced by any other optimal portfolios satisfying (5). In particular, if X_m^* is substituted by X_{GLS}, X_{OLS}, and X_{MV} in (9), (12) and (14), respectively, then equations (16)–(20) are equilibrium asset pricing models.

In the approximate form of the APT, the factor risk premiums may not be unique. However, the following corollary shows that the risk premiums are uniquely determined by the optimal portfolio in the equilibrium asset pricing models (16)–(20):

Corollary I. Given a positive definite V, the risk premiums in an equilibrium asset pricing model must be uniquely determined by the factor beta matrix B and the optimal portfolio satisfied (5).

Proof: If the equilibrium asset pricing model can be represented by both $R - r = B\lambda_A + \delta_A VX$ and $R - r = B\lambda_B + \delta_B VX$ with the same optimal portfolio X, then $B(\lambda_A - \lambda_B) = (\delta_A - \delta_B) VX$, which implies either VX can be generated by B or $\lambda_A = \lambda_B$ and $\delta_A = \delta_B$. If VX can be generated by B, says $VX = B\lambda^*$ for some λ^*, then $R - r = B(\lambda_A + \delta_A\lambda^*) = B(\lambda_B + \delta_B\lambda^*)$. Pre-multiplying $(B^T B)^{-1} B^T$ in both sides results in $\lambda_A + \delta_A\lambda^* = \lambda_B + \delta_B\lambda^*$.

Q.E.D.

The sufficient and necessary condition for the exact APT has been extensively explored in the literature. The other implication of (5) is related to the exact APT and is stated in the following Proposition:

Proposition 3. Under a linear factor model, if there exists a vector λ and parameter δ such that an optimal portfolio X^* held by an investor satisfies (5), then a necessary and sufficient condition for the exact APT is that $\delta V X^*$ be generated either by B or by the null space $\{\ 0\ \}$.

Proof (Sufficiency): Proving Exact APT is equivalent to showing linear dependence between $R - r$ and B. If an optimal portfolio X^* held by an investor satisfies (5) and $\delta VX^* = B\lambda^+$, for some $k \times 1$ vector λ^+, then (5) can be rewritten as $R - r = B(\lambda + \lambda^+)$. This implies that the expected excess returns vector $R - r$ is linearly dependent on factor loadings matrix B, thus the exact APT holds. If $\delta VX^* = 0$, then (5) implies $R - r = B\lambda$.

(Necessary): If $R - r$ is linearly dependent on B, then there exists a $k \times 1$ vector λ^* such that $R - r = B\lambda^*$, which implies the vector $\delta VX^* = B(\lambda^* - \lambda)$ in (5). That is, δVX^* is generated either by B if $\lambda^* \neq \lambda$ or by $\{\ 0\ \}$ if $\lambda^* = \lambda$.

Q.E.D.

A necessary and sufficient condition for exact APT derived by Ross (1978) and Connor (1984) is that all mutual funds are idiosyncratic risk free. This condition is very restrictive and is later relaxed by Chen and Ingersoll (1983) to requiring only an idiosyncratic risk-free optimal portfolio held by investors as a sufficient condition for exact APT. Indeed, from (5) an idiosyncratic risk-free optimal portfolio (i.e., $X^T\tilde{\varepsilon} = 0$) held by the investors will be sufficient to guarantee the linear dependence of the expected excess return vector and factor loadings matrix and hence the exact APT. It should be noted that the condition $X^T\tilde{\varepsilon} = 0$ is equivalent to $VX = 0$ because $X^T\tilde{\varepsilon} = 0$ implies $VX = 0$, and $VX = 0$ in turn implies $X^T VX = 0$ and $X^T\tilde{\varepsilon} = 0$.

The condition $X^T\tilde{\varepsilon} = 0$ (or $VX = 0$) for nonzero X indicates that the idiosyncratic risks are dependent; this can happen if and only if V is not of full rank in a finite economy.[19] Although it is impossible to have a nonzero solution for $VX = 0$ when V is positive definite in a finite economy, it is likely that $VX = 0$ may satisfy $X \neq 0$ in an infinite economy (see Huberman, 1982; Ingersoll, 1984). Since both the portfolio formulation (2)–(4) and the necessary condition (5) in the infinite economy are the same as that in a finite economy, the equilibrium asset pricing models (16)–(20) may be extended to the infinite economy. In particular, the well-diversified mean-variance efficient portfolio $X^T_{MV}\tilde{\varepsilon} = 0$ condition derived by Chamberlain (1983) for the exact APT in a limit economy is a direct result of (20).

The other sufficient condition for exact APT is that either an optimal portfolio X held by investors satisfies (5) and $VX = B\lambda^+$ for some $k{\times}1$ vector λ^+ or there exist an idiosyncratic risk neutral investor, whose investment can be formulated from (2)–(4). Recall that neutral idiosyncratic risk implies $\xi = \infty$ in (4) and $\delta = 0$ in (5). A zero idiosyncratic risk premium from an investor results in the exact APT, according to (5). The condition $VX = B\lambda^+$ implies the linear dependence of the expected excess returns vector $R - r$ and the factor loadings matrix B and thus the exact APT. For a positive definite V, $VX = B\lambda^+$ is equivalent to $X = V^{-1}B\lambda^+$. That is, if an optimal portfolio X can be constructed from the k factor risk mutual funds $V^{-1}B$ without the optimal idiosyncratic risk mutual fund $V^{-1}(R - \text{r})$, it is also a sufficient condition for exact APT. This demonstrates that in a risk aversion world and a finite economy, the exact APT may hold in cases when the portfolio's idiosyncratic risk cannot be diversified completely.[20]

In the case of uncorrelated idiosyncratic risk $\tilde{\varepsilon}$, however, the asset pricing model (16) might underpredict the expected excess return if the aggregative supply of assets are positive and the idiosyncratic risk is not priced.[21] The uncorrelated idiosyncratic risk assumption implies a diagonal covariance matrix V, and the positive aggregative supply implies all positive weights in the optimal portfolio X^*_m. The result is stated in the following corollary:

Corollary II.   Under a risk aversion world and a finite economy, if idiosyncratic risks are uncorrelated and the aggregate supply of assets is positive, then $R - r > B\lambda_m$.

Proof: Positive δ_m, V, and X^*_m implies $\delta_m VX^*_m > 0$ in (16). Therefore, $R - r > B\lambda_m$.

Q.E.D.

If the factor loadings is a zero matrix (i.e., $B = 0$), all optimal portfolios used in (16)–(20) reduce to an identical portfolio $V^{-1}(R - r)$, and the expected excess returns are priced by the relation, $R - r = \delta VX$. Even in the absence of common factors, a nonzero correlation of the asset returns with the return on the optimal idiosyncratic risk mutual fund $V^{-1}(R - r)$ alone can produce nonzero expected excess returns, according to the models (16)–(20). This result can be used to illustrate that a repackaging of assets would not alter the asset pricing models (16)–(20). For example, if (1) is rewritten as

$$\tilde{R} - r = R - r + BF + \tilde{\varepsilon}, \tag{1'}$$

pre-multiplying a matrix A, which satisfies $AB = 0$, to both sides of (1'), yields,

$$A(\tilde{R} - r) = A(R - r) + A\tilde{\varepsilon}. \tag{21}$$

The covariance matrix of the repackaged idiosyncratic risk, $A\tilde{\varepsilon}$, is AVA^T. With no common factors in (21), the repackaged portfolio's expected excess return, $A(R - r)$, is determined as,

$$A(R - r) = \delta\, AVA^T Y, \tag{22}$$

for an optimal portfolio Y. It is easy to show that (22) is a direct result of (5) by setting $X = A^T Y$ and after multiplying A to both sides of (5) (or (16)–(20)). Therefore, repackaging would not alter the equilibrium asset pricing models (16)–(20). The main reason for Shanken's (1982) observation that repackaging alters asset pricing is that the idiosyncratic risk premium is absent in Ross's (1976b, 1977) APT. If the idiosyncratic risk is priced according to (16)–(20), then the result is invariant to repackaging.

V. AN ERROR-BOUND DEVIATION FROM EXACT APT

The error-bound deviation from the exact APT studied by Dybvig (1983) in terms of pricing, and Grinblatt and Titman (1983) in terms of return, depends on (i) the independence of idiosyncratic risks $\tilde{\varepsilon}$, and (ii) the size of the risk aversion measure. They argue that the error bound is small relative to the measurement error in expected returns.[22] The assumption of independent idiosyncratic risks implies that all common factors are known in advance or can be correctly estimated by investigators so that there are no missing factors in (1). This may not be likely as the identification and the number of common factors in the asset market is still not resolved. For instance, Roll and Ross (1980) show a five-factor model through a factor analysis to generate the factors which were priced in the capital markets. Brown and Weinstein (1983) find that the number of common factors across securities is between three and five. Chen, Roll, and Ross (1986) document four macroeconomic variables which are significantly priced. Furthermore, Dhrymes, Friend, and Gultekin (1984) report the number of factors implied by Chi-squared tests increases as more securities are analyzed. The uncertain number of common factors may thus cause a misspecification problem. In the presence of missing factors, the error bound calculated from assuming no idiosyncratic risks may not be tenable.

Various risk aversion measures have been estimated in the literature. For example, the value of relative risk aversion measure as documented by Brown and Gibbons (1985) is 1; estimates by Hansen and Singleton (1983) range from .07 to .62; and from Ferson (1982) varies from −1.4 to 5.4. Higher figures such as those by Hall (1981) that range from −26.3 to 25.6; and from Cecchetti and Mark (1990), suggesting values that range from 14 to 30. These different risk aversion measures could produce vastly different error bounds. Another shortcoming of using risk aversion measure in error bound is that it is not observable on a daily or monthly basis. Therefore, the error bounds formulated by Grinblatt and Titman (1983) and Dybvig (1983) may not be tested with daily (or monthly) data.

In this paper an equilibrium asset pricing model (16) is used to investigate the error-bound deviation from the exact APT. A merit in using (16) is to circumvent having to explicity specify a risk aversion measure and the assumption of multi-variate normality used by Grinblatt and Titman (1983). The error bound from (16) is $R - r - B \lambda_m = \delta_m V X_m^*$. To obtain an explicit error bound, the aggregate supply portfolio X_m^* is assumed to be the mean-variance efficient market portfolio. Hence, the first equality in (14) can be used to calculate the market risk premium $\delta_m = (R_m - r)/\sigma_m^2$, where R_m is the expected market return, and σ_m^2 is the variance of market return. Ibbotson and Sinquefield (1989) document that the average expected excess return $R_m - r$ is 8.5% and the standard deviation σ_m of market return is 20.9% over the period 1926–1988. Grinblatt and Titman (1983) assume that the proportion of aggregate wealth in each asset is .1% and an asset's yearly variance of idiosyncratic risk is 20%. Substituting these figures into $\delta_m V X_m^*$, the annualized error bound in terms of return under the uncorrelated idiosyncratic risks is .0389%, which is tighter than the .2% explicit error bound calculated by Grinblatt and Titman (1983), which is good. As shown in the portfolio analysis, the importance of the individual variance of asset return diminishes drastically, whereas covariances of asset returns are more important in determining the portfolio risk as the number of assets in the portfolio becomes larger. Therefore, only a negligible error bound is to be expected if the idiosyncratic risks are indeed uncorrelated.

The ith element of VX_m^* is $cov(\tilde{\varepsilon}_i, R_m) = \rho_{im}\sigma_i\sigma_m$, where R_m is the market return, σ_i is the standard deviation of $\tilde{\varepsilon}_i$, ρ_{im} is the correlation coefficient between $\tilde{\varepsilon}_i$ and R_m, and cov(.) is the covariance operator. Now, using the same figures as above, and let correlation coefficient $\rho_{im} = .1$, the error bound increases to 1.8188%, according to $\delta_m VX_m^*$. Since 1.8188% is no longer considered small, the exact APT may not provide good approximation for expected excess returns if V is non-diago-nal.[23] The market factor which explains the major part of security return is documented by Brown (1989) and Trzcinka (1986). Their findings may be used to explain the importance of the market idiosyncratic risk $X_m^{*T}\tilde{\varepsilon}$ in (16).

Finally, we address the issue of testability of equations (16)–(20). Recall the equilibrium asset pricing models (16)–(20) are equivalent. If any one of the models is rejected, then all models (16)–(20) would also be rejected. Since an asset pricing model is equivalent to an optimal portfolio constructed from the $k + 1$ risky mutual funds, to test an asset pricing model is then equivalent to testing the optimality of the corresponding portfolios. Hence, if it is possible to construct or observe an optimal portfolio such as X_{GLS} in (9), X_{OLS} in (12), X_{MV} in (14), or the aggregate supply portfolio X_m^* in (16) from the economy, then (16)–(20) may be testable. Furthermore, the idiosyncratic risk premium δ should be positive under a risk aversion world because of the positive Lagrangian multiplier in the idiosyncratic risk constraint; a nonpositive δ would be sufficient to reject the equilibrium asset pricing models (16)–(20). For instance, (16)–(20) can be rejected if the δ_m in (16) is nonpositive.[24] Since the models presented in this paper can be applied to any finite assets economy, and since any subset of assets from the market can be used to derive the equilibrium asset pricing models like (16)–(20), if the asset return follows a linear factor model and the number of common factors is less than the number of assets in the subset, unlike the CAPM, the models (16)–(20) may be tested only on a subset of assets.

VI. CONCLUSIONS

This paper formulates the investor's portfolio choice into a quadratic programming problem to maximize the expected excess rate of return subject to both constraints on factor betas and idiosyncratic risk within a finite economy with positive definite covariance matrix of idiosyncratic risks. The necessary condition for optimal portfolio is also a sufficient condition. The mutual funds separation theorem is derived from the necessary condition. The resulting $k + 1$ risky mutual funds need not be free of idiosyncratic risk. The k factor risk mutual funds are constructed from the product of the inverse covariance matrix of idiosyncratic risks and the factor loadings, while the optimal idiosyncratic risk mutual fund is constructed from the product of the covariance matrix of idiosyncratic risks and the expected excess return vector. In addition, an aggregate portfolio is optimal but not necessarily mean-variance efficient.

The aggregation of the $k + 1$ mutual funds over all investors yields an equilibrium asset pricing model with an idiosyncratic risk premium. The approach does not assume normally distributed returns nor there be an idiosyncratic risk-free market portfolio. The resulting model allows some factors to be missed in the linear factor generating process because the effects of the missing factors on asset returns would be captured by the idiosyncratic risk factor, which is priced in our equilibrium asset pricing model.

In contrast, the necessary and sufficient condition for the exact APT is that the expected excess return's vector be linearly dependent of the factor loadings matrix. Beside the existence of an idiosyncratic risk-free optimal portfolio, the existence of either (i) an idiosyncratic risk neutral investor, or (ii) an optimal portfolio constructable from the k factor risk mutual funds is a sufficient condition for exact APT.

Since finding an optimal portfolio and deriving an equilibrium asset pricing model are equivalent, empirical tests of the asset pricing equation can be conducted by testing the optimality of the portfolio. Hence, if some optimal portfolios can be constructed or observed, then the equilibrium asset pricing models presented in this paper will also be testable in a finite economy. Furthermore, the test may be conducted by examining a one-sided test where a positive idiosyncratic risk premium supports the alternative hypothesis. What distinguishes this proposed empirical test of the APT from previous attempts is that it has a refutable hypothesis. The proposed test may be conducted under either a subset of assets or in a missing factors framework.

The error bound from the exact APT is examined under the presence of positive definite covariance matrix for idiosyncratic risks. An explicit return error bound is estimated and is shown to be negligible if all of factors can be extracted and estimated correctly. Otherwise, the error bound is found to be significantly larger and Ross's APT is no longer a good approximation for the expected excess return in a finite economy, where there are missing factors in the linear factor generating process.

ACKNOWLEDGMENT

We acknowledge helpful comments from Andrew Chen and Ko Wang. This paper was presented at the 1991 FMA annual meeting in Chicago. The usual disclaimer applies.

NOTES

1. For the reply see Dybvig and Ross (1985).
2. In this paper the exact APT is defined as the case when expected excess return's vector can be recovered from the factor loadings matrix.
3. See Lemma 1 in Grinblatt and Titman's (1987). Furthermore, as they have realized, in the limit economy these reference portfolios, which are formed from an infinite number of assets, that are unobservable (see pp. 101–102).
4. For example, Roll (1977) proves that testing the mean-variance efficiency of the market portfolio is equivalent to testing the Capital Asset Pricing Model (CAPM).
5. For a sample of conflicting empirical studies, see Roll and Ross (1980), Brown and Weinstein (1983), Dhrymes, Friend, and Gultekin (1984), Cho, Elton, and Gruber (1984), and Dhrymes, Friend, Gultekin, and Gultekin (1985a, 1985b).
6. Equations (3) and (4) consist of $k + 1$ linear equations with n variables, therefore the feasible solution set is nonempty if the number of securities n is greater than the number of factors k plus one. Furthermore, since the Lagrangian function is a quadratic function of X, the solution to the necessary condition is also the sufficient condition for the optimal solution.
7. In the optimal solution λ is determined by the constraint (3), thus b may be interpreted as a "consensus" value, which may depend on risk aversion.
8. It should be noted that mutual funds $V^{-1}(R - r)$ and $V^{-1}B$ may not have the sum of their entries equals to one. However, it is possible to rescale the mutual funds to make the sum of entries equal to one.

9.   Namely, $(BB^T + V)^{-1}B = V^{-1}B[I_k - B^T(BB^T + V)^{-1}B]$. $[BB^T + V]^{-1}B$ are the mimicking portfolios formed by Huberman and colleagues (1987, pp. 3 and 8) to serve in place of factors under the diagonal matrix V and the exact APT. Since the mimicking portfolios can be generated from the k risk mutual funds $V^{-1}B$, (i) the mimicking portfolios, $[BB^T + V]^{-1}B$, and the k mutual funds, $V^{-1}B$, may be interchangeable under the exact APT, and (ii) the results developed from mimic portfolios may extend to this paper Fama (1996) shows $[BB^T + V]^{-1}B$ are mean variance efficient portfolios.

10.   Black (1972) constructed the optimal zero beta portfolio by minimizing the variance of the idiosyncratic risk subject to the zero beta constraint.

11.   In the absence of arbitrage opportunities and a nonsingular covariance matrix of idiosyncratic risks, Ingersoll (1984) uses an alternate approach to construct a zero factor beta portfolio whose expected excess return is one and the variance is bounded in an infinite economy to prove the existence of an error bound for APT in an infinite assets economy. For detailed construction see equations (10)–(13) in Ingersoll (1984, p. 1025).

12.   As shown by Ingersoll (1984), the λ_{GLS} in (10) is not the generalized least-square estimator of λ in (5) since V is not the cross-sectional covariance structure of the residuals (see Ingersoll, 1984, p. 1024).

13.   This can be proved by applying the transpose of X_{GLS} to both sides of (5). Given the positive idiosyncratic risk premium δ under risk aversion and $X_{GLS}^T(R - r) = \delta_{GLS} > 0$, the covariance $X_{GLS}^T VX = \delta_{GLS}/\delta > 0$.

14.   It is clear that X_{OLS} is not a zero factor beta portfolio. However, X_{OLS} can be an optimal portfolio held by some investors subject to some specific constraints on factor beta and idiosyncratic risk. For example, if the constraint on the factor beta in (3) and on the idiosyncratic risk in (4) are $b_{OLS} = (R - r)^T[I - B(B^TB)^{-1}B^T]V^{-1}B$ and $\xi_{OLS} = (R - r)^T[I - B(B^TB)^{-1}B^T]V^{-1}[I - B(B^TB)^{-1}B^T](R - r)$, respectively, then X_{OLS} will be the optimal portfolio derived from maximizing its expected excess return and satisfying the factor beta and idiosyncratic risk constraints.

15.   Fama's (1996) formulation is to minimize total portfolio risk subject to different factor risks and rates of return constraints. To derive Fama portfolios (see his equation (7)) from our equation (14), set $r = 0$, the Fama portfolio $\Omega^{-1}R$, and $\Omega^{-1}B$ come from our mutual funds combinations $V^{-1}(R - r)$ and $V^{-1}B$, and $(BB^T + V)^{-1}B = V^{-1}[I - BB^T V^{-1}(I + BB^TV^{-1}]B = V^{-1}B[I - B^T V^{-1}(I + BB^TV^{-1})^{-1}B]$.

16.   If an investor's portfolio is denominated in terms of his wealth, then portfolio X in equations (2)–(4) can be replaced by wX, where w is investor's wealth. The necessary and sufficient condition (5) for the optimal portfolio becomes $R - r = B\lambda + \delta wVX$. Dividing by δ in both sides, aggregating this first order condition over all investors, defining δ_m as the total wealth in the market times the reciprocal of the summation of $1/\delta$, and λ_m as the product of the summation of λ and the reciprocal of the summation of $1/\delta$ result in the same form of (16).

17.   Substituting X_m^* by $V^{-1}B(\lambda_{GLS} - \lambda_m)/\delta_m + (\delta_{GLS}/\delta_m) X_{GLS}$, $V^{-1}B(\lambda_{OLS} - \lambda_m)/\delta_m + (\delta_{OLS}/\delta_m) X_{OLS}$, and $V^{-1}B(\lambda_{MV} - \lambda_m)/\delta_m + (\delta_{MV}/\delta_m) X_{MV}$, obtains equilibrium asset pricing models (17), (18), and (19), respectively.

18.   Namely, $\delta_{OLS} = \delta_{GLS}/X_{GLS}^T VX_{OLS}$, and $\delta_{MV} = \delta_{GLS}/X_{GLS}^T VX_{MV}$.

19.   A sufficient condition for an idiosyncratic risk-free portfolio is the existence of a derivative (or nonprimitive, see Ross, 1976a) asset.

20.   Wei (1998) obtains idiosyncratic risk-free portfolio by including an additional factor, the market excess return factor, in the return generating process. We take the more general case when all random errors are not dependent, and thus all linear combinations of these terms are still random variables and not deterministic.

21.   The same conclusion is reached by Grinblatt and Titman (1983) from maximizing the expected utility of terminal wealth under the existence of zero cost basis portfolios with no idiosyncratic risk (for details see Grinblatt & Titman, 1983, pp. 499–500).

22.   Specifically, the annualized price error bound found from Ross's APT by Dybvig (1983) is .04% under the assumption that the index of relative risk aversion is 5, while the annualized return error bound found by Grinblatt and Titman (1983) is .2% when relative risk aversion is assumed to be 2.

23.   Some readers may argue that the $\rho_{im} = 0.1$ is too high. Hence the real error bound may not be as large. Whether the $\rho_{im} = 0.1$ is too high depends on how many factors are missing in empirical modeling (1). However, even if the $\rho_{im} = .05$, the error bound is still .9094%, and it is still not small. Furthermore, as shown in (17)–(20), the equilibrium asset pricing model depends on the particular optimal portfolio. The error bound could be conceivably greater than 1% for some optimal portfolios used in asset pricing model.

24.   An alternative is to test whether or not the expected excess return, either on the optimal zero factor beta or on the mean-variance efficient portfolio, if these portfolios can be constructed, is greater than zero.

REFERENCES

Black, F. (1972). Capital market equilibrium with restrict borrowing. *Journal of Business, 40*, 444–455.

Brown, D., & Gibbons, M. (1985). A simple econometric approach for utility-based asset pricing model. *Journal of Finance, 40*, 359–381.

Brown, S. (1989). The number of factors in security returns. *Journal of Finance, 44*, 1247–1262.

Brown, S., & Weinstein, M. (1983). A new approach to testing asset pricing models: the bilinear paradigm. *Journal of Finance, 38*, 711–743.

Cecchetti, S., & Mark, N. (1990). Evaluating empirical tests of asset pricing models: alternative interpretations. *American Economic Review, 80*, 48–51.

Chamberlain, G., & Rothschild, M. (1983). Arbitrage, factor structure, and mean-variance analysis on large asset markets. *Econometrica, 51*, 1281–1304.

Chamberlain, G. (1983). Funds, factors, and diversification in arbitrage pricing models. *Econometrica, 51*, 1305–1323.

Chen, N., & Ingersoll, J. (1983). Exact pricing in linear factor models with finitely many assets: A note. *Journal of Finance, 38*, 985–988.

Chen, N., Roll, R., & Ross, S. (1986). Economic forces and the stock market. *Journal of Business, 59*, 383–403.

Cho, D., Elton, E., & Gruber, M. (1984, March). On the robustness of the roll and ross arbitrage pricing theory. *Journal of Financial and Quantitative Analysis, 19*, 1–10.

Connor, G. (1984). A unified beta pricing Theory. *Journal of Economic Theory, 34*, 13–31.

Dhrymes, P., Friend, I., & Gultekin, N. (1984). A critical reexamination of the empirical evidence on arbitrage pricing theory. *Journal of Finance, 39*, 323–346.

Dhrymes, P., Friend, I., Gultekin, N., & Gultekin, M. (1985a). An empirical examination of the implications of arbitrage pricing theory. *Journal of Banking and Finance, 9*, 73–99.

Dhrymes, P., Friend, I., Gultekin, M., & Gultekin, N. (1985b). New tests of the APT and their implications. *Journal of Finance, 40*, 659–674.

Dybvig, P. (1983, December). An explicit bound on deviations from APT pricing in a finite economy. *Journal of Financial Economics, 12*, 483–496.

Dybvig, P., & Ross, S. (1985). Yes the APT is testable. *Journal of Finance, 40*, 1173–1188.

Fama, E. (1996). Multifactor portfolio efficiency and multifactor asset pricing. *Journal of Financial and Quantitative Analysis*, 441–465.

Ferson, W. (1982). *Expected real interest rates and consumption in efficient financial markets: Theory and tests*. Ph.D Dissertation, Graduate School of Business, Stanford University.

Grinblatt, M., & Titman, S. (1983). Factor pricing in a finite economy. *Journal of Financial Economics, 12*, 497–507.

Grinblatt, M., & Titman, S. (1987). The relation between mean-variance efficiency and arbitrage pricing. *Journal of Business, 60*, 97–112.

Hall, H. (1981). *Intertemporal substitution in consumption*. Unpublished Working Paper, Department of Economics, Stanford University.

Hansen, L., & Singleton, K. (1983). Stochastic consumption, risk aversion, and the temporal behavior of asset returns. *Journal of Political Economy*, *91*, 249–265.

Huberman, G. (1982). A simple approach to arbitrage pricing theory. *Journal of Economic Theory*, *28*, 183–191.

Huberman, G., Kandel, S., & Stambaugh, R. (1987). Mimicking portfolios and exact arbitrage pricing. *Journal of Finance*, *42*, 1–9.

Ibbotson, R., & Sinquefield, R. (1989). *Stocks, Bonds and Inflation (SBBI)*. 1989 Yearbook. Chicago, IL: Ibbotson Associates.

Ingersoll, J. (1984). Some results in the theory of arbitrage pricing. *Journal of Finance*, *39*, 1021–1039.

Roll, R. (1977). A critique of the asset pricing theory's tests. *Journal of Financial Economics*, *4*, 129–176.

Roll, R., & Ross, S. (1980). An empirical investigation of the arbitrage pricing theory. *Journal of Finance*, *35*, 1073–1104.

Ross, S. (1976a). Options and efficiency. *The Quarterly Journal of Economics*, *90*, 75–89.

Ross, S. (1976b). The arbitrage theory of capital asset pricing. *Journal of Economic Theory*, *13*, 341–360.

Ross, S. (1977). Return, risk and arbitrage. In I. Friend & J. Bicksler (Eds.), *Risk and return in finance*. Cambridge, MA: Ballinger.

Ross, S. (1978). Mutual funds separation in financial theory—the separating distributions. *Journal of Economic Theory*, *17*, 454–486.

Shanken, J. (1982). The arbitrage pricing theory: Is it testable? *Journal of Finance*, *37*, 1129–1140.

Shanken, J. (1985, September). Multi-beta CAPM or equilibrium—APT?: A reply. *Journal of Finance*, *40*, 1189–1196.

Stambaugh, R. (1983). Arbitrage pricing with information. *Journal of Financial Economics*, *12*, 357–369.

Trzcinka, C. (1986). On the number of factors in the arbitrage pricing model. *Journal of Finance*, *41*, 347–368.

Wei, J. (1988). An asset-pricing theory unifying the CAPM and APT. *Journal of Finance*, *43*, 881–892.

MACROFORECASTING ACCURACY AND GAINS FROM STOCK MARKET TIMING

Kie Ann Wong, Chi-Keung Woo, and
Richard Yan-Ki Ho

ABSTRACT

This is a study to determine the levels of macroforecasting accuracy required to produce positive return advantages from market timing with large-firm or small-firm stocks at different levels of transaction costs. It is not another study on evaluating market timing performance of mutual fund managers. We find that market timing strategies could be attractive to managers of large funds. The results are sensitive to the levels of transaction costs. The returns of small-firm stocks are not necessarily higher than those of large-firm stocks after accounting for different degrees of variations in returns.

How to evaluate the performance of investments is a topic of considerable interest to both practitioners and academics. This interest reflects the immediate relevance of the subject for investors and its important implications for the theory of finance

Research in Finance, Volume 16, pages 127–139.
Copyright © 1998 by JAI Press Inc.
ISBN: 0-7623-0328-X

with respect to the efficiency of asset prices in allocating capital. As the topic is so significant, a major application of modern capital market theory is to provide a structural specification to measure investment performance. Within this structure, Fama (1972) suggests that the forecasting skills can be partitioned into two components: "microforecasting" which forecasts price movements of individual stocks relative to stocks generally, and "macroforecasting" which forecasts price movements of general stock market relative to fixed income securities. The former is frequently referred to as "stock selection" and the latter as "market timing." In other words, market timing attempts to predict equity market movements as the basis for short-term shifts into and out of common stock investments.

Treynor and Black (1973) show that investment managers can effectively separate actions related to stock selection from those related to market timing. They can vary the risk levels of their portfolios through recomposition in anticipation of general stock market movements. This is confirmed by Kon and Jen (1979) who find that many mutual funds do have discrete changes in the level of market-related risk over time. This suggests that investment managers do attempt to incorporate market timing with their portfolio strategies. Recently, a study of stock recommendations by security analysts at major U.S. brokerage firms showed that even the analysts appear to have market timing and stock selection abilities (Womack, 1996).

Most of the recent empirical studies of investment performance focus on microforecasitng and are based on a mean-variance capital asset pricing model (CAPM) framework (Fama, 1972; Jensen, 1972). Within this framework a portfolio's excess return is a linear function of the excess return on the market portfolio. Treynor and Mazuy (1966) argue that if an investment manager can forecast general stock market movements, he will hold a greater proportion of the market portfolio when the market return is high and a smaller proportion when the market return is low. Thus, the portfolio return will be a nonlinear function of the market return. Graham and Harvey (1996) analyze the advices contained in a sample of 237 investment newsletter strategies over 1980–1992. They find, however, no evidence that letters systematically increase equity weights before market rises or decrease weights before market declines.

Grant (1977) shows that in the empirical tests that focus only on microforecasting skills, market timing ability will cause the regression estimate of alpha in the standard CAPM equation to be a downward-biased measure of the excess returns resulted from microforecasting ability. Empirical findings by Chang and Lewellen (1984), Henriksson (1984), and Lee and Rahman (1990) corroborate Grant's contention. These and other studies (Roll, 1977; Admati & Ross, 1985; Dybvig & Ron, 1985; Lehmann & Modest, 1987) suggest that standard security market line tests of investment performance cannot provide reliable inferences; new techniques must be brought to bear in evaluating the performance of actively managed portfolios.

Henriksson and Merton (1981) devise a parametric and a nonparametric test for measuring market timing ability. Chang and Lewellen (1984) and Henriksson

(1984) employ the Henriksson-Merton model in evaluating mutual fund performance and find no evidence of significant market timing skill by fund managers. Kon
(1983) examines the performance of 37 mutual funds and finds that 14 had positive
overall timing estimates but none was statistically significant. Lehmann and Modest
(1987) combine a version of the arbitrage pricing theory with the Treynor and
Mazuy (1966) quadratic regression technique to evaluate portfolio performance.
They find statistically significant abnormal timing and selection performance by
mutual funds. Lee and Rahman (1990) use a modified security-market line approach developed by Bhattacharyal and Pfleiderer (1983) to produce separate
measures of timing and stock-selection ability. Their results indicate that at the
individual fund level, there is some evidence of superior market timing and selection
ability on the part of the fund manager. Coggin, Fabozzi, and Rahman (1993)
examine the selectivity and market timing performance of a sample of equity
pension fund managers. They find that the average excess return of timing measure
is negative and that of selectivity measure positive, regardless of the choice of
benchmark portfolio or estimation model. It can be summarized that there appears
to be inconsistent findings of recent studies about the market timing ability of fund
managers.

It is not our purpose here to add another piece of study in the controversy on
evaluating market timing performance of mutual fund managers. We aim at determining the level of macroforecasting accuracy required to produce positive return
advantages from market timing in conjunction with cash equivalents. The required
level of accuracy will also be determined at different levels of transaction costs for
large-firm and small-firm stocks. It is important to have reliable evidence on
whether it is possible for fund managers to beat the market through market timing
before considering what techniques should be used to evaluate their market timing
ability. According to Fuller and Kling (1994), profitable market timing models have
been difficult to identify ex ante. Brocato and Chandy (1994) also cast doubt on the
market timing argument, which claims that active timing produces superior risk-
adjusted returns relative to an unmanaged equity fund with buy-and-hold strategy.
However, Wagner, Shellans, and Paul (1992) find that the 25 market timers in their
study generated superior performance over a buy-and-hold strategy over a five-year
period in terms of variability and risk-adjusted returns.

We use a simulation approach and define "good" and "bad" periods differently
from those used by Sharpe (1975), who ignores transaction costs in his definition.[1]
We define a good period as one in which stocks have a higher return than the return
from cash equivalents (Treasury bills) plus transaction costs and a bad period as
one in which cash equivalents have a higher return than the return from stocks plus
transaction costs. Based on monthly return data for the 1975–1990 period, monthly
portfolio revisions and transaction costs of 0.5%, we find that market timing in
Treasury bills and large-firm or small-firm stocks would be successful if macroforecasting accuracy could exceed 56% of the time, a level that is probably within
the abilities of many fund managers. The results are sensitive to the level of

transaction costs. When transaction costs increase, the required forecasting accuracy also increases, probably to a level beyond the abilities of most investors.

The remainder of the paper is organized in four sections. Section I discusses the simulation model and method. Section II briefly describes the data for the study. Section III examines the results, while Section IV presents concluding remarks.

I. THE SIMULATION MODEL AND METHOD

This section describes the simulation model used to analyze the effect of transaction costs θ and prediction accuracy α on expected return $E(R_t)$ and standard deviation σ, of R_t for $t = 1, \ldots, T$.[2] To better understand this model, it is fruitful to first describe the net returns generated by a buy-and-hold (B&H) strategy when applied to two types of assets: cash (C) and stocks (S). This is followed by a discussion on the returns under perfect foresight and under imperfect prediction. The last part of this section explains the simulation process.

A. Holding Strategy

For the sake of exposition without any loss of generality, we assume a wealth-seeking investor who is endowed with cash at time 0 and wishes to hold cash at the end of time period T. Let R_{ct} and R_{st} denote the (random) returns from C and S, respectively. Under the B&H strategy the cash return for each time period is simply R_{ct}. The transaction costs for cash equivalents are not considered in our computation as the amount involved is insignificant. However, if the investor decides to hold stocks, the return for the first period R_1 is not R_{s1} because of the presence of the (one-way) transaction costs θ. To wit,

$$R_1 = [(1 + R_{s1})/(1 + \theta)] - 1 \tag{1}$$

as each \$1 of cash can only purchase \$$(1 + \theta)^{-1}$ worth of stock. For $T > t > 1$, $R_t = R_{st}$ since there is no stock purchase or sale. At the end of the period the net return is:

$$R_T = (1 + R_{sT})(1 - \theta) - 1 \tag{2}$$

because the investor receives only \$$(1 - \theta)$ of every \$1 worth of stock sold.

B. Perfect Foresight

We can extend the above line of reasoning to the case of perfect foresight. Conditional on the event R of correctly predicting the actual returns in period t, the net return in period t ($< T$) to an investor with cash holding is:

$$R_{t<T} \mid C, R = \text{Max} \{R_{ct}, [(1 + R_{st})/(1 + \theta)] - 1\} \tag{3}$$

Alternatively, if the investor's initial holding is stock, the (conditional) net return is:

$$R_{t<T} \mid S, R = \text{Max. } \{R_{st}, [(1 + R_{ct})(1 - \theta)] - 1\} \tag{4}$$

Obviously (3) and (4) implicitly define the holding at the beginning of the next period $(t + 1)$.

Though slightly different, the conditional return in period T can be derived in a similar manner. The (conditional) net return in period T to an investor with cash holding is:

$$R_T \mid C, R = \text{Max. } \{R_{ct}, [(1 + R_{st})(1 - \theta)/(1 + \theta)] - 1\} \tag{5}$$

The transaction cost term enters the right-hand side of (5) twice since switching from cash to stock then to cash involves two transactions. If the investor's initial holding is stock, the (conditional) net return is:

$$R_T \mid S, R = \text{Max. } \{[(1 + R_{ct})(1 - \theta)] - 1, [(1 + R_{st})(1 - \theta)] - 1\} \tag{6}$$

because the investor wishes to have cash at the end of the period.

C. Imperfect Prediction

It is unrealistic for an investor to possess perfect foresight. The investor may realize a lower return if he or she fails to predict the actual returns correctly. In this case the net returns conditional on initial holding and the event W of being wrong are as follows:

$$R_{t<T} \mid C, W = \text{Min. } \{R_{ct}, [(1 + R_{st})/(1 + \theta)] - 1\} \tag{7}$$

$$R_{t<T} \mid S, W = \text{Min. } \{R_{st}, [(1 + R_{ct})(1 - \theta)] - 1\} \tag{8}$$

$$R_T \mid C, W = \text{Min. } \{R_{ct}, [(1 + R_{st})(1 - \theta)/(1 + \theta)] - 1\} \tag{9}$$

and

$$R_T \mid S, W = \text{Min. } \{[(1 + R_{ct})(1 - \theta)] - 1, [(1 + R_{st})(1 - \theta)] - 1\} \tag{10}$$

D. Simulation Method

To evaluate the effect of transaction costs θ and prediction accuracy α on expected return $E(R_t)$ and risk σ, we simulate the outcomes of the strategy using the monthly return data to be described in the next section. The simulation process consists of the following steps:

Step 1: Select one value for α from {0.5, 0.6, . . . , 0.9, 1.0} to determine the number of correct prediction.[3] Select one value for θ from {0.005, 0.015, 0.03}. Finally, set J, the number of replications: J = 500 if α < 1.0; and $J = 1$, if α = 1.0 (i.e., perfect foresight).

Step 2: Assign to each monthly observation a randomly generated binary variable to indicate whether the prediction is correct. This constitutes one sample for step 3 described below.

Step 3: Determine conditional net returns using equations (3) to (10).

Step 4: For the jth replication, compute the sample mean x_j and variance s_j^2 using the (conditional) net returns found from step 3.

Step 5: Go to step 2 if $j < J$; otherwise, go to step 6.

Step 6: Compute $(\Sigma_j x_j / J)$ and $(\Sigma_j s_j^2 / J)$ which are maximum likelihood estimates of $E(R_t)$ and σ^2 for a given pair of θ and α.

II. DATA

The data series used in this study are the monthly returns for cash equivalents, large-firm stocks, and small-firm stocks over the 1975–1990 period, complied by Ibbotson Associates. The returns on cash equivalents and large-firm stocks are represented by the total returns on 30-day U.S. Treasury bills and the S&P 500 Composite Index, respectively. The returns on small-firm stocks are represented by the total returns on the stock price index of small companies as complied by Dimensional Fund Advisors (DFA) Small Company Fund.

In this paper the average monthly returns over the 1975–1990 period on a timing strategy with monthly portfolio revisions are examined and compared with a buy-and-hold stocks strategy. In addition, we conduct a sensitivity analysis to determine the effect of transaction costs on returns. Transaction costs of 0.5, 1.5, and 3% are used for shifts from one asset class to another. The 0.5% is considered to be more representative of the transaction costs incurred by large institutional investors, while 1.5% to be more representative of the transaction costs by small trust funds and large individual investors. The 3% is considered to be the transaction costs incurred by small individual investors.

III. RESULTS

As shown in Table 1, with transaction costs of 0.5%, the average monthly returns by holding small-firm stocks were 1.72%, compared with 1.29% for large-firm stocks, a difference of 0.43%. The returns for small-firm stocks were also more disperse, as measured by the standard deviation of returns, 6.36% for small-firm

Table 1. Investment Strategies and Monthly Returns by Market Timing Accuracy
with Transaction Costs of 0.5 percent Sample Period:
January 1975 to December 1990

Investment Strategy	Timing Accuracy	Proportion Holding Stocks[a]	Mean Returns[b]	t-Statistics	Standard Deviation[c]	Mean Returns/std Deviation
Holding Treasury bills		0.0000	0.00654	40.5134	0.00224	2.9238
S & P 500 Stocks						
Holding Stocks[d]		1.0000	0.01292	3.8907	0.04600	0.2808
Market Timing:						
A	1.0	0.5625	0.02503	12.2053	0.02841	0.8808
B	.9	0.5493	0.02129	9.7692	0.03020	0.7050
C	.8	0.5363	0.01780	7.8348	0.03148	0.5654
D	.7	0.5235	0.01425	6.1179	0.03227	0.4415
E	.6	0.5126	0.01076	4.5490	0.03277	0.3283
F	.5	0.5005	0.00729	3.0968	0.03263	0.2235
Small-Firm Stocks						
Holding Stocks[d]		1.0000	0.01723	3.7507	0.06364	0.2707
Market Timing:						
A	1.0	0.5990	0.03273	11.1284	0.04076	0.8031
B	.9	0.5755	0.02778	8.9776	0.04287	0.6479
C	.8	0.5553	0.02309	7.2316	0.04424	0.5219
D	.7	0.5342	0.01845	5.6784	0.04502	0.4098
E	.6	0.5153	0.01391	4.2642	0.04520	0.3077
F	.5	0.4996	0.00935	2.8586	0.04531	0.2063

Notes: [a]Number of months holding stocks/192 months.
[b]Sample average if timing accuracy = 1.0; mean of 500 sample averages if timing accuracy < 1.0.
[c]Sample standard deviation if timing accuracy = 1.0; square-root of mean of 500 sample variances if timing accuracy < 1.0.

stocks versus 4.6% for large-firm stocks. The results are similar when the transaction costs increase to 1.5 and 3%, respectively (as shown in Tables 2 and 3). Investing in Treasury bills provides the lowest average monthly returns (0.65%) and variability of returns (0.22%). This result is expected as Treasury bills were often treated as risk-free assets.

Table 1 also shows the average monthly return with market timing accuracy ranging from perfect market timing (timing accuracy = 1.0) to being accurate half of the time (timing accuracy = 0.5) for large-firm stocks and for small-firm stocks. The average monthly returns of a buy-and-hold strategy of the respective type of stocks are also presented. The monthly return advantage from perfect market timing

Table 2. Investment Strategies and Monthly Returns by Market Timing Accuracy
with Transaction Costs of 1.5 percent Sample Period:
January 1975 to December 1990

Investment Strategy	Timing Accuracy	Proportion Holding Stocks[a]	Mean Returns[b]	t-Statistics	Standard Deviation[c]	Mean Returns/std Deviation
Holding Treasury bills		0.0000	0.00654	40.5134	0.00224	2.9238
S & P 500 Stocks						
Holding Stocks[d]		1.0000	0.01280	3.8684	0.04587	0.2792
Market Timing:						
A	1.0	0.6250	0.02037	9.5941	0.02943	0.6924
B	.9	0.5858	0.01663	7.4745	0.03082	0.5394
C	.8	0.5584	0.01304	5.6378	0.03204	0.4069
D	.7	0.5328	0.00959	4.0699	0.03267	0.2937
E	.6	0.5127	0.00586	2.4438	0.03323	0.1764
F	.5	0.4994	0.00215	0.8922	0.03342	0.0644
Small-Firm Stocks						
Holding Stocks[d]		1.0000	0.01711	3.7395	0.06339	0.2699
Market Timing:						
A	1.0	0.6198	0.02863	9.6708	0.04102	0.6979
B	.9	0.5880	0.02351	7.5753	0.04301	0.5467
C	.8	0.5642	0.01868	5.8206	0.04447	0.4201
D	.7	0.5385	0.01386	4.2349	0.04535	0.3056
E	.6	0.5164	0.00906	2.7368	0.04587	0.1975
F	.5	0.5034	0.00430	1.3042	0.04563	0.0941

Notes: [a]Number of months holding stocks/192 months.

[b]Sample average if timing accuracy = 1.0; mean of 500 sample averages if timing accuracy < 1.0.
[c]Sample standard deviation if timing accuracy = 1.0; square-root of mean of 500 sample variances if timing accuracy < 1.0.

strategy with large-firm stocks was 1.21% over a buy-and-hold strategy and was 1.85% over holding Treasury bills given transaction costs of 0.5%. The selection of asset classes used for market timing has a significant effect on the results. The monthly return advantage from perfect market timing with small-firm stocks was 1.55% over a buy-and-hold strategy and 2.62% over holding Treasury bills. The monthly return advantage from perfect market timing with small-firm stocks over large-firm stocks was 0.77%. This result clearly indicates that if the transaction costs are the same, the selection of small-firm stocks for market timing is more profitable than the selection of large-firm stocks before taking the risk factor into consideration. As shown in Tables 2 and 3, similar results are obtained when the transaction costs increase to 1.5 and 3%, respectively. If the transaction costs of

Table 3. Investment Strategies and Monthly Returns by Market Timing Accuracy
with Transaction Costs of 3 percent Sample Period:
January 1975 to December 1990

Investment Strategy	Timing Accuracy	Proportion Holding Stocks[a]	Mean Returns[b]	t-Statistics	Standard Deviation[c]	Mean Returns/std Deviation
Holding Treasury bills		0.0000	0.00654	40.5134	0.00224	2.9238
S & P 500 Stocks						
Holding Stocks[d]		1.0000	0.01264	3.8310	0.04572	0.2765
Market Timing:						
A	1.0	0.6406	0.01672	7.7153	0.03003	0.5568
B	.9	0.5885	0.01179	5.1606	0.03166	0.3724
C	.8	0.5574	0.00751	3.1209	0.03333	0.2252
D	.7	0.5311	0.00323	1.2981	0.03443	0.0937
E	.6	0.5136	–0.00109	–0.4303	0.03515	–0.0311
F	.5	0.5005	–0.00531	–2.0708	0.03554	–0.1494
Small-Firm Stocks						
Holding Stocks[d]		1.0000	0.01693	3.7203	0.06307	0.2685
Market Timing:						
A	1.0	0.6406	0.02458	8.1989	0.04155	0.5917
B	.9	0.5888	0.01855	5.8463	0.04397	0.4219
C	.8	0.5565	0.01294	3.9389	0.04552	0.2843
D	.7	0.5348	0.00736	2.1868	0.04666	0.1578
E	.6	0.5162	0.00205	0.6060	0.04688	0.0437
F	.5	0.4996	–0.00316	–0.9352	0.04686	–0.0675

Notes: [a]Number of months holding stocks/192 months.

[b]Sample average if timing accuracy = 1.0; mean of 500 sample averages if timing accuracy < 1.0.
[c]Sample standard deviation if timing accuracy = 1.0; square-root of mean of 500 sample variances if timing accuracy < 1.0.

small-firm stocks are 1.0% higher than that of large-firm stocks, the market timing accuracy has to be above 75% for small-firm stocks to perform better than large-firm stocks before accounting for risk difference (refer to Tables 1 and 2).

To take into consideration the different levels of risk involved in different market timing strategies, the average monthly returns per unit of risk (standard deviation) are computed for comparison purposes. The results are shown in the last column of Tables 1, 2, and 3. It can be seen that the monthly return advantage after risk adjustment is the reverse of that before the risk adjustment, given transaction costs of 0.5%. The performance of perfect market timing strategy with large-firm stocks was better than that with small-firm stocks. However, the results are mixed when the transaction costs increase to 1.5 and 3%, respectively. There is no obvious difference in return advantage per unit of risk with transaction costs of 1.5%. For transaction costs of 3%, the perfect market timing strategy with small-firm stocks performs better than that with large-firm stocks after risk adjustment.

The above discussion was based on the idealistic assumption of perfect market timing. The benefits of market timing with large-firm stocks or small-firm stocks, if successful, are attractive. However, two questions remain to be answered: Is the level of macroforecasting skill needed for successful market timing attainable by an average investor? Is the minimum required forecasting accuracy significantly affected by the level of transaction costs?

With the assumption of equal accuracy in forecasting "good" and "bad" periods and same transaction costs for small-firm and large-firm stocks, we use historical returns data and the simulation model developed in Section I to generate net expected monthly returns (after transaction costs) at five different levels of predictive accuracy (0.9, 0.8, 0.7, 0.6, and 0.5) for each of the three different levels of transaction costs (0.5, 1.5, and 3%). These are computed by 500 rounds of simulation for each of the two asset-class combinations: large-firm stocks with Treasury bills and small-firm stocks with Treasury bills. To determine the return advantages (or disadvantages) of market timing strategy at different levels of predictive accuracy, the net expected returns are compared with the average monthly returns (after transaction costs) of the buy-and-hold stocks strategy. From these comparisons, the approximate minimum levels of predictive accuracy required to produce positive return advantages from market timing with each asset-class combination and each level of transaction costs are determined. These results are also presented in Tables 1, 2, and 3.

Table 1 shows that with monthly portfolio revisions and transaction costs of 0.5%, the minimum required predictive accuracy over the 1975–1990 period is about 67% for timing large-firm stocks and about 66% for timing small-firm stocks before taking risk into consideration. The return advantage from timing small-firm stocks is smaller after adjusting for risk difference as measured by average returns per standard deviation (as shown in the last column of Table 1), and the minimum required predictive accuracy is significantly lower based on adjusted returns. With these adjusted returns, the minimum required predictive accuracy is about 56% for timing large-firm stocks and about 57% for timing small-firm stocks, a level that is likely to be within the ability of many professional managers of large funds. However, the data in Tables 2 and 3 show that, as the level of transaction costs increases, the minimum required predictive accuracy needed for successful market timing also increases. It is interesting to note that the variations in returns stabilize for both large-firm stocks and small-firm stocks when the predictive accuracy of timing drops to 70% and below though the mean returns decline substantially.

The minimum required predictive accuracy for timing large-firm and small-firm stocks is very sensitive to the level of transaction costs. With transaction costs of

1.5%, the minimum predictive accuracy increases to about 80% for large-firm stocks and to about 77% for small-firm stocks before adjusting for risk difference. The respective percentage decreases to about 67% for both large-firm and small-firm stocks based on adjusted returns. The minimum predictive accuracy increases to a level beyond the reach of both fund managers and individual investors given the transaction costs of 3%. Based on adjusted returns, the minimum predictive accuracy is about 83% for large-firm stocks and about 79% for small-firm stocks, not to mention the required accuracy based on returns before adjusting for risk difference.

The above analyses may suffer from two weaknesses: (a) the transaction costs (including bid-ask spreads) for small-firm stocks are likely to be higher than that for large-firm stocks; (b) the survival bias of the stock price index of small firms is different from that of the S&P 500 Composite Index. However, it is believed that these two weaknesses would not alter our results; that the returns from market timing small-firm stocks are not necessarily higher than those from large-firm stocks after adjusting for different risk involved. If the transaction costs of small-firm stocks are higher, then the returns for small-firm stocks presented in Tables 1, 2, and 3 will be somewhat lower. This is clear when we compare the results for large-firm stocks at 0.5% transaction costs in Table 1 with those for small-firm stocks at 1.5% transaction costs in Table 2. As for survival bias, it is likely that the returns for large-firm stocks would be more favorably affected as the mortality rate of large firms is lower than that of small firms.

IV. CONCLUSION

Based on monthly return data for the 1975–1990 period in the U.S. stock market, a monthly portfolio revision strategy, and transaction costs of 0.5%, we find that market timing returns (after accounting for risk difference) for large-firm or small-firm stocks are attractive if macroforecasting accuracy is more than 56% of the time, which could be attainable by fund managers. This result is sensitive to the level of transaction costs. For investors who pay a transaction cost of higher than 1.5%, the minimum required forecasting accuracy is probably beyond the abilities of most if not all of them.

There is not much difference in required predictive accuracy between the timing of large-firm stocks and small-firm stocks for a given level of transaction costs. Beyond the minimum required predictive accuracy, the return advantages are sensitive with the increase in predictive accuracy, with the sensitivity of large-firm stocks being greater than that of small-firm stocks. The returns of small-firm stocks are not necessarily higher than those of large-firm stocks after accounting for different degrees of return variations. This is especially clear when the difference in transaction costs for large-firm and small-firm stocks is taken into consideration.

NOTES

1. Sharpe (1975) defines a "good" year as one in which stocks have a higher return (including dividends) than cash equivalents (Treasury bills), and a "bad" year as one in which cash equivalents have a higher return than stocks (S&P Composite Index). These definitions are adopted in subsequent studies by Jeffrey (1984), Droms (1989), and Kester (1990). Using a simple characterization for a complex process, Sharpe (1975, p. 67) concludes that "unless a manager can predict whether the market will be good or bad each year with considerable accuracy (e.g., be right at least seven times out of 10), he should probably avoid attempts to time the market altogether." Jeffrey (1984) shows that the risks inherent in market timing outweigh the rewards to be gained from it. Using more updated data and less restrictive assumptions, Droms (1989) and Kester (1990) find that the potential gains from market timing are higher than that reported by Sharpe (about 5%) and required prediction accuracy for successful timing is lower.

2. It is appropriate to use standard deviation as a measure of risk as we are using a portfolio of S&P 500 stocks or small-firm stocks which is composed of a large number of stocks.

3. For instance, if there are 192 monthly observations for a 16-year period, for a 10% accuracy level the number of correct predictions is 20 (= .1 × 192).

REFERENCES

Admati, A. R., & Ross, S. A. (1985). Measuring investment performance in a rational expectations equilibrium model. *Journal of Business, 58*, 1–26.

Bhattacharya, S., & Pfleiderer, P. (1983). A note on performance evaluation. *Technical Report 714*. California: Stanford University, Graduate School of Business.

Brocato, J., & Chandy, P. R. (1994). Does market timing really work on the real world? *Journal of Portfolio Management, 20*(2), 39–44.

Chang, E. C., & Lewellen, W. G. (1984). Market timing and mutual fund investment performance. *Journal of Business, 57*, 57–72.

Coggin, T. D., Fabozzi, F. J., & Rahman, S. (1993). The investment performance of U.S. equity pension fund managers: An empirical investigation. *Journal of Finance, 48*, 1039–1055.

Droms, W. G. (1989, January/February). Market timing as an investment policy. *Financial Analysts Journal*, 73–77.

Dybvig, P. H., & Ross, S. A. (1985). Differential information and performance measurement using a security market line. *Journal of Finance, 40*, 383–399.

Fama, E. F. (1972). Components of investment performance. *Journal of Finance, 27*, 551–567.

Fuller, R. J., & Kling, J. K. (1994). Can regresion-based models predict stock and bond returns? *Journal of Portfolio Management, 20* (3), 55–63.

Graham, J. R., & Harvey, C. R. (1996). Market timing ability and volatility implied in investment newsletters' asset allocation recommendations. *Journal of Financial Economics, 42*, 397–421.

Grant, D. (1977) Portfolio performance and the cost of timing decisions, *Journal of Finance, 32*, 837–846.

Henriksson, R. D. (1984). Market timing and mutual fund performance: An empirical investigation. *Journal of Business, 57*, 73–96.

Henriksson, R. D., & Merton, R. C. (1981). On market timing and investment performance II: Statistical procedures for evaluating forecasting skills. *Journal of Business, 54*, 513–533.

Jeffrey, R. H. (1984, July/August). The folly of stock market timing. *Harvard Business Review*, 102–110.

Jensen, M. C. (1972). Optimal utilization of market forecasts and the evaluation of investment performance. In G. P. Szogo & K. Sheel (Eds.), *Mathematical Methods in Investment and Finance*. Amsterdam: Elsevier.

Kester, G. W. (1990, September/October). Market timing with small versus large-firm stocks: Potential gains and required predictive ability. *Financial Analysts Journal*, 63–69.

Kon, S. J. (1983). The market timing performance of mutual fund managers. *Journal of Business, 56*, 323–347.

Kon, S. J., & Jen, F. C. (1979). The investment performance of mutual funds: An empirical investigation of timing, selectivity and market efficiency. *Journal of Business, 52*, 263–289.

Lee, C. F., & Rahman, S. (1990). Market timing, selectivity, and mutual fund performance: An empirical investigation. *Journal of Business, 63*, 261–278.

Lehman, B. N., & Modest, D. M. (1987). Mutual fund performance evaluation: A comparison of benchmarks and benchmarket comparisons. *Journal of Finance, 42*, 233–265.

Roll, R. W. (1977). A critique of the asset pricing theory's tests—Part I: On past and potential testability of the theory. *Journal of Financial Economics, 4*, 129–176.

Sharpe, W. F. (1975, March/April). Likely gains from market timing. *Financial Analysts Journal*, 60–69.

Treynor, J. L., & Black, F. (1973) How to use security analysis to improve portfolio selection. *Journal of Business, 46*, 66–86.

Treynor, J. L., & Mazuy, K. K. (1966, July/August) Can mutual funds outguess the market? *Harvard Business Review*, 131–136.

Wagner, J., Shellans, S., & Paul, R. (1992). Market timing works where it matters most in the real world. *Journal of Portfolio Management, 18*(4), 86–90.

Womack, K. L. (1996). Do brokerage analysts' recommendations have investment value? *Journal of Finance, 51*, 137–167.

THE EFFECT OF SEASONED EQUITY
OFFERINGS ON STOCK PRICES:
A CASE OF DIVERSIFICATION VERSUS GROWTH
OPPORTUNITIES

Sia Nassiripour, Khondkar E. Karim,
Philip H. Siegel, and Mojib U. Ahmed

ABSTRACT

This paper examines the market reaction to the seasoned equity offerings after controlling for corporate diversification and growth opportunities. The results of studies that investigate the market reaction to the announcement of seasoned equity offerings are inconclusive. The mixed results indicate that the models used in prior studies had misspecification problems due to omitted variables. This paper uses alternative measures of corporate diversification and growth opportunities. The results show an insignificant relationship between growth opportunities and the value of the firm. However, the results demonstrate a significant negative market reaction to the issue of seasoned equity by diversified firms.

Research in Finance, Volume 16, pages 141–156.
Copyright © 1998 by JAI Press Inc.
All rights of reproduction in any form reserved.
ISBN: 0-7623-0328-X

I. INTRODUCTION

This paper investigates the market reaction to seasoned equity offerings after controlling for growth opportunities and level of diversification. The results of studies that investigate the market reaction to the announcement of seasoned equity offerings are inconclusive. The mixed results indicate that the models used in prior studies had misspecification problems due to omitted variables.

Most papers studying the market reaction to announcement of equity offerings have reported a negative abnormal return (Asquith & Mullins, 1986; Barclay & Litzenberger, 1988; Eckbo & Masulis, 1992; Hess & Bhagat, 1986; Kalay & Shimrat, 1987; Mikkelson & Partch, 1985). The explanations provided for this negative reaction rely on the theory of the nature of negative information conveyed to the market. New offerings may signal overvaluation of the firm's assets (Myers & Majluf, 1984); the inability of the firm to generate funds internally (Miller & Rock, 1985); or the overinvestment of free cash flow (Jensen, 1986).

Other theories predict a positive relationship between the profitability of investment opportunities and the announcement effects of equity offerings. The signaling model of Ambarish, John, and William (1987) and the free cash-flow theory of Jensen (1986) predict that the market would react positively to equity offerings of high-growth firms. The adverse selection-based models of Myers and Majluf (1984) and Choe, Masulis, and Nanda (1993) also predict that the usual negative announcement effect will be attenuated if the market believes that the issuing firm has the opportunity to undertake profitable investments.

Several studies have reported positive market reaction upon the issues of new equity. Pilotte (1992) reported the effect of growth opportunities to be a possible factor for the positive market reaction. Cooney and Kalay (1993), using a model based on Myers and Majluf's (1984) pecking order hypothesis, reported a positive market reaction to the announcement of seasoned equity offering by high-growth firms. Denis (1994) also found a positive relationship between various growth proxies and announcement-period price changes for a very small sample of high-growth firms. However, he concluded that something other than growth opportunities must explain the cross-sectional variations in market reactions to seasoned equity offering announcements.[1]

This paper also examines the role of diversification in explaining market reaction to the issue of new equity. Weston (1970) proposed that diversified firms are capable of allocating resources more efficiently because they create a larger internal market. He contends that resource allocation is more efficient in an internal rather than in an external market. Lewellen (1971) showed the benefit of coinsurance through diversification and found that diversified firms have greater debt capacity. Chandler (1977) found that a multidivisional firm would be able to create specialized divisions and thus will benefit from inherent efficiency. Stulz (1990) showed that diversified firms, by creating a larger internal market, reduce the underinvestment problem described by Myers (1977). Therefore it can be argued that the market should react positively to less focused (i.e., diversified) firms when issuing equity.

Jensen (1986) argues that as long as lines of business have access to more cash flow as a part of a diversified firm than on their own, the diversified firms invest more in negative net present value projects than their segments would if operated independently. Meyer, Milgrom, and Roberts (1992) extended Jensen (1986), as well, by proposing that unprofitable lines of business create greater value losses in conglomerates than they would in single-industry firms. Myerson (1982) and Harris, Kreiebel, and Raviv (1982) examined the information asymmetry cost between central management and divisional managers in decentralized firms. They hypothesized that information asymmetry costs are higher in conglomerates than in more focused firms; since information is more dispersed within the conglomerates. Therefore, they propose that diversified firms are less profitable than their lines of business would be if operated independently.

The above studies all predict a negative market reaction to the issue of new equity by diversified firms. Based on the assertions made by the proponents of the focus theory there should be a positive (negative) relationship between more (less) focused (i.e., less diversified) firms issuing equity and abnormal market returns. Comment and Jarrell (1995), Lang and Stulz (1995), and Berger and Ofek (1995) show that an increase in focus results in an increase in market value. Contrary to the above finding, John and Ofek (1995) find that increased focus is a significant deterrent of seller's gains from asset sales. This paper reexamines the market reaction to focus increasing (decreasing) firms issuing equity by using different proxies for measuring focus.

Our overall results fail to support the focus theory. Our sample firms that increase their focus by reducing the number of segments do not show any significant increase in their market value. However, our cross-sectional regression of the overall sample supports the diversification theory. We observe that the focus-increasing variables have significant negative coefficients when regressed on three days abnormal returns around the event date. We also use other variables to control for factors such as growth opportunities, agency theory, and investment profile. None of these variables are independently significant when regressed on three days abnormal returns around the event date except the proxy for the agency theory measured by ratio of issue proceeds to the value of common stock outstanding ($PRCD\_SO$). Jensen (1986) explains that season equity offerings increase the free cash flow in the hand of managers, thus creating a negative market reaction to such issues. The $PRCD\_SO$ coefficient is highly significant and negative, and confirms this view.

Test results did not show any significant relationship between growth opportunities and segment information and the value of the firm. These results are similar to the Denis (1994) study, which concluded that something other than growth and focus is more prevailing in the determination of the impact of such offerings.

The remainder of this paper is organized as follows. The data collection is described in Section II. The methodology is developed in Section III. The empirical findings are reported in Section IV. Section V concludes the paper.

II. DATA COLLECTION

The initial sample contains seasoned equity offerings for the period 1991 through 1994. The sample was collected from the August 1995 issue of *Compact Disclosure* on new issues, which contains new financing announcement dates from 1991 through July 1995. *Compact Disclosure* reports four different dates associated with each issue, however, in most cases all dates were not available.[2] The registration date was used as the event date except when the registration date was not available then the earliest date among other dates was taken as the event date.

Sample firms were matched with Compustat Annual Industrial Tape-1994 and Center for Research on Security Prices (CRSP) daily records of stock price and return tape-1994. Compustat's CD-ROM was used to collect segment data since the annual industrial tape does not contain segment data. Firms listed on the National Association of Security Dealers Automated Quotations (NASDAQ) as well as New York Stock Exchange (NYSE) and American Exchange (AMEX) were included in the sample to overcome the limitation of not including firms in the over-the-counter (OTC) market (Brous & Kini, 1992; Barclay & Litzenberger, 1988).

In the first phase of selecting sample firms, all public utilities and financial companies including banks, financial services, and insurance companies were deleted in compliance with previous studies in this area.[3] This brought the sample down to 557 from 1,122 issues available in the disclosure database. The final sample of firms were selected based on the following criteria:

1. If there was more than one issue per issuer within the sample period, then each issue must be at least 730 days apart, so that the impact of one issue on the market as well as in the financial statement of the issuers would not effect the other issue. If two subsequent issues are less than 730 days apart but more than 365 days apart, the second issue was dropped from the sample. If both issues were within 365 days of each other, then both issues were dropped from the sample.[4]
2. In order to accommodate a 30-day post-event period in the initial 61-day event window, any issue with an event date after November 30, 1994 was also eliminated.[5]
3. In order to be included in the study a firm must have both price and return data in the CRSP daily master data file and segment data in the Compustat CD-ROM.

Table 1. The Distribution of Sample by Event Year and Type of Issue (primary vs combined) and by Exchange where it is Traded

Exchange	1991	1992	1993	1994	Total
NYSE & AMEX	1	10	97	46	154
NASDAQ	0	5	63	22	90
Issue Type					
Primary	1	10	108	45	164
Combined	0	5	52	23	80
Total	1	15	160	68	244

The final sample size consisted of 244 issue announcements of which 154 firms were listed in the NYSE and AMEX, with the remaining 90 firms listed on the NASDAQ. Out of 244 issue announcements, 164 issues were exclusively primary issues while 80 issues were combined primary and secondary issues. Table 1 contains the sample breakdown by year.

III. METHODOLOGY

This study uses Tobin's Q as a basis for understanding a firm's growth opportunities. Tobin's Q is the ratio of the market value of a firm to the replacement cost of its assets. Tobin (1969) introduced this ratio in order to examine the causal relationship between Q and investment. He argues that if at the margin Q exceeded unity, a firm would have incentive to invest since the value of its new capital investment would exceed its cost. If all such investment opportunities are exploited, the marginal value of Q should tend toward unity.[6,7] This paper uses the sample firms Q ratio as well as industry median adjusted Q ratio to distinguish between firms that have and do not have future growth opportunities. High (low) Q firms are those which possess favorable (unfavorable) growth at the time of making seasoned equity offering.

The calculation of Tobin's Q is practically impossible due to the nonavailability of replacement cost estimated for the sample firms. The procedure used by Lindenberg and Ross (1981) to estimate Tobin's Q is also very complicated due to the difficult computational efforts and the problem of data availability. Chung and Pruitt (1994) developed a simple formula to approximate Lindenberg and Ross's estimate of Tobin's Q.[8] The primary advantage of this method is that all data needed to calculate Tobin's Q is readily available in the Compustat annual database, and that approximation is capable of explaining 96.9% of the variability of Lindenberg and Ross's method of approximating Q. Therefore, Chung and Pruitt's approximation was employed.

A calculated Tobin's Q of the firms was adjusted by using the industry median of Tobin's Q. Event year was defined as the financial year within which a firm made the equity issue announcement. Out of 244 issue firms during the sample period, 90 issue firms had a Tobin's Q greater than one. The remaining 154 issue firms had Tobin's Q of equal or less than one. When calculated Tobin's Q were adjusted for industry median, 154 issue firms had Tobin's Q greater than zero and 90 issue firms had negative Tobin's Q. A more restricted definition of growth proxy was used in this paper. A firm is labeled a high-Q firm (one which possesses greater growth opportunities) if and only if its Tobin's Q is greater than one and the industry median adjusted Q is greater than zero. Using this classification, 88 firms were grouped into high-Q firms and 156 firms into the low-Q firms group.

Segment information was used as a proxy for measuring the level of a firm's diversification. If a firm had decreased (increased) its number of segments in the recent past (last two years) the firm was classified as a high (low) focus in diversification. Furthermore, those firms that decrease the number of segments were classified as focus-increasing firms. Diversification theories predict that a decrease in diversification should have a negative impact on the value of a firm. However, the proponents of focus theory argue that an increase in focus, measured as a decrease in the number of segments, would have a positive impact on the value of a firm resulting from a positive market return.

Compustat database was used to calculate the two measures of focus. The first measure was the number of lines of business reported by Compustat as indicated by the four-digit SIC codes assigned to each firm. Compustat assigns as many as two four-digit SIC codes to each segment. The second measure was a net sales based on the Herfindahl index[9] which indicates the degree to which revenues are concentrated in just a few of a company's business segments. It is calculated across n business segments as the sum of squares of each segment (i's) sales, S_i, as a proportion of total sales:

$$H_t = \sum_{i=1}^{n} - \left(S_{it} / - \sum_{i=1}^{n} S_{it} \right)^2$$

where H_t takes values between zero and one. The closer H_t is to one, the more concentrated is the firm's sales within a few segments, and therefore the more focused its operations. The change in focus was calculated as the first and second difference in H_t, the t subscript representing the period in consideration.

High (low)-focused firms were defined as those that have H in the event year greater (less) than the median H in the event period for the entire sample. As an alternative measure, median number of segments in each industry was calculated in the event period and if the number of segments of a firm were greater (less) than the median we classified that firm as a high (low)-focused firm. In order to determine if focus has increased in the event period, an increasing focus firm was classified as a firm that has increased its focus in the event period when compared with its two preceding years. Out of 244 sample issue firms, 193 issue firms did not increase their focus over the previous two-year period in relation to the event period.[10]

The stock market reaction to seasoned equity offering announcements was measured using daily excess stock returns. These excess returns were estimated from the daily stock return file provided by CRSP tape. The daily excess return for any security was estimated as

$$AR_{jt} = R_{jt} - (\alpha_j - \beta_j R_{mt})^{11,12}$$

where

$t =$ day measured relative to the event,

$AR_{jt} =$ excess return to security j for day t,

$R_{jt} =$ return on security j during day t,

$R_{mt} =$ daily equally weighted index for all common stocks on NYSE and AMEX and NASDAQ firms on the CRSP tape on the event date t (a proxy for the market portfolio of the risky assets)

$\alpha_j =$ estimated period intercept of firm j

$\beta_j =$ OLS estimates of firm j's market model parameters.

A 120-day estimation window was used for the estimation of the market model parameters, and a 61-day event window was used for capturing the announcement effect of seasoned equity offerings on the daily return of the issuer stock. Five cumulative abnormal returns (CAR) – CAR_00(event day) $CAR\_10(-1,0)$, $CAR\_01(0,1)$ $CAR\_11(-1.1)$, $CAR\_51(-5,0)$ and $CAR\_55(-5,5)$ were calculated. Day 0 was the announcement day.

Cross-sectional regression was used to examine the relationship between the segment parameter and other parameters. The impact on the value of the firm was measured as three days abnormal returns around the event date. The sample firms were partioned by the level of growth opportunities and degree of corporate diversification.

IV. RESULTS

Table 2 indicates that there is no significant difference in cumulative abnormal returns around the event date when the sample was grouped by growth proxy (high Q vs. low Q). High-Q firms were those firms which have a Q ratio greater than one and an industry median adjusted Q ratio greater than zero. Three different measures of Q ratio (Q ratio greater than one, Q ratio greater than respective industry median, and both Q ratio greater than one and industry median adjusted Q ratio greater than zero) were used.

There was no significant difference in abnormal returns between the firms when they were grouped based on the level of focus.[13] Similarly, the number of segments

Table 2. Cumulative Average Abnormal Returns around the Event Date for Overall Sample. High-q firms are defined as firms with both Q ratio greater than 1 and industry median adjusted Q ratio greater than 0 in the year before the seasoned equity offering in the sample period. Focus increasing firms (Incsng_HI) are those firms that have increased their focus by reducing the number of segments their business operations over the last two years. That is in the event period the Herfindahl index must be smaller than either the year before or two years before the event period.

Event Date	Overall (n = 244)	High_Q (n = 88)	Low_Q (n = 156)	Difference	Incsng_HI (n = 50)	Dcrsng_HI (n = 194)	Difference
(0,0)	-0.017454[a]	-0.015018[a]	-0.018829[a]	0.003811	-0.015601[a]	-0.017932[a]	0.002331
(0,1)	-0.025353[a]	-0.018508[a]	-0.029214[a]	0.010706	-0.018233[a]	-0.027188[a]	0.008955
(-1,0)	-0.017580[a]	-0.017704[a]	-0.017511[a]	-0.000190	-0.015628[b]	-0.018083[a]	0.002455
(-1,1)	0.025479[a]	-0.021194[b]	-0.027896[a]	0.006702	-0.018260[b]	-0.027339[a]	0.009079
(-5,5)	-0.035393[a]	-0.036942[b]	-0.029724[a]	-0.007220	-0.024628[b]	-0.038168[a]	0.013540

Notes: [a] Significant at less than 1% level.
[b] Significant at less than 5% level but not less than 1% level.
[c] Significant at less than 10% level but not less than 5% level.

were used, as well as Herfindahl index to proxy for focus increase. Although these results are not reported they are consistent with the results reported in Table 2.[14]

Table 3 shows the market reaction using Herfindahl Index as the Proxy for the level of focus as the only controlling variable. Firms were classified as high (low)-focus firms if the firms had a Herfindahl index greater (less) than the sample median. The market reaction for high focus firms was significantly different from the low focus firms.

Table 3 shows that there is a significant differential impact of seasoned equity offerings based on the level of focus at the event period. Further, the impacts of growth were more negative for the high-focus (less-diversified) firms than low-focus (greater diversification) firms. These results lend support to the diversification theory, and thus, refute the focus theory which advocates that the increase in focus gives the market a signal that firms are now more efficient. The other proxy for number of segments (the number of segments reported by Compustat) were also similar, therefore, these results are reported here.

The sample once more was grouped by the level of focus, and of growth opportunities. This was done to investigate whether both high-Q and low-Q firms have similar market impact when separated by the level of focus in the period of seasoned equity offering.

Table 4 shows that if the firms growth opportunity was low, the market would react more negatively to the announcement of seasoned equity offerings by the high-focus (i.e., less-diversified) firms than by the low focus (or more-diversified) firms. These differences were statistically significant. These results do not indicate such significance for high-growth firms. This suggests that there exist some other

Table 3. Cumulative Average Abnormal returns around the Event Date for Overall Sample. High Focused firms are those firms which have increased their Herfindahl index in the last two years in relation to the event year, all other firms are low focused firms.

Event Date	Overall (n = 244)	High Focused Firms (n = 162)	Low Focused Firms (n = 82)	Difference
(0,0)	−0.017454[a]	−0.021019[a]	−0.010411[a]	−0.01061[b]
(0,1)	−0.025335[a]	−0.030338[a]	−0.015504[a]	−0.01483[a]
(−1,0)	−0.017580[a]	−0.021001[a]	−0.010823[b]	−0.01018[b]
(−1,1)	−0.025479[a]	−0.030320[a]	−0.015916[b]	−0.01440[b]
(−5,5)	−0.035393[a]	−0.044186[a]	−0.018024[c]	−0.02616[b]

Notes: [a]Significant at less than 1%
[b]Significant at less than 5% level but not less than 1% level.
[c]Significant at less than 10% level but not less than 5% level.

factors that probably are influencing the negative impact of seasoned equity offerings.

Cross-sectional regression analysis was used to investigate the relationship between the proxies for growth opportunities, focus, and the market value of the firms measured by the abnormal return around the event date. The days $(-1,1)$ abnormal return around the event date was used as the dependent variable. The results of the regression analysis are shown in Table 5.

Table 5 contains the results for the overall sample. When the variables were used independently, the dependent variable—three days cumulative abnormal returns— was negatively related both to the event period Herfindahl index (HI), and to the

Table 4. Cumulative Average Abnormal Returns around the Event Date for the Overall Sample when grouped by the level of growth opportunities and by the focus level of the firm. A high growth opportunities firm is defined as a firm having both a Q ratio greater than one and also an industry median adjusted Q ratio greater than zero. A high-focus firm is a firm that has increased its Herfindahl index in the last two years with respect to event year.

Total Sample (n = 244)		High-Focused Firms	Low-Focused Forms	Differences
High_Q Firm's		(n = 69)	(n = 19)	
	(0,0)	−0.01615257	−0.01089948	−0.0052500
	(0,1)	−0.01962637	−0.01444871	−0.0051800
	(−1,0)	−0.19712280	−0.01041070	−0.1867100
	(−1,1)	−0.02318608	−0.01395930	−0.0092300
	(−5,5)	−0.04399210	−0.01133867	−0.0326500
Low_Q Firm's		(n = 93)	(n = 63)	
	(0,0)	−0.02463022	−0.01026417	−0.0143700[a]
	(0,1)	−0.01582287	−0.03828546	0.0224630[a]
	(−1,0)	−0.02195683	−0.01094688	−0.0110100[c]
	(−1,1)	−0.03561207	−0.01650558	−0.0191100[a]
	(−5,5)	−0.04432901	−0.02003975	−0.0242900[c]
Differences	(0,0)	0.008478	−0.0006400	
between	(0,1)	−0.003800	0.0238370	
High_Q	(−1,0)	−0.175170	0.0005360	
and	(−1,1)	0.012426	0.0025460	
Low_Q	(−5,5)	0.000337	0.0087010	

Notes: [a]Significant at less than 1% level.
[b]Significant at less than 5% level but not less than 1% level.
[c]Significant at less than 10% level but not less than 5% level.

Table 5. Cross Sectional Regression Analysis

	Intercept	TQ	HI	CFTA	NITA	CX3G	PRCD	RD	FRGN	XCHNG	SNDRY	Adj-R^2	F-Value
Total Sample													
Model-1	-0.030613[a]	0.004255										0.0002	0.3071
Model-2	-0.003895		-0.026027[b]									0.0114	0.0536
Model-3	-0.023212[a]			-0.045273								0.0012	0.2575
Model-4	-0.025940[a]				-0.039177							0.0027	0.2018
Model-5	-0.025908[a]					-0.00006						-0.0048	0.9494
Model-6	-0.010747[b]						-0.075199[a]					0.0741	0.0001
Model-7	-0.029071[a]							-0.039177				-0.0067	0.5678
Model-8	-0.023021	0.006955	-0.26001	0.050821	0.003609	0.004707	-0.031454	0.012470	-0.002901	0.021033	-0.008100	0.0401	0.2201
High Focus													
Model-1	-0.041182[a]	0.009302										0.0123	0.0876
Model-2	0.195595		-0.226853									0.0022	0.2459
Model-3	-0.029349[a]			-0.013850								-0.0060	0.7853
Model-4	-0.028295[a]				-0.019071							-0.0049	0.6285
Model-5	-0.031929[a]					-0.000047						-0.0074	0.9630
Model-6	0.000776[a]						-0.094091[a]					0.0460	0.0038
Model-7	-0.033484[a]							-0.012839				-0.0103	0.6528
Model-8	-0.142965	0.014491	0.075765	-0.056460	0.072463	0.003425	0.007254	-0.011409	0.004328	0.018183	0.000657	-0.0426	0.6856

(continued)

Table 5. Continued

Total Sample	Intercept	TQ	HI	CFTA	NITA	CX3G	PRCD	RD	FRGN	XCHNG	SNDRY	Adj-R²	F-Value
Low Focus													
Model-1	-0.014463[b]	-0.003000										-0.0097	0.6197
Model-2	-0.020140		0.005116									-0.0126	0.8612
Model-3	-0.013472[a]			-0.090049								0.0131	0.1577
Model-4	-0.00972b				-0.079455[b]							0.0272	0.0784
Model-5	-0.016164[a]					0.003181						0.0130	0.1685
Model-6	-0.017457						-0.063472[a]					0.1472	0.0002
Model-7	-0.020502[a]							0.172950				-0.0236	0.4908
Model-8	-0.041182	0.005896	0.081128	0.221207	-0.058153	0.02083[b]	-0.050035	-0.199742	-0.018728	0.010535	-0.017979	0.5533	0.0330

Notes: [a]Significant at less than 1% level.
[b]Significant at less than 5% level.
[c]Significant at less than 10% level.

The dependent variable is the three days (–1,1) cumulative abnormal returns for all the model (although other cumulative returns were tested). *TQ* is the Tobin's Q, *HI* is the Herfindahl Index, *CFTA* - Cash Flow to Total Assets, *NITA* is Net Investment to Total Assets, *CX3G* is Pre-event Three Years Capital Expenditure Growth, *PRCD* is the Proceed from the offering in relation to market value of capital stock, *RD* is the Research and Development. All variables are for the event year period. The dummies are used – *FRGN* represent whether the offering included Foreign market, *SNDRY* distinguish between only primary, and combined primary and Secondary offers, and XCHNG determines whether the issue is made either in NYSE and AMEX or in the NASDAC market.

152

proceeds of the issue relative to the value of common stock outstanding (*PRCD*). Both independent variables were statistically significant.

Among all the eight models only the models that included the independent variables *HI* and *PRCD* and had a significant *F*-value were used. The multiple regression model (Model-8) did not have a significant *F*-value. The only significant variable in the model was the past three years capital expenditure growth (*CX3G*).

The sample issue firms were divided into high-focus firms and low-focus firms groups and the same regressions were performed. The results indicated that the high-focus firms *Q* ratio (*TQ*) and *PRCD* were significantly positive when regressed independently. The low-focus firms net investment to total assets (*NITA*) and the *PRCD* were significant when regressed independently. In the multiple regression model (Model-8) none of the variables were significant for the high-focus firm. However, for the low-focus firms *CX3G* still remained statistically significant. The multiple regression model was significant for low-focus firms only.

V. CONCLUSION

This paper examined the market reaction to the seasoned equity offerings after controlling for corporate diversification and growth opportunities. The results of the prior studies that investigate the market reaction to the announcement of seasoned equity offerings are inconclusive. The mixed results indicate that perhaps the models used had misspecification problems due to omitted variables. This paper used alternative measures of corporate diversification and growth opportunities. The results showed insignificant relationship between growth opportunities and the value of the firm. However, the results demonstrate a significant negative market reaction to the issue of seasoned equity by diversified firms. The research findings failed to support the current phenomenon in finance literature that by increasing the focus, thereby decreasing the operational segments of a business, a firm can signal to the market that it is now more efficient than before. The analysis did not find the reduction in diversification produced any significant positive market reaction. On the contrary there is a negative market reaction for low-growth firms. Therefore, the results support the diversification theory at least for the low-*Q* firms.

NOTES

1. For a more specific discussion please see Healy and Palepu (1990) and Choe, Masulis, and Nanda (1993) for the overpricing argument and Dierkens (1991), and Brous and Kini (1992), who do not find positive relationship between various proxies for growth opportunities and changes in the stock prices on the announcement of equity offers. For positive reaction to announcements please see Wruck (1989) and Hertzel and Smith (1993).

2. Registration date is the date at which issuers register the issue with SEC. Effective date is the date at which an issuer gets the approval for the issue. Prospectus date is the date at which the issuer issues the prospectus; and the withdrawn date is the date on which the issue is withdrawn.

3.   See Eckbo and Masulis (1995) for a discussion on the reasons why utility offerings are different from other equity offerings. See Cornett and Tehranian (1994) for a discussion of the market reaction to involuntary bank equity offerings.

4.   This is done in compliance with the argument of Thakor (1993) that for two successive issues, the market always reacts negatively to the second equity issue announcement.

5.   The reason for using a longer event period is to be able to calculate beta for estimated returns away from the event date.

6.   In the finance literature Q has been employed to explain a number of diverse corporate phenomena, such as cross-sectional differences in investment and diversification decisions (Malkiel, Fursenberg, & Watson, 1979), the relationship between managerial equity ownership and firm value (McConnell & Servaes, 1990; Morck, Shleifer, & Vashny, 1988), the relationship between managerial performance and tender-offer gains (Lang, Stulz, & Walking, 1989), investment opportunities and tender-offer espouses (Lang, Stulz, & Walking, 1989), and financing, dividend, and compensation policies (Smith & Watts, 1992).

7.   We also used marginal Q calculated as the increase of Tobin's Q over the preceding year, and our results are not significantly different than what is reported here, when we used marginal Q.

8.   Approximate $Q = (MVA + PS + DEBT)/TA$
where:

> MVA = product of a firm's share price and the number of common stock shares outstanding
> ($DI\_25^{*}DI\_199$ of Compustat)
> PS = Liquidating value of firm's outstanding preferred stock(DI_10)
> $DEBT$ = Short-term liabilities *net* of short term assets (DI_5-DI_4) *plus* the book
> value of the firm's long-term debt(DI_9)
> TA = Book value of the total assets of the firm (DI_6).

9.   This item represents gross sales (the amount of actual billings to customers for regular sales completed during the period) reduced by cash discounts, trade discounts, and returned sales and allowances for which credit is given to customers, for each industry segment. For more details please refer to Compustat user's manual.

10.   As both measures of focus produce the same results we only report results using the Herfindahl index.

11.   Special care has been taken to ensure that during the estimation period no seasoned equity offering took place for each firm.

12.   The potential bias of the Ordinary Least Square (OLS) estimate of β_j due to nonsynchronous and infrequent trading has been recognized and corrected by Eades, Hess, and Kim (1984) using methodology developed by Scholes and Williams (1977).

13.   High-focus firms are those which have a higher Herfindahl index in the event year compared to a year before the event year and/or two years before the event.

14.   The results are not different when alternative measures of growth proxy and/or alternative measures of focus proxy were used.

REFERENCES

Ambarish, R., John, K., & William, J. (1987, June). Efficient signalling with dividends and investments. *Journal of Finance, 42*, 321–344.

Asquith, P., & Mullins, D. (1986, January/February). Equity issues and offering dilution. *Journal of Financial Economics, 15*, 61–90.

Barclay, M., & Litzenberger, R. (1988, May). Announcement effects of equity issues and the use of intraday price data. *Journal of Financial Economics, 21*, 71–100.

Berger, P., & Ofek, E. (1995, January). Diversification's effect on firms value. *Journal of Financial Economics, 37,* 39–65.

Brous, P., & Kini, U. (1992, Winter). Equity issues and Tobin's Q: Some new evidence. *Journal of Financial Research, 15,* 323–340.

Choe, H., Masulis, R., & Nanda, V. (1993, June). On the timing of seasoned common stock issue: Theory and evidence. *Journal of Empirical Finance, 1,* 3–32.

Chandler, A. (1977). *The Visible Hand.* Cambridge, MA: Belknap Press.

Chung, K., & Pruitt, S. (1994, Autumn). A sample approximation of Tobin's Q. *Financial Management, 23,* 70–74.

Comment, R., & Jarrell, G. (1995, January). Corporate focus and stock returns. *Journal of Financial Economics, 37,* 76–87.

Cooney, J., & Kalay, A. (1993, April). Positive information from equity issue announcements. *Journal of Financial Economics, 33,* 149–172.

Cornett, M., & Tehranian, H. (1994, February). An examination of voluntary versus involuntary security issuance by commercial banks: The impact of capital regulations on common stock returns. *Journal of Financial Economics, 35,* 99–122.

Denis, D. (1994, June). Investment opportunities and the market reaction to equity offerings. *Journal of Financial and Quantitative Analysis, 29,* 159–178.

Dierkens, N. (1991, June). Information asymmetry and equity issues. *Journal of Financial and Quantitative Analysis, 26,* 181–200.

Eckbo, E., & Masulis, R. (1992, December). Adverse selection and the right offer paradox. *Journal of Financial Economics, 32,* 293–332.

Eckbo, E., & Masulis, R. (1995). Seasoned equity offerings: A survey. In R. A. Jarrow, V. Maksimovic, & W. T. Ziemba (Eds.), *Handbooks of operations research and management science: Finance.* Amsterdam, The Netherland: North-Holland.

Eades, K., Hess, P., & Kim, E. (1984, March). On interpreting security returns during the exdividend period. *Journal of Financial Economics, 13,* 3–34.

Harris, M., Kriebel, C. H., & Raviv, A. (1982, June). Asymmetric information, incentives and intrafirm resource allocation. *Management Science, 28,* 604–620.

Healy, P., & Palepu, K. (1990, Spring). Earning and risk change surrounding primary stock offerings. *Journal of Accounting Research, 28,* 25–48.

Hertzel, M., & Smith, R. (1993, June). Market discount and shareholders gains for placing equity privately. *Journal of Finance, 48,* 459–485.

Hess, A., & Bhagat, S. (1986, October). Size effect of seasoned equity issues: empirical evidences. *Journal of Business, 59,* 567–584.

Jensen, M. (1986, May). Agency cost of free cash flow, corporate finance, and takeover. *American Economic Review, 76,* 323–329.

John, K., & Ofek, E. (1995, January). Asset sales and increase in focus. *Journal of Financial Economic, 37,* 105–122.

Kalay, A., & Shimrat, A. (1987, September). Firm value and seasoned equity issues: price pressure, wealth redistribution, or negative information. *Journal of Financial Economics, 19,* 109–126.

Lang, L., Stulz, R., & Walking, R. (1989, September). Managerial performance, tobin's Q, and the gains from successful tender offers. *Journal of Financial Economics, 24,* 137–154.

Lang, L., Stulz, R., & Walking, R. (1995). Tobin's Q, corporate diversification and firm performance. *Journal of Political Economy, 102,* 1248–1280.

Lewellen, W. (1971). A pure financial rational for the conglomerate merger. *Journal of Finance, 26,* 521–537.

Lindenberg, E., & Ross, S. (1981, January). Tobin's Q ratio and industrial organization. *Journal of Business, 54,* 1–32.

Malkiel, B., Furstenberg, G., & Watson, H. (1979, May). Expectations, Tobin's Q and industry investment. *Journal of Finance, 34,* 543–560.

McConnell, J., & Servaes, H. (1990, October). Additional evidence on equity ownership and corporate value. *Journal of Financial Economics, 27*, 595–612.

Meyer, M., Milgrom, P., & Roberts, J. (1992). Organizational prospects, influence costs, and ownership changes. *Journal of Economics and Management Strategy, 1*, 9–35.

Mikkelson, W., & Partch, M. (1985, June). Stock price effect and costs of secondary distribution. *Journal of Financial Economics, 14*, 165–194.

Miller, M., & Rock, K. (1985, September). Dividend policy under asymmetric information. *Journal of Finance, 40*, 1031–1050.

Morck, R., Shleifer, A., & Vishny, R. W. (1988, January/March). Management ownership and market valuation: An empirical analysis. *Journal of Financial Economics, 20*, 293–316.

Myers, S. (1977, November). Determinants of corporate borrowing. *Journal of Financial Economics, 5*, 147–176.

Myers, S., & Majluf, N. (1984, June). Corporate financing and investment decision when firms have information investors do not have. *Journal of Financial Economics, 13*, 187–222.

Myerson, R. (1982, June). Optimal coordination mechanisms in generalized principle-agent problems. *Journal of Mathematical Economics, 10*, 67–81.

Pilotte, E. (1992, July). Growth opportunities and the stock price response to new financing. *Journal of Business, 65*, 371–394.

Scholes, M., & Williams, J. (1977, December). Estimating betas from nonsynchronous data. *Journal of Financial Economics, 5*, 309–328.

Smith, C., & Watts, R. (1992, December). The investment opportunity set and corporate financing, dividend, and compensation policies. *Journal of Financial Economics, 32*, 263–292.

Stulz, R. (1990, January). Managerial discretion and optimal financing policy. *Journal of Financial Economics, 26*, 3–27.

Thakor, A. (1993, December). Information, investment horizon, and price reactions. *Journal of Financial and Quantitative Analysis, 28*, 459–482.

Tobin, J. (1969, February). A general equilibrium approach to monetary theory. *Journal of Money Credit and Banking, 1*, 15–29.

Weston, J. (1970). The nature and significant of conglomerate firms. *St. John's Law Review, 44*, 66–80.

Wruck, K. (1989, January). Equity ownership concentration and firm value: Evidence from private equity financing. *Journal of Financial Economics, 23*, 3–28.

TAX UNCERTAINTY AND EQUITY RISK:
SOME EMPIRICAL EVIDENCE

R. Gene Stout and Raymond A. K. Cox

ABSTRACT

This paper examines financial statement data and finds that the increasing frequency of tax code changes can be associated with a weakening of the correlation between before-tax cash flows and after-tax cash flows, and an increase in the volatility of after-tax cash flows relative to before-tax cash flows. Financial statement data is incorporated into a regression model to find that tax uncertainty adds explanation to the riskiness of equity returns. However, the risk is idiosyncratic and therefore, in a world where the Capital Asset Pricing Model holds, tax uncertainty would not impact the cost of equity capital.

More than two centuries have passed since Adam Smith admonished that "certainty ... in taxation (is) a matter of so great importance that a very considerable degree of inequality ... is not near so great an evil as a small degree of uncertainty." In spite of that warning, the history of U.S. tax policy has shown increasing uncertainty.

At its inception in 1913 the federal tax regulations were 16 pages in length. But between 1955 and 1994 the number of sections of the tax regulations increased

Research in Finance, Volume 16, pages 157–169.
Copyright © 1998 by JAI Press Inc.
All rights of reproduction in any form reserved.
ISBN: 0-7623-0328-X

578% while the number of words grew from 744,000 to 5,557,000.[1] Since 1980 the total number of changes in the tax code would exceed 5,000, and there have been at least five major tax code revisions.[2]

Several studies have examined the pervasive impacts of uncertain income tax policies. Alm (1988) analyzed individual behavior under uncertain tax policies, and Watson (1992) modeled individual saving and portfolio decisions. Cheung and Heany (1993), Bizer and Judd (1989), and Auerbach and Hines (1987) studied the impacts of tax uncertainty on business investment; and Bizer and Judd (1989) and Skinner (1988) drew (somewhat different)[3] conclusions regarding the welfare or inefficiency cost of tax policy uncertainty.

Considerably less research has been performed to analyze the effects of tax uncertainty on business cash flows and, ultimately, on the returns and risks of the securities markets. Such research is important because market reactions to tax uncertainty may cause wealth changes among taxpayers. In addition and perhaps more importantly, as stated by Beaver, Kettler, and Scholes (1970), such research is important because "Our knowledge of risk determination is incomplete as long as we do not know what exogenous variables (i.e., nonprice data) are impounded in assessments of security prices and price changes." Auerbach and Hines (1987) proposed to predict changes in the market value of securities in an uncertain tax environment, but acknowledged that important aspects of firm valuation remain poorly understood, and numerous studies (Auerbach, 1987; Cox, Kleiman, & Stout, 1994; Cutler, 1988; Downs & Demigures, 1992; Downs & Tehranian, 1988; Downs & Hendershott, 1987) have examined the impact of tax code revisions on changes in wealth.

This paper examines tax uncertainty. The purposes of the research are (1) to test for the existence of tax uncertainty; and (2) to test financial markets for the impacts of tax uncertainty.

Our first hypothesis is that the increasing frequency of tax code changes has caused greater volatility in the effective tax rate on before-tax cash flows, and thereby weakened the link (correlation) between before-tax cash flow and after-tax cash flow. This hypothesis is tested in the first section of the paper.

The first hypothesis is important because such a finding would imply that the Congress has, over time, taken a more powerful role in influencing after-tax cash flows. This realization would generate a set of tax uncertainty-induced changes in firm and, possibly, investor behavior. Auerbach and Hines (1988) modeled anticipated tax reforms in an attempt to identify the impact of anticipated tax reforms on investment incentives. More generally, tax uncertainty-induced changes in firm behavior could be termed tax uncertainty management. Firms, for example, would have a stronger interest in planning toward expected tax changes or maintaining the flexibility to minimize the tax liability under uncertain provisions. Possible behaviors might include changing the timing of potentially impacted decisions (wait and see attitude or accelerating/delaying investments), expanding the effort to influence tax changes (lobbying), and offsetting tax change impacts through tax change diversification or possibly hedging on the present value of after-tax cash flow (Smith & Stulz, 1985).

Our second hypothesis is that tax uncertainty *does* increase the variability of shareholder returns, and further, that the increased variability has both systematic and nonsystematic components. These issues are examined in the second section of the paper.

We expect that tax uncertainty increases the variability of shareholder returns because changes in the effective tax rate on before-tax cash flows have been increasingly guided by equity, political, and federal budget concerns rather than cyclical dampening. Hence, the effective tax rate on before-tax cash flows is less correlated with before-tax cash flows. Further, we expect that tax change management is not completely effective, so the rather random changes in the effective tax rate on before-tax cash flows is at least partially transmitted to after-tax cash flows, and thereby impacts the variability of investor returns.[4]

Some of the tax uncertainty-induced variability in investor returns is expected to be systematic because the tax change uncertainty impacts all firms in the market. Some of the uncertainty is expected to be nonsystematic because of tax change targeting (leasing, real estate investment trusts). Continued exposure to tax change targeting may induce firms to engage in tax uncertainty diversification. Leasing firms, for example, were treated very favorably under the tax code change of 1981 (Economic Recovery Tax Act, ERTA), and they became desirable acquisitions for the tax advantages that they could generate. Conglomeration of this fashion could, conceivably, generate negative tax change covariances leaving the firm subject only to the average tax change. To the extent that such tax uncertainty diversification is incomplete, tax uncertainty would have a nonsystematic impact on the variability of investor returns.

I. THE EXISTENCE OF TAX UNCERTAINTY

A review of the relatively recent tax code changes provides some direct evidence of more frequent changes and increased "tax code tinkering" over time. The Tax Reform Act of 1969 was the first of what could be termed the "major" tax acts amending the 1954 code. There were four tax code changes in the 1970s (the Revenue Act of 1971, the Employee Retirement Income Security Act [ERISA] of 1974, the Tax Reform Act [TRA] of 1976, and the Revenue Act of 1978), but only the TRA could be classified as a "major" change. The 1980s, however, contained 10 tax code changes (the Crude Oil Windfall Profit Tax Act of 1980, the Installment Sales Revision Act of 1980, the Economic Recovery Tax Act [ERTA] of 1981, the Tax Equity and Fiscal Responsibility Act [TEFRA] of 1982, the Subchapter S Revision Act of 1982, the Tax Reform Act of 1984, the Tax Reform Act of 1986, the Revenue Act of 1987, the Technical and Miscellaneous Revenue Act [TAMRA] of 1988, and the Revenue Reconciliation Act of 1989), and more importantly, the acts of 1982, 1984, 1986, and possibly 1988 would be considered "major" changes in the tax code.

To measure the impacts of tax uncertainty, we compute two statistics: (1) the correlation between after-tax cash flow and before-tax cash flow ($\rho_{ATCF,BTCF}$) for firm i in time period t, and (2) the natural logarithm of the coefficient of variation of the effective tax rate on before-tax cash flow for firm i over time period t ($LN(CVTR_{i,t})$).

For $\rho_{ATCF,BTCF}$, we compute measures of before-tax and after-tax cash flow annually for firm i in fiscal year y. Before-tax cash flow ($BTCF_{i,y}$) is income before extraordinary items and discontinued operations,[5] plus depreciation and amortization, plus taxes deferred from current income. After-tax cash flow ($ATCF_{i,y}$) is before-tax cash flow minus taxes paid. $\rho_{ATCF,BTCF}$ is the simple correlation between $ATCF_{i,y}$ and $BTCF_{i,y}$ for firm i over time period t.

In computing $LN(CVTR_{i,t})$, we begin with taxes paid as a fraction of before-tax cash flow, that is, the effective tax rate on before-tax cash flow for firm i in fiscal year y. The coefficient of variation of the effective tax rate on before-tax cash flow ($CVTR_{i,t}$) is computed for firm i over time period t, to measure the volatility of the effective tax rate on before-tax cash flows relative to or corrected for the size of the average effective tax rate. The distribution of $CVTR_{i,t}$ is normalized by the natural logarithm transformation. Hence, the natural logarithm of the coefficient of variation of effective cash flow tax rate, $LN(CVTR_{i,t})$, is a normally distributed measure of the volatility of the effective cash flow tax rate.

To test the hypothesis that more frequent tax code changes have weakened the connection between $ATCF$ and $BTCF$ over time, two study periods, calendar years 1972 through 1979 and calendar years 1980 through 1987, are chosen for comparison. The periods are selected to be of equal length, and 1980 is selected as the dividing point because it marks the beginning of a new period of tax policy activism.[6]

Our primary sample consists of all firms whose stock traded continuously (monthly) and under the same ticker symbol over 20 calendar years (1972–1991). We constructed the sample by screening Standard & Poor's (S&P) COMPUSTAT PC PLUS for all such securities traded on the New York Stock Exchange (NYSE), the American Stock Exchange (AMEX), and the National Association of Securities Dealers Automated Quotation System (NASDAQ). The screening yielded 738 NYSE firms, 178 AMEX firms, and 192 NASDAQ firms for a total sample of 1,108 firms.

Our first test of the impact of greater tax policy activism relies on $\rho_{ATCF, BTCF}$ over time. It is hypothesized that $\rho_{ATCF, BTCF}$ has decreased over time, providing support for the relative weakening of the connection of $BTCF$ to $ATCF$ and greater tax uncertainty. Fiscal years are numbered by the calendar year in which they end.[7] Accordingly, we hypothesize:

$$\rho_{ATCF,BTCF}^{1973-1980} > \rho_{ATCF,BTCF}^{1981-1988}$$

Table 1. Increasing Tax Uncertainty as Measured by the Relationships Between After-tax Cash Flow and Before-tax Cash Flow Over 1973–1980 and 1981–1988

	1973–1980		1981–1988		t-Statistic	F-Statistic
	Mean	Variance	Mean	Variance	Means	Variances
NYSE						
Correlation, after-tax cash flow to before-tax cash flow	.9725	.054	.9507	.078	4.85**	2.09**
Natural logarithm of the coefficient of variation of the effective tax rate on before-tax cash flow	−2.4318	.892	−2.0392	.976	−9.84**	1.20
AMEX						
Correlation, after-tax cash flow to before-tax cash flow	.9689	.058	.9588	.068	1.57**	1.37*
Natural logarithm of the coefficient of variation of the effective tax rate on before-tax cash flow	−1.7833	1.013	−1.5109	1.077	−2.87**	1.13
NASDAQ						
Correlation, after-tax cash flow to before-tax cash flow	.9714	.055	.9538	.078	2.49**	2.01**
Natural logarithm of the coefficient of variation of the effective tax rate on before-tax cash flow	−2.1252	1.097	−1.8825	1.043	−2.38**	0.90
ALL MARKETS (NYSE, AMEX, NASDAQ)						
Correlation, after-tax cash flow to before-tax cash flow	.9717	.055	.9526	.077	4.85**	1.96**
Natural logarithm of the coefficient of variation of the effective tax rate on before-tax cash flow	−2.2772	.979	−1.9295	1.021	−9.83**	1.09

Note: The sample consists of the 738 NYSE firms, 178 AMEX firms, and 192 NASDAQ firms whose common stock traded continuously and under the same ticker symbol from 1973 to 1992. After-tax cash flow is before-tax cash flow minus taxes paid, and before-tax cash flow is income before extraordinary items and discontinued operations, plus depreciation and amortization, plus taxes deferred from current income. Statistical significance at $\alpha = .05$ and $\alpha = .01$ are designated by * and **, respectively.

Further, it is postulated that tax change "targeting" has increased the across firm variability (σ^2) in $\rho_{ATCF, BTCF}$ in the latter period, that is:

$$\sigma_\rho^2 \ ^{1973-1980} < \sigma_\rho^2 \ ^{1981-1988}$$

Our second test of greater tax code uncertainty examines, by LN(*CVTR*), the volatility of the tax rate on before-tax cash flow. We hypothesize that LN(*CVTR*) has decreased over time, indicating greater tax uncertainty (because *CVTR* is less than one), hence:

$$LN(CVTR)^{1973-1980} > LN(CVTR)^{1981-1988}$$

In addition, we theorize again, that the increased variability in tax changes across firms has caused greater variability in LN(*CVTR*), so:

$$\sigma^2_{LN(CVTR)}{}^{1973-1980} > \sigma^2_{LN(CVTR)}{}^{1981-1988}$$

Table 1 shows the results of two comparisons of the study periods. The first comparison is $\rho_{ATCF,BTCF}$, the correlation between $ATCF_{i,y}$ and $BTCF_{i,y}$, and the second comparison is the LN($CVTR_{i,t}$). The table shows the results of the comparisons for each security market and across all three markets.

With regard to the first comparison, we find that the correlation between *ATCF* and *BTCF*, has weakened, quite uniformly, over time. The average correlation between *BTCF* and *ATCF* for the NYSE firms dropped from .9725 to .9507 (*t*-statistic = 4.85), the average correlation among AMEX firms declined from .9689 to .9588 (*t*-statistic = 1.57), and the average correlation for NASDAQ firms declined from .9714 to .9538 (*t*-statistic = 2.49). This result is summarized across all three markets showing a correlation of .9717 in the earlier period but only .9526 in the later period (*t*-statistic = 4.85). The declines in the correlation between *ATCF* and *BTCF* are statistically significant at $\alpha = .01$ for all tests *except* the AMEX.

Test results for $\sigma^2_\rho{}^{1973-1980} > \sigma^2_\rho{}^{1981-1988}$ are similar. The variance of the correlation between *ATCF* and *BTCF* has increased, showing greater across-firm variability in the later period, in each of the markets and in all of the markets. The *F*-statistics are statistically significant at $\alpha = .01$ for all tests *except* the AMEX, which is significant at $\alpha = .05$. Changes in the correlation between before-tax and after-tax cash flow could be the result of changes in timing between cash flows and taxable income. We would argue that such changes, particularly those which result from tax management, are in response to, and thereby result from, tax uncertainty.

Our comparison of the two time periods shows that LN($CVTR_{i,t}$) has increased. We view $CVTR_{i,t}$ as a measure of tax uncertainty for firm *i* and conclude, possible timing differences notwithstanding, that the latter period is characterized by greater tax uncertainty. The LN($CVTR_{i,t}$) increased from −2.4318 to −2.0392, from −1.7833 to −1.5109, and from −2.1252 to −1.8825, in the NYSE, AMEX, and NASDAQ markets, respectively. Across all three markets the combined LN(*CVTR*) increased from −2.2772 to −1.9295. The declines in LN($CVTR_{i,t}$) are all statistically significant at $\alpha = .01$ with *t*-statistics of −9.84, −2.87, −2.38, and −9.83, respectively. The *F*-statistics, however, cannot reject the hypothesis of equal variances in LN(*CVTR*).

Investor behavior would respond to tax uncertainty if it increases the variability of security returns. And, to the extent that tax uncertainty increases nondiversifiable security risk, it would increase firms' cost of equity capital. These issues are examined in the following section.

II. TAX UNCERTAINTY AND SECURITY RETURNS

The total risk of security returns is the variance of returns. Empirically we compute the variance of monthly returns over the current and prior 59 months at year-end. We restrict the study period to post (fiscal) 1981, those years thought to be characterized by more frequent and significant tax code changes. Allowing 59 months for the variance computation, we compute for each of the firms' fiscal 1987–1992,

$$VARR_{i,y} = \sum_{j=m}^{m-59} (R_{i,j} - \overline{R}_{i,y})^2/60 \tag{1}$$

where $VARR_{i,y}$ is the variance of monthly returns for firm i over the 60-month period ending in the year-end month of fiscal year y,

$R_{i,j}$ is the return to security i in month j, and

$R_{i,y}$ is the average monthly return for firm i over the 60-month period ending in the year-end month of fiscal year y.

Our measure of tax uncertainty, *CVTR*, is computed from annual statement data extracted from S&P's COMPUSTAT PC PLUS, a 20-year database. We now compute $CVTR_{i,y}$ over 15-year periods ending in fiscal years 1987 to 1992. We chose 15-year periods to allow the longest possible tax history in the 20-year data set.

We further restrict the sample to firms having *CVTRs* that are between zero and one in each fiscal year. The restriction that the *CVTRs* be greater than zero confines the sample to firms with positive tax rates on before-tax cash flows over each of the six 15-year periods; the restriction that the *CVTRs* be less than one eliminates firms with tax rates close to zero. In total, the restriction confines the final sample to 491 firms which had significantly positive average after-tax cash flows over each of the six 15-year periods. Such firms would, arguably, have the greatest concern for tax uncertainty.[8]

To decompose the impacts of tax uncertainty into systematic and nonsystematic components, we compute a fiscal year-end 60-month beta ($\beta_{i,y}$). We begin with $R_{i,m}$, the monthly holding period return to security i:

$$R_{i,m} = (P_{i,m} - P_{i,m-1} + D_{i,m})/P_{i,m-1} \tag{2}$$

where $R_{i,m}$ is the holding period return to security i in month m,

$P_{i,m}$ is the closing price of security i in month m, and

$D_{i,m}$ is the dividend, by *ex dividend* date, to security i in month m.

We then employ the market equilibrium version of the simplified CAPM (market model) by Sharpe (1964), Lintner (1965), and Mossin (1966) which attributes differential expected returns across securities solely to systematic (market) risk.

We estimate the market model from fiscal year-end 60-month least squares regressions of:

$$R_{i,m} = a_i + b_{i,y} (RM_m) + e_{i,m} \tag{3}$$

where $R_{i,y}$ is the *ex post* holding period return to security i in month m,

RM_m is the market return in month m,

$e_{i,m}$ is the residual, unsystematic return to security i in month m, and

$b_{i,y}$ is the estimated beta (β_i) of security i at fiscal year-end y.

The cross-sectional regression of $VARR_{i,y}$ on $CVTR_{i,y}$ measures the impact of tax uncertainty on total risk, and the regression of $VARR_{i,y}$ on the fiscal year-end $\beta_{i,y}$ measures and tests the relationship between total risk and systematic risk. We hypothesize that total risk ($VARR_{i,y}$) is a function of *both* tax uncertainty ($CVTR_{i,y}$) and systematic risk ($\beta_{i,y}$).

We begin by testing the impacts of the variables separately. The regression results in Table 2 show that total risk is significantly related to both tax uncertainty and systematic risk in each of the study years, and (therefore) over all years as well.

Panel A reports the regression results of:

$$VARR_{i,y} = \alpha_0 + \alpha_1 CVTR_{i,y} + \varepsilon_i \tag{4}$$

The regression results are reported across all years (1987–1992) using the restricted ($0 < CVTR < 1$) sample of 491 observations (firms) in each year and 2,946 observations over the entire period. Tax uncertainty, as measured by $CVTR_{i,y}$, positively impacts total riskiness of stock returns, as measured by $VARR_{i,y}$. The coefficient of $CVTR$ is statistically significant at $\alpha = .01$ and the single-variable $CVTR$ model explains a small (about 2.5%) but statistically significant ($F = 72.6$) portion of the variability in the riskiness of total returns.

These results are of practical value. From the perspective of financial managers, the findings suggest that financial decisions which ameliorate changes in tax rates reduce shareholder risk. Such decisions might involve project timing to accelerate investments expected to be negatively impacted by tax code changes or to delay investments expected to be more favorably impacted by the changes. Perhaps more surprisingly, from a government perspective, the findings suggest that changes in taxation, regardless of the intended effect, have a "tinkering" impact which increases shareholder risk. Even the investment tax credit, for example, carried tax uncertainty impacts. These unanticipated effects were contrary to, and to some extent offset, the desired outcome. Moreover, the findings suggest that the taxation authority should *not* view tax changes as exogenous shocks, but rather, recognize the tax uncertainty (feedback) effects.

Table 2. Regression Results of Total Risk on Tax Uncertainty; Beta

	Panel A $VARR_{i,y} = \alpha_0 + \alpha_1 CVTR_{i,y} + \varepsilon_i$				Panel B $VARR_{i,y} = \alpha_0 + \alpha_1 \beta_{i,y} + \varepsilon_i$			
	Estimated Coefficients:				Estimated Coefficients:			
	Intercept (α_0)	$CVTR_{iy}$ (α_1)	Adjusted R^2	F-Statistic	Intercept (α_0)	$\beta_{i,y}$ (α_1)	Adjusted R^2	F-Statistic
Time Period								
1987–1992	.0065** (29.36)	.0041** (8.522)	0.0237	72.625**	.0010** (3.220)	.0074** (25.354)	0.1790	642.817**

Notes: The dependent variable is the variance of the holding period return on the stock of firm i over the fiscal year-end month and the prior 59 months. The sample consists of the 491 firms which were traded on the NYSE and AMEX exchanges and the NASDAQ continuously and under the same ticker symbol over 1973–1992 and which also had coefficients of variation of effective tax rates on before-tax cash flow ($CVTR_{i,y}$) between 0 and 1 in each of fiscal years 1987 to 1992. The independent variable of Panel A is $CVTR_{i,y}$, the coefficient of variation of taxes paid relative to before-tax cash flow over fiscal year y and the prior 14 years. The independent variable of Panel B is $\beta_{i,y}$, the beta of firm i over the fiscal year-end month of year y and the prior 59 months. T-statistics are in parentheses; * and ** denote statistical significance at $\alpha = .05$ and $\alpha = .01$, respectively.

165

The tax uncertainty effects *may be* transmitted to corporate decisions by increasing the volatility of returns which increases the firms' weighted average cost of capital. Such would be the case *only if* the tax uncertainty impacted the systematic risk. Otherwise, and to the extent that tax uncertainty is not impounded in beta, investors might devise trading rules which target expected changes in the tax code or consider the diversification of tax change uncertainty.

Panel B reports regression results of another single-variable model:

$$VARR_{i,y} = \alpha_0 + \alpha_1 \, \beta_{i,y} + \varepsilon_i \qquad (5)$$

The results are reported across all years and for the same firms. The results show that the variability of total returns is positively impacted by $\beta_{i,y}$, the fiscal year-end beta over the current and prior 59 months. The coefficient of β is statistically significant at $\alpha = .01$. Across the study period, β explains about 18% of total risk. And, once again, the F-statistic is statistically significant at $\alpha = .01$ ($F = 642.8$).

Table 3 reports the results of regressing total security risk, $VARR_{i,y}$, on both $CVTR_{i,y}$ and $\beta_{i,y}$ for the same observations as Table 2.

The regression coefficients in this two-variable model are statistically significant at $\alpha = .01$. Taken together, the variables explain about 21% of the variability is total security riskiness. In addition, the reported F-statistic is statistically significant at $\alpha = .01$ with $F = 393$.

Moreover, the regression coefficients in the two-variable model are remarkably stable when compared to those of the single-variable models of Table 2. The inclusion of both variables in the same model changes the coefficient of *CVTR* from .0041 to .0047 and the coefficient of β from .0074 to .0076. And further, the *adjusted*

Table 3. Regression Results of Total Risk on Tax Uncertainty and Beta

$$VARR_{i,y} = \alpha_0 + \alpha_1 \, CVTR_{i,y} + \alpha_2 \, \beta_{i,y} + \varepsilon_i$$

	Estimated Coefficients:				
Time Period	Intercept (α_0)	$CVTR_{i,y}$ (α_1)	$\beta_{i,y}$ (α_2)	Adjusted R^2	F-Statistic
1987–1992	−.0011	.0047	.0076	0.2103	393.199**
	(−3.12)*	(10.86)**	(26.39)**		

Notes: The dependent variable is the variance of the holding period return on the stock of firm *i* over the fiscal year-end month of year *y* and the prior 59 months. The sample consists of the 491 firms which were traded on the NYSE and AMEX exchanges and the NASDAQ continuously and under the same ticker symbol over 1973–1992 and which also had coefficients of variation of effective tax rates on before-tax cash flow ($CVTR_{i,y}$) between 0 and 1 in each of fiscal years 1987 to 1992. The independent variables are $CVTR_{i,y}$, the coefficient of variation of taxes paid relative to before-tax cash flow over fiscal year *y* and the prior 14 years and $\beta_{i,y}$, the beta of firm *i* over the fiscal year-end month and the prior 59 months. *T*-statistics are in parentheses; * and ** denote statistical significance at $\alpha = .05$ and $\alpha = .01$, respectively.

R^2 of the two-variable model is approximately additive of the single-variable models. For example, the sum of the adjusted R^2s of the single-variable models is .2027 and the adjusted R^2 for the two-variable model is .2103. This suggests that tax uncertainty and systematic risk have separate and (nearly) additive impacts on the total variability in security returns. A decomposition of the explanatory impacts, however, reveals that the *unadjusted R^2* of the two-variable model (.2109) consists of a direct affect of systematic risk (.1868), a direct affect of tax uncertainty (.0317) and a joint affect (−.0076) attributable to the slightly negative linear association between the regressors.[9]

III. SUMMARY

We explore the existence and impacts of uncertain tax policies. First, we examine financial statement data for evidence to support the existence of tax uncertainty. In particular, we examine the data for evidence that the increasing frequency of tax code changes can be associated with a relative weakening of the correlation between before-tax and after-tax cash flows and an increase in the volatility of after-tax cash flows relative to before-tax cash flows. An examination of two study subperiods, 1973 through 1980 and 1981 through 1988, reveals that the correlation between after-tax cash flows and before-tax cash flows *has* weakened and the effective tax rate on before-tax cash flows *has* become more volatile. This finding suggests that uncertain tax policies have, over time, increased the volatility of after-tax cash flows.

Next, we examine data from financial markets to investigate the impact of tax uncertainty in financial markets. We employ a capital asset pricing model with fiscal year-end observations to calculate security βs and to test the association between β and the total variability in shareholder returns. We find that systematic risk explains about 18% of the total variability in shareholder returns. Furthermore, we find that tax uncertainty adds explanation to the variability in shareholder returns. Tax uncertainty seems to explain a small but statistically significant portion of the variability. When incorporated into the capital asset pricing model, tax uncertainty improves the explanation of total riskiness of shareholder returns by about 3%. Since our measure of tax uncertainty is *not* correlated with beta, tax uncertainty seems to be largely unsystematic.

These findings suggest that the increasing frequency of tax code changes, possibly "tax code tinkering," increases the riskiness of shareholder returns, but since the impact is idiosyncratic, investors could diversify the risk and it would not cause higher capital costs. Nonetheless, insofar as tax uncertainty does increase total security risk, the legislators might heed the early warnings of Adam Smith, that "certainty of taxation is more important than equality," and establish a more permanent tax code to refrain from continual fiscal fine tuning.

NOTES

1. See Hall (1994). Additionally, Auerbach and Hines (1988) noted that Congress changed investment incentives in 16 of the years 1953 to 1985.

2. The five *major revisions* referred to are the Economic Recovery Tax Act of 1981, the Tax Equity and Fiscal Responsibility Act of 1982, the Tax Reform Act of 1986, the Omnibus Budget Reconciliation Act of 1990, and the Revenue Reconciliation Act of 1993.

3. Skinner estimated the welfare cost, in terms of annual GNP, to be substantial enough to promote the indexing of capital gains to inflation, but Bizer and Judd argued that even randomization of capital income taxation has a low efficiency cost.

4. Let X = before-tax cash flows, t = the effective tax rate on before-tax cash flows, μ = the mean, E = the expected value operator, Var = the variance, and Cov = the covariance. If *both* X and t are random variables, then $\text{Var}[X(1-t)] = \mu_{(1-t)}^2 \text{Var}[X] + \mu_X^2 \text{Var}[t] - 2\mu_X(1-\mu_t)\text{Cov}[X, t] - \text{Cov}[X, t]^2 + E[(X-\mu_X)^2 (t-\mu_t)^2] - 2(1-\mu_t)E[(X-\mu_X)^2(t-\mu_t)] + 2\mu_X E[(X-\mu_X)(t-\mu_t)^2]$. The variability of after-tax cash flows clearly becomes a function of the variability of before-tax cash flows, the variability of the tax rate, and the covariability between the variables.

5. Extraordinary items are omitted because of the erratic and sporadic nature of these items, presumably uncorrelated to tax payments or before-tax cash flow.

6. The initial years were certainly active, with two major tax code revisions only one year apart. The Economic Recovery Tax Act was enacted August 13, 1981 but the long periods of debate would be expected to create serious announcement impacts in calendar 1980. Also, see note 1.

7. The earliest month is July 1981, the first month of fiscal 1982 for a firm with a June fiscal year; and the latest month is May 1992, the last month of fiscal 1992 for a firm with a May fiscal year.

8. This restriction does not seem to introduce any bias in the sample with respect to beta. Across all years, the final sample has an average beta (β_i) of 0.996 and an average R^2 of 0.372.

9. There is a slight negative correlation between *CVTR* and β. The correlation, however, is significantly different from zero only in 1988.

REFERENCES

Alm, J. (1988). Uncertain tax policies, individual behavior, and welfare. *American Economic Review, 78*, 237–245.

Auerbach, A. (1987). The tax reform act of 1986 and the cost of capital. *Economic Perspectives, 1*, 73–86.

Auerbach, A., & Hines, J., Jr. (1987). Anticipated tax changes and the timing of investment. In Feldstein (Ed.), *The effects of taxation on capital accumulation.* Chicago, IL,University of Chicago Press for NBER.

Auerbach, A., & Hines, J., Jr. (1988). Investment tax incentives and frequent tax reforms. *American Economic Review, 78*, 211–216.

Beaver, W., Kettler, P., & Scholes, M. (1970). The deviation between market determined and accounting determined risk measures. *The Accounting Review*, 654–682.

Bizer D., & Judd, K. (1989). Taxation and uncertainty. *American Economic Review, 79*, 331–336.

Cheung, J., & Heaney, J. (1993). Tax uncertainties and the investment decision. *Journal of Business Finance and Accounting, 20*, 905–910.

Cox, R., Kleimam, R., & Stout, R. (1994). Tax policy and shareholder wealth: Some evidence from the tax reform act of 1986. *Financial Review, 29*, 249–274.

Cutler, D. (1988). Tax reform and the stock market: An asset price approach. *American Economic Review, 78*, 1107–1117.

Downs, T., & Demirgures, C. (1992). The asset price theory of shareholder revaluations: Tests with the tax reforms of the 1980's. *Financial Review, 27*, 151–184.

Downs, T., & Hendershott, P. (1987). Tax policy and stock prices. *National Tax Journal, 40,* 183–190.

Downs, T., & Tehranian, H. (1988). Predicting stock responses to tax policy changes. *American Economic Review, 78,* 1118–1130.

Hall, A. (1994, November 28). Growth of federal government tax 'industry' parallels growth of tax code. *Tax Notes,* 1133–1138.

Lintner, J. (1965, February). The valuation of risk assets and the selection of risky investments in stock portfolios and capital budgets. *The Review of Economics and Statistics,* 13–37.

Mossin, J. (1966, October). Equilibrium in a capital asset market. *Econometrica,* 768–783.

Sharpe, W. F. (1964, September). Capital asset prices: A theory of market equilibrium under conditions of risk. *Journal of Finance,* 425–442.

Skinner, J. (1988). The welfare cost of uncertain tax policy. *Journal of Public Economics, 37,* 126–146.

Smith, A. (1976). *An inquiry into the nature and causes of the wealth of nation.* New York: Oxford University Press.

Smith, C., & Stulz, R. (1985). The determinants of firms' hedging policies. *Journal of Financial and Quantitative Analysis, 20,* 391–405.

Watson, H. (1992). The effects of income tax rate uncertainty in a dynamic setting. *Southern Economic Journal, 58,* 682–689.

BETA CHANGES AROUND STOCK DISTRIBUTIONS: AN EXTENSION

Taylor W. Foster, III and Edmund Scribner

ABSTRACT

This study updates and extends prior beta-shift studies to (1) all stock splits and (2) stock dividends. In addition, the sample is partitioned into NYSE and AMEX stocks. The initial results for all stock splits parallel those of Wiggins (1992) for large splits, but an apparent exchange effect is observed. Specifically, NYSE splits exhibit a significant increase in beta, even when weekly data and three-week estimators are used. On the other hand, AMEX splits do not evidence a significant increase in beta based on weekly data. This suggests that the effect that Wiggins attributed to the measurement interval differs across exchanges. No significant changes in beta are found following stock dividend ex-dates irrespective of the measurement interval or exchange.

Research in Finance, Volume 16, pages 171–181.
Copyright © 1998 by JAI Press Inc.
All rights of reproduction in any form reserved.
ISBN: 0-7623-0328-X

I. INTRODUCTION

Lamoureux and Poon (1987) and Brennan and Copeland (1988), using daily data, report evidence of a permanent increase in average beta following stock splits. Wiggins (1992) replicates and extends the Brennan and Copeland study and finds that for splits of size two-for-one and greater the increase in beta is sensitive to the return measurement interval. Specifically, he reports that the apparent beta increase disappears when using weekly or monthly rather than daily returns.

This study extends the work of Wiggins by covering all stock splits (rather than two-for-one and greater), by including stock dividends as well as stock splits, and by partitioning the sample into New York Stock Exchange (NYSE) and American Stock Exchange (AMEX) stocks. By far the majority of studies of the market effects of stock distributions focus on stock splits, and many of these studies exclude smaller splits. As a result, little has been reported concerning the effect of distribution size on observed market reactions. In particular, no studies have examined the behavior of beta for both stock splits and stock dividends, nor have any beta-shift studies tested the possibility of an exchange effect corresponding to that observed by Dubofsky (1991) for variance of returns.

The initial results for all stock splits parallel those of Wiggins for large splits. Nevertheless, there appears to be a significant exchange effect. Specifically, NYSE splits exhibit a significant increase in beta, even when weekly data and three-week estimators are used, suggesting that the effect Wiggins attributed to the measurement interval differs across exchanges. Also, in contrast to Wiggins's findings for splits, the stock dividend results indicate insignificant changes in beta following stock dividend ex-dates irrespective of the measurement interval or exchange.

The next section describes the data set. Subsequent sections contain the results for stock splits, the analysis for stock dividends, and a summary and concluding comments.

II. DATA

The data set was obtained from a combination of the December 31, 1992 and December 31, 1993 CRSP daily master tapes. First, 10,838 stock distributions occurring between July 1, 1962 and December 31, 1992 were found on the 1992 tape. Of these, 22 had split factors of zero and 272 did not have a NYSE or an AMEX exchange listing. In addition, 311 had ex-dates in early 1962 and did not have enough data preceding the ex-date for the monthly calculations (see below). Eliminating these events reduced the data set to 10,233 distributions. Second, the 1993 tape was used to obtain returns, thereby eliminating any problem with insufficient data following events that occurred relatively late in 1992. Finally, 1,937 distributions were dropped because they had at least one missing return during the period under examination. The final sample consisted of 8,296 events, broken down as follows:

	NYSE	AMEX	TOTAL
Stock split sample	3,648	784	4,432
Stock dividend sample	2,510	1,354	3,864
Totals	6,158	2,138	8,296

Betas were estimated using two different procedures, as performed by Brennan and Copeland and Wiggins. First, the market model with the CRSP equally weighted index was applied to time-series data for each stock distribution. Second, beta was estimated cross-sectionally for all firms by day (month or week) relative to the ex-date, using the cross-sectional procedure of Ibbotson (1975). Ordinary least squares (OLS) betas were computed, along with the three-day and five-day betas used by Wiggins to adjust for nonsynchronous trading and to mitigate bias from price-adjustment delays. Three separate regressions were employed to obtain each three-day estimator; the return on day t was regressed against the market return on days $t - 1$, t, and $t + 1$. The three-day estimator was the sum of the betas from the three separate regressions. The five-day estimators were obtained in a similar fashion. As Wiggins (1992, pp. 633–634) notes, the three-day estimators are proportional to Scholes-Williams (1977) betas and the five-day estimators are proportional to Fowler-Rorke (1983) betas.

Analogous computations were then made using weekly and monthly data.[1] All betas were calculated according to the format used by Wiggins.[2] For the daily calculations, the pre-event beta was estimated over the 80-day period from day -80 through day -1. The post-event beta was calculated over the 80-day period from day $+5$ through day $+84$. Weekly betas were estimated from 16-week regressions both before and after the event week. Monthly regressions used a six-month period on each side of month zero. The weeks consisted of five trading days, and the months consisted of 25 trading days. Wiggins's monthly calculations differ in that he used (1) excess returns and (2) returns based on actual month-ends rather than returns based on trading-day months. In addition, Wiggins changed his sample for the monthly data, using 2,380 observations for his monthly calculations and only 2,330 for his daily and weekly computations. The present study, to make a clearer comparison of the effect of using different return intervals, used the same number of observations for all three (daily, weekly, and monthly) calculations. Consequently, it was required that each stock distribution have sufficient daily data prior to the ex-date to support the monthly calculations.[3]

To examine beta behavior for stock splits versus stock dividends, the data set was partitioned into two categories. As noted by Fama, Fisher, Jensen, and Roll (1969), Grinblatt, Masulis, and Titman (1984), and Dravid (1987), a split factor of 25% is the conventional dividing line between stock "dividends" and stock "splits." Thus, we categorized stock distributions of 25% or more as splits and those less than 25% as stock dividends. The sample consists of 4,432 stock splits and 3,864 stock dividends. (The largest stock dividend was 20%.)

III. STOCK SPLITS

Table 1 presents beta estimates around the ex-dates of all sizes of stock splits. The top half of Table 1 displays the time-series estimates. The bottom half of Table 1 presents the cross-section estimates. Table 1 also shows the daily, weekly, and monthly betas for all three estimators (OLS, three-period, and five-period), as well as a stock exchange breakout.

For daily data the patterns exhibited in Table 1 for all split factors (the first three columns) are similar to those reported by Wiggins in his tests of large splits. All three daily estimators indicate significant increases in both time-series and cross-section betas. The post-ex-date OLS time-series beta exhibits an 18% increase over the pre-event beta, and the OLS cross-section beta exhibits a 15% increase. The differences in the mean OLS betas are more than 10 standard errors greater than zero. Consistent with the Wiggins large stock-split results, the three-day and five-day betas also increase, but the increases are slightly smaller in percentage terms than those shown by the OLS betas. The three-day time-series and cross-section betas increase by 17.5 and 13%, respectively. The five-day time-series and cross-section betas increase by about 15 and 9%, respectively. This decrease in the upward shift in beta for the three-day and five-day estimators as compared to OLS is consistent with the pattern found by Wiggins. As he notes, the Brennan and Copeland sample did not reveal such a pattern.

The first three columns of Table 1 also present the weekly and monthly results for all sizes of stock splits. Again, the findings are consistent with the large split results reported by Wiggins. For weekly data only the OLS beta exhibits a statistically significant increase for both time-series and cross-sectional regressions. For monthly data neither the OLS nor the three-month betas exhibit a statistically significant increase.

The last six columns of Table 1 present the NYSE and AMEX breakout for splits. For daily data the results for both the NYSE and AMEX subgroups are consistent (with one exception) with the aggregate data presented in the first three columns. For weekly data, however, the time-series three-week estimator is significant for the NYSE subgroup but not for all splits. Similarly, the cross-sectional three-week estimator is significant at the 9% level for the NYSE subgroup but is insignificant for all splits. None of the AMEX weekly estimators (time-series or cross-sectional) is significant.[4]

Table 1. Mean Beta Estimates Around Ex-Dates of Stock Splits (25% or greater)

Time-Series Betas

Daily Data	All Splits			NYSE Splits			AMEX Splits		
	OLS	3-Day	5-Day	OLS	3-Day	5-Day	OLS	3-Day	5-Day
Pre-event	1.124	1.771	1.887	1.099	1.743	1.860	1.235	1.911	2.031
Post-event	1.325	2.081	2.174	1.323	2.072	2.167	1.335	2.114	2.203
Difference	0.202*	0.310*	0.287*	0.224*	0.329*	0.307*	0.100*	0.202*	0.171*
Std. error	(0.010)	(0.020)	(0.027)	(0.011)	(0.021)	(0.029)	(0.028)	(0.056)	(0.077)

Weekly Data	OLS	3-Wk.	5-Wk.	OLS	3-Wk.	5-Wk.	OLS	3-Wk.	5-Wk.
Pre-event	1.138	1.333	1.219	1.115	1.294	1.185	1.235	1.503	1.362
Post-event	1.270	1.383	1.221	1.276	1.365	1.194	1.243	1.433	1.331
Difference	0.131*	0.050	0.001	0.160*	0.071*	0.009	0.008	-0.070	-0.031
Std. error	(0.017)	(0.030)	(0.040)	(0.018)	(0.032)	(0.042)	(0.048)	(0.086)	(0.115)

Monthly Data	OLS	3-Mo.		OLS	3-Mo.		OLS	3-Mo.	
Pre-event	1.028	0.814		0.995	0.794		1.183	0.924	
Post-event	1.072	0.865		1.050	0.840		1.180	0.994	
Difference	0.044	0.050		0.055*	0.046		-0.003	0.069	
Std. error	(0.023)	(0.040)		(0.024)	(0.041)		(0.071)	(0.121)	

(continued)

175

Cross-Sectional Betas

Table 1. Continued

Daily Data

	All Splits			NYSE Splits			AMEX Splits		
	OLS	3-Day	5-Day	OLS	3-Day	5-Day	OLS	3-Day	5-Day
Pre-event	1.110	1.808	1.964	1.082	1.776	1.924	1.228	1.969	2.171
Post-event	1.277	2.041	2.135	1.272	2.028	2.124	1.298	2.107	2.213
Difference	0.167*	0.232*	0.171*	0.190*	0.252*	0.200*	0.070*	0.138*	0.042
Std. error	(0.012)	(0.026)	(0.033)	(0.011)	(0.027)	(0.035)	(0.030)	(0.056)	(0.079)

Weekly Data

	All Splits			NYSE Splits			AMEX Splits		
	OLS	3-Wk.	5-Wk.	OLS	3-Wk.	5-Wk.	OLS	3-Wk.	5-Wk.
Pre-event	1.078	1.532	1.671	1.052	1.475	1.607	1.189	1.772	1.931
Post-event	1.177	1.544	1.600	1.168	1.523	1.569	1.218	1.636	1.753
Difference	0.099*	0.013	-0.071	0.116*	0.048	-0.038	0.029	-0.137	-0.178
Std. error	(0.017)	(0.031)	(0.055)	(0.014)	(0.028)	(0.053)	(0.050)	(0.098)	(0.123)

Monthly Data

	All Splits		NYSE Splits		AMEX Splits	
	OLS	3-Mo.	OLS	3-Mo.	OLS	3-Mo.
Pre-event	0.993	1.231	0.947	1.163	1.191	1.506
Post-event	1.004	1.289	0.979	1.239	1.116	1.532
Difference	0.010	0.057	0.032	0.076	-0.076	0.026
Std. error	(0.026)	(0.067)	(0.031)	(0.062)	(0.049)	(0.083)

Notes: *Significant difference between post-ex-date and pre-ex-date beta estimate at 5% level. Standard errors are the square root of the sum of the squared standard errors of mean pre-event and post-event betas.

Table 2. Mean Beta Estimates Around Ex-Dates of Stock Dividends (smaller than 25%)

Time-Series Betas

	All Stock Dividends			NYSE Stock Dividends			AMEX Stock Dividends		
Daily Data	OLS	3-Day	5-Day	OLS	3-Day	5-Day	OLS	3-Day	5-Day
Pre-event	1.069	1.712	1.824	1.093	1.719	1.799	1.013	1.669	1.839
Post-event	1.064	1.719	1.822	1.085	1.715	1.808	1.023	1.703	1.818
Difference	-0.004	0.007	-0.001	-0.008	-0.003	0.009	0.009	0.034	-0.022
Std. error	(0.013)	(0.024)	(0.031)	(0.015)	(0.028)	(0.037)	(0.024)	(0.045)	(0.060)
Weekly Data	OLS	3-Wk.	5-Wk.	OLS	3-Wk.	5-Wk.	OLS	3-Wk.	5-Wk.
Pre-event	1.041	1.361	1.297	1.025	1.289	1.228	1.060	1.475	1.409
Post-event	1.050	1.333	1.265	1.054	1.310	1.201	1.038	1.353	1.329
Difference	0.010	-0.028	-0.033	0.029	0.021	-0.027	-0.022	-0.122	-0.080
Std. error	(0.020)	(0.034)	(0.044)	(0.023)	(0.041)	(0.052)	(0.037)	(0.063)	(0.083)
Monthly Data	OLS	3-Mo.		OLS	3-Mo.		OLS	3-Mo.	
Pre-event	1.077	0.845		1.069	0.835		1.092	0.885	
Post-event	1.046	0.844		1.035	0.832		1.063	0.882	
Difference	-0.030	0.000		-0.034	-0.003		-0.030	-0.003	
Std. error	(0.025)	(0.041)		(0.032)	(0.052)		(0.049)	(0.082)	

(continued)

177

Table 2. Continued

Cross-Sectional Betas

	All Stock Dividends			NYSE Stock Dividends			AMEX Stock Dividends		
Daily Data	*OLS*	*3-Day*	*5-Day*	*OLS*	*3-Day*	*5-Day*	*OLS*	*3-Day*	*5-Day*
Pre-event	1.046	1.824	2.032	1.075	1.848	2.030	0.990	1.769	2.029
Post-event	1.060	1.848	2.050	1.064	1.826	2.001	1.047	1.873	2.111
Difference	0.014	0.024	0.017	-0.011	-0.021	-0.029	0.057*	0.104*	0.082
Std. error	(0.013)	(0.027)	(0.033)	(0.013)	(0.028)	(0.039)	(0.024)	(0.046)	(0.058)
Weekly Data	*OLS*	*3-Wk.*	*5-Wk.*	*OLS*	*3-Wk.*	*5-Wk.*	*OLS*	*3-Wk.*	*5-Wk.*
Pre-event	1.036	1.581	1.800	1.028	1.509	1.718	1.052	1.709	1.949
Post-event	1.055	1.598	1.846	1.033	1.537	1.748	1.082	1.676	1.972
Difference	0.019	0.017	0.046	0.005	0.027	0.030	0.030	-0.032	0.024
Std. error	(0.021)	(0.027)	(0.051)	(0.027)	(0.044)	(0.060)	(0.024)	(0.063)	(0.110)
Monthly Data	*OLS*	*3-Mo.*		*OLS*	*3-Mo.*		*OLS*	*3-Mo.*	
Pre-event	1.056	1.162		1.024	1.074		1.113	1.298	
Post-event	1.041	1.311		1.012	1.301		1.080	1.289	
Difference	-0.015	0.148		-0.012	0.227		-0.033	-0.009	
Std. error	(0.021)	(0.095)		(0.039)	(0.174)		(0.036)	(0.079)	

Notes: *Significant difference between post-ex-date and pre-ex-date beta estimate at 5% level. Standard errors are the square root of the sum of the squared standard errors of mean pre-event and post-event betas.

IV. STOCK DIVIDENDS

Table 2 presents the corresponding results for stock dividends (size under 25%). The most noticeable difference between Table 1 for splits and Table 2 for stock dividends is that the significant increases in beta for splits are not evident for stock dividends. In fact, based on daily data, none of the six aggregate beta changes (time-series and cross-section OLS, three-day, and five-day) for stock dividends is statistically significant. All six were significant for stock splits. Thus, as far as results using daily data are concerned, there is no evidence of a beta change for stock dividends but there is evidence of a highly significant beta increase for stock splits.

Table 2 also presents stock dividend results using weekly and monthly data as well as a breakout by stock exchange. In contrast to the OLS results in Table 1, when weekly and monthly returns are used, no stock dividend betas show a significant change after the ex-date. Generally (with two exceptions), there does not appear to be an exchange difference for stock dividends. Overall, the results support Dravid's (1987) suggestion that stock dividends and stock splits are different types of events.

V. SUMMARY AND CONCLUDING COMMENTS

This paper updates and extends the study of beta shifts to all sizes of stock splits and to stock dividends. Possible exchange effects are examined by partitioning the sample into NYSE and AMEX stocks. Beta is estimated using daily, weekly, and monthly returns. The results for all splits are similar to those reported elsewhere in the literature for large splits. Specifically, there is evidence of a significant increase in beta following split ex-dates, but such evidence weakens as the return measurement interval increases.

For NYSE splits, the evidence of a beta increase persists somewhat longer, with even the three-week beta exhibiting a significant increase. This is not the case for splits in the aggregate. AMEX splits, on the other hand, do not exhibit any significant beta changes beyond those reflected in the daily data. These results for beta are similar to those reported by Dubofsky for volatility. Specifically, Dubofsky observes that, using daily data, there is an increase in post-split volatility for both NYSE and AMEX securities. However, when weekly returns are used, AMEX stocks show no increase in volatility while NYSE stocks still exhibit a post-split volatility increase (yet smaller than that found with daily data).

In the absence of a theory explaining differential behavior on the two exchanges, it is natural to seek out institutional differences that might shed some light on the observed results. Cohen and colleagues (1983, p. 273) assert that, for securities with relatively long (short) price-adjustment delays, OLS will tend to underestimate (overestimate) beta. They further assert that there are possible reasons for price-adjustment delays other than nonsynchronous trading that would limit the effectiveness of the Scholes-Williams (1977) procedure. It is plausible that the incidence of price-adjustment lags differs between the two exchanges. In addition, Dubofsky points out that (1) specialists are more likely to participate in trades of low-volume stocks than high-volume stocks in order to maintain price stability, (2) AMEX stocks are typically lower priced than NYSE securities, and (3) institutions dominate ownership and trading on the NYSE but not on the AMEX. Dubofsky also notes that AMEX rule 132 requires that specialists adjust open limit orders to sell by the split factor; NYSE rule 118 requires that open orders to sell not be adjusted on the ex-date. Although not noted by Dubofsky, there is also a difference in the NYSE and AMEX accounting requirements for stock splits. The *NYSE Listed Company Manual* (1996) requires the issuing company to capitalize *paid-in-capital* for splits where par or stated value per share remains unchanged. The AMEX does not have a similar requirement. The link between these institutional factors and shifts in the covariance between market and firm returns is not clear.

The results for stock dividends contrast sharply with those for stock splits. For the combined sample of stock dividends, evidence of beta changes is absent even when using daily returns. It is unclear why illusory beta shifts for stock splits that appear with daily data do not also appear for stock dividends. This finding supports previous conclusions in the volatility literature, notably Dravid (1987), that stock splits and stock dividends are fundamentally different events. It should be noted that there is an accounting difference between stock dividends and splits. Typically, stock dividends are accounted for by capitalizing retained earnings at fair value. Some stock splits are reported by capitalizing retained earnings at par, but many splits involve no change in retained earnings.

NOTES

1.   The Wiggins (1992) large split study was replicated for daily and weekly data to confirm the consistency of the procedures used in this study with those of Wiggins. The results closely matched those reported by Wiggins.

2.   As in Wiggins (1992), five-month betas were not estimated.

3.   Sufficient daily data preceding the ex-date consisted of 187 days, comprising seven 25-trading-day months (six months for the OLS regressions plus one for the three-month estimators). An additional 12 days were needed to place the ex-date in the center of month zero.

4.   The two exchanges were compared as to average size of stock distribution and average pre-ex-date price. The average size factor was 32% on the AMEX and 52% on the NYSE. The average pre-ex-date price was $15.18 on the AMEX and $27.60 on the NYSE. As a precaution to determine whether these differences might be driving the observed exchange effect, the difference between post- and pre-event three-week beta was regressed on three independent variables—size, price, and exchange (as a dummy variable). Of the three, only exchange had a significant coefficient (significant at the 0.01 level, as compared with 0.24 and 0.40 for size and price, respectively).

REFERENCES

Brennan, M., & Copeland, T. (1988, September). Beta changes around stock splits: A note. *Journal of Finance, 43*, 1009–1013.

Cohen, K., Hawawini, G., Maier, S., Schwartz, R., & Whitcomb, D. (1983, August). Friction in the trading process and the estimation of systematic risk. *Journal of Financial Economics, 12*, 263–278.

Dravid, A. (1987, March). A note on the behavior of stock returns around ex-dates of stock distributions. *Journal of Finance, 42*, 163–168.

Dubofsky, D. (1991, March). Volatility increases subsequent to NYSE and AMEX stock splits. *Journal of Finance, 46*, 421–431.

Fama, E., Fisher, L., Jensen, M., & Roll, R. (1969, February). The adjustment of stock prices to new information. *International Economic Review, 10*, 1–21.

Fowler, D., & Rorke, C. H. (1983, August). Risk measurement when shares are subject to infrequent trading: Comment. *Journal of Financial Economics, 12*, 279–283.

Grinblatt, M., Masulis, R., & Titman, S. (1984, December). The valuation effects of stock splits and stock dividends. *Journal of Financial Economics, 13*, 461–490.

Ibbotson, R. G. (1975, September). Price performance of common stock new issues. *Journal of Financial Economics, 2*, 235–272.

Lamoureux, C., & Poon, P. (1987, December). The market reaction to stock splits. *Journal of Finance, 42*, 1347–1370.

New York Stock Exchange (1996). *Listed company manual.* (Loose-leaf) Section 703.02: Stock split/stock dividend listing process. New York: NYSE.

Scholes, M., & Williams, J. (1977, December). Estimating betas from nonsynchronous data. *Journal of Financial Economics, 5*, 309–327.

Wiggins, J. (1992, December). Beta changes around stock splits revisited. *Journal of Financial and Quantitative Analysis, 27*, 631–640.

COMMON STOCHASTIC TRENDS IN THE TERM STRUCTURE OF INTEREST RATE SWAPS

S. V. Jayanti, Sorin Tuluca, and Alan K. Reichert

ABSTRACT

This study examines the long-run dynamics of the term structure of interest rate swaps for five maturities ranging from two to five years. Using Johansen's cointegration analysis procedures we find that the swap series are cointegrated. In addition, we find substantial, if not conclusive, support for the expectations hypothesis theory (EHT) as it applies to the term structure of swap rates. Finally, we demonstrate that an error correction model (ECM) incorporating the information from the cointegration analysis outperforms a vector autoregressive model (VAR) when forecasting out of sample swap rates.

I. INTRODUCTION

In the last 10 years interest rate swaps have become one of the most important instruments in hedging interest rate risk. The spectacular growth in the swap market

Research in Finance, Volume 16, pages 183–200.
ISBN: 0-7623-0328-X

is illustrated by the fact that the notional principal of interest rate swaps outstanding increased from $5 billion at the end of 1982 to $889 billion at the end of 1987 and $6.241 trillion at the end of 1994.[1] During this period the number of swap market participants increased dramatically; swaps are standardized and traded as a commodity. It is possible that these developments resulted in increased efficiency in the swap market and reduced arbitrage opportunities.[2]

In one of the earliest empirical studies on interest rate swaps, McNulty (1990) estimates a pricing model using data on individual swap transactions during the period December 1982 to May 1984. His results indicate a high degree of integration between the swap and Treasury markets. To the authors knowledge there are no studies on the long-run dynamics of interest rate swaps of various maturities. However, several studies examine the Treasury yield curve using cointegration techniques and report a long-term relationship between yields of different maturities. For example, Bradley and Lumpkin (1992) find empirical evidence that the seven Treasury rates with maturities from three months to 30 years are cointegrated. Hall, Anderson, and Granger (1992) analyze the very short-term (one–11 months) maturities, while Engsted and Tanggaard (1994) include two, five, and 10-year yields to the short-term rates. This last study reports that the term structure of interest rates is cointegrated and is driven by a common stochastic trend which they identify as the short-term rate. They confirm in that the expectation hypothesis of the term structure holds for Treasury securities.

This study examines both long-run relationships and short-term dynamics among the prices of interest rate swaps of various maturities. Specifically, we analyze swap prices quoted as mid-market spread (i.e., average of bid and offer spreads) over the comparable Treasury rates for maturities of two, three, five, seven, and 10 years. The data period runs from July 1991 through August 1995. We employ the maximum likelihood analysis of cointegration developed by Johansen (1988, 1991) and Johansen and Juselius (1990). Johansen's multivariate cointegration procedure has several advantages over the single equation approach of Engle and Granger (1987). For example, Johansen method does not assume that the cointegrating vector is unique and identifies the appropriate number of cointegrating vectors. Since it treats all variables as endogenous, one is not forced to make a priori judgments with respect to whether the variables are exogenous or endogenous.

The empirical results indicate that the prices of the five swap maturities under consideration are cointegrated, implying that a long-run equilibrium condition prevents these rates from drifting too far apart. The expectations hypothesis of term structure implies $n - 1$ independent cointegrating vectors in a system of n interest rates. This condition is approximately satisfied with three out of four possible vectors found to be cointegrated. Thus, our findings generally support the EHT in the term structure of swap rates. We also find that an error-correction model, which utilizes the lagged error-correction terms from the cointegrating vectors, outperforms an unrestricted vector autoregressive model in forecasting swap rates.

II. METHODOLOGY

Many economic time series involving interest rates are considered to be nonstationary, drifting in time.[3] One means of achieving stationarity is to difference the data series which unfortunately results in loss of information about the long-run relationship between the levels of the variables. The cointegration framework introduced by Engle and Granger (1987), and later extended by Johansen (1988, 1991), permits the analysis of time series in level form without the need for transformation. The main advantage of cointegration is that it takes into account the dynamic linkages among time series. Our analysis of swap rates proceeds in three steps:

Step 1: Testing for Unit Roots

There are two widely used tests for detecting the presence of unit roots in time series: the Augmented Dickey-Fuller test (ADF) and the Phillips-Perron test (PP). In the ADF test the following regression is estimated:

$$\Delta y_t = \alpha_0 + \alpha_1 y_{t-1} + \alpha_2 t + \sum_{i=1}^{p} \delta_i \Delta y_{t-i} + e_t \tag{1}$$

where y_t represents the swap rates and e_t is an error term.

The value of p, the number of lagged differences, is chosen from a visual examination of the autocorrelations and partial autocorrelations as well as portmanteau tests in order to eliminate the autocorelation of the error term. The α coefficients in equation (1) are tested for statistical significance against critical values to determine if the series have a unit root and is nonstationary.

The Phillips and Perron (1988) procedure (PP) corrects the standard errors used to compute the t-statistic using the Newly and West (1987) correction. Although ADF and PP tests lead to similar results, the PP test is robust to serial autocorrelations because it uses a nonparametric correction; therefore, it avoids the standard stringent normality assumptions.

Step 2: Testing for Cointegration

The next stage of analysis involves testing for cointegration using the multivariate tests developed by Johansen (1988, 1991) and Johansen and Juselius (1990). Johansen's method is preferred to the univariate test developed by Engle and Granger (1987) because it enables one to analyze systems of more than two series simultaneously.

Johansen suggests that a vector of time series written as a k order vector autoregressive (VAR) model in levels:

$$Y_t = \sum_{i=1}^{k} A_t Y_{t-i} + e_t \qquad (2)$$

can be transformed to an error correction model (VECM) in the first difference and lagged levels:

$$\Delta Y_t = \sum_{i=1}^{k-i} \Gamma_i \Delta Y_{t-k} + \Pi Y_{t-k} + \varepsilon_t \qquad (3)$$

where:

$$\Gamma_i = -I + A_1 + \ldots + A_i \ (I \text{ is a unit matrix}),$$

$$\Pi = -(I - A_1 - \ldots - A_k)$$

Equation (3) will have the same degree of integration on both sides only if $\Pi = 0$ (no cointegration) or if ΠY_{t-k} is $I(0)$, which implies cointegration. The rank of the matrix Π gives the number of cointegrating vectors. Π can be written as

$$\Pi = \alpha\beta' \qquad (4)$$

where β is the matrix of cointegrating vectors, and α is the feedback matrix of factor loadings or feedback coefficients.

The number of cointegrating vectors (r) is determined by two tests:

The *trace test* is based on the statistic

$$LR_{trace} = -T \sum_{i=r+1}^{n} \ln(1 - \lambda_i) \qquad (5)$$

and the *maximal eigen value test* is based on

$$LR_{\lambda_{max}} = -T\ln(1 - \lambda_{r+1}) \qquad (6)$$

where the lambdas are the estimated eigenvalues obtained by the maximum likelihood procedure in Johansen and Juselius (1990).

The test statistics in equations (5) and (6) do not represent regular chi-square distributions but weakly converge to a function of $(p - r)$ dimensional Brownian motion (see Johansen 1991). Critical values for up to five dimensions are provided by Johansen and Juselius (1990, see Table A1).

If cointegration exists in the swap series, then the series can be represented as an error correction model (ECM). Engle and Granger (1987) demonstrate that such ECMs incorporate both the level and difference of variables and preserve the stationarity of the error term. The ECM is a dynamic model since it contains both the cointegrating error term and lagged variables. If the coefficient of the error correction term is found to be statistically significant, it confirms the existence of cointegration in the series under consideration.

Step 3: Comparing Relative Forecasting Performance

If ECM is a valid representation of the swap series then forecasts based on ECM should outperform the forecasts lacking such information. To test this proposition, we evaluate the forecasting performance of two alternative models. The first method employs an unrestricted vector autoregressive (VAR) model. The error correction model is used to produce an alternate second set of forecasts. The root mean square error (RMSE) and the Theil's U inequality coefficient are used to assess the relative performance of the two methods. If one procedure produces a reduction in either RMSE or Theil's U compared to the other method, then that method is said to have superior prediction accuracy. In order to ascertain if the difference between the two models is statistically significant the Ashley, Granger, and Schmalensee (AGS) (1980) procedure is employed. The AGS procedure tests for a statistically significant difference between the mean square error (MSE) of alternative forecast results. The null hypothesis of no significant difference between MSE is equivalent to the hypothesis that both α and β, in the following regression, are equal to zero:

$$\varepsilon_{var} - \varepsilon_{vecm} = \alpha + \beta[(\varepsilon_{var} + \varepsilon_{vecm}) - (\overline{\varepsilon}_{var} + \overline{\varepsilon}_{vecm})] + \eta \tag{7}$$

where, ε_{var} and ε_{vecm} represent the forecast error of the VAR and VECM models, respectively. The bar notation indicates the average of each of the two error terms. If α is significantly different from zero then a meaningful difference in the mean absolute error exists between the two methods, while if β is significantly different from zero there exists a meaningful difference in the prediction error variances.

A. Data

The data are obtained from Swaps Monitor Market Information Service. The data consists of daily quotations on mid-market spreads (average of bid and offer spreads) on plain vanilla U.S. dollar denominated interest rate swaps during the period July 15, 1991 and August 14, 1995 with maturities of two (SWAP2), three (SWAP3), five (SWAP5), seven (SWAP7), and 10 years (SWAP10). The quotes pertain to the fixed side of the swap and the prices are quoted as spreads (basis points) over the Treasury rate. The quote is the average of the quotes of three leading firms of brokers: Prebon Yamane, Eurobrokers, and Tullett & Tokyo. Each of the three firms was asked where it currently sees well-supported bid and offer spreads over the "on-the-run" Treasury rate at each maturity. "Well-supported" means the spread at which more than one counterparty whose credit is generally accepted in the market for that maturity would be willing to enter into a swap of at least $50

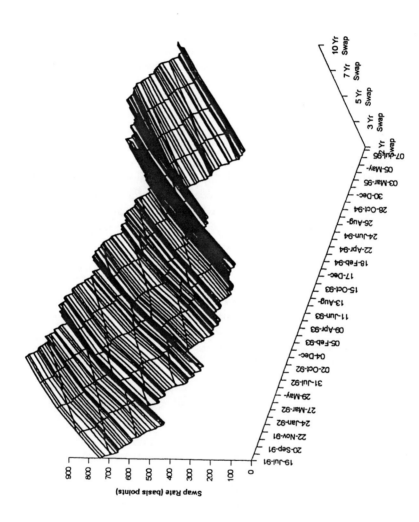

Figure 1. History of Swap Rate Term Structure (selected maturities)

million with other acceptable counterparties. The data on weekly Treasury rates were obtained from the Federal Reserve Bank of St. Louis.

Daily spreads on swaps are averaged over a week and added to the average Treasury yield for that week. Thus, weekly swap prices are employed in this study. Figure 1 depicts the history of the swap yield curve over the period under consideration (July 19, 1991 to August 11, 1995). The graph indicates that swap yields have generally declined over the four-year period and that the term structure of swap rates has become significantly flatter.

III. EMPIRICAL RESULTS

A. Unit Root Tests

To test the presence of unit roots (nonstationary) we used both ADF and PP tests on each of the five swap-rate series. The results are reported in Table 1. The null hypothesis for each test is that the series has a unit root. If the absolute value of the test statistic is greater than the critical value, the null hypothesis is rejected. From Table 1 it is clear that each series is nonstationary. Tests for the presence of a trend term indicate that the model without trend is more appropriate for each series. Tests for presence of unit roots in first differences suggest that the null hypothesis is rejected for all five series. The number of lags, different for each equation, was chosen using autocorrelation and partial autocorrelation diagrams as well as portmanteau tests. Thus, both ADF and PP indicate that the five swap series are nonstationary when measured in levels but stationary in first differences.

B. Cointegration Tests

The results for Johansen tests are shown in Table 2. For both the trace and the maximal eigenvalue test, the null hypothesis is that there are at most r cointegrating vectors. The critical values are obtained from Johansen-Juselius (1990). If the values of trace and λ_{max} are smaller than the critical values, it suggests acceptance of the null hypothesis. The test starts from $r = 0$, the hypothesis that there is no cointegrating relationship in a VAR model. If the null hypothesis cannot be rejected the procedure stops. If the hypothesis is rejected, we examine sequentially the hypothesis that $r \leq 1$, $r \leq 2$, and so on. If the null hypothesis cannot be rejected for $r \leq k$, but has been rejected for $r \leq k - 1$, the conclusion is that the number of vectors, or the rank of β is equal to k.

Examining the results of Table 2, both tests clearly reject the null hypothesis for $r = 0$ at a 10% level of significance. For $r = 1$ and $r = 2$ the two tests yield slightly different results. For $r = 1$, using the trace test we reject the null hypothesis, while the results of the maximal eigenvalue test marginally fails to reject the null hypothesis. At $r = 2$, for all practical purposes, the maximal eigenvalue test rejects the null hypothesis, while the trace test come close to rejecting the null hypothesis.

Table 1. Augmented Dickey-Fuller (ADF) and Phillips-Peron (PP) Unit Root Tests
for Swap Rates Levels and First Differences

| | Swap Maturity | | | | | |
Test	2 YR	3 YR	5 YR	7 YR	10 YR	Critical Values 10%
ADF Levels						
CONSTANT	−1.5896	−1.7201	−1.9389	−1.9992	−1.9699	−2.57[a]
NO TREND	1.2640	1.4891	1.9121	2.1226	2.1009	3.78[b]
CONSTANT	−2.1124	−2.0113	−2.0131	−1.9805	−1.8900	−3.13[c]
TREND	1.7035	1.5211	1.5233	1.6028	1.4525	4.03[d]
	2.5546	2.2719	2.525	2.2803	2.0188	5.34[e]
ADF Difference						
CONSTANT	−3.6203	−3.4151	−3.4316	−3.3690	−3.274	−2.57[a]
NO TREND	6.5828	5.8551	5.9134	5.7080	5.3778	3.78[b]
CONSTANT	−3.6823	−3.4699	−3.4901	−3.3992	−3.2989	−3.13[c]
TREND	4.5458	4.0379	4.0775	3.8759	3.6402	4.03[d]
	6.7892	6.0334	6.0910	5.7809	5.4420	5.34[e]
PP Levels						
CONSTANT	−1.6144	−1.8526	−2.0369	−2.0943	−2.0488	−2.57[a]
NO TREND	1.4844	2.0065	2.5278	2.7126	2.6927	3.78[b]
CONSTANT	−2.5113	−2.3480	−2.1185	−2.0086	−1.8523	−3.13[c]
TREND	3.6488	3.1798	2.7660	2.4463	2.1091	4.03[d]
	5.2825	4.4690	3.6866	3.1446	2.5680	5.34[e]
PP Difference						
CONSTANT	−10.765	−11.086	−11.347	−11.894	−11.699	−2.57[a]
NO TREND	57.932	61.442	64.369	70.727	68.434	3.78[b]
CONSTANT	−10.947	−11.230	−11.465	−11.982	−11.759	−3.13[c]
TREND	39.936	42.030	43.809	47.854	46.085	4.03[d]
	59.901	63.044	65.708	71.778	69.125	5.34[e]

Notes: All critical values are identical for ADF and Phillips-Peron tests.
[a]Test for the unit root coefficient H_0: coefficient is zero.
[b]Joint test for the constant and unit root coefficient. H_0: all coefficients are zero.
[c]Test for the unit root coefficient. H_0: coefficient is zero.
[d]Joint test for the constant, trend and unit root coefficient. H_0: all coefficients are zero.
[e]Joint test for the trend and unit root coefficient. H_0: all coefficients are zero.

Table 2. Johansen Cointegration Tests with Cointegrating and the Feedback
Matrices

Panel A

H_0	λ max	Critical Values 1%	λ trace	Critical Values 1%
$r \leq 4$	.139	2.82	.139	2.82
$r \leq 3$	5.259*	12.10	5.398*	13.34
$r \leq 2$	18.668	18.70	24.066	26.79
$r \leq 1$	22.067	24.71	46.133	43.96
$r = 0$	40.595	30.77	86.727	65.06

Panel B

β_1^{*}	β_2	β_3	β_4	β_5
−0.3300	−0.0077	0.0870	−0.0261	0.0405
0.6893	0.0281	0.0065	0.0669	−0.0318
−0.4943	0.1054	−0.3086	−0.0579	−0.0160
0.0549	−0.2919	0.0810	−0.0175	0.0199
0.0661	0.1624	0.1550	0.0494	−0.0125

Panel C

α_1^{*}	α_2	α_3	α_4	α_5
1.5330	−1.1126	0.9752	−1.5626	−0.0633
0.6638	−1.3456	1.2036	−1.5909	−0.0308
1.0975	−1.2606	1.0551	−1.4547	0.0225
0.6732	−1.1647	0.4491	−1.5413	0.0475
0.6198	−1.6554	0.2240	−1.2965	0.0481

Notes: Panel A presents tests for the number of cointegrating vectors. * denotes the values for which the null
hypothesis of *r* cointegrating vectors cannot be rejected. Panel B presents the matrix of cointegrating
vectors. * denotes significant vector. Panel C presents the matrix of adjustment coefficients (feedback
matrix.) * denotes the significant vector.

For $r = 3$, both tests clearly indicate that the null hypothesis should not be rejected.
Hence, it seems reasonable to conclude that the number of cointegrating vectors is
three.

The evidence of cointegration among the five swap series implies that there is a
long-run equilibrium relationship that prevents any one rate from drifting away too
far from equilibrium. This result is consistent with the empirical findings of Bradely
and Lumkins (1992) and Hall, Anderson, and Granger (1992) of a conintegrating
relationship in the term structure of Treasury rates.

The expectations hypothesis of the term structure (EHT) implies that one common integrated factor (e.g., short-term interest rates) drives the entire system of

both short- and long-term interest rates. In a system of n interest rates the number of common trends, or the number of independent cointegration vectors, should be $n - 1$. Further, all those vectors should satisfy the zero-sum restrictions for the coefficients of the cointegrating vectors.[4] Rejecting one or both of these conditions constitutes evidence against the EHT (Engsted & Tanggaard, 1994). Our results indicate the existence of three cointegration vectors in a system of five rates. These results provide considerable but not total support for the EHT in regards to the term structure of swap rates. On the other hand, our results are somewhat stronger than the findings of Arshanapalli and Doukas (1994) who report only two cointegrating vectors in a system of five Eurocurrency rates. At the same time our results are not quite as strong as those reported in Engsted and Tanggaard (1994) where EHT was unambiguously found to hold for the term structure of U.S. interest rates.

In Table 2 we report the eigenvectors (β) and feedback coefficients (α). The significant cointegrating vector represented by the largest eigenvalue normalized by the coefficient of the two-year swap rate is given by:

$$2YR = 2.0888\,(3YR) - 1.467\,(5YR) + .166\,(7YR) + 0.200\,(10YR) \qquad (8)$$

This equation represents the long-term relationship among the system of five swap rates. As previously mentioned, the choice of expressing the two-year rate as endogenous is arbitrary. As an equilibrium relationship, the coefficients should theoretically sum to 1.0. The estimated coefficients in equation (8) actually sum to 0.989, a value insignificantly different from 1.0. As discussed before, the Johansen procedure considers all the variables as endogenous. The error in this long-term relationship, with the appropriate number of lags, is the correction applied to the system. The error has all the characteristics of a normal variable. This in itself is an improvement over the error of an unrestricted VAR model where the error can display significant nonnormality.

C. Error Correction Model

The cointegrated system obtained above can be represented as an error correction model that incorporates both levels and differences of variables such that stationarity is preserved (Engle & Granger, 1987). The error correction model is a dynamic model which exploits the possible long-term relations among the variables. The results of the model augmented with the fifth lag of the error correction (VECM) are shown in Table 3. The model employs the entire sample of 213 observations incorporating four lags of each variable. This specification was chosen based on the Akaike Information (AIC) and Schwarz (SW) criteria, reported in Table 3. It can be seen that the error correction coefficient for two-year swap is -1.533 and is significant with a p-value of 0.077. The coefficients for other maturities are not statistically significant.[5]

These results confirm that the five swap series are cointegrated and that the ECM is a valid representation of the relationships inherent in the data. The significance

Table 3. Vector Error Correction Model for the Full Sample (213 observations)

	Swap Maturity				
	2 YR	3 YR	5 YR	7 YR	10 YR
SWAP2[-1]	-0.0878	-0.2738	-0.4390	-0.5455	-0.62423
	(.802)	(.436)	(.181)	(.09)*	(.037)**
SWAP3[-1]	0.4765	0.6234	0.7454	0.6918	0.7978
	(.332)	(.208)	(.106)	(.126)	(.058)*
SWAP5[-1]	0.0914	0.2768	0.0788	0.3625	0.2643
	(.877)	(.643)	(.887)	(.506)	(.601)
SWAP7[-1]	-0.8022	-0.9554	-0.6075	-0.6001	-0.7706
	(.136)	(.078)*	(.228)	(.224)	(.093)*
SWAP10[-1]	0.5079	0.5159	0.3791	0.2377	0.4851
	(.231)	(.227)	(.339)	(.541)	(.18)
SWAP2[-2]	0.3320	0.6470	0.2219	0.2575	0.2014
	(.34)	(.065)*	(.496)	(.42)	(.497)
SWAP3[-2]	-0.0628	-0.7207	-0.0782	-0.3514	-0.2909
	(.898)	(.144)	(.864)	(.434)	(.485)
SWAP5[-2]	-0.1958	0.2195	-0.1394	0.2790	.02076
	(.744)	(.716)	(.804)	(.613)	(.685)
SWAP7[-2]	0.6214	0.6690	0.6876	0.5313	0.5937
	(.269)	(.237)	(.192)	(.303)	(.215)
SWAP10[-2]	-0.7122	-0.8082	-0.7074	-0.7490	-0.7184
	(.111)	(.072)*	(.091)*	(.068)*	(.059)*
SWAP2[-3]	-0.4680	-0.3546	-0.5086	-0.3363	-0.3391
	(.232)	(.368)	(.166)	(.35)	(.31)
SWAP3[-3]	1.0460	0.8737	1.2211	1.0097	0.9425
	(.08)*	(.145)	(.029)**	(.065)*	(.064)*
SWAP5[-3]	-0.7145	-0.6302	-0.9555	-0.8911	-0.8515
	(.274)	(.338)	(.119)	(.138)	(.127)
SWAP7[-3]	0.3261	0.2383	0.3378	0.3066	0.3869
	(.558)	(.671)	(.517)	(.549)	(.416)
SWAP10[-3]	-0.1386	-0.0543	0.0046	0.0002	-0.0628
	(.756)	(.904)	(.991)	(1.)	(.869)
SWAP2[-4]	-0.9134	-0.6492	-0.6504	-0.3642	-0.3566
	(.02)**	(.099)*	(.076)*	(.309)	(.284)
SWAP3[-4]	0.8705	0.3756	0.6191	0.1782	0.2328
	(.14)	(.525)	(.261)	(.741)	(.642)
SWAP5[-4]	0.6973	0.8360	0.5957	0.6906	0.6030
	(.279)	(.198)	(.323)	(.243)	(.273)
SWAP7[-4]	-0.1601	0.1766	-0.0571	-0.0078	0.0354
	(.767)	(.745)	(.91)	(.987)	(.939)
SWAP10[-4]	-0.4834	-0.7447	-0.5207	-0.5400	-0.5739
	(.259)	(.085)	(.195)	(.17)	(.117)

(continued)

Table 3. Continued

	Swap Maturity				
	2 YR	3 YR	5 YR	7 YR	10 YR
ECV [–5]	1.533	0.66385	1.0975	0.67323	0.61983
	(.077)*	(.445)	(.175)	(.396)	(.4)
CONSTANT	–0.1422	–0.2699	–0.4116	–0.5165	–0.5245
	(.872)	(.761)	(.618)	(.524)	(.486)
ADJ R^2	.1258	.1120	.0958	.069	.0824
AIC	5.1393	5.1512	5.0077	4.9691	4.8205
SC	5.4923	5.5042	5.3607	5.3221	5.1735
F	2.419	2.244	2.044	1.73	1.885
p-value	.001	.002	.006	.029	.014
DW	2.0352	2.0231	2.0150	2.0077	2.0117

Notes: * denotes p-values (in parentheses) of less than 10%, ** denotes p-value of less than 5%.

Table 4. VAR Model for the Full Sample (213 observations)

	Swap Maturity				
	2 YR	3 YR	5 YR	7 YR	10 YR
SWAP2[–1]	0.1137	–0.18656	–0.29473	–0.457	–0.54276
	(.732)	(.574)	(.343)	(.133)	(.055)*
SWAP3[–1]	0.1062	0.46303	0.4803	0.52916	0.64808
	(.812)	(.301)	(.251)	(.196)	(.088)*
SWAP5[–1]	0.41895	0.41862	0.31326	0.50634	0.39669
	(.46)	(.46)	(.554)	(.328)	(.409)
SWAP7[–1]	–0.97512	–1.0302	–0.73126	–0.676	–0.84053
	(.067)*	(.053)*	(.141)	(.164)	(0.063)*
SWAP10[–1]	0.54754	0.53304	0.40742	0.25508	0.50113
	(.199)	(.21)	(.305)	(.511)	(.165)
SWAP2[–2]	0.44424	0.6956	0.30228	0.30684	0.2468
	(.197)	(.044)**	(.346)	(.328)	(.397)
SWAP3[–2]	–0.40815	–0.87024	–0.32542	–0.50309	–0.43053
	(.366)	(.055)*	(.44)	(.223)	(.261)
SWAP5[–2]	0.27762	0.42454	0.19955	0.48694	0.399
	(.608)	(.432)	(.692)	(.324)	(.384)
SWAP7[–2]	0.39496	0.57092	0.5255	0.43186	0.50216
	(.473)	(.299)	(.306)	(.389)	(.281)
SWAP10[–2]	–0.6977	–0.80193	–0.697	–0.74262	–0.71249
	(.12)	(.074)*	(.096)*	(.07)*	(.061)*

(continued)

Table 4. Continued

	Swap Maturity				
	2 YR	3 YR	5 YR	7 YR	10 YR
SWAP2[–3]	–0.19009	–0.2343	–0.30963	–0.21425	–0.22671
	(.598)	(.516)	(.358)	(.515)	(.458)
SWAP3[–3]	0.34739	0.57115	0.72098	0.70292	0.66002
	(.438)	(.203)	(.086)*	(.087)*	(.083)*
SWAP5[–3]	–.001	–0.32129	–0.44473	–0.57779	–0.56302
	(.998)	(.535)	(.358)	(.222)	(.2)
SWAP7[–3]	.0680	0.12654	0.15304	0.19327	0.28258
	(.9)	(.815)	(.762)	(.695)	(.538)
SWAP10[–3]	–0.14322	–.0563	.001	–.0017	–.0647
	(.75)	(.9)	(.998)	(.997)	(.865)
SWAP2[–4]	–0.62779	–0.52551	–0.44596	–0.23879	–0.24118
	(.08)*	(.142)	(.181)	(.464)	(.425)
SWAP3[–4]	0.20128	.085	0.13999	–0.1157	–.0378
	(.657)	(.85)	(.741)	(.78)	(.922)
SWAP5[–4]	1.3736	1.1288	1.0799	0.98757	0.87645
	(.009)***	(.031)**	(.028)**	(.039)**	(.049)**
SWAP7[–4]	–0.4857	.0355	–0.29023	–0.15081	–.0962
	(.343)	(.945)	(.543)	(.747)	(.824)
SWAP10[–4]	–0.41991	–0.71719	–0.47517	–0.51211	–0.54823
	(.328)	(.095)	(.236)	(.192)	(.132)
CONSTANT	–.0173	–0.21577	–0.32213	–0.46164	–0.474
	(.984)	(.807)	(.696)	(.567)	(.527)
ADJ R^2	.1157	.114	.0916	.0703	.0838
AIC	5.146	5.1447	5.008	4.9634	4.8147
SC	5.4835	5.4817	5.345	5.3004	5.1517
F	2.354	2.332	2.044	1.783	1.947
p-value	.002	.002	.007	.025	.012
DW	2.0386	2.024	2.0136	2.0035	2.0072

Notes: * denotes p-values (in parenthesis) of less than 10%, ** denotes p-values of less than 5%.

of the error correction coefficient for the two-year swap suggests that the two-year swap tends to wander more often from equilibrium, but the long-run relationship expressed in equation (8) ultimately causes rates to return to equilibrium. It may also be noted that the two-year swap is the most popular swap, with a volume considerably larger than swaps of other maturities.

For comparison purposes the same results are reported in Table 4 for an unrestricted VAR model. Comparing the results in Tables 3 and 4 it is clear that the most noticeable improvement across all criteria is obtained for the two-year swap rate.

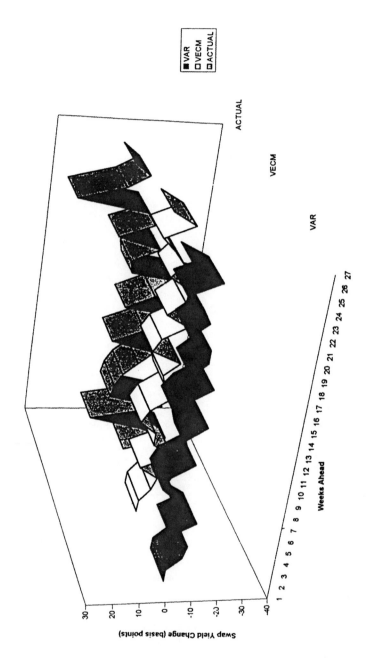

Figure 2. Relative Forecasting Performance of VAR and VEC Models for the Two Year Swap

Table 5. Statistics and Comparison of the Forecasting Models

	2 Year		3 Year		5 Year		7 Year		10 Year	
	VECM	VAR	VECM	VAR	VECM	VAR	VECM	VAR	VECM	VAR
RMSE	14.27	14.38	14.34	14.44	13.69	13.75	13.09	13.15	11.98	12.08
Theil U	.796	.802	.783	.789	.766	.77	.764	.767	.761	.767
R^2	.038	.018	.007	.003	.001	.001	.002	.001	.018	.012
AGS TEST	α	β	α	β	α	β	α	β	α	β
	1.93	.019	.97	.007	1.48	.019	.88	.012	.87	.015
t-value	(5.66)*	(.98)	(6.08)*	(.73)	(5.60)*	(1.24)	(5.65)*	(1.24)	(5.96)*	(1.43)

$$U = \frac{\sqrt{1/T\Sigma(Y_t^f - Y_t^a)^2}}{\sqrt{1/T\Sigma(Y_t^f)^2} + \sqrt{1/T\Sigma(Y_t^a)^2}}$$

Notes: RMSE is the root mean square error between actual values and the forecast. R^2 is computed between actual and predicted values. Theil U is the Theil's inequality coefficient, a measure of forecast accuracy defined by the following formula:

where Y^f is the forecast and Y^a is the actual value, and T is the total number of predictions.

AGS is a test for significant differences in the mean square error of forecasts. The null hypothesis is that α and β in the following regression, are both zero:

$$\varepsilon_{var} - \varepsilon_{vecm} = \alpha + \beta[(\varepsilon_{var} + \varepsilon_{vecm}) - (\bar{\varepsilon}_{var} + \bar{\varepsilon}_{vecm})] + \eta$$

where ε_{var} and ε_{vecm} represent the forecast error of the VAR respectively VECM model and the bar notation represent the errors' average. In parenthesis are the t-test for coefficients' statistical significance. *represents values with a significance below the 1% level. The unmarked values are not significant at conventional levels.

197

The fact that the error correction term is not significant for the other regressions makes the VECM and the VAR models quite similar for all maturities but the two-year swap. However, this does not discard the possibility put forth by Engle and Granger (1987) for VECM to be superior in forecasting performance to an unrestricted VAR.

D. Relative Forecasting Performance

To determine the relative forecasting ability of the two models, a VEC model and an unrestricted VAR model are both estimated using the first 187 observations in the data set.[6] The remaining 26 observations are employed as a holdout sample to determine the ex ante performance of the two models. The prediction results that represent the forecasted change in weekly two-year swap rates generated by the two models are graphed in Figure 2. While the graph shows the two models as being similar in their predictive capability a more rigorous assessment is presented in Table 5. The Root Mean Squared Error (RMSE), Theil's U, and the R^2 between the observed and predicted values are consistently lower for the VECM compared to the VAR model. To test if this difference is statistically significant the AGS procedure is employed. As reported in Table 5, α is significantly different from zero for all maturities with the mean absolute error for the VAR model consistently greater than the mean absolute error for the VEC model. These results suggest the conclusion that the VEC model is a valid representation of the system of five interest rate swap rates.

IV. CONCLUSION

This study finds that interest rate swaps with maturities from two to 10 years have unit roots and are cointegrated. The existence of one cointegrating vector suggests that a common relationship binds these rates together in a long-run equilibrium. Hence, four common integrate factors apparently drive the system (see Stock & Watson, 1988). Common integrating factors might include among others, inflation, credit risk, and interest rate risk. For example, Jayanti, Reichert, and Tuluca (1996) show that swap spreads of different maturities are related to the yield spread between Baa and Aaa bonds and the slope of the yield curve. Fama and French (1989) provide evidence that stock and bond returns are related to default and term premiums. Thus, it is possible that default risk and term premiums may also be responsible for the behavior of the system of the swap rates.

The existence of a cointegrating relationship among the five swap series implies that the rates cannot drift too far away from long-run equilibrium. This study finds that the requirement of $n - 1$ independent cointegrating vectors in a system of n interest rates implied by the expectations hypothesis of term structure is approximately but not entirely supported. Thus, the results provide substantial but not conclusive support for the EHT. This suggests the possibility that small pricing inefficiencies may exist in the market for interest rate swaps. However, the swap market is still relatively immature compared to the market for Treasury securities and further research is needed before a definitive conclusion regarding market inefficiencies can be reached.

Finally, we demonstrate that the equilibrium relationship implied by cointegration can be used to improve forecasting performance. For example, an error correction model incorporating the information from the cointegration analysis outperformed a VAR model.

NOTES

1. Source is the International Swaps and Derivatives Association Survey, June 1995.

2. In a typical plain vanilla interest rate swap one party pays fixed interest rate to another party in exchange for a variable rate interest on the notional principal amount. The rates on the fixed side of the swap are typically quoted as spreads on comparable maturity Treasury yields. Thus, we can have a yield curve for swap rates of different maturities, similar to the Treasury yield curve.

3. For example, studies of the cointegration of US Treasury rates include Bradley and Lumpkin (1992), Hall, Anderson, and Granger (1992), and Engsted and Taggaard (1994).

4. For details the reader is referred to Engsted and Tanggaard (1994).

5. Cointegration requires the error correction be significant in at least one of the regressions (Engle & Granger, 1987).

6. The Johansen procedure applied to the first 187 observations was similar in all respects to the results reported for the full sample. Hence, only the results for the full models are reported.

REFERENCES

Ashley, R. Granger, C. W., & Schmalensee R. (1980). Advertising and aggregate consumption: An analysis of causality, *Econometrica, 48*, 1149–1167

Arshanapalli, B., & Doukas J. (1994). Common stochastic trends in a system of Eurocurrency rates. *Journal of Banking and Finance, 18*, 1047–1061.

Bradley, M. G., & Lumpkin S. A. (1992, Sept). The treasury yield curve as a cointegrated system. *Journal of Financial and Quantitative Analysis*, 449–459.

Engle, R. F., & Granger, C. W. (1987). Cointegration and error-correction: Representation, estimation and testing. *Econometrica, 55*, 251–276.

Engsted, T., & Tanggaard, C. (1994). Cointegration and the US term structure. *Journal of Banking and Finance, 18*, 167–181.

Fama, E., & French, K. (1989). Business conditions and expected returns on stocks and bonds. *Journal of Financial Economics, 25*, 23–49.

Granger, C. W. (1986). Developments in the study of cointegrated economic variables. *Oxford Bulletin of Economics and Statistics, 48*, 213–228.

Hall, A. D., Anderson, H. M., & Granger, C. W. (1992). A cointegration analysis of treasury bill yields. *The Review of Economics and Statistics, 74*, 116–126.

Jayanti, S., Reichert, A., & Tuluca (1996). *Determinants of bid-offer spreads in interest rate swaps.* Working paper, Department of Finance, Cleveland State University.

Johansen, S. (1988). Statistical analysis of cointegrating vectors *Journal of Economic Dynamics and Control, 12*, 231–254.

Johansen, S. (1991). Estimation and hypothesis testing of cointegration vectors in Gaussian vector autoregressive models. *Econometrica, 59*, 1551–1580.

Johansen, S., & Juselius, K. (1990). Maximum likelihood estimation and inference on cointegration-ith application to the demand for money. *Oxford Bulletin of Economics and Statistics, 52*, 169–210.

McNulty, J. (1990). The pricing of interest rate swaps. *Journal of Financial Services Research, 4*, 53–63.

Newey, W., & West, K. (1987). A simple positive semi-definite, heteroskedasticity and autocorrelation consistent covariance matrix. *Econometrica, 51*.

Phillips, P. C., & Perron, P. (1988). Testing for a unit root in time series regression. *Biometika, 75*, 335–346.

Stock, J., & Watson, M. (1988). Testing for common trends, *Journal of the American Statistical Association, 83*, 1097–1107.

AN EMPIRICAL ANALYSIS OF GAP MANAGEMENT AND NET INTEREST MARGIN FOR THE U.S. COMMERCIAL BANKS

Van Son Lai and M. Kabir Hassan

ABSTRACT

In order to examine the determinants of GAP and NIM for U.S. commercial banks, we develop a simultaneous-equations model that jointly determines net interest margin and various maturity gaps. We estimate our model using annual data for the population of insured commercial banks for the years 1984 through 1987. For banks with assets up to $1 billion, we find net interest margin significantly associated with various maturity gaps. For 12 months banks had negative gaps; for five years they had positive gaps. Although we are able to identify the determinants of gap, these factors vary with the maturity of the gaps. We show that banks of any size do not follow a zero-gap policy. Our study also establishes that for large banks NIM and GAPs are weakly related. Our framework is highly relevant for thousands of "community banks" for which accounting flows (such as net interest income) are the primary indicators of the effectiveness of asset-liability management.

Research in Finance, Volume 16, pages 201–220.
Copyright © 1998 by JAI Press Inc.
All rights of reproduction in any form reserved.
ISBN: 0-7623-0328-X

I. INTRODUCTION

The purpose of this paper is to examine empirically the determinants of bank asset-liability management (ALM) within the context of net interest margin (NIM) and various maturity gaps (GAP). In order to examine the determinants of GAP and NIM for U.S. commercial banks, we develop a simultaneous-equations model that jointly determines net interest margin and various maturity gaps. We estimate our model using annual data for the population of insured commercial banks for the years 1984 through 1987. Interest rate risk is important because *unexpected* changes in interest rates can adversely affect bank cash flows and equity values. Managing bank assets and liabilities to minimize both the short- and long-run effects of interest rate risk is the objective of asset-liability management (ALM). The risk-based capital requirements consider only credit risk and bank capital. The Federal Deposit Insurance Corporation Improvement Act of 1991 (FDICIA) requires U.S. bank regulators to add an interest rate component to their capital guidelines. This condition, within the backdrop of the thrift crisis, provides an impetus for the development of a consistently accurate and cost effective means for regulators to assess interest rate risk.

Holding market interest rates constant, we estimate cross-sectional time-series relations between net interest margin (NIM) and various maturity gaps (GAP) for U.S. insured commercial banks, divided into three subgroups, for the years 1984 to 1987. Since market values of bank equities are available only for a few hundred commercial banks compared to our samples of over 13,000 banks, our approach is per force an accounting one. Our theoretical foundation is a simultaneous-equations model that jointly determines NIM and maturity gaps ranging from 12 months to five years.

The financial intermediaries have expanded into a variety of securities as an alternative to traditional lending activities. The extent, volume, and nature of these activities including purchasing, originating, and selling securities has led to questions regarding the inconsistent accounting for and financial statement presentation of such securities by insured financial institutions. The FASB 115 addresses the accounting and reporting for investments in equity securities with determinable fair values and for all investments in debt securities. (Financial Accounting Standards Board, FAS 115 Summary, 1993). FASB 115 has implications for GAP management. Securities classified as available for sale reduces the measured duration of bank earning portfolios. FASB 115 conditions the selection of securities; for example, banks select shorter duration classes classified as available for sale to protect their accounting capital.

The Federal Deposit Insurance Corporation Improvement Act of 1991 (FDICIA) requires U.S. bank regulators to revise capital adequacy standard for banks and to add an interest rate component to their risk-based capital guidelines. While bank regulators have historically relied on an accounting model of interest rate risk (GAP or repricing model), the Federal Reserve's new method is closely related to the economic model of interest rate risk (duration model). A proposed quantitative screen would exempt smaller banks identified as potentially low-risk institutions from additional reporting and, most likely, from any capital requirement for interest rate risk. Greater use of a bank's internal risk measure would be permitted for evaluating interest rate risk when the methodology and key assumptions of that measure are deemed adequate by examiners (Federal Reserve Board, March 1993; *American Banker*, April 1, 1993).

Our study extends the existing literature of bank interest rate risk in the following ways. First, we investigate the determinants of both NIM and GAP in a simultaneous equation system by exploiting a unique data set for all insured commercial banks, collected only for the years 1984 through 1987. To our knowledge this is the first attempt to cover the entire banking population in such a study of bank ALM decisions. Second, we establish the interdependency of capital adequacy, hedging, net interest margin, and gap management. While market discipline may exist only for a few hundred banks whose stocks are traded, regulatory discipline may be more important for community banks, which number in the thousands, because they are not subject to the same kind of market discipline as larger banks. Our results suggest that accounting repricing information plays an important role in detecting interest rate risk for banks with assets less than $1 billion. Repricing data may help bank regulators monitor interest rate risk for banks whose stocks are not traded in the capital market.

This paper consists of five sections. Following a review of the literature in Section II, we present our model in Section III. The data and empirical methodology are presented in Section IV. We present our empirical results in Section V. Section VI concludes our paper.

II. LITERATURE ON MEASURING INTEREST RATE RISK

Much has been written on measuring, managing, and controlling bank interest rate risk. Under the rubric of asset-liability management three major on-balance sheet methods have been discussed: (1) the maturity-gap approach, (2) the duration-gap approach, and (3) the simulation approach. The first method simply attempts to match stated or contracted maturities of assets with liabilities whereas the second relies on the more meaningful notion of effective time to repricing of rate-sensitive cash flows. The simulation approach blends the first two methods into "dynamic" scenario or contingency analyses. Each method offers advantages and disadvantages to the management of interest rate risk (see for instance, Toevs & Haney, 1986; Roll, 1987).

Financial innovation provides contingent and synthetic ways (e.g., futures, swaps, and options) for financial institutions to hedge both symmetric (i.e., risk due to changes in interest rate levels and/or margins) and asymmetric (i.e., risk due to pre-payable assets and/or contract features such as "caps") interest rate risk.[1] Batlin

(1983), Koppenhaver (1985), Goldfarb (1987), and Brodt (1988) derive the optimal financial futures position to minimize the bank's risks for a given balance sheet. Brodt (1988) also considers these decisions as a joint problem. The adoption of one or more of the above complementary approaches hinges on the level of sophistication of the financial institution's management and its information system.

Without access to internal information on the asset/liability/hedging data, empirical researchers have relied on two alternative data sources: (1) reported accounting data (i.e., the bank profitability/net income or net interest margin approach) associated with Flannery (1981), Maisel and Jacobson (1978), Ho and Saunders (1983), and Simonson and Hempel (1983), and (2) equity values of traded banks (i.e., the market-return approach) associated with Flannery (1981), Flannery and James (1984), Unal and Kane (1988), Tarhan (1987), among others. The former approach examines whether interest rate changes have significant effect on bank profitability while the latter tests the nominal contracting hypothesis using stock prices. Based on data in different test periods before 1984, the results are mixed with the exception of Kane and Unal (1990; Unal & Kane 1988) whose sample periods extend into 1985. Most of the studies have used data from large institutions in pre-deregulation eras when off-balance sheet activities were minimal.[2] A growing stream of literature (Deshmukh, Greenbaum, & Kanatas, 1983; Morgan & Smith, 1987) questions the "traditional" prescription of a zero gap to immunize banks from interest rate risk. These authors attempt to derive the optimal or minimal maturity gap for financial institutions. In a two-period model Morgan and Smith (1987) analyze the maturity intermediation and lending decision of banks. When a bank's loan demand is casually linked to the loan rate, they find the strategy of matching the maturity of assets and liabilities is not generally optimal or even the one with minimum risk, which is due primarily to the "built-in" or natural hedge that the intermediary has as a result of rolling over short-term loans while continuing to finance long-term loans. Other authors derive a minimum gap, risk exposure that incorporates both capital and off-balance sheet items. Although these items are not gap related to interest rate risk, they are correlated with interest rate changes. Because of this non-gap risk, the minimum-risk strategy is to diversify by holding a nonzero gap.

Deshmukh, Greenbaum, and Kanatas (1983) considers the financial intermediary's choice of operating as either a broker with minimal risk exposure, because interest rate risk is shifted to borrowers and/or lenders, or an asset transformer (like an inventory producer) willing to actively assume interest rate risk from balance-sheet mismatching. Drawing on the development of the hedging literature, Ho and Saunders (1983), Koppenhaver (1985), Goldfarb (1987), Brodt (1988), and others take up applications of interest rate management in conjunction with hedging instruments in financial institutions. However, without access to detailed data (e.g., spreads on cost of funds and earnings assets, hedging portfolios of financial futures and swaps, etc.), external analysts cannot test these hedging models empirically.[3]

Given the availability of data from regulatory agencies, we opt for the net interest margin approach as it assures the widest representation of all U.S. banks. Lee and Zumwalt's (1981) empirical results support the use of both NIM as an important source of extra-market information in asset pricing. Although analyses based on accounting data potentially suffer from "window dressing" of the financial statements, nonuniformity, and changes in accounting standards, book income (such as net interest margin) cannot consistently and indefinitely be smoothed over the long run. The use of large samples will mitigate this problem since not all banks "window-dress" at the same time.

III. A MODEL OF DETERMINANTS OF BANK NIM AND GAP MANAGEMENT

The accounting model of the firm focuses on reported earnings per share (EPS) in the short run as the key determinant of value. Net interest income (NII = interest income minus interest expense) provides the lifeblood of a bank's earnings. The focal variable of ALM from the accounting perspective is net interest income (or its ratio form net interest margin (NIM = NII/earning assets)). In this context the ALM objective is to maximize net interest income for a given level of risk as reflected by the variability of net interest income or vice versa (i.e., minimize risk for a target level of NII). The following simple formula captures the relationship between expected and unexpected changes in interest rates (Δr) and changes in net interest income (ΔNII):

$$\Delta NII = \Delta r GAP = \Delta r[RSA - RSL], \tag{1}$$

where GAP = the difference between rate-sensitive assets (RSA) and rate-sensitive liabilities (RSL) over a particular maturity horizon (e.g., 12 months). The accounting model of ALM focuses on the sensitivity of NII to unexpected changes in interest rates. Mismanagement of interest rate risk, as the thrift crisis has proven, first manifests itself in reported earnings and, if unchecked, results in liquidity and solvency problems.

Although the accounting model of ALM or management of interest rate risk is important, it is not complete because it ignores how changes in interest rates affect the market value of the bank's equity, broadly defined to include the value of unbooked equity associated with off-balance sheet activities (OBSAs). This focus on the sensitivity of the market value of the bank's assets and liabilities is the heart of the economic model of interest rate risk. It is important because of its emphasis on market values, which serve as signals about current interest rate risk and future earnings.

Since the economic model has a time horizon beyond the short-term focus of the accounting model and since it considers off-balance sheet activities, it is a more comprehensive measure of interest rate risk. Nevertheless, this model is less widely used than the accounting model because of its difficulty to apply. Both approaches provide insights about the management of interest rate risk, and they should be viewed as complements and not substitutes. In either case, however, the focus is on the sensitivity of a particular variable (NII or reported earnings versus market value of equity to changes in interest rates).

Although theories on the determinants of NIM are fairly well developed, those on gap analysis are not. We are not aware of a theoretical model treating the determinants of NIM and gap in an integrative fashion. Since our empirical approach does not test a general theoretical relationship, it simply endeavors to understand observed bank phenomena. To do this we use available data in conjunction with existing theories in the context of a simultaneous-equation framework in the spirit of Graddy and Kyle (1979, 1980). We associate the tradeoff between GAP/NIM to the risk/return paradigm. Since these decisions are jointly determined by bank managers, we highlight the simultaneity of asset-liability-hedging management decisions and include NIM as one of the joint determinants of a bank's various gap positions.[4] To derive the determinants of NIM and gap and then cast them into simultaneous structural equations, we integrate and synthesize different streams of literature on asset-liability-hedging management (ALHM).

Our synthesis of the determinants of NIM and gap leads us to the following linear system of simultaneous equations and expected signs for the variables:

$$\text{NIM} = f(\overset{+/-}{\text{GAP12}}, \overset{+/-}{\text{GAP60}}, \overset{+/-}{\text{GROWTH}}, \overset{+}{\text{FFR}}) + U \qquad (2)$$

$$\text{GAPI} = h(\overset{+}{\text{NIM}}, \overset{+}{\text{CDRATE}}, \overset{-}{\text{TAXSHLD}}, \overset{+/-}{\text{CAPITAL}}, \overset{-}{\text{LNGFUTR}},$$

$$\overset{+}{\text{SHTFUTR}}, \overset{-}{\text{SIZE}}, \overset{+}{\text{INLFUND}}, \overset{+/-}{\text{LTLOAD}}, \overset{+}{\text{MORTG}},$$

$$\overset{+}{\text{CR3}}, \overset{+/-}{\text{SWAP}}) + V_I \qquad (3)$$

where $I = 12, 60$ represents the indexing of GAP.[5] The variables in equations (2) and (3) are defined in Table 1; U and V_I are error terms. Due to heterogenous expectations included in the error terms, gaps vary across institutions and over time. The jointly determined (endogenous) variables are NIM and GAPI while the other variables are predetermined (exogenous) ones. Although the specifications of equations (2) and (3) are ad hoc, the basic structure of the model and the determinants of NIM and GAPI are well established in the literature. Basically, we extend the O'Hara (1983) model to develop our NIM equation, and Morgan and Smith (1987) to develop GAP equation.

To avoid singular design matrices, we ignore interest rate volatility and the yield curve as they are the same across banks. Furthermore, the short-run, interes trate effects on annual NIM are expected to be negligible. Since during our test period

Table 1. Variable Definitions

NIM	=	Net interest income/Total assets
GAP12	=	Six month-to-one year maturity gap/Total assets
GAP60	=	One-to-five year maturity gap/Total assets
GROWTH	=	Equity growth (annual rate of change)
FFR	=	Free Funds Ratio = Non-interest bearing deposit/Earning assets
CDRATE	=	Interest expense on time certificates of deposit of $100,000 or more/Time certificates of deposit of $100,000 or more
TAXSHLD	=	Tax exempt income, tax credit and provisions for loans and lease losses/Total assets
CAPITAL	=	Total equity capital/Total assets
LNGFUTR	=	Long (buy) futures and forward contracts/Total assets
SHTFUTR	=	Short (sell) futures and forward contracts/Total assets
SWAP	=	Notional value of all outstanding interest rate swaps/Total assets
SIZE	=	Logarithm of total assets in $ millions
INLFUND	=	Inventory of loanable funds
	=	Cash, securities and assets held in trading accounts/Total assets
LTLOAN	=	Loans and lease financing receivables over 5 years/Total assets
MORTG	=	Loans secured by real estate/Total assets
CR3	=	Three-firm concentration ratio for county-wide deposits
TASSET	=	Total assets ($ million)

(1984 to 1987), interest rates declined rather steadily and then rose slightly at the end of 1987, we do not have a complete interest rate cycle for our experiments. We did not include the volatility of NIM as a regressor, since with annual data we have only four observations to estimate it for each bank. Simonson and Hempel (1982) show that gap interest rate risk also stems from variations in net-margin dollar flows associated with rate-sensitive assets (liabilities) financed by nonsensitive-rate liabilities (assets). To account for this and to proxy for the fixed-cost rate on gap nonsensitive liabilities booked in previous periods, we include the gap of maturity longer than one year (GAP_{60}).

IV. DATA, VARIABLE DEFINITION, AND EMPIRICAL METHODOLOGY

A. Data Sources

Data are taken from December 31 Reports of Conditions and Income files prepared on magnetic tapes by the Fed, FDIC, and OCC for the years 1984 through 1987. Schedule J on "Repricing Opportunities for Selected Balance Sheet Categories" and Schedule L entitled "Commitments and Contingencies," both available only since June 1983, are used to calculate maturity gap ratios and hedging volumes in futures and swaps. Since December 1987, Schedule J has been discontinued by the regulatory agencies and only available for savings banks. Our sample period is of special interest because of the opportunity to examine systematically the interaction between NIM and GAPI. We divide our sample into the following three asset-size groups (average total assets for the four years shown in parentheses):

Group 1:   Total assets between $100 and $300 million ($161 million)
Group 2:   Total assets between $300 million and $1 billion ($511 million)
Group 3:   Total assets larger than $1 billion ($4.5 billion)

Our sample sizes change from year to year because of asset growth and the deletion of banks with missing data from the sample.

The definitions of the variables used in our empirics are presented in Table 1 and described below. NIM is the tax equivalent net interest margin divided by total assets. Tax-exempt interest income arises from the obligations and securities of states and political subdivisions in the United States and the lease financing receivables. Data for the calculations of gap ratios are extracted from Schedule J. For instance, GAP3 reflects assets maturing or repriced in three months or less minus liabilities maturing or repriced in three months or less, all divided by total assets.[6] To proxy a bank's growth, we use either the annual rate of change in equity or total assets (*GROWTH*).[7]

The free-funds ratio (*FFR*) is represented by the ratio of non-interest-bearing deposits to earning assets. We proxy interest rates via the liability rate, an indicator of the rate effect, by the pseudo-CD rate which is the bank interest expense on time certificates of deposit of $100,000 or more divided by the volume of time certificates of deposits of $100,000 or more (*CDRATE*).[8] Tax shields comprise the income from obligations and securities issued by state and political subdivisions in the United States, provisions for loan and lease losses, estimated tax-exempt lease income, investment tax credit, and foreign tax credit (*TAXSHLD*).

Futures and swaps data are off-balance sheet items taken from Schedule L, which banks have been required to report since June 1983 (*LNGFUTR, SHTFUTR, SWAP*). We proxy the inventory of loanable funds of Deshmukh, Greenbaum, and Kanatas (1983) by the total of cash, marketable securities, and assets held in trading accounts (*INLFUND*). This index of a bank's "financial slack" or liquidity pool reflects its inclination toward either the brokerage or intermediation mode. We define long-term loans as loan and lease financing receivables over five years (*LTLOAD*). To proxy for prepayment we use the loans secured by real estate (*MORTG*). As indicated earlier CR3 proxies the competitiveness of a bank's market.[9] All the variables are scaled by total bank assets, except *SIZE*. Since *SIZE* is expressed in terms of the logarithm of total assets, it captures any nonlinearities in the relationship between bank asset size and the other variables in the simultaneous-equations system (Koppenhaver, 1990). It also smooths the size variable and reduces the undesirable effects of outliers.

B. Empirical Methodology

The conventional method of analyzing the performance of financial institutions with a single equation ordinary least squares (OLS) is inadequate in capturing the simultaneity of bank asset-liability management. In this context the explanatory variables of GAP and NIM will not be independent of error terms. We use a three-stage least squares (3SLS) to construct a simultaneous equations model of NIM and GAP management. A 3SLS estimator permits us to use fully the information contained in the covariances among the errors of our reduced-form equations, which increases asymptotically the efficiency of the estimators. Furthermore, to test the simultaneity hypothesis between NIM and GAPI with the joint estimation of the parameters in the system, the use of the 3SLS method is most appropriate.

V. ANALYSIS OF EMPIRICAL RESULTS

We present our empirical findings in two parts: descriptive analysis and 3SLS time-series and cross-section results of our simultaneous-equations model.

A. Descriptive Statistics

Tables 1, 2, and 3 present data definitions and summary statistics for the variables used in our simultaneous equation system. Table 2 provides the descriptive statistics for the second group of banks (assets between 100 to 300 million). The group means generally follow the same stable pattern from 1984 to 1987. The average NIM for all banks varies from 1.87 to 3.78% with the group means for the smallest banks being higher, which is consistent with the findings of Ho and Saunders (1981) and Flannery (1981).[10] Gap ratios range from a negative −1.7% for GAP12 to over 22% of total assets in GAP60. All GAP12 and GAP60 are negative and positive respectively with average magnitudes of 3.3 and 19% of total assets, respectively. For GAP60 at the end of 1984, the gap ratios of large banks are less than those of small ones; at the end of 1987 as long-term interest rates were expected to rise, gaps of large banks exceed those of small banks. Also we note that the GAP60s do not change drastically over time and hover around 20% of total assets. These findings suggest that financial institutions are relatively "passive" in managing gaps over one-year maturity, suggesting the existence of some target level. We observe that GAP12 fluctuates the most while GAP60 show some regularities over time and across banks.[11] Regardless of gap signs, we observe from 1984 to 1986 gaps ratios that are narrowing while in 1987 gaps ratios tend to widen. These findings are consistent with the strategy to narrow gap when interest rates are expected to decline and to widen gap when interest rates are expected to rise. On balance, banks behaved as if they were asset sensitive during 1984 to 1987.

Table 2. Summary Statistics
Banks with Assets From $100 to $300 Million

Variable	1984 N = 1656		1985 N = 1755		1986 N = 1858		1987 N = 1837	
	Mean	Std. Dev.	Mean	Std. Dev.	Mean	Std. Dev.	Mean	Std. Dev.
NIM	0.0389	0.0083	0.0401	0.0081	0.0378	0.0087	0.0391	0.0096
GAP12	-0.0378	0.0493	-0.0333	0.0554	-0.0204	0.0594	-0.0187	0.0630
GAP60	0.2039	0.0988	0.1844	0.1044	0.1847	0.1077	0.1965	0.1180
GROWTH	0.1324	0.4098	0.1074	0.3040	0.2233	3.4377	0.1017	0.3344
FFR	0.1766	0.0625	0.17808	0.0660	0.1619	0.0826	0.1450	0.0714
CDRATE	0.1002	0.0496	0.0865	0.0311	0.0760	0.0286	0.0623	0.0219
TAXSHLD	0.0103	0.0084	0.0119	0.0102	0.0131	0.0109	0.0195	0.0081
CAPITAL	0.0737	0.0211	0.0738	0.0187	0.075	0.0243	0.0781	0.0262
LNGFUTR	0.0004	0.0113	0.0003	0.0051	0.0002	0.0023	0.0001	0.0010
SHTFUTR	0.0013	0.0330	0.0002	0.0051	0.0002	0.0045	0.0002	0.0045
SWAP	0	0	0.0012	0.0136	0.0012	0.010	0.0012	0.010
SIZE	5.0282	0.3073	5.0251	0.3053	5.0379	0.3019	5.0451	0.3047
INLFUND	0.3466	0.1211	0.3397	0.1257	0.3377	0.1366	0.3266	0.1411
LTLOAN	0.0748	0.065	0.0673	0.0622	0.0632	0.0589	0.0634	0.0656
MORTG	0.2145	0.0954	0.2276	0.1032	0.2625	0.1387	0.2970	0.1572
CR3	0.3835	0.1946	0.3947	0.2004	0.3844	0.2010	0.398	0.2020
TASSET ($million)	160.342	52.57	159.735	51.941	161.610	51.913	162.900	52.583

Table 3. Summary of U.S. Commercial Bank Maturity Gaps in December 31
(Means with Standard Error of the Mean in Parentheses)

	Banks with Assets from $100 to $300 Million			
	1984	*1985*	*1986*	*1987*
GAP12	–0.0378*	–0.0333*	–0.0204*	–0.0187*
	(0.0012)	(0.0013)	(0.0013)	(0.0014)
GAP60	0.2039*	0.1844*	0.1847*	0.1965*
	(0.0024)	(0.0025)	(0.0025)	(0.0028)
	Banks with Assets from $300 Million to $1 Billion			
GAP12	–0.0288*	–0.0248*	–0.0065**	–0.004
	(0.0022)	(0.0019)	(0.0024)	(0.0026)
GAP60	0.1843*	0.1828*	0.1864*	0.1875*
	(0.0042)	(0.0053)	(0.0054)	(0.0058)
	Banks with Assets Over $1 Billion			
GAP12	–0.0266*	–0.0269*	–0.0014**	–0.0051**
	(0.0048)	(0.0037)	(0.0042)	(0.0045)
GAP60	0.1989*	0.194*	0.1943*	0.2157*
	(0.0127)	(0.0114)	(0.0085)	(0.0119)

Notes: *Significantly different from zero at 1% level.
**Significantly different from zero at 10% level.

Since Table 3 shows that invariably all gap ratios are highly significantly different from zero, U.S. banks do not adopt a zero maturity-gap policy. Instead they take advantage of either their "built-in"/natural hedge or they follow a hedging program.

All groups of banks, with the exception of the one over $1 billion, show a reduction in the tax shield ratio in 1987 as compared to 1986. This finding is no doubt related to the Tax Reform Act of 1986, which eliminated the investment tax credit and lengthened depreciation periods. The 1986 tax law also repealed the deduction for interest expense to purchase or carry tax-exempt securities. This change combined with the volume cap on municipal bond issuance caused the decline in tax-shields for commercial banks (on average over 1% of total assets). Over our period of study the use of swaps became more widespread increasing from 0% in 1984 to 1.24% of total assets in 1987 (for banks over $1 billion). Only the largest banks increased their use of futures over time. Swap volume amount to 0.07% of total assets versus 0.03% of total assets in futures. Because swaps do not have margin requirements, they are more effective than financial futures and options in hedging interest rate risk beyond two to three years.

Like Koppenhaver (1990), we record that over time banks are taking larger positions in futures, and in total have changed from a net-short (sell) position in all contracts to the net-long (buy) position. In 1987, for all banks, loans secured by real estate increased to over 24% of total assets. The savings and loan crisis, declining interest rates, and the new tax law in 1986, which eliminated most personal tax shelters, except mortgage deductibility, could have caused this increase. Long-term loans constitute over 5% of total assets for the average bank.

B. 3SLS Estimates of the Determinants of NIM and GAP

NIM Equation

Table 4 shows results of the NIM equation. We report the pooled cross-section results for the entire population of banks and for three size groups separately. Each of the jointly determined variables is shown with the estimated coefficients for their predetermined variables.[12]

The regression coefficients for the jointly determined variable NIM are consistent with the prediction from equation (2) for the full sample, and three groups of banks up to over $1 billion in assets. The variable GROWTH is significant and negative for group 1 and group 3 banks. This result is consistent with those of Graddy and Karna (1984) for small banks. But, NIMs decrease as asset increases for group 2

Table 4. 3SLS Regression Estimates of NIM and GAP Determinants Dependent Variable: Net Interest Margin (NIM)

Explanatory Variables	Full Sample	Groups by Size		
		1	2	3
Intercept	0.037***	+	+	+
	(8.29)			
GROWTH	–0.007***	–	+	–
	(–3.22)			
FFR	0.059***	+	+	+
	(4.92)			
0-to-12 Month Maturity GAP	–0.0034***	–	–	•
	(–4.25)			
12-to-60 Month Maturity GAP	–0.002	–	•	–
	(–1.56)			
System Weighted R^2	.52	.54	.52	.50

Notes: Results appear for the entire sample of FDIC-insured commercial banks over the 1984–1987 period. T-statistics appear in parentheses beneath the regression coefficients. * indicates significance at the .10 level, ** indicates significance at the .05 level, and *** indicates significance at the .01 level. For each of the subgroups, a "+" sign indicates that the coefficient in the regression is positive and significant, a "–" sign indicates that the coefficient in the regression is negative and significant, and a "•" indicates that the coefficient in the regression was not significant at the least restrictive .10 level.

banks (assets between $300 and $1 billion), consistent with the theoretical and empirical work of Ho and Saunders (1981) and Allen (1988).

The free-funds ratio (FFR) is consistently positive and significant. Also, the signs on GAPI are consistent with the declining interest-rate cycle during 1984 to 1987. We obtain negative coefficients for GAP12 and GAP60. The 0 to 12 month gap has a highly significant negative coefficient. Since the majority of banks have negative gaps in the 0–12 month range, a decrease in GAP12 reflects an increase in interest rate risk, ie, a move toward a more negative gap, and such an increase in interest rate risk results in a statistically significant increase in NIM.

For small banks with assets up to 1 billion, most of the regression coefficients are highly significant. For the third group of banks over $1 billion of assets, the results are much less significant. Large banks, however, are more sensitive to longer maturity gaps since they have more long-term loans than smaller banks. Current gaps affect the net interest margins in the future and given our annual data, if past gaps equal current gaps, one would expect NIMs to be sensitive to gaps. Our results suggest that large banks' interest-rate risk, as manifested through annual NIM, depends much less on maturity gaps.[13]

GAP Equations

The regression results for gap equations (equation (3)) appear in Tables 5 and 6. The results for the 0–12 months GAP (Table 5) and for 12–60 month GAP (Table 6) are consistent with each other, and we make reference to both tables as we discuss the empirical results. In general, for a bank of average size, the intercepts in the GAP equations are significant. These terms capture other contemporaneous (and exogenous) variables such as the interest rate volatilities and term-structure factors as posited in our general model. Our inclusion of NIM as a jointly determined variable in the GAP equation is empirically supported since it has the expected sign and is significant. The sign of the coefficient for NIM is negative and significant, indicating that, as NIM increases, gaps become more negative ie, they increase.

Our interest rate proxy and control variable, *CDRATE*, is in general significant for banks up to group 2 although its sign fluctuates depending on the maturity of the GAP. This rate, however, which proxies for short-term effects, does not affect "long" maturity gaps. Also for banks with assets over $1 billion, it appears that interest rates did not affect GAPI probably because larger banks have greater access to purchase funds while making variable-rate loans.

TAXSHLD is significant and has the predicted sign in accord with the theory of Gurel and Pyle (1984) which has never been tested. The variable *CAPITAL*, which is the proxy of the equity-liquidity linkage to maturity mismatching (Maisel & Jacobson, 1978), is significant only for the group 1 banks and not significant for banks over $1 billion. The sign of the coefficient of *CAPITAL* is negative, indicating that as capital levels increase, gaps become more negative. This suggests that interest rate risk increases as institutions are more able to bear it.

Table 5. 3SLS Regression Estimates of NIM and GAP Determinants
Dependent Variable: 0–12 Month GAP

Explanatory Variables	Full Sample	Groups by Size		
		1	2	3
Intercept	0.176**	+	+	+
	(2.85)			
NIM	0.059***	+	+	•
	(–10.22)			
CDRATE	.371*	+	+	•
	(1.79)			
TAXSHLD	–0.617***	–	–	–
	(–8.58)			
CAPITAL	–0.112*	–	•	•
	(–1.97)			
LNGFUTR	–.190***	–	–	–
	(6.40)			
SHTGFUTR	.190***	+	+	+
	(7.41)			
SIZE	–0.060**	•	–	–
	(–2.587)			
INLFUND	0.561***	+	+	+
	(9.88)			
LTLOAN	–.1480***	•	+	+
	(–4.81)			
MORTG	4.76***	+	+	+
	(3.375)			
CR3	.1480*	+	+	•
	(1.81)			
SWAP	0.76**	+	–	+
	(2.75)			

Notes: _T_–statistics appear in parentheses beneath the regression coefficients. * indicates significance at the
.10 level, ** indicates significance at the .05 level, and *** indicates significance at the .01 level. For
each of the subgroups, a "+" sign indicates that the coefficient in the regression is positive and
significant, a "–" sign indicates that the coefficient in the regression is negative and significant, and
a "•" indicates that the coefficient in the regression was not significant at the least restrictive .10 level.
Three-stage least squares does not produce equation-specific R^2 figures, producing instead a system
weighted R^2. This R^2 figure can be found in Table 4.

Table 6. 3SLS Regression Estimates of NIM and GAP Determinants
Dependent Variable: 12–60 Month GAP

Explanatory Variables	Full Sample	Groups by Size		
		1	2	3
Intercept	−0.167**	−	+	−
	(-2.05)			
NIM	4.059***	+	+	•
	(7.22)			
CDRATE	.016*	+	•	+
	(1.79)			
TAXSHLD	−0.27***	•	−	−
	(−6.82)			
CAPITAL	0.52***	−	+	+
	(3.77)			
LNGFUTR	−2.120***	•	−	−
	(-4.40)			
SHTGFUTR	.190***	•	+	+
	(7.41)			
SIZE	−0.160**	•	−	−
	(−2.87)			
INLFUND	0.61***	+	•	+
	(3.88)			
LTLOAN	−.0807***	−	+	+
	(−3.81)			
MORTG	0.76***	+	+	+
	(4.375)			
CR3	.180*	+	+	•
	(1.71)			
SWAP	0.06**	+	−	+
	(2.25)			

Notes: *T*–statistics appear in parentheses beneath the regression coefficients. * indicates significance at the .10 level, ** indicates significance at the .05 level, and *** indicates significance at the .01 level. For each of the subgroups, a "+" sign indicates that the coefficient in the regression is positive and significant, a "−" sign indicates that the coefficient in the regression is negative and significant, and a "•" indicates that the coefficient in the regression was not significant at the least restrictive .10 level. Three-stage least squares does not produce equation-specific R^2 figures, producing instead a system weighted R^2. This R^2 figure can be found in Table 4.

The coefficients of *LNGFUTR* and *SHTFUTR* exhibit the expected sign and are statistically significant. The *SWAP* variable sign is also significant. The results for futures and swaps should be also interpreted with caution since banks are currently required to report only the consolidated notional amounts outstanding. Thus, the amounts include transactions motivated both by fee generating and hedging activities. The *SIZE* variable is in general significant but its expected negative sign occurs for GAP12 and GAP60. Due to economies of scope and scale and diversification, larger institutions can reduce the size of their longer gap ratios.

The concept of inventory of loanable funds is applicable only for "small banks" and the expected sign valid only for gaps of long maturity. An increase in loanable funds would be associated with a larger (more negative) gap. Larger banks having greater access to money-market funds do not hold large inventory of loanable funds. The coefficients of *LTLOAN* are significantly positive, which means an institution, ceteris paribus, with more short-term assets has less interest rate risk.

The significance and expected sign of *LTLOAN* in explaining GAP occur only for small banks and for short maturity gaps where a more stringent credit standard probably is employed. The prepayment variable proxied by *MORTG* is significant and carries the expected sign for GAP12 and GAP60 and for banks in all three groups, indicating that prepayable assets are a major concern to bankers. Finally, our proxy for the degree of competitiveness of a bank's market (CR3) shows significance for small banks and for GAP12 and GAP60, suggesting that these institutions are more sensitive to market power and customer relationships associated with long-term transactions.

VI. SUMMARY AND POLICY IMPLICATIONS

This paper examines the determinants of NIM and GAP jointly in an integrative and systemic fashion for the years 1984 to 1987, a period of deregulation when off-balance sheet hedging and fee-based activities experienced rapid expansion. Based on "unique" and complete GAP data for the population of U.S. commercial banks (the collection of these data were discontinued in 1988), our evidence lends support to a model linking NIM and GAP simultaneously for U.S. banks having assets up to $1 billion.[14] Although the simultaneous equations model works less well for large banks, our empirical evidence strongly supports the determinants posited for NIM. On the other hand, the determinants of GAP depend on the maturity of the gap for significance and sign. We also find that banks had negative gaps ($RSA - RSL < 0$) for GAP12 but positive ones ($RSA - RSL > 0$) for GAP60. In the theoretical literature the term "gap" often is used loosely without specifying its length (e.g., Deshmukh, Greenbaum, & Kanatas, 1983; Morgan & Smith, 1987).

For a bank of a given size, our results suggest that hypotheses advanced in the literature may be consistent with certain GAP measures. Nevertheless, our determinants of gap for small banks are significant regardless of maturity which suggest that small banks rely essentially on maturity gap management to cope with interest rate risk. We show that banks of any size do not follow a zero-gap policy. Our study also establishes that for large banks with assets over $1 billion, NIM and GAPs are not related. One possible explanation may be that large banks do not focus on gap analyses but manage their asset/liability/hedging activities using duration or synthetic contracts or both.

Since our results suggest that repricing information plays an important role in detecting interest rate risk for banks with assets of less than $1 billion, the regulators should consider collecting such data (Schedule RC-J of "Repricing Opportunities for Selected Balance-Sheet Categories"; discontinued in 1988) again, at least for these banks. We also conclude that larger banks use more sophisticated methods for managing interest rate risk such as duration and the financial-engineering tools (e.g., forwards, futures, options, and swaps) associated with off-balance sheet activities. Our framework is highly relevant for thousands of "community banks" for which accounting flows (such as net interest income) are the primary indicators of the effectiveness of asset-liability management. Since capital market information is available for large banks, it is more appropriate for large banks to conform with the FAS 115, but inappropriate for smaller banks. This is also consistent with the Federal Reserve's proposed interest rate risk management model.

ACKNOWLEDGMENTS

The authors thanks especially the editor, Andrew Chen, for his valuable comments and assistance. Lai acknowledges financial support from the SSHRC of Canada and funds FCAR of Quebec. Hassan acknowledges a University of New Orleans summer research grant.

NOTES

1. Although whether a firm should choose to hedge and the determinants of hedging are issues related to gap management, these questions are beyond the scope of this paper. See for instance, Smith and Stulz (1985) and Campbell and Kracaw (1987), for an analysis of hedging, deposit insurance, bank risk taking, and incentive compatibility.

2. Flannery (1981, 1983) employing a bank profitability model, Flannery and James (1984) using an ex post market model augmented by an interest rate sensitivity index show that banks are well hedged although the interest rate sensitivity is related to the degree of maturity mismatch of the assets and liabilities. These findings are consistent with the maturity-mismatch hypothesis. On the other hand, Tarhan (1987) also finds banks are well hedged but their interest rate sensitivities are not related to the maturity gap. Unal and Kane (1988) and Kane and Unal (1990) attribute the conflicting interest rate sensitivities to differences in interest regimes.

3. An alternative method, the market-return approach to assessing interest rate sensitivity of depository institutions, has several shortcomings (1) only 20% or so of U.S. commercial banks are publicly traded and they are the largest ones, (2) the subjective assignment of the holding company's traded stock value to its lead bank, and (3) the nonstationarity of market interest rate betas as shown by Unal and Kane (1988).

4. Most studies use one year gap data. Our approach employs gap data of maturities of one year and five years (as specified in Schedule J of the Report of Condition). Our model departs from previous

studies since it deals jointly with NIMs and various maturity gaps. Flannery (1981, 1983) does not directly relate NIMs and GAPs but net income with SHORT (one-year maturity gap) an includes all non-interest and operating revenues and expenses.

5. The justifications for our simultaneous-equations framework and the individual variables can be found in Graddy and Karna (1984) for the "spirit" of the simultaneity of NIM and gap and for the determinants of NIMs for small banks; Rose (1989) for background and measuring and managing interest rate risk; Simonson and Hempel (1982) for optimization of NIM; Wetmore and Brick (1990) for the endogeneity of gaps; Olson and Simonson (1982) and Simonson and Hempel (1982) for the determinants of NIM, Hanweck and Kilcollin (1984) and Flannery (1981) for the effects of interest rates and portfolio rebalancings; Ho and Saunders (1981) and Flannery (1981, 1983) for the effects of both the level and variability of rates; Koppenhaver and Lee (1987); Morgan and Smith (1987), and Allen (1988) for the effects of purchased funds, potential economies of scope, and portfolio shifts, respectively; Deshmukh, Greenbaum, and Kanatas (1983) for the effects of acting more as an asset transformer than a broker and discussion of credit and fundings risks; Morgan, Shome and Smith (1988) for the effects of futures hedging and capital; Gurel and Pyle (1984) for the effects if tax shields; and Samuelson (1945) for the effects of monopoly power.

6. The definitions of the GAP categories ("buckets") are those used in the Report of Condition published by the Board of Governors of the Fed. We assume these stated book maturities are effective maturities (see Flannery, 1981; Kwan, 1991) for a discussion of the problem of ambiguous maturities of assets and liabilities). This ambiguity also applies to the duration approach, which requires more micro-information such as cash flow, time to repricing, and market values of balance-sheet items not available from public accounting reports.

7. Whether we used changes in equity or total assets to proxy growth made little difference in our empirical results. We report GROWTH measured by equity capital defined as the sum of perpetual and preferred stock, common stock, surplus, undivided profits and capital reserves, and cumulative foreign currency translation adjustments.

8. We used either average CD volume or year-end volume to calculate CDRATE. Both measures produced similar results. The results reported here were based on the year-end CD figures. Although we assume the level of the interest rate to be exogenous in our theoretical exposition, it becomes endogenous in our empirical model through the CD rate.

9. While CR3 appears to be a reasonable measure of market competition for banks in rural areas, it may not be the case in urban areas. For urban areas, the use of county-wide deposits to measure market share will likely bias the calculated degree of market power downward. On the other hand, the exclusion of thrifts in the measure biases the calculation upward.

10. Ho and Saunders (1981) report NIM varying from 4.44 to 4.91% with an average of 4.68% of earning assets for 53 banks over the 1976 to 1979. For the period 1976–1981 when interest rates were rising, Hanweck and Kilcollin (1984) find that the mean NIM of 21 large banks of over $1 billion assets was 2.74%, the NIM of 12 banks of $0.1–1 billion assets was 4.41%, and the NIM of 12 small banks of assets less than $100 million averaged 4.8%. During a period of falling market rates (December 1975 to June 1977), Graddy and Karna (1984) find (for 98 banks with asset size varying from $26 million to over $1 billion), average NIM varied from 3.9 to 4.41% with rate sensitive gap varying from –8 to 35 % of average earning assets.

11. The relatively stable gap structure across all bank sizes seems to indicate that demand conditions affect maturity structure. That is, there appears to be much more customer demand for short-term bank liabilities than for short-term bank assets. Moreover, for longer terms, demand for long-term assets (e.g., loan demand) exceeds demand for bank liabilities. This is not surprising since it is in these markets that banks have a comparative advantage over nonbank financial intermediaries. In the market for short-term assets, banks faced competition from securities markets (e.g., commercial paper). Similarly, for long-term liabilities, banks faced competition from well organized debt markets (domestic and Euro-bond markets). On balance, banks' maturity gap structure should be a function of customer demand for bank services.

12.   To detect the presence of multicollinearity among the predetermined variables, we analyzed simple correlations among the regressors. A priori, we anticipate some correlation between the variables *CAPITAL, SIZE, INLFUND, LTLOAN,* and *MORTG.* The covariance matrix varies with the groupings and years. Our results show MORTG is both negatively correlated with *INLFUND* and positively correlated with *LTLOAN.* The larger the bank group, the higher is the correlation between variables. For the small-bank groups (group 1), the coefficients of correlation between *MORTG* and *INLFLTND* (range from −0.28 to −0.58) are higher than those between *MORTG* and *LTLOAN* (range from 0.26 to 0.39). Only for group 3 is the correlation between *MORTG* and *INLFUND* not significant. Also in group 3, *SIZE* and *INLFUND* were negatively correlated (−0.26 to −0.43), which we do not observe for the smaller-bank group. To judge the severity of multicollinearity, we check for the stability of the estimated regression coefficients from year to year. In general, since regression coefficients are not erratic from year to year multicollinearity does not appear to be a major concern.

13.   These results may be linked to those of Tarhar (1987). For a sample of 46 large banks during 1979 to 1982, he finds that although bank stock prices are affected by unanticipated interest-rate movements, the reaction does not appear to be related to the maturity structure of bank assets and liabilities. On the contrary, in extending the work of Flannery and James (1984) it was found for bank holding companies that interest-rate betas were a function o maturity structure for the period 1976 to 1983. Although we do not follow the market-return approach, our results for banks in group 1 support Flannery and James's findings. On the other hand, our results for banks larger than $300 million concur with those of Tarhan.

14.   In 1987, although "large" banks (i.e., assets greater than $300 million) represent only 7.4% of the population of insured banks ($N = 13,382$), they accounted for 74% of the industry's total assets of over $2.7 trillion.

REFERENCES

Allen, L. (1988, June). The determinants of bank interest margins: A note. *Journal of Financial and Quantitative Analysis, 23,* 231–235.

Batlin, A.C. (1983). Interest rate hedging, prepayment risk, and the future market hedging strategies of financial intermediaries. *Journal of Futures Markets,* 177–184.

Brodt, A.I. (1988). Optimal bank asset and liability management with financial futures. *Journal of Futures Markets,* 457–481.

Campbell, T., & Kracaw, W. (1987). Optimal managerial incentive contracts and the value of corporate insurance. *Journal of Financial and Quantitative Analysis,* 315–328.

Deshmukh, S. D., Greenbaum, S.I., & Kanatas, G. (1983, March). Interest rate uncertainty and the financial intermediary's choice of exposure. *Journal of Finance,* 141–147.

Financial Accounting Standards Board, FAS 115 Summary (1993).

Flannery, M.J. (1981, December). Market interest rates and commercial bank profitability: An empirical investigation. *Journal of Finance,* 1085–1101.

Flannery, M.J. (1983, August). Interest rates and bank profitability: Additional evidence. *Journal of Money, Credit, and Banking,* 355–362.

Flannery, M.J., & James, C. (1984, November). Market evidence of the effective maturity of bank assets and liabilities. *Journal of Money, Credit, and Banking,* 435–445.

Goldfarb, D.R. (1987). Hedging interest rate risk in banking. *Journal of Futures Markets,* 35–47.

Graddy, D.B., & Kyle, R. (1979). The simultaneity of bank decision-making, market structure, and bank performance. *Journal of Finance,* 1–18.

Graddy, D.B., & Kyle, R. (1980). Affiliated bank performance and the simultaneity of financial decision-making. *Journal of Finance,* 952–957.

Graddy, D.B., & Karna, A.S. (1984, Winter). Net interest margin sensitivity among banks of different sizes. *Journal of Bank Research,* 283–290.

Gurel, E., & Pyle, D. (1984, September). Bank income taxes and interest rate risk management: A note. *Journal of Finance*, 1199–1206.

Hanweck, G.A., & Kilcollin, T.E. (1984). Bank profitability and interest rate risk. *Journal of Economics and Business*, 77–84.

Ho, T.S.Y., & Saunders, A. (1981, November). The determinants of bank interest margins: theory and empirical evidence. *Journal of Financial and Quantitative Analysis*, 581–600.

Ho, T.S.Y., & Saunders, A. (1983, December). Fixed-rate loan commitment, take-down risk, and the dynamics of hedging with futures. *Journal of Financial and Quantitative Analysis*, 499–516.

Kane, E.J., & Unal, H. (1990, March). Modelling structural and temporal variation in the market valuation of banking firms. *Journal of Finance, 45*, 113–136.

Koppenhaver, G.D. (1985, March). Bank funding risks, risk aversion, and the choice of futures hedging instrument. *Journal of Finance*, 241–255.

Koppenhaver, G.D. (1990). An empirical analysis of bank hedging in futures markets. *Journal of Futures Markets*, 1–12.

Kwan, Simon H. (1991). Re-examination of interest rate sensitivity of commercial bank stock returns using a random coefficient model. *Journal of Financial Services Research, 5*(1), 61–76.

Lee, C.F., & Zumwalt, J.K. (1981, March). Associations between alternative accounting profitability measures and security returns. *Journal of Financial and Quantitative Analysis*, 71–92.

Maisel, S.T., & Jacobson, R. (1978, November). Interest rate changes and commercial bank revenues and costs. *Journal of Financial and Quantitative Analysis*, 687–700.

Morgan, G.E., & Smith, S.D. (1987, September). Maturity intermediation and intertemporal lending policies of financial intermediaries. *Journal of Finance*, 1023–1034.

Morgan, G.E., Shome, D.K., & Smith, S.D. (1988, March). Optimal futures positions for large banking firms. *Journal of Finance*, 175–195.

O'Hara, M. (1983). A dynamic theory of the banking firm. *Journal of Finance, 38*, 127–140.

Olson, R.L., & Simonson, D.G. (1982, Spring). Gap management and market rate sensitivity in banks. *Journal of Bank Research*, 53–58.

Roll, R. (1987). *Managing risk in thrift institutions: Beyond the duration gap*. Federal Home Loan Bank Board Grant Paper C55020.

Rose, S. (1989, June). The two faces of A-L management. *The American Banker, 5*, 1, 9.

Samuleson, P. A. (1945, March). The effect of interest rate increases on the banking systems. *American Economic Review*, 16–27.

Simonson, D., & Hempel, G. (1982). Improving GAP management for controlling interest-rate risk. *Journal of Bank Research*, 109–115.

Smith, C., & Stulz, R. (1985). The determinants of firms' hedging policies. *Journal of Financial and Quantitative Analysis*, 391–405.

Tarhan, V. (1987). Unanticipated interest rates, bank stock returns and the nominal contracting hypothesis. *Journal of Banking and Finance*, 99–115.

Toevs, A.L., & Haney, W.C. (1986). Measuring and managing interest rate risk: A guide to asset/liability models used in banks and thrifts. In R.B. Platt (Ed.), *Controlling interest rate risk* (pp. 256–350). New York: John Wiley & Sons.

Unal, H., & Kane, E.J. (1988). Two approaches to assessing the interest rate sensitivity of deposit institutions' equity returns. In A. Chen (Ed.), *Research in Finance*. Greenwich, CT: JAI Press.

THE INTERDEPENDENCY OF FIRMS' FINANCING CHOICES AND INVESTMENT DECISIONS:
SOME CANADIAN EVIDENCE

Bill B. Francis

ABSTRACT

This paper utilizes a discrete choice/continuous outcome econometric model to examine the interdependency of the firm's real and financial decisions. Using Canadian data, the financial decision examined is the firm's choice between debt and equity, conditional on the firm raising new capital with a seasoned public issue. The investment decision is the firm's capital expenditures that are financed with the acquired funds. Evidence indicates the presence of self-selection bias, which suggests that parameter estimates of previous discrete choice studies that have addressed the issue of the firm's choice of financing instrument without accounting for the use of these funds may be inconsistent and inefficient. In addition, I find that the firm's choice of financing instrument and its investment decision are interdependent and that operating and financial leverage are complements. In general the results provide some support for both the pecking order hypothesis and the static trade-off model.

Research in Finance, Volume 16, pages 221–252.
Copyright © 1998 by JAI Press Inc.
All rights of reproduction in any form reserved.
ISBN: 0-7623-0328-X

I. INTRODUCTION

A central issue in finance is the relationship between the firm's financial and investment decisions. It is of interest in corporate finance because the financing of investment is a central purpose of capital structure. Until little more than a decade ago capital structure issues were examined under the assumption that real decisions were exogenously determined. However, recent work indicates that a firm's financing and investment decisions are interdependent. Most of this research is theoretical and, as yet, is not supported by sufficient empirical evidence that would allow us to ascertain which set of hypothesized interactions is more important from a practical viewpoint. Harris and Raviv (1991) point out that not much work has been done empirically to verify or refute any specific set of hypothesized interactions. This statement still holds true today. In this paper I examine the relationship between the firm's choice of financing instrument and the investment decision as one piece of the interaction of the real and financial decisions puzzle. Specifically, this study examines the interdependence of the firm's choice between debt and equity, conditional on the firm raising new capital with a public issue, and its capital expenditure decision.

Traditional corporate finance capital structure models are based on the premise that firms trade off the incentive and tax benefits of debt against the costs of financial distress holding the firm's assets and investment plans constant. In these models firms are assumed to substitute debt for equity or equity for debt until an optimum capital structure is attained. Several testable hypotheses emerge from these models. For example, they predict that there will be a reversion of the firm's actual capital structure to its optimum. Additionally, they predict that there is a cross-sectional relationship between leverage, taxes, profitability, and bankruptcy costs.

Empirical evidence has provided some support for the static trade-off models. Marsh (1982), Jalilvand and Harris (1984), and Mackie-Mason (1990) find that firms adjust to a target capital structure. Titman and Wessels (1988) find mixed support, with only profitability and asset uniqueness being significant. Mackie-Mason and Jung, Kim, and Stulz (1996) find support for the tax hypothesis.

However, other evidence reported does not support the static trade-off model. It is well documented that there are negative valuation effects following equity issues and, in general, no effect following debt issues. If in fact, changes in debt ratios are movements to an optimum capital structure there should be positive valuation effects following debt or equity issues. Additionally, as noted by Titman and Wessels, among others, there is a negative relationship between leverage and profitability. This result is counter to the predictions of the static trade-off models.

Myers (1984) and Myers and Majluf (1984) noting the failure of the static trade-off models to adequately characterize the behavior of firms seeking external financing provide an alternative hypothesis known as the "pecking order model." In this model, because of asymmetric information and signaling problems associated with external financing, firms' financing patterns follow a financing hierarchy based on the safest security. Specifically, firms prefer internal financing, and if external funds are needed, then debt is chosen and as a last resort equity. It is important to note that there is no well-defined optimal debt ratio in this model.

Results of empirical studies, which test the pecking order hypothesis, are mixed. Shyam-Sunder and Myers (1994) provide evidence indicating that the pecking order model has much greater explanatory power than the traditional static trade-off models. However, Helwege and Liang (1996) provide evidence that rejects the pecking order theory and supports the optimal capital structure model. In other less direct tests, Choe, Masulis, and Nanda (1993) and Jung, Kim, and Stulz (1996) report that firms are more likely to issue equity during periods of economic expansions when moral hazard is less severe. Opler and Titman (1996) in examining firms' debt-equity choice find some support for both models.

More recently, following new theoretical developments that demonstrate a relationship between investment and financing decisions, empirical studies have turned to the investigation of the relationship between leverage and investment. Using approaches that differ significantly than the one used in this paper, different studies report conflicting results. In an earlier study Long and Malitz (1985) report a positive relationship between capital expenditures and leverage. Shyam-Sunder and Myers (1994) report a positive relationship between capital expenditures and the firm's debt-to-equity ratio. Lang, Ofek, and Stulz (1996) document a negative relationship between leverage and investment for firms with low Tobin's q. Similarly, Smith and Watts (1992) document a negative relationship between debt and growth opportunities. Thus, the evidence indicates that it is not clear as to which model best characterizes the relationship between the firm's financing and investment decisions.

In this paper I examine the relationship between the firm's decision to issue debt or equity and its investment decision. This study differs from previous studies on several accounts. First, a discrete choice/continuous outcome model is used to examine the relationship between the firm's investment and financing decisions. Specifically, the firm's choice between debt and equity is modeled as a discrete choice. Its investment decision is modeled as a continuous outcome. Previous researchers, who utilized discrete choice analysis to examine the firm's financing decisions, kept the usage of the funds obtained exogenous. Myers (1977), Jensen (1986), and Stulz (1990), among others, point out that with voluntary corporate decisions such as the choice of financing instrument and investment expenditures, economically motivated managers can control the type, timing, and/or magnitude of these decisions. Rational managers voluntarily make decisions only if they provide some personal or corporate benefit. Further, the benefits emanating from financing decisions are not independent of the planned usage of the funds obtained. An additional feature of this methodology is that it allows for the testing of whether the manager's choice of financing instrument is consistent with managerial enhancement behavior.

The second feature of this study is that by separating the firm's investment decision by method of financing we are able to disentangle the role of cash flows in firms' financing and investment decisions. This issue has recently received considerable attention in the finance and economics literature.

The third feature of this paper is the utilization of Canadian data. Previous empirical studies of the firm's choice of financing instrument or of the relationship between the firm's real and financing decisions have utilized American or European data. The use of a Canadian data set permits an examination of the determinants of the firm's debt/equity choice and the relationship between the firm's financing and investment decisions in a different economic environment.

In brief, the results support the hypothesis that the firm's financing and investment decisions are interdependent and, in particular, that the firm's operating and financial leverage are complements. There is also evidence indicating that previous discrete choice models, that examine firms' debt/equity choice, are characterized by self-selectivity bias. Further, by interpreting the coefficient of the self-selectivity variable, results indicate that management chooses the financing instrument that maximizes the value of the firm. Finally, I find evidence indicating that the impact of cash flow on investment depends on whether debt or equity funds the investment.

The rest of the paper is organized as follows. Section II presents a brief review of the relationship between investment and financing decisions. Section III develops the econometric model relating the firm's financing and investment decisions. The specific financial decision examined is the firm's choice between debt and equity, conditional on the firm raising new capital with a public issue. The investment decision is the firm's capital expenditures that are financed with the acquired funds. Section IV describes the data. Additionally, the variables utilized in the financing choice and investment modules are defined. Section V discusses the results of the financing choice model. In Section VI, the empirical findings of the investment module are presented. Section VII summarizes and concludes the paper.

II. FINANCING CHOICE AND INVESTMENT DECISION

In their seminal paper, Modigliani and Miller (1958) established that, in a perfect and competitive capital market the financing decisions of the firm are irrelevant. An implication of this is that the firm's real and financial decisions are independent and, thus, can be analyzed separately. Since then much work has been done demonstrating the interdependency of these decisions. Relying on the tax advantage of debt, Hite (1977) shows that there should be a positive relationship between the firm's level of capital intensity and financial leverage. DeAngelo and Masulis (1980) noting that non-debt tax shields are substitutes for debt-related tax shields, demonstrate that there is a negative relationship between non-debt tax shields (proxying for the degree of capital utilization in Hite's model) and the intensity of the firm's usage of financial leverage.

More recently several papers have explicitly endogenized the firm's investment and financing decisions. Dotan and Ravid (1985) show that operating and financial leverage (as defined by the level of investment expenditures and the level of debt financing, respectively) are negatively related (i.e., substitutes) to exogenous shocks in the firm's debt level. Dammon and Senbet (1988) and Aivazian and Berkowitz (1992) show that by allowing investment expenditures to affect the level of output (income), increases in allowable non-debt tax shields do not necessarily decrease the firm's debt level. Instead, the net effect depends on the magnitudes of the output and substitution effects. If the output effect is greater than the substitution effect operating and financial leverage are complements. However, they are substitutes if the output effect is less than the substitution effect. Thus, the relationship is ambiguous.

Theoretical results based on the existence of agency costs depend on the models' underlying assumptions. Myers (1977) shows that firms that are characterized as having a substantial amount of discretionary investment opportunities will be beset with relatively higher agency costs for a given level of leverage. Thus, lower levels of leverage should characterize these firms. An implication of this model is that in extreme cases, due to a firm's "debt overhang" valuable investment projects will not be undertaken.

Jensen (1986) and Stulz (1990) present models in which leverage plays a disciplinary role and reduces the agency costs of managerial discretion. In these models the disciplinary role of debt prevents managers from undertaking poor projects, thus, the value of the firm is increased. However, the relationship between leverage and investment is ambiguous since, as the authors show, leverage can also have an opposite effect on the value of firms that are highly leveraged. Specifically, because of the negative impact of adverse liquidity shocks, firms that are characterized by a relatively high level of debt in their capital structure are less able to take advantage of valuable investment projects in comparison to their less leveraged counterparts.

In summary, the relationship between the firm's investment decision and the firm's choice of financing instrument and thus its capital structure is ambiguous. The question I therefore want to address is whether the firm's investment and choice of financing instrument decisions are complements or substitutes or as pointed out by Miller (1991, p. 481) we should not "waste our limited worrying capacity on second-order and largely self-correcting problems like leveraging."

III. THE METHODOLOGY

A. Econometric Model

The phenomenon that some firms choose to issue debt and others choose to issue equity to finance their investment projects suggests that there is a self-selection problem. If the choice process is not made independently of potential gains from debt versus gains from equity, the choice of financing method should not be treated exogenously. Rather, if firms that choose to issue equity are the ones that can most benefit from the choice and vice versa for those who choose debt, then the choice decision should be treated as endogenous.

The net impact of this endogenous choice process is that the observed investment data are not the outcome of a random selection. The expression random selection refers to the sample of investment decisions financed with the full set of financing choices (including convertible debt, retained earnings, bank debt, etc.) that would be observed if one could simultaneously measure each firm's investment decisions financed by the full set of financing choices. In order to correct for this simultaneity and hence nonrandomness in the observed data, a discrete choice/continuous outcome model is used. More specifically, the model utilized has the following general reduce form specification:

$$I_D = X_D \beta_D + \varepsilon_D \qquad \text{(1a)}$$

$$I_E = X_E \beta_E + \varepsilon_E \qquad \text{(1b)}$$

$$F^* = Z\theta - \varepsilon. \qquad \text{(1c)}$$

I_D and I_E represents the firm's gross capital expenditures financed by debt and equity respectively. F^* represents the unobservable underlying objective function of the manager of the firm. Maximization of the manager's goal may or may not be consistent with shareholder wealth maximization depending on the existence and size of the agency costs of managerial discretion. The manager chooses whether to issue debt or equity based on which one has the most favorable impact on his objective. Therefore, if the firm issues debt, it must be that $F^* \geq 0$ and if the firm issues equity it must be that $F^* < 0$. X_D and X_E represent explanatory variables that determine the firm's capital expenditures financed by debt and equity, respectively. Z is a set of explanatory variables that determine the firm's choice of financing instrument. β_D, β_E, and θ are parameter vectors. Finally ε_D, ε_E, and ε are vectors of random errors and are assumed to be normally distributed. The model represented by equations (1a)–(1c) is known as a switching regression model with known sample separation in the sense that the choice of debt or equity is known information.

Although the index F^* is unobservable, we observe the choice of whether the firm issues debt or equity, and the firm's capital expenditures I_i, where $i = 1, 2, \ldots, J$ observations. Because I_{Di} and I_{Ei}, the firm's capital expenditures financed with debt and equity respectively, are assumed mutually exclusive, they cannot be observed simultaneously for any one firm. Thus, the criterion function (F_i^*) can be scaled such that $F_i = 1$ iff $\varepsilon_i \leq Z_i\theta$ ($F_i^* \geq 0$) and $F_i = 0$ iff $\varepsilon_I > Z_i\theta$ ($F_i^* < 0$). The model to be estimated has the following specification:

Regime 1: $I_{Di} = X_D\beta_D + \varepsilon_D$ iff $\varepsilon_i \le Z_i\theta$, (i.e., $F_i = 1$)   (2a)

Regime 2: $I_{Ei} = X_E\beta_E + \varepsilon_E$ iff $\varepsilon_i > Z_i\theta$, (i.e., $F_i = 0$)   (2b)

Given the exogenous variables X_{Di}, X_{Ei}, and Z_i, equations (2a) and (2b) have the following interpretation: If $\varepsilon_i \le Z_i\theta$, the observation I_i is generated by regime 1. That is, firm i chooses debt financing and $F_i = 1$. Conversely if $\varepsilon_i > Z_i\theta$, the observation I_i is generated by regime 2, that is, firm i chooses equity financing and $F_i = 0$.

The model can be described as a switching regression model with endogenous switching. With sample separation known the capital expenditure observations I_i are available and parameter estimates of β_D and β_E can be obtained. Assuming that ε_i is correlated with ε_{Di} and ε_{Ei}, ordinary least squares estimation of the investment expenditure equations will give biased and inconsistent estimates. This occurs because the expected values of ε_{Di} and ε_{Ei} are nonzero (Judge, Griffiths, Lee, & Hill, 1982 p. 514). Thus a different estimation technique will be required.

Parameter estimates of this model can be obtained by maximum likelihood. However, in models of this type quite often the likelihood function is not well behaved and is generally characterized by a lack of convergence. An alternative two-stage procedure which avoids these problems is presented in Maddala (1983, chap. 8) and is briefly summarized below.

With sample separation known for the criterion function we can obtain estimates of the parameter vector θ by probit maximum likelihood techniques (ML). To obtain parameter estimates of β_D and β_E, estimates of the residuals ε_D and ε_E in (2a) and (2b) are required. Maddala shows that:

$$E(\varepsilon_D \mid \varepsilon_i \le Z\theta) = E(\sigma_{D\varepsilon}\varepsilon_i \mid \varepsilon_i \le Z\theta)$$

$$= -\sigma_{D\varepsilon}[\phi(Z\theta)/\Phi(Z\theta)]$$

$$= -\sigma_{D\varepsilon}J_D. \qquad (3)$$

And similarly,

$$E(\varepsilon_E \mid \varepsilon_i > Z\theta) = E(\sigma_{E\varepsilon}\varepsilon_i \mid \varepsilon_I > Z\theta)$$

$$= -\sigma_{E\varepsilon}[\phi(Z\theta)/\Phi(Z\theta)]$$

$$= -\sigma_{E\varepsilon}J_E. \qquad (4)$$

J_D and J_E are the selectivity bias correction terms and $\phi(.)$ and $\Phi(.)$ are the density function and the distribution function of the standard normal respectively. The terms J_D and J_E are known as the inverse of Mill's ratio and are monotone decreasing functions of the probability that an observation is selected into the sample. $\sigma_{D\varepsilon}$ and $\sigma_{E\varepsilon}$ are the covariances of the errors between equation (1a) and (1c), and equation

(1b) and (1c). Based on equation (3) and (4), equation (2a) and (2b) can be written as:

$$I_{Di} = X_D \beta_D + \sigma_{De} J_D + e_D \tag{5a}$$

$$I_{Ei} = X_E \beta_E + \sigma_{Ee} J_E + e_E. \tag{5b}$$

Where, e_D and e_E are the new disturbances, with zero conditional means and are defined as:

$$e_D = \varepsilon_D + \sigma_{De} J_D \tag{6a}$$

$$e_E = \varepsilon_E + \sigma_{Ee} J_E. \tag{6b}$$

And have conditional variances:

$$\sigma^2(e_D \mid F_i = 1) = \sigma_{DD} - \sigma_{De} J_D (X_D \beta_D + J_D) \tag{7a}$$

$$\sigma^2(e_E \mid F_i = 1) = \sigma_{EE} + \sigma_{Ee} J_E (X_E \beta_E + J_E). \tag{7b}$$

Equation (5a) and (5b) can then be estimated using standard OLS techniques.

Equation (2a), (5a), and (5b) represent the general form of the econometric model to be estimated. It is important to note that the residuals in equation (5a) and (5b) are heteroscedastic. This is because the variance expressions in (7a) and (7b) are not constant over observations due to the last term in both equations. The procedure utilized to make the heteroscedastic corrections is outlined in Maddala (1983). Finally, predicted values of the investment equations are used in the discrete choice model to obtain an estimate of the structural model.

B. The Investment Module

At present there is no widely accepted structural model of investment spending. Along with the neoclassical investment production, the Tobin's q model of investment has also been used in the finance literature. However, it has met with very limited success (see, for e.g., Oliner & Rudebusch, 1992). Whereas, work by Abel and Blanchard (1986), among others, provide evidence indicating an important role for accelerator effects from sales or output. Based on this evidence, the investment equation is based on the neoclassical investment model.

In the empirical literature on neoclassical investment the underlying production function on which the econometric specification is based is usually the Cobb-Douglas (CD) or Constant Elasticity of Substitution (CES). Due to the very tight restrictions imposed by the former, the latter is chosen as the underlying production function. In logarithmic form, and adjusting for the simultaneity between the investment and financing decisions, the investment equations have the following form:

$$\ln I_{Di} = \beta_{0D} + \beta_{1D}\ln(p/c_d)_i + \beta_{2D}\ln Q_i + \sigma_{De}J_D \tag{8a}$$

$$\ln I_{Ei} = \beta_{0E} + \beta_{1E}\ln(p/c_e)_i + \beta_{2E}\ln Q_i + \sigma_{Ee}J_E. \tag{8b}$$

Where p is the output price; and Q_i is output. The variable c is the firm's user cost of capital and is defined as:[1]

$$c = g(1-k)\{1 - [t_c v/(v + r(1 - lt_c))]\}\{r(1 - t_c) + \zeta - \dot{g}/g\}(1 - t_c)^{-1}.$$

Where g is the price of capital goods; t_c is the corporate income tax rate; v is the discounted value of the capital allowance on a dollar's worth of investment; r is the firm's discount rate; k is the investment tax credit; l is the rate at which loans can be offset against tax; ζ is the rate of depreciation; and a dot over a variable represents the time derivative.

As equations (8a) and (8b) now stand they assume that the firm's user cost of capital is the same for both debt and equity financed investment expenditures. But due to the tax deductibility of interest payments, two different user cost of capital are obtained depending on the choice of financing instrument. Specifically, if debt is the chosen form of finance, $l = 1$ and the firm's user cost of capital is:

$$c_d = g(1-k)(v+r)\{[((\zeta - (\dot{g}/g)) + r(1 - t_c)]/[v + r(1 - t_c)]\}.$$

Similarly, if equity is chosen, $l = 0$ and c takes the following form:

$$c_e = g(1-k)[v + (r/(1 - t_c))][(r + \zeta - \dot{g}/g)(v + r)].$$

Equations (8a) and (8b) adjusted for differences in the user cost of capital are the specific forms of the investment equations to be estimated.

A test for simultaneity and therefore selectivity bias is to test for $\sigma_{De} = 0$ and/or $\sigma_{Ee} = 0$ in equations (8a) and (8b). The standard t-test is used to ascertain the significance of these coefficients and, thus, whether simultaneity and hence selectivity bias is an issue. If there is selectivity bias, OLS estimates of the investment equation parameters are biased and inconsistent if uncorrected. In addition, the parameters of the probit equation are inefficient. An alternative test of selectivity bias is obtained by pooling all the observations of the sample. Specifically, by using the observations on all firms—both debt issuers and equity issuers—and performing the same two-stage estimation procedure, estimates of σ_{Pe} can be obtained. In this procedure σ_{Pe} is the correlation between the errors of the criterion function and the errors of the regression equation when all the observations are pooled. If $\sigma_{Pe} = 0$, selectivity bias is not an issue and the OLS results are consistent and unbiased. An additional test that is usually performed with switching regression models is the likelihood ratio test for difference in regimes. Define β_R and $L(\beta_R)$ as the restricted (that is, $\sigma_{P\varepsilon} = 0$) parameter estimates and likelihood value, respectively. Similarly, define β_{UR} and $L(\beta_{UR})$ to be unrestricted (that is, $\sigma_{P\varepsilon} \neq 0$) parameter estimates and likelihood value, respectively. Then the likelihood ratio statistic, $-2\ln[L(\beta_R)/L(\beta_{UR})]$, has an asymptotic χ^2 distribution with one degree of freedom. A test of the presence of sample selectivity bias is a test for $-2\ln[L(\beta_R)/L(\beta_{UR})] = 0$. The two-stage estimation procedure presented in this section provides a complete model of the investment and financing decisions of the firm.

IV. THE DATA

A. The Sample

The data set used in this study was compiled from various sources of information on registered Canadian corporations. The primary source of data was the Financial Post Industrial data tape (FPID). This is a data set that contains yearly balance sheet and stock market information on registered Canadian corporations. Although the FPID data set is fairly complete, at times observations were missing or incomplete. Whenever possible these were completed with data from prospectuses of firms; the Globe and Mail Business Review; the Bank of Canada Review; Corporate Taxation Statistics; Statistics Canada publications; the McLeod Young and Weir Bond Record; and the Financial Post Industrial Manual.

The sources of issue information were the Financial Post data cards, firms' prospectuses (whenever available), the Financial Post Industrial Manual, and the Financial Post Record of Bond and Stock Issues. In order for a specific stock or bond issue to be included in the sample several criteria had to be met. The most important of these was that the proposed use of funds from the security issue had to be for capital expenditures. This information was obtained by hand-searching the various sources of information indicated above, with the main source being the Financial Post data cards. Only 320 firms met this criterion given its restrictive nature. Second, a continuous history of accounting data of at least six years was required given that at least five years prior to the security issue were necessary to compute the firm's long-term leverage ratios. Third, the net proceeds had to exceed $1,000,000.

In addition to the above criteria other factors determining the final sample size were (1) Issues were dropped if the issuing firm was not on the FPID data tape. This was necessary in order to obtain stock market information and data on firm characteristics. (2) The sample was restricted to those firms traded on the Toronto Stock Exchange. This restriction was necessary because stock market data on firms quoted on the other Canadian exchanges over the entire sample period were not available. (3) Firms included must have made a cash issue of either common stock or bonds during the time period. (4) Firms belonging to utilities and financial

Table 1. Sample Issue Statistics

Year	Total Issues	Debt Issues	Total Value($000)	Debt Issue($000)	% Debt Issues
1966	6	6	99500	99500	100
1967	10	10	199500	199500	100
1968	3	2	76000	70000	66.7
1969	1	1	20000	20000	100
1970	15	14	437713	427500	93.3
1971	13	12	435500	455095	92.3
1972	9	7	232888	230075	77.7
1973	6	4	223000	184000	66.7
1974	9	8	443625	430777	88.8
1975	20	19	1056705	856300	95.0
1976	13	10	518886	394500	76.9
1977	8	8	325500	325500	100
1978	8	6	377010	335500	75.0
1979	14	6	328584	163653	42.9
1980	10	4	393250	248500	40.0
1981	5	2	193323	110000	40.0
1982	16	7	785814	402500	43.8
1983	26	6	1185229	285000	23.1
1984	15	3	358917	210000	20.0
TOTAL	207	135			

Note: This table provides annual issue statistics on the total number of issues and on the number of debt issues included in the sample.

services were also not included. As a result of all the above restrictions and criteria, the final sample consisted of 207 observations on new, seasoned security offerings covering the time period 1966 to 1984.

Descriptive statistics for the sample of debt and equity issues used in this study are shown in Table 1. The sample issue statistics demonstrate a higher percentage of debt issues from 1966–1978. However, starting in 1979 the relative importance of equity as a means of obtaining external financing increased dramatically. This increase in the percentage of equity issues suggests that there may be a structural change in the data starting in 1979. A possible explanation for this phenomenon is the onset of double-digit inflation. This possibility will be tested for below. The dollar amount value of the issues also reflects this general pattern.[2]

B. Variables Used in the Financing Module

In this section the variables used in the estimation of the financing choice model are presented. Except where noted, all accounting data are for the end of the fiscal year prior to the issue. Detailed definitions are presented in Appendix A.

Fi (Observed Choice)

This is an index variable representing the chosen financing instrument and is used as the dependent variable in the discrete choice model. It is coded as one if debt is chosen, zero if equity is chosen.

Investment (Operating Leverage)

Following Anderson (1981, 1990) the firm's investment decision is represented by the nominal value of its gross capital expenditure.[3] The logarithmic transformation of investment expenditure (LINV) is used as a means of controlling for the effect of size on the firm's choice of financing instrument via its investment expenditures.[4] The sign of the coefficient of the investment variable depends on the relative magnitudes of the "output and substitution effects." A positively (negatively) signed coefficient can be interpreted as being consistent with the "output effect" being greater (less) than the "substitution effect" which would be consistent with operating and financial leverage being complements (substitutes).

Moral Hazard Costs

Myers (1977) and Harris and Raviv (1990), among others, hypothesize that the firm's optimal debt ratio is inversely related to the moral hazard costs of debt. Two measures of agency costs are used. First, Harris and Raviv argue that firms with assets that can be used, as collateral should, ceteris paribus, issue more debt. As an indicator of collateral value, the measure, gross plant plus inventory scaled by total assets, is used (COL) (Titman & Wessels, 1988). Given that this variable is positively related to collateral value, it is expected that this variable will have a positive effect on the probability of the firm issuing debt.

The other measure used is the ratio of the firm's cash flow to its capital stock (CFLK). Myers (1977) hypothesizes that the cost of moral hazard is related to the fraction of firm value that is accounted for by firm growth opportunities. In particular, he argues that there is an inverse relationship between the firm's optimal debt ratio and the amount of growth opportunities. Several authors (see, e.g., Gilchrist & Himmelberg, 1995) present evidence that controlling for profitability, the firm's cash flow also reflects growth opportunities. Thus, it is expected that this variable will have a negative effect on the probability of the firm issuing debt. The variables, earnings per share (EPS) and return on asset (ROA), are used to control for the firm's profitability. It should be noted that the pecking order model contends that for firms seeking external funds, there should be an inverse relationship between profitability and equity issues. We would therefore expect a positive relationship between EPS and ROA and the probability of the firm issuing equity.

Tax Effects

DeAngelo and Masulis (1980) note that although the firm faces a statutory tax rate its effective tax rate is affected by the levels of both debt and non-debt tax shields. As an indicator of non-debt tax shields (NDT) I utilize the ratio of the firm's non-debt tax shields scaled by the firm's total assets. Non-debt tax shields are measured as earnings before interest and taxes (EBIT) less interest, and income tax payments divided by the appropriate tax rate (Titman & Wessels, 1988). DeAngelo and Masulis (1980) point out that non-debt tax shields are substitutes for the tax benefits of debt financing. However, Dammon and Senbet (1988) have shown that if the investment decision is endogenized its effect is ambiguous due to the existence of both output and substitution effects. Thus, it is not possible, a priori, to give a sign to the coefficient on NDT. However, a positively (negatively) signed coefficient would be consistent with the output effect exceeding (being less than) the substitution effect.

Several authors have argued that, ceteris paribus, the firm's financial leverage is an increasing function of its debt-related tax shields. As a measure of the firm's debt-related tax shields (DT), the amount of the security issue multiplied by the appropriate corporate tax rate scaled by the firm's (EBIT) is utilized. As the value of debt-related tax shields increases, debt financing becomes cheaper at the margin. Thus, it is expected that this variable will have a positively signed coefficient.

Bankruptcy Costs and Financial Distress

The static trade-off model contends that the firm's optimal capital structure is inversely related to the size of expected bankruptcy costs. The data, which are required to estimate the impact of bankruptcy costs on the firm's choice of financing instrument, are unobservable. Although it may be possible to obtain some form of measurement that represents the magnitude of bankruptcy costs, it is highly improbable that reliable estimates of the probability of bankruptcy could be obtained. With this limitation in mind I use the standard deviation of EBIT scaled by total assets (VEARN) as a proxy for operating risk (Bradley, Jarrell, & Kim, 1984). Operating risk increases the probability of bankruptcy, and thus bankruptcy costs; it is, therefore, expected that the sign of the coefficient of this variable will be negative.

Optimal Debt Ratio

Several studies have shown that firms adjust to long-run target leverage ratios (see, e.g., Bradley, Jarrell, & Kim, 1984). In adjusting to their long-run target ratio it is expected that if firms are above their long-run target ratio they should issue equity, and if below they should issue debt. Like Marsh (1982), I employ a variable defined as the difference between the firm's current and long-run debt to value ratios (DSTR). It is expected that this variable will have a positively signed coefficient.

The advantages of this measure are twofold. First, it allows us to determine whether or not firms adjust to a long-run target capital structure when seeking public funds. Second, it avoids the potential problem of endogeneity of the firm's capital structure. As a proxy for the firm's long-run target ratio, five-year averages of its leverage ratio is used.[5] It is expected that this variable will have a positively signed coefficient.

Asymmetric Information

Myers and Majluf (1984), among others, point out that issuing debt is cheaper than equity when there is more information asymmetry between bondholders and shareholders. Lucas and McDonald (1990) and Choe, Masulis, and Nanda (1993) note that firms tend to have good projects during favorable economic times. Additionally, asymmetric information tends to be smaller during these periods. Two variables representing capital market conditions are included to capture this effect. Capital market conditions are unobservable variables. In obtaining measures of capital market conditions, forecasts of equity market conditions and debt market conditions are utilized (Marsh, 1982). The forecasting equation for equity issues is:

$$E_t = b_0 + b_1 E_{t-1} + b_2 E_{t-2} + b_3 TR_{t-1} + b_4 TR_{t-2} + e_t. \tag{9}$$

Where, E_t, E_{t-1}, and E_{t-2} are the amount of equity issued in quarter's t, $t-1$ and $t-2$, respectively; TR_{t-1} and TR_{t-2} are the total returns on the Toronto Stock Exchange in quarter $t-1$ and $t-2$ respectively. The predicted values of E_t are used to represent equity market conditions (TS). High values of TS are assumed to indicate conditions conducive to issuing equity.

The timing variable for debt (TD) is defined analogously. It is measured as the forecast of the three-month Treasury bill yield during the corresponding quarter in which debt was issued. The forecasting equation is:

$$R_t + a_0 + a_1 R_{t-1} + a_2 R_{t-2} + e_t. \tag{10}$$

R_{t-1} and R_{t-2} are the three-month Treasury bill yields in quarter's, $t-1$, $t-2$, respectively. The predicted values of R_t are used as a proxy for market conditions TD. High values of TD are assumed to correspond to high promised coupon payments. This would lead to a negative impact on the probability of a firm issuing debt since, ceteris paribus, high coupon payments would indicate low yield on proceeds from the bond issue.

Other Factors

Titman and Wessels (1988) provide evidence that leverage ratios are related to size. Further, evidence provided by Smith (1977) indicates that small firms pay substantially more to issue equity than do large firms. As a proxy for transaction costs, the logarithm of total assets (LTASS) is used. All else constant, it is expected that LTASS will have a negatively signed coefficient.

Recent research supports the hypothesis that firms within the same industry tend to have similar capital structures (Bradley, Jarrell, & Kim, 1984; Mackie-Mason, 1990). This finding may be due to similar investment opportunities or possibly similar economic and financial factors affecting the capital structure decisions of all the firms in the industry. To control for industry effects, dummy variables representing two-digit SIC codes are used.

C. Variables Used in Investment Module

Investment (I): The dependent variable used in the investment expenditure equations is the logarithm of gross capital expenditures. This variable is discussed in Section II. Given the switching regression specification, the variable is partitioned into two groups, $LINV_{Di}$ if debt is the chosen form of financing and $LINV_{Ei}$ if equity is the chosen form of financing.

Output and Relative Prices

Neoclassical investment theory posits that the investment decision is a function of the demand for the firm's output and relative prices of the firm's product. One of the problems associated with using micro data to estimate investment expenditure equations is that of obtaining a "true" measurement of an individual firm's output. Data that could be considered as the "true" firm's output is usually not available. Various proxies such as net sales, gross national product, and output have been used. Researchers have had mixed results in the use of these proxies in terms of both significant coefficients and goodness of fit criteria.[6] As a proxy for the demand for the firm's output, I use the firm's net sales scaled by its industry's product price (LSLS).[7] Theory dictates that this variable should have a positively signed coefficient.

The other variable utilized is the natural logarithm of the ratio of the firm's industry product price to the user cost of capital (LRP). A substantial amount of discussion was devoted to the firm's user cost of capital above.[8] In developing historical data on the variables that are used in calculating the user-cost of capital variable, an attempt is made to develop as many firm specific and investment specific data as possible. However, for some variables it is impossible to meet this objective. In these instances industry-specific and economy-wide variables are used as proxies.[9] It is expected that, ceteris paribus, as the product price facing the firm increases relative to the user cost of capital, there will be an increase in the firm's capital expenditure. As a result, it is expected that the coefficient will be positively signed.

One of the advantages of separating the investment equation by type of financing method is that it allows me to shed light on the relative impact of both relative prices and the demand for the firm's output on the firm's leverage decision. In a recent paper Maksimovic (1988) shows that the firm's leverage increases with the elasticity of demand for its product. It is therefore expected that, ceteris paribus, the elasticity of demand should be higher in the debt financed investment equation. Additional evidence is provided by the probit equations that are used to obtain the inverse of Mill's ratio. It is expected that both LSLS and LRP will have a positive effect on the probability that the firm will issue debt.

Other Factors

Oliner and Rudebusch (1992) and Gilchrist and Himmelberg (1995) provide evidence that the firm's investment decision is related to its cash flows. There is considerable debate as to what role is being played by cash flows when it is included in the investment function. If it is a measure of profitability then it should have a positive effect on both debt and equity financed investment decisions. However, if it is proxying for growth opportunities, then we should expect a negative relationship in the debt-financed equation and a positive relationship in the equity-financed equation (see, e.g., Myers, 1977). As an indicator I utilize the firm's cash flow scaled by its capital stock (CFLK).

It is assumed in the estimation that all firms face fundamentally the same technology. Clearly this is an oversimplification in that firms are generally characterized by different technologies. However, due to the limited sample size, attempts to separate the sample into different industries and perform estimation on each of these subsamples were not successful. To compensate for this, dummy variables representing the respective industries are utilized. The rationale is that these dummy variables will pick up disparities in technology and tax policies across the various industries.

V. EMPIRICAL RESULTS OF FINANCING CHOICE MODULE

A. Probit Models

The results of estimating the financing choice module corrected for both simultaneity and self-selectivity are summarized in Table 2. Columns 2–3 contain the estimates with the industry dummies. Results without dummy variables are presented in columns 4–5 for comparison purposes. A positive sign indicates a greater probability of debt being issued relative to equity. The former model is the focus of the discussion that follows.

The principal hypothesis is that the firm's investment and financing decisions are independent. The coefficient of the investment variable (LINV) is positive and significant at the 95% confidence level. The positive sign is consistent with the notion that the "output effect" exceeds the "substitution effect." This result does not support Dotan and Ravid's (1985) theoretical prediction. However, it is consistent with explanations given by Hite (1977) and Aivazian and Berkowitz (1992).

Table 2. Results of Financing Choice Module Corrected for Self-Selection Bias and Simultaneity

Variable	Coeff.	T-stat	Coeff.	T-stat
INTCPT	0.519	0.217	0.497	0.232
DSTR	−0.039	−0.407	−0.060	−0.485
DT	0.297	3.528	0.238	3.280
NDT	0.4E-6	0.735	−0.5E-6	−1.119
TS	−0.1E-5	−3.994	−0.1E-5	−4.238
TD	−0.169	−2.339	−0.189	−2.720
EPS	0.423	2.014	0.539	2.763
ROA	9.491	2.214	8.482	2.130
VEARN	−0.011	−0.498	−0.014	−0.719
LINV	1.312	3.938	0.957	3.350
COL	1.261	2.314	1.470	2.470
LTASS	−1.161	−3.177	−0.790	−2.618
CFLK	−2.195	−1.971	−2.560	−2.144
DSIC0	−1.653	−2.358		
DSIC1	0.195	0.369		
DSIC2	0.560	0.826		
DSIC3	−0.225	−0.382		
DSIC5	1.038	1.324		
DSIC6	0.080	0.073		
DSIC7	0.474	0.836		
ρ^2		0.58		0.55
% Correct		90.8%		88.2%

Notes: This table reports the estimation results of the probit model corrected for selectivity bias. The model estimated with industry dummy variables is reported in columns 2–3. Columns 4–5 contain results of the estimation without industry dummy variables. Explanatory variables are defined as follows: DSTR = deviation from optimal capital structure; DT = debt related tax shield; NDT = non-debt tax shield; TS = equity market conditions; TD = debt market conditions; EPS = earnings per share; ROA = return on assets; VEARN = expected bankruptcy costs; LINV = log (gross capital expenditures); COL = gross plant and inventory scaled by total assets; LTASS = log (total assets); CFLK = cash flow scaled by the firm's capital stock; DSICi is the two-digit SIC code industry dummy variables.

More importantly, however, for the first time, evidence is provided which indicates that the firm's *choice* of financing instrument is dependent upon its use of the funds obtained in the issue. This suggests that studies which have ignored the use of the funds while using discrete choice models to analyze the firm's debt/equity choice may in fact be misspecified (see, e.g., Jung, Kim, & Stulz, 1996; Mackie-Mason, 1990; Marsh, 1982).

The signs of the coefficients of the variables used to test the moral hazard costs hypothesis are consistent with theory. The positive and significant coefficient of

COL indicates that as the collateral value of the firm's assets increases, there is an increase in the probability of the firm issuing debt. This finding supports the secured debt hypothesis which states that firms can obtain more favorable terms when issuing debt if the firm's debt can be collateralized (e.g., Harris & Raviv, 1990; Myers, 1977).

CFLK, which is proxying for firms' future growth opportunities, has the expected negative sign and is significantly different from zero. This finding lends support to the agency costs explanation put forth by Jung, Kim, and Stulz (1996) that there is a negative relation between leverage and future growth opportunities. Note that if this interpretation is correct we should observe a negatively signed coefficient of the variable CFLK in the investment equation which is characterized by debt financing; and conversely, a positively signed coefficient in the investment equation which is characterized by equity financing. This issue will be addressed below when the results of the investment equations are discussed.

Turning to the profitability variables, both EPS and ROA have the expected positive sign and are statistically significant. This indicates that the likelihood of a firm issuing debt is much higher when its recent profitability has been relatively high. These results are consistent with the Myers (1984) and Myers and Majluf (1984) hypothesis of a hierarchy of financing choices.

The evidence strongly supports the asymmetric information hypothesis. The coefficient of TS demonstrates the expected negative sign and is significantly different from zero at conventional levels. This suggests that during periods of strong stock market conditions, which on average indicate high share prices, there is an increased probability that firms will issue equity. The coefficient of the debt-timing variable TD has the expected negative sign and is also statistically significant at conventional levels. This result indicates that, ceteris paribus, firms are less likely to issue debt during periods of high interest rates. Previous studies of the firm's choice between debt and equity financing did not find that firms time their debt issues.

The variable used to control for economies of scale has a large significant effect with the predicted sign. This result lends support to the hypothesis that, ceteris paribus, large firms enjoy a comparative advantage over small firms when issuing equity. The negative relationship exhibited by the variable LTASS is not consistent with the results of Marsh (1982), Titman and Wessels (1988), and Jung, Kim, and Stulz (1996) that indicate a positive relationship. A possible explanation for this difference is that the latter two studies do not allow for the interaction of the firm's investment and financing decisions. Thus, the positive effect in those studies could be due to the variable LTASS proxying for firm's capital expenditures and not debt capacity or asymmetric information as they suggest. Furthermore, studies that have used firm size as a proxy for debt capacity should note Myers's (1977) conclusion that there should be no consistent relationship between diversification and debt capacity.

The financial distress hypothesis, in general, and the bankruptcy costs hypothesis in particular is not supported. The coefficient of VEARN which, measures operating risk has the expected negative sign but is not significantly different from zero. This finding is not consistent with results of studies by Marsh (1982) and Mackie-Mason (1990) using U.K. and U.S. data respectively. Possible explanations for the finding reported in this paper are: (a) in general, expected bankruptcy costs are not of sufficient magnitude to be an important determinant of the firm's choice of financing instrument or (b) Canadian corporations do not attach much weight to exposure to operating risk when making capital structure decisions.

The results documented so far are consistent with the "output effect" being greater than the "substitution effect." Given this finding it is expected that DT will have a positively signed coefficient and NDT will have a negatively signed coefficient. The evidence on the debt-related tax shield variable is strongly significant with the expected sign. This result supports the earlier findings that are consistent with the "output effect" exceeding the "substitution effect." Further, this finding suggests that, ceteris paribus, as the value of the firm's tax shields is increased, there is an increased probability that the firm will issue debt. This result provides support for the optimal capital structure model. In addition, it provides some of the first clear evidence that the firm's *choice* of financing instrument is positively related to debt-related tax shields. Marsh (1982) did not examine the issue of tax effects. And Mackie-Mason (1990) did not explicitly address the issue of the effect of debt-related tax shields on the firm's choice of financing instrument. The findings reported here suggest that studies which purport to examine the firm's optimal capital structure in general, and choice of financing instrument in particular, should explicitly model the firm's debt-related tax shields.

The evidence on NDT is weak. Although having the expected negative sign, it is not significant. The insignificance of this variable may be due to the countervailing "output and substitution effects" resulting from the higher capital investment. This finding is similar to that reported by Long and Malitz (1985). The result reported here suggests that conclusions pertaining to the importance of firm's non-debt tax shields, which are based on studies not allowing for the interaction of financing and investment decisions, may be erroneous. The variable DSTR has the expected negative sign but is not significant. This suggests that firms have a tendency, albeit weak, to adjust toward a long-run target leverage ratio. The finding that DSTR is not significantly different from zero does not support the static trade-off theories of financing decisions. This evidence suggests that there are other, more important, firm specific factors that determine the probability of a firm's choice of issuing debt or equity given that it is making a public issue. This finding is important because it is not consistent with Marsh's (1982), Mackie-Mason's (1990), and Opler and Titman's (1996) results. These authors tested this hypothesis and found evidence that firms adjust to their long-run target leverage ratios. The difference in results may be due to the inclusion of the capital expenditure variable. Several authors (e.g., Myers & Majluf, 1984; Oliner & Rudebusch, 1992) have argued that the firm's investment decision plays an important role in the "hierarchy" theory of financing decisions.

Of the seven dummy variables included in the model, only one is significantly different from zero at conventional levels. A likelihood ratio test (χ^2, seven degrees of freedom) for the model without the industry dummies against the model containing the industry dummy variables is 12.60. The zero restrictions on the industry dummies are rejected at the 90% confidence level. These results indicate that, jointly, the industry dummy variables have some impact on the firm's choice

Table 3. Estimates of Financing Choice Module with LINV Replaced by its Determinants

Variable	Coeff.	T-stat	Coeff.	T-stat
INTCPT	−0.494	−1.768	−0.513	−1.417
DSTR	−0.058	−0.477	−0.002	−0.010
DT	0.223	2.836	0.325	3.254
NDT	−0.7E-6	−1.372	−0.2E-5	−1.925
TS	−0.1E-5	4.338	−0.1E-5	−3.784
TD	−0.213	−3.118	−0.215	−2.664
EPS	0.381	2.155	0.353	1.639
ROA	8.499	1.829	13.521	2.589
VEARN	−0.021	−0.957	−0.013	−0.561
LSLS	0.447	2.044	0.918	2.837
LRP	1.327	3.908	1.883	4.199
COL	1.391	2.035	1.466	1.719
LTASS	−0.496	−1.720	−1.024	−2.388
CFLK	−3.141	−2.665	−4.929	−2.909
DSIC0			−1.296	−1.773
DSIC1			−1.529	−2.060
DSIC2			0.550	0.719
DSIC3			0.668	0.969
DSIC5			0.718	0.871
DSIC6			1.751	1.409
DSIC7			−0.489	−0.687
$\bar{\rho}^2$	0.51		0 .54	
% Correct	89.1%		88.2%	

Notes: This table reports estimation results of the probit model with *LSLS* = log (net sales/product price), and *LRP* = log(product price/user cost of capital), substituted for *LINV* = log (gross capital expenditures). The remaining explanatory variables are defined as follows:*DSTR* = deviation from optimal capital structure; *DT* = debt-related tax shield; *NDT* = non-debt tax shield; *TS* = equity market conditions; *TD* = debt market conditions; *EPS* = earnings per share; *ROA* = return on assets; *VEARN* = expected bankruptcy costs; *COL* = plant and inventory scaled by total assets; *LTASS* = log (total assets); *CFLK* = cash flow scaled by the firm's capital stock; *DSICi* is two-digit SIC code industry dummy variables.

of financing instrument. A comparison of the model with and without the industry dummy variables yields similar results.

Table 3 presents results of the reduced form probit model. This yields estimates of the inverse of Mill's ratio which are used in the investment equations to correct for sample selectivity bias and, hence, simultaneity. Additionally it allows for the ascertaining of the impact of LSLS and LRP on the firm's financing choice. The results without the industry dummy variables are included to facilitate comparison with the former results.

Maksimovic (1988) suggests that the firm's leverage is an increasing function of demand for its output. The positive and significant coefficient of LSLS provides support for his hypothesis. Additionally, this finding, along with the positive and significant coefficient of LRP provides additional evidence that is consistent with the "output effect" exceeding the "substitution effect." Note also that the results are consistent with those contained in Table 2.

B. Summary Statistics and Specification Analysis

Looking to the summary statistics, $\overline{\rho}^2$ in a discrete choice model is analogous to $\overline{R}^2$ in a regression equation. When interpreting this statistic, it is important to note that $\overline{\rho}^2$ for a discrete choice model is usually much lower than $\overline{R}^2$ for a comparable fit in a classical regression model. This is because the dependent variable takes on only two values, both of which are at the extremes of the range of the right side of the equation. In comparing the structural model to the reduced form model, the results indicate that the former model has a higher explanatory power. This is shown by the higher $\overline{\rho}^2$, 0.58 as opposed to 0.54, and the higher log likelihood statistic.

Another summary statistic is the ability of the model to correctly predict the observed choices in the sample. The models depicted in Tables 2 and 3 correctly classify 90 and 88% of the decisions, respectively. These correct classification rates are much higher than that reported in Marsh (1982) that correctly classifies 75% of the decisions and those reported in Jung, Kim, and Stulz (1996) which had a range of 74 to 81% of the decisions.[10]

VI. INVESTMENT MODULE

This section presents and discusses the results obtained from the estimation of the investment equation. The section is organized in the following manner. First, the effect of the demand for the firm's output (LSLS) and relative prices (LRP) is analyzed. Second, the role of cash flows (CFLK) in the investment equation is discussed. In addition, the ability of CFLK to distinguish between the agency cost hypothesis and the pecking order hypothesis is highlighted. Third, the importance of industry specific factors is analyzed. The section concludes with a discussion of the significance and interpretation of the inverse of Mill's ratio.

A. Investment Equations

Table 4 presents the results of the investment equation when debt is the source of financing. Table 5 contains estimates of the equity financing equation. Columns 2–3 in Tables 4 and 5 present the results uncorrected for simultaneity and sample selectivity bias. The investment equations corrected for simultaneity and sample selectivity bias and adjusted for the heteroscedastic errors are presented in columns 4 through 5. The issue of sample selectivity bias will be determined by the significance of the coefficient (Lambda) of the inverse of Mill's ratio that was obtained from the probit equation when LINV was replaced by its determinants. In addition, a likelihood ratio test between the estimates of the coefficients corrected

Table 4. Results of Debt Financed Investment Expenditures Corrected for Self-selection Bias and Heteroscedasticity

Variable	Coeff.	T-stat	Coeff.	T-stat
INTCPT	−0.245	−0.339	−0.368	−0.526
LSLS	0.932	14.393	0.939	15.083
LRP	0.530	6.404	0.530	6.552
CFLK	−1.133	−2.280	−1.379	−2.783
DSIC0	0.307	0.917	0.314	0.978
DSIC1	−0.649	−2.467	−0.559	−2.162
DSIC2	−0.583	−2.290	−0.505	−2.025
DSIC3	1.198	5.091	1.230	5.415
DSIC5	0.918	4.009	1.012	4.459
DSIC6	1.458	3.776	1.523	4.047
DSIC7	−0.810	−3.327	−0.785	−3.319
Lambda			−0.582	−2.552

	Summary Statistics	
	Uncorrected	Corrected
Number of Observations	135	135
R^2	.78	.79
R^2	.75	.77
$F(11, 123)$	41.92	42.11
Log-Likelihood	−154.52	−151.54
Chi-square	204.80	210.77

Notes: This table reports the estimation results of the debt-financed investment equation corrected for both self-selection bias and heteroscedasticity. These results are reported in columns 4–5. Columns 2–3 contain uncorrected results. LSLS = log(net sales/industry product price); LRP = log(industry product price/user cost of capital); CFLK = cash flow scaled by the firm's capital stock; and DSICi is the two-digit SIC code industry dummy variable.

Table 5. Results of Equity Financed Investment Expenditures Corrected for Self-selection Bias and Heteroscedasticity

Variable	Coeff.	T-stat	Coeff.	T-stat
INTCPT	–0.260	–0.240	–0.245	–0.245
LSLS	0.582	8.601	0.582	9.253
LRP	0.850	5.202	0.849	5.616
CFLK	0.117	1.434	0.117	1.671
DSIC0	1.182	2.850	1.178	3.075
DSIC1	0.081	0.255	0.073	0.243
DSIC2	–0.750	–2.292	–0.752	–2.476
DSIC3	1.262	4.219	1.256	4.505
DSIC5	1.125	1.484	1.129	1.616
DSIC6	1.296	2.359	1.288	2.531
DSIC7	–0.372	–1.289	–0.377	–1.402
Lambda			0.020	0.124

	Summary Statistics	
	Uncorrected	Corrected
Number of Observations	72	72
R^2	.81	.79
R^2	.78	.76
$F(11, 60)$	26.19	23.43
Log-Likelihood	–71.91	–71.90
Chi-squared	119.98	120.00

Notes: This table presents the estimation results of the equity financed investment equation corrected for self-selection bias and heteroscedasticity. These results are reported in columns 4–5. Columns 2–3 contain uncorrected results. LSLS = log(net sales/industry product price); LRP = log(industry product price/user cost of capital); CFLK = cash flow scaled by the firm's capital stock; and DSICi is the two-digit SIC code, industry dummy variable.

for selectivity bias and uncorrected for selectivity bias will provide additional evidence on the issue of simultaneity.

The estimated coefficient of LSLS has the expected positive sign and is significantly different from zero in both equations. This result suggests that as the demand for the firm's product increases, there is an increase in the firm's investment expenditures.

One of the advantages of separating the investment equation by the type of financing is that interesting insights are obtained as to the relative size of the output parameters. A likelihood ratio test was conducted to test for equality of coefficients between the investment equations when debt and equity are the sources of financing. The likelihood ratio test statistic is 44.912. The 5% critical value from the chi-square distribution with 11 degrees of freedom is 21.03, thus the null hypothesis of equality of coefficients across equations can be rejected. The results suggest that, in general, the coefficients from the debt-financed equation and the equity-financed equation are statistically different from each other. Specifically, the coefficient of LSLS in the debt-financed investment equation is larger than that of the equity-financed equation. This finding is consistent with Maksimovic's (1988) hypothesis that the firm's leverage ratio increases with the elasticity of demand.[11] The variable has the expected positive sign and is significant at conventional confidence levels in both equations. These results suggest that as the firm's product price increases relative to its user cost of capital, it will increase its capital expenditures.

It was argued earlier that the variable CFLK is proxying for firms' growth opportunities. To be consistent with the results of the financing module, we should expect a positively signed coefficient in the equity-financed equation and a negatively signed coefficient in the debt-financed equation. The present results are consistent with these, a priori, expectations. In the investment equation characterized by debt issue, the coefficient is negative and significant at the 95% confidence level. In the investment equation characterized by equity issue the variable is positive and significant at the 90% confidence level. These results are consistent with those reported by Smith and Watts (1992) and Lang, Ofek, and Stulz (1996).

Oliner and Rudebusch (1992), among others, argue that the relationship between the firm's operating cash flow, (CFLK), and its corporate capital structure is difficult to interpret, because it could also be proxying for internal sources of funds if the pecking order hypothesis is correct. If the pecking order hypothesis is correct,[12] then we should observe a positively signed coefficient of CFLK in both investment equations. However, if it is proxying for firm specific and intangible opportunities, CFLK should have a positive coefficient in the equity financed equation and a negative coefficient in the debt financed equation. The finding that the coefficient is positive in the equity financed equation and negative in the debt financed equation supports the hypothesis that CFLK is proxying for future growth opportunities. This evidence is consistent with that obtained in the financing module equation. Thus, by using a discrete choice model in conjunction with a switching regression model, one is able to identify which hypothesis is tested using the firm's operating cash flow.

In the debt-financed equation, six of the seven dummy variables utilized to control for industry specific effects are significant at the 95% confidence level. In the investment equation financed by equity, five of the seven dummy variables used to control for industry specific effects are significant at the 95% confidence level. A sixth is significant at the 80% confidence level. These results suggest that industry specific effects play an important part in explaining the variation of firms' capital expenditures.

B. Sample Selection Bias Results

The inverse of Mill's ratio is used to test the hypotheses of (a) endogeneity of the switching regime and (b) sample selectivity bias characterizing the investment equations. Results indicate that the coefficient of this variable is negative and significantly different from zero at the 95% confidence level in the debt-financed equation. However, it is not significant in the equity-financed equation.[13] These findings provide support for the endogeneity of the switching regime. The endogeneity of the switching regime provides evidence of the interdependency of the firm's financing and investment decisions.

Besides testing for the endogeneity of the firm's choice of financing instrument, the inverse of Mill's ratio tests for selectivity bias. The significance of the coefficient of this variable in the debt financed investment equation indicates that selectivity bias is an issue in this study. A comparison of the results when corrected for and uncorrected for sample selectivity bias shows that in all cases the standard errors of the coefficients are reduced when the inverse of Mill's ratio is included as an explanatory variable. By making this correction, the efficiency and consistency of the parameters are improved. Furthermore, the diagnostic statistics that are used to indicate the statistical fit of the model are generally improved. Additionally, the coefficients of the regression equation corrected for self-selectivity bias have improved.

Given the result that the sample selectivity variable is not significant in the investment equation when equity is the chosen form of financing, it is instructive to reestimate the investment equation using the entire sample with and without the correction for sample selectivity bias. By performing these estimations a more robust test of whether or not simultaneity is an issue can be performed. In particular, a likelihood ratio test using the log-likelihood statistic from these two regressions will provide additional evidence on the issue of simultaneity between the firm's choice of financing instrument and the investment decision (Lee & Trost, 1978).

Table 6 presents results of the pooled sample, with and without the selectivity criterion variable. Columns 2 and 3 give the results without the sample selectivity variable. Columns 4 and 5 give the results with the sample selectivity variable.

The likelihood ratio statistic of no difference in regimes between the models with and without the selectivity variable, (χ^2 with one degree of freedom), is 6.206. This finding indicates that the null hypothesis of exogeneity of the firm's choice of financing instrument can be rejected, thus providing additional evidence of the interdependence of the firm's financing and investment decisions.

In the literature on self-selection, a major concern has been with testing for self-selectivity. However, an equally important issue concerns the signs and magnitudes of the covariances (Lambda). By focusing on the signs and magnitudes of the covariances, not only can statements of the firm's expected capital expenditures be made, but also more importantly, conclusions as to the viability of the value

Table 6.   Results of Investment Expenditures Based on the Combined Sample
Corrected for Self-selection Bias and Heteroscedasticity

Variable	Coeff.	T-stat	Coeff.	T-stat
INTCPT	0.354	0.588	0.664	1.092
LSLS	0.730	7.164	0.751	7.520
LRP	0.624	8.329	0.623	8.410
CFLK	0.115	1.276	0.109	1.228
DSIC0	1.219	5.272	1.125	4.856
DSIC1	−0.491	−2.298	−0.523	−2.475
DSIC2	−0.707	−3.335	−0.726	−3.466
DSIC3	1.211	6.239	1.163	6.035
DSIC5	0.953	4.309	1.047	4.723
DSIC6	1.352	4.012	1.371	4.119
DSIC7	−0.749	−3.832	−0.801	−4.126
Lambda			−0.711	−2.436

Summary Statistics

	Uncorrected	Corrected
Number of Observations	207	207
R^2	.73	.75
$\bar{R}^2$	.72	.74
$F(10, 196)$	56.50	53.16
Log-Likelihood	−249.00	−245.90
Chi-squared (11)	280.67	286.88

Notes: This table presents the estimation results of the investment equation for the combined sample corrected
for self-selection bias and heteroscedasticity. These results are reported in columns 4–5. Columns 2–3
contain uncorrected results. *LSLS* = log(net sales/industry product price); *LRP* = log(industry product
price/user cost of capital); *CFLK* = cash flow scaled by the firm's capital stock; and DSICi is the two-
digit SIC code, industry dummy variable.

maximization premise can be drawn. The following interpretation of the selectivity
variable is based on work by Roy (1951) and Trost (1981).

The results in Tables 4 and 5 show that $\sigma_{E\varepsilon} > 0$ and $\sigma_{D\varepsilon} < 0$ respectively. This
means that the expected (mean) debt-financed investment expenditures is greater
than $(X_{Di}\beta_D))$ and the expected (mean) equity-financed expenditures is greater than
$(X_{Ei}\beta_E)$. Assuming that the value of the firm is an increasing function of its capital
expenditures,[14] and that managers' compensation, and therefore their utility, is an
increasing function of capital expenditures, the implication of the interpretation of
the error covariances can be stated as follows.[15] For managers faced with the choice
between debt and equity, those who benefited most from issuing debt (in terms of
managerial enhancement) chose to issue debt and similarly, those who benefited
most from issuing equity chose to issue equity. Thus, it can be concluded that based

on the choice set available to the firms included in this sample, managers chose to issue the financing instrument that maximized their utility.

VII. SUMMARY AND CONCLUSION

The results of this study support the hypothesis that, in general, the firm's financing and investment decisions are interdependent, and specifically, that the firm's *choice* of financing instrument is endogenous. The results are also consistent with the "output effect" being larger than the "substitution effect," thus providing evidence that is consistent with operating and financial leverage being complements. At a more specific level the results indicate that agency costs are important determinants of firms' choice of financing instruments. Larger firms seem to prefer issuing equity. There are also indications that firms attempt to time the issuing of debt and equity securities to coincide with favorable market conditions. Mixed results are obtained with regards to the costs of financial distress hypothesis. Also, while the debt related tax shields hypothesis is supported, the non-debt-related tax shields hypothesis is not supported. Thus, the results provide mixed support for both the pecking order hypothesis and the static trade-off model.

This study corrects for the selectivity bias and hence simultaneity bias, which characterized previous discrete choice, models. Further, evidence provided by the selectivity variable indicates that management chooses the financing instrument that maximizes self-enhancement. Additionally, by being able to separate the investment equations, I am able to show that cash flows are proxying for future growth opportunities.

From a methodological point of view, the finding of the presence of sample selectivity bias indicates that parameter estimates of previous empirical studies that examine the firm's choice of financing instrument are inconsistent. This further suggests that future studies of the firm's choice of financing instrument should utilize a structural approach. Clearly, the econometric methodology used in this paper is a valid candidate.

APPENDIX A

Data Definitions

$LINV$ =   Log (gross capital expenditures).

COL =   Gross plant plus inventory scaled by total asset.

$CFLK$ =   (Net Income + interest expense + depreciation + amortization)/net property plant and equipment.

NDT =   [$ebit - int - (itax/t_c)$]/total assets; $ebit$ = earnings before interest and taxes; $itax$ = reported income tax payments; int = interest expense; t_c = (tax figure reported on its income statement – deferred taxes)/cash flows.

$DT =$ (issue size)T_c/ebit.

$VEARN =$ The standard deviation of the difference in EBIT scaled by total assets.

$ROA =$ Earnings after taxes scaled by total assets.

$TS = -267.46 + .051E_{t-1} + .27E_{t-2} + 1.62Tr_{t-1} - 1.01TR_{t-2}$; E_{t-1} and E_{t-2} are the amount of equity issued in quarter $t-1$ and $t-2$, respectively; TR_{t-1} and TR_{t-2} are returns on the Toronto stock exchange in quarters $t-1$ and $t-2$, respectively.

$TD = 1.013 + .87R_{t-1} - .0015R_{t-2}$; R_{t-1}, and R_{t-2} are three month treasury bill yields in quarters $t-1$, $t-2$, and $t-3$ respectively.

$EPS =$ Earnings per share.

$DSTR = acstr - lcstr$; $acstr =$ book value of long-term debt at end of previous fiscal year/(long-term debt + market value of equity); $lcstr$ is the five-year average of $acstr$; market value of equity = shares outstanding times stock price at end of previous fiscal year.

$LTASS =$ Log (total assets).

$LSLS =$ Log (net sales/product price); the two-digit SIC industry product price is used as a proxy for the firm's product price.

$LRP =$ Log (the two-digit industry product price/user cost of capital).

$c_d = g(1 - k)(v + r)\{[(\zeta - (\dot{g}/g)) + r(1 - t_c)]/[v + r(1 - t_c)]\}.$

$c_e = g(1 - k)[v + (r/(1 - t_c))][(r + \zeta - \dot{g}/g))(v + r)].$

$g =$ Data on individual firm's acquisition price of capital are not available to researchers. As a proxy I use the ratio of the corresponding industry's investment deflators, defined as the current acquisition price of capital goods divided by the output price deflator. The level of aggregation is the two-digit SIC level.

$\dot{g}/g =$ Ratio of the inflation rate of the producer price index to the acquisition price of capital.

$k =$ The firm's investment tax credit.

$v =$ Information required to construct this variable is not available. Following Nickell (1977, p. 200) I assume that v is equal to the depreciation variable d. This variable is discussed in Appendix B.

$\zeta =$ The firm's depreciation rate. The construction of this variable is described in Appendix B.

$r =$ The discount rate of the firm is unobservable and as such, there is much debate as to which proxy variable is the most appropriate. Although the weighted average cost of capital variable is appealing, evidence indicates that corporate bond yields is a much better approximation for this unobservable variable (Nickell, 1978). In the estimation, the Mcleod Young and Weir industrial long-term bond rate is used.

APPENDIX B

Several studies, for example Titman and Wessels (1988), have used the ratio of the depreciation allowances claimed by the firm to its capital stock as a measure of the firm's depreciation rate. However, Anderson (1990) argues that this variable is spuriously correlated with the dependent variable in the investment equation. He suggests regressing the ratio of the firm's depreciation charges to its capital stock against a set of industry dummies with the predicted values from the regressors used as the depreciation rates as a method to overcome this problem. He further points out that these depreciation rates can be interpreted as an instrumented version of the variable with industry dummies serving as instruments. The results are presented in Table A1.

Table A1.

Variable	Coefficient	Std. Error	Implied Dep
Intercept (Energy)	.267	.055 (*)	.267
DSIC01 Mining	–.061	.024 (*)	.206
DSIC02 Paper/Forest	–.170	.073 (*)	.097
DSIC03 Manufacturing	–.044	.016 (*)	.223
DSIC04 Consumer Prod	–.070	.039 (**)	.197
DSIC05 Construction	–.035	.017 (*)	.232
DSIC06 Transport	–.043	.015 (*)	.224
DSIC07 Retail	–.022	.010 (*)	.245

Notes: (*) and (**) signify an economic depreciation rate based on a significant parameter estimate at a 95 and 90% confidence level, respectively. The depreciation rates obtained by this procedure appear to be higher than what is to be expected. Further, the relative rates between industries seem to be out of line with expectations. However, in noting that over the sample period accelerated depreciation rates (on a straight-line basis) were applied to machinery and buildings the results become more plausible. Buildings are generally written off at a rate of 5%, however, during the period, 1963–1966, buildings were written off at the rate of 20%. Machinery, is generally written off at an average rate of 20%. However during the periods, 1963–1966, and from 1972–1984, durable machinery for processing and manufacturing industries were written off at a rate of 50%.[16] Thus, the most likely explanation for the apparently high depreciation rates and the unlikely relative rates were the accelerated depreciation rates available to firms over the sample period in general, and to non-natural resource industries in particular. The results obtained by Anderson (1990) are similar to the ones reported here.

ACKNOWLEDGMENT

I am grateful for helpful comments from Varouj Avaizian, Michael Berkowitz, and Andrew Chen (the editor).

NOTES

1. The specification of the firm's user cost of capital outlined here is based on the derivation by Nickell (1978, pp. 200–201). A weakness of the current specification is that it does not take into account agency costs, and ignores the implications of future financing decisions on the tax rate and financial distress. However, as Nickell points out, deriving a firm's user cost of capital in a model that adjusts for these factors in an intertemporal optimization framework quickly becomes intractable and does not lend itself to empirical implementation. The assumption here is that using the specification outlined here much is not lost.

2. Population issue statistics also reflect this general trend. These are not reported due to space limitations.

3. Investment models that have used the neoclassical framework are typically expressed in real terms. However, Anderson (1981) points out that all transactions between economic agents are conducted in current value. He further argues that the economic theory underlying the neoclassical framework offers testable hypotheses of the way agents react in current value; thus, there seems little point in converting nominal capital expenditures to real capital expenditures unless specific interest is to be focused on real capital. Further, given that the major focus of this paper is the interdependency of the financial and investment decisions, it would seem that defining capital expenditures in current value would be more beneficial in terms of defining the role finance plays in the model which generated the data.

4. The variable LINV is more than likely correlated with the measure of non-debt tax shields which is included as an explanatory variable in the financing module equation. However, the degree of correlation should not be very high because data used in constructing the non-debt tax shields variable are based on information from the year prior to the one in which the issue was registered. Whereas, the capital expenditure variable is based on information from the year the issue was registered.

5. The choice of five-year averages is based on data availability as opposed to any theoretical reason. In studies which have used averages of debt ratios as proxy for the firm optimal capital structure, the time period has ranged from five years to 20 years (Bradley, Jarrell, & Kim, 1984). For a discussion of the advantages (disadvantages) of the use of book value as opposed to market value see Titman and Wessels (1988).

6. For a discussion of this issue see for example Nickell (1978, pp. 284–286).

7. Ideally, one would like to be able to use the individual firm's product price. This information is generally not available to researchers. As a proxy variable the industry's product price is used. The level of aggregation is the SIC two-digit industry code.

8. In the construction of the user-cost of capital, it is assumed that the firm's capital gains is equal to zero. This assumption is fairly standard, see for example Nickell (1978, p. 289), and Anderson (1981, 1990).

9. In the theoretical econometrics literature, it is argued that the use of aggregate data leads to a loss in efficiency because of the loss in information due to data aggregation. However, Judge and colleagues (1980, p. 353) have shown that using macro data will not lead to aggregation bias if the coefficients obtained (from using macro data) can be viewed as random drawings from the same probability distribution. Thus, aggregation bias should not be a major issue and the coefficient obtained should be efficient.

10. In Section II it was indicated that the onset of double-digit inflation may have led to a structural change. However, a likelihood ratio test could not reject the null hypothesis of no structural change.

11. The specification of the variable in logarithmic form allows for this interpretation.

12. The pecking order being correct means those firms would first raise capital from retained earnings, then from debt and as a last resort from equity. Thus, ceteris paribus, the higher the firm's earnings the lower the probability of equity being issued.

13. The finding of an insignificant coefficient of lambda in the equity financed equation does not indicate that sample selectivity bias is absent, and therefore that there is exogenous switching. A

sufficient condition for sample selectivity bias and hence endogeneity is for one of the two error covariances to be significant (Maddala, 1983, p. 284).

14.   McConnell and Muscarella (1985) have shown that announcements of increases in planned capital expenditures are associated with significant positive excess stock returns.

15.   Note that the interpretation that follows would also hold if both coefficients are positive. In fact, the only necessary condition is that the coefficient of error covariance (Lambda) from the debt financed investment equation be less than the coefficient of the error covariance (Lambda) from the equity financed equation.

16.   This information was obtained from Boadway, Bruce, and Mintz (1984). In addition they also provide evidence that the breakdown of investment during the sample period was the following: land accounted for, 4%; inventories for, 32%; depletable assets, 7%; buildings, 19%; and machinery, 38% of total physical capital.

REFERENCES

Abel, A., & Blanchard, O. (1986). The present value of profits and cyclical movements in investment. *Econometrica, 54*, 249–273.

Aivazian, V., & Berkowitz, M. (1992). Precommitment and financial structure: An analysis of the effects of taxes. *Economica, 49*, 93–106.

Anderson, G. (1981). A new approach to the empirical investigation of investment expenditures. *Economic Journal, 91*, 88–103.

Anderson, G. (1990). *Is the cost of capital really independent of the level of investment and the financial structure of the firm.* Mimeo, University of Toronto.

Boadway, R., Bruce, N., & Mintz, J. (1984). Taxation, inflation, and the effective marginal tax rate on capital in Canada. *Canadian Journal of Economics, 17*, 63–80.

Bradley, M., Jarrell, G. A., & Kim, E. H. (1984). On the existence of an optimal capital structure: Theory and evidence. *Journal of Finance, 39*, 857–878.

Choe, H., Masulis, R., & Nanda, V. (1993). Common stock offerings across the business cycle: Theory and evidence. *Journal of Empirical Finance, 1*, 3–31.

Dammon, R., & Senbet, L. (1988). The effect of taxes and depreciation on corporate investment and financial leverage. *Journal of Finance, 43*, 357–373.

DeAngelo, H., & Masulis, R. (1980). Optimal capital structure under corporate and personal taxation. *Journal of Financial Economics, 8*, 3–29.

Dotan, A., & Ravid, S. (1985). On the interaction of real and financial decisions of the firm under uncertainty. *Journal of Finance, 40*, 501–517.

Gilchrist, S., & Himmelberg, C. (1995). Evidence on the role of cash flow for investment. *Journal of Monetary Economics, 36*, 541–572.

Harris, M., & Raviv, A. (1990). Capital structure and the informational role of debt. *Journal of Finance, 45*, 321–349.

Harris, M., & Raviv, A. (1991). The theory of capital structure. *Journal of Finance, 46*, 297–355.

Helwege, J., & Liang, N. (1996). Is there a pecking order? Evidence from a panel of IPO firms. *Journal of Financial Economics, 40*, 429–458.

Hite, G. (1977). Leverage, output effects, and the M-M theorems. *Journal of Financial Economics, 4*, 177–202.

Jalilvand, A., & Harris, R. (1984). Corporate behavior in adjusting to capital structure and dividend targets: An econometric study. *Journal of Finance, 39*, 127–145.

Jensen, M. (1986). Agency costs of free cash flow, corporate finance and takeovers. *American Economic Review, 76*, 323–329.

Judge, G., Griffiths, W., Lee, T., & Hill, R. (1985). *The theory and practice of econometrics.* New York: John Wiley & Sons.

Jung, K., Kim, Y., & Stulz, R. (1996). Timing, investment opportunities, managerial discretion, and the security issue decision. *Journal of Financial Economics, 42*, 159–185.

Lang, L., Ofek, E., & Stulz, R. (1996). Leverage, investment and firm growth. *Journal of Financial Economics, 40*, 1996, 3–30.

Lee, L., & Trost, R. (1978). Estimation of some limited dependent variable models with applications to housing demand. *Journal of Econometrics, 8*, 357–382.

Long, M., & Malitz, I. (1985). Investment patterns and financial leverage. In B. Friedman (Ed.), *Corporate Capital Structures in The United States* (pp. 325–352). Chicago: University of Chicago Press.

Lucas, D., & McDonald, R. (1990). Equity issues and stock price dynamics. *Journal of Finance, 45*, 1019–1043.

Mackie-Mason, J. (1990). Do taxes affect corporate financing decisions? *Journal of Finance, 45*, 1471–1493.

Maddala, G. (1983). *Limited-dependent and qualitative variables in econometrics.* Cambridge University Press.

Maksimovic, V. (1988). Capital structure in repeated oligopolies. *Rand Journal of Economics, 19*, 389–407.

Marsh, P. (1982). The choice between equity and debt: An empirical study. *Journal of Finance, 37*, 121–144.

McConnell, J., & Muscarella, C. (1988). Corporate capital expenditure decisions and the market value of the firm. *Journal of Financial Economics, 14*, 399–422.

Miller, M. (1991). Leverage. *Journal of Finance, 46*, 479–488.

Modigliani, F., & Miller, M. H. (1958). The cost of capital, corporation finance, and the theory of investment. *American Economic Review, 48*, 262–297.

Myers, S. (1977). The determinants of corporate borrowing. *Journal of Financial Economics, 5*, 147–175.

Myers, S. (1984). The capital structure puzzle. *Journal of Finance, 39*, 575–592.

Myers, S., & Majluf, N. (1984). Corporate financing and investment decisions when firms have information investors do not have. *Journal of Financial Economics, 13*, 187–221.

Nickell, S. J. (1978). *The investment decisions of firms.* Cambridge University Press.

Oliner, S., & Rudebusch, G. (1992). Sources of the financing hierarchy for business investment. *Review of Economics and Statistics, 74*, 643–654.

Opler, T., & Titman, S. (1996). *The debt-equity choice: An analysis of issuing firms.* Working paper, Ohio State University.

Roy, A. (1951). Some thoughts on the distribution of earnings. *Oxford Economics Papers, 3*, 135–146.

Shyam-Sunder, L., & Myers, S. (1994). *Testing static trade-off against pecking order models of capital structure.* Working paper, NBER No. 4722.

Smith, C., Jr. (1977). Alternative methods for raising capital: rights versus underwritten offers. *Journal of Financial Economics, 4*, 273–307.

Smith, C., Jr., & Watts R. (1992). The investment opportunity set and corporate financing, dividend and compensation policy. *Journal of Financial Economics, 32*, 263–292.

Stulz, R. (1990). Managerial discretion and optimal financing policies. *Journal of Financial Economics, 26*, 3–27.

Titman, S., & Wessels, R. (1988). The determinants of capital structure choice. *Journal of Finance, 43*, 1–19.

Trost, R. (1981). Interpretation of error covariances with nonrandom data: An empirical illustration of returns to college education. *Atlantic Economic Journal, 9*, 5–90.

CPSIA information can be obtained at www.ICGtesting.com
Printed in the USA
LVOW070240061112

305990LV00004B/221/P

9 780762 303281